STUDIES ON THE DEVELOPMENT OF
BEHAVIOR AND THE NERVOUS SYSTEM

Volume 3

NEURAL AND BEHAVIORAL SPECIFICITY

STUDIES ON THE DEVELOPMENT OF
BEHAVIOR AND THE NERVOUS SYSTEM

Volume 3

NEURAL AND BEHAVIORAL SPECIFICITY

Edited by

GILBERT GOTTLIEB

Psychology Laboratory
Division of Research
North Carolina Department of Mental Health
Raleigh, North Carolina

ACADEMIC PRESS • New York San Francisco London   1976
A Subsidiary of Harcourt Brace Jovanovich, Publishers

ACADEMIC PRESS, INC.
111 Fifth Avenue, New York, New York 10003

United Kingdom Edition published by
ACADEMIC PRESS, INC. (LONDON) LTD.
24/28 Oval Road, London NW1

LIBRARY OF CONGRESS CATALOG CARD NUMBER: 72–12194

ISBN 0–12–609303–2

PRINTED IN THE UNITED STATES OF AMERICA

CONTENTS

Section 1   HISTORICAL AND THEORETICAL ASPECTS

Section 3   NEUROSPECIFICITY: EXPERIENCE

Section 4   BEHAVIORAL SPECIFICITY

Perceptual Development in Mammals

Richard C. Tees

LIST OF CONTRIBUTORS

Numbers in parentheses indicate the pages on which the authors' contributions begin.

KAO LIANG CHOW (155), Department of Neurology, Stanford University School of Medicine, Stanford, California

J. D. DANIELS (195), Division of Biology, California Institute of Technology, Pasadena, California

GILBERT GOTTLIEB (25, 237), Psychology Laboratory, Division of Research, North Carolina Department of Mental Health, Raleigh, North Carolina

PAUL GROBSTEIN (155), Department of Pharmacological and Physiological Sciences, University of Chicago, Chicago, Illinois

M. J. KEATING (59), Division of Developmental Biology, National Institute for Medical Research, London, England

WILLIAM R. LIPPE (5), Psychology Laboratory, Division of Research, North Carolina Department of Mental Health, Raleigh, North Carolina

RONALD L. MEYER (111), Division of Biology, California Institute of Technology, Pasadena, California

J. D. PETTIGREW (195), Division of Biology, California Institute of Technology, Pasadena, California

R. W. SPERRY (111), Division of Biology, California Institute of Technology, Pasadena, California

RICHARD C. TEES (281), Department of Psychology, University of British Columbia, Vancouver, British Columbia, Canada

PREFACE

Historically speaking, a large measure of the progress in neurobiology and biopsychology has come from the recognition of neural specificities of various sorts, such as Descartes' reflex paths (an inevitable reaction to an external stimulus because of the connection between stimulus and response via a specific nervous pathway); Charles Bell's law (the ventral spinal cord is specifically motor in function, while the dorsal cord is specifically sensory in function); Johannes Müller's "specific energies of nerves" (each sensory nerve, however stimulated, gives rise to its own sensory process); and Charles Sherrington's notion of "adequate stimulation" (each sense organ responds optimally to a specific form of stimulation—each organ of sense is specifically irritable, as Müller put it).

In this century, particularly in the last decade, the specificity of peripheral–central neural connections has been added to the list in the neurobiological sphere, and the species-specificity of motor movement (fixed or modal action patterns), perception, and even learning has been added in the behavioral and psychological spheres.

Specificity, whether behavioral or neural, is a phenotype—it is the outcome of a developmental process. Such a multilevel process involves not only molecular biology and biochemistry, but intrinsic and extrinsic functional factors as well. The fact that a developing organism's spontaneous and evoked sensory and motor experience may play an important role in the attainment of neural and behavioral specificity is a relatively new idea, one that is explored rather fully in this volume.

While specificity is a problem which is best experimentally analyzed from a developmental point of view, it is also a comparative problem, one that must be studied in various animal groups in order to appreciate singularity (if it be so) or multiplicity of "mechanism." Thus, the comparative coverage is fairly broad, including fish, amphibians, birds, and mammals. Finally, there are some long-standing conceptual problems common to the behavioral and neural realms and these are described in the two introductory chapters and the final chapter.

A word about the term "specificity." It is used in several different senses throughout the volume. Whereas certain authors (Keating, and Meyer and Sperry) mean to refer to the biochemical individuality of neurons by the term neural specificity, other authors (Daniels and Pettigrew, and Gottlieb) use the term to refer to specific or selective electrophysiological functions of neurons (orientation-selective visual cells, for example) and/or highly specific anatomical pathways (as, from certain points in the retina to certain points in the visual cortex). The meaning each author has in mind for neural specificity is usually made clear, either by the context or by overt definition. The term "behavioral specificity," on the other hand, always refers to behavior which is typical or characteristic of a species at a given stage of development.

I am grateful to William R. Lippe and Ronald W. Oppenheim, the two consulting editors for this volume, for their editorial suggestions. Mary Catharine Vick provided her usual careful and cheerful assistance with copyediting. Paul G. Roofe graciously lent a portrait of C. Judson Herrick.

GILBERT GOTTLIEB

C. Judson Herrick (1932)

DEDICATION TO
C. JUDSON HERRICK (1868–1960)

In view of the fact that Charles Judson Herrick died only 16 years ago, it is startling to realize that his life began in "frontier" days. Minnesota had entered the Union only a scant 10 years before his birth, and the city of Minneapolis, his birthplace, was incorporated only the year before he was born.

C. Judson Herrick's academic career intertwined with that of his older brother Clarence. In 1885, when Clarence became professor of geology at Denison University in Granville, Ohio, Judson accompanied him and enrolled in the preparatory department of the college. In 1888, Clarence resigned from Denison to accept a similar appointment at the University of Cincinnati. In 1889, Judson followed Clarence to the University of Cincinnati, where, in the following year, he was appointed laboratory assistant in biology. In 1891, Judson became an instructor in the preparatory department at Denison and soon thereafter was awarded his B.S. degree from Cincinnati. Meanwhile, his brother accepted an appointment at the University of Chicago, one which he was to resign in only a few months, once again returning to Denison. In that year (1892), Judson had accepted a professorship of natural science in Ottawa University, Kansas. In 1893, however, he rejoined Clarence at Denison as a teaching fellow. Several months later, Clarence became incapacitated by pulmonary tuberculosis and Judson assumed most of his brother's teaching duties, as well as management of the *Journal of Comparative Neurology*, which Clarence had founded three years earlier. (Judson was to serve in a key editorial capacity on this journal until 1927, at which time he resigned as Managing Editor, and was succeeded by G. E. Coghill.) In 1895, Clarence moved to New Mexico, and, in the following year, Judson pursued his Ph.D. research at Columbia University, returning to Denison in 1897. The following year, he was promoted to Professor of Zoology (from Assistant Professor of Biology). He received his Ph.D. degree from Columbia in 1900 for the research completed there in 1896 (on the cranial nerves of *Menidia*, smelt-like fishes). Seven years later, Herrick moved to the University of Chicago, where he took up duties as Professor of Neurology in the Department of Anatomy. He stayed at Chicago for the remaining 30 years of his active academic life.

While Herrick worked primarily on the neural structure and function of fish and amphibian brains, he had very broad philosophic and scientific interests, so he kept himself abreast of general developments in psychology, zoology, and physics, as well as other fields. He numbered among his friends and colleagues the comparative physiological psychologists R. M. Yerkes, Heinrich Klüver, and Karl Lashley, as well as the neuroanatomists George E. Coghill and Gerhardt von Bonin, all of whom had strong interests in psychological development and the evolution of the brain. In 1924, Herrick published a book on the *Neurological Foundations of Animal Behavior*.

Although a regular contributor to the scientific literature throughout his career, Herrick described himself as a slow study. (He was here no doubt comparing himself to Clarence, who was an intellectual collossus by anyone's standards.) In any event, C. J.'s variegated interests culminated in several general books, published many years after his retirement from the University of Chicago. The first of these volumes, published in 1948, summarized his lifelong study of the tiger salamander's brain and was titled simply *The Brain of the Tiger Salamander*. (It is by no means a straight-forward empirical treatment but includes a theoretical synthesis of the probable course of cerebral development and evolution in vertebrates as a whole. It was Herrick's assumption that the urodele amphibians represent the most generalized version of the primitive brain and early behavior of vertebrates, so, for him, they were the choice starting point for evolutionary study.) The next year he published *George Ellett Coghill, Naturalist and Philosopher*, in which he not only summarized Coghill's doings, but also the content of innumerable philosophic conversations which he and Coghill had engaged in over the years (Coghill had died in 1941). By his own admission, there is considerable of Herrick's own philosophizing in that book; he makes it clear that he shared Coghill's interest in such abstract conceptions as "space, time, and consciousness."

The abiding question had to do with "psychogenesis"—the evolution of mental development. When does consciousness (awareness) enter the phylo-genetic picture? What features of the brain account for human intelligence, perception, and cognition? In answer to the first question, in an imaginary dialog which concludes the biography, Herrick has Coghill say:

There are ample precedents for giving "mind" a wider connotation than "consciousness." If you prefer some other expression, like "experience," that can be split into conscious and unconscious experience, I have no quarrel with that.... The thing that we agree upon is that integrative experience, as you call it, and mentation, as I call it, is a total-pattern type of activity common to all organisms and that there has been progressive expansion and individuation of this pattern in evolutionary history and in personal development. As you have suggested, this organic property may have its roots in what you call pattern of performance in the inorganic realm; it probably does. In any case the organic pattern is different from anything known in the inorganic realm. Somewhere in this series a conscious component of the pattern emerges. We don't know where, but there is no evidence at all that it is anywhere present in the inorganic realm. Consciousness is a true emergent. Are we agreed about this?

Herrick has himself reply:

Yes, and in this connection I would refer again to ... [the] conception of integrative levels. .... In discussing psychogenesis I prefer to stress the emergent capacities inherent in all natural processes. In animals the total pattern of integration is necessarily changed, and the apparatus employed undergoes differentiation parallel with every complication of the partial patterns as these are successively individuated. Translating this clumsy verbiage into the vernacular, this means that, during organic evolution and the struggle for existence, every individual preserves his own life despite the multitude of different things he had to do about it. And the fullness of that life is enlarged with every increase in his control of the environment which sustains him. When conscious control is added to unconscious control, life is enriched by opening up an entirely new domain of experience.

Herrick answered the question of the neural basis of perception and cognition in the last book he published, *The Evolution of Human Nature* (1956). The former ("analytic processes") he identified with the projection areas of the brain; the latter ("synthetic or integrative processes") he identified with the association areas of the brain. He wrote:

The brain is a glorified sorting machine and the projection centers of the cortex make the final refinements of this analysis of the data of experience. In the remainder of the cortex the raw data are rearranged in patterns which are in large measure determined by the use made of them, that is, by experience. This is an integrative process which employs mechanisms and mechanical principles of different order from those of the analytic systems.

While certain of Herrick's psychological terms and concepts may seem a bit "dated" (as no doubt ours will to those who succeed *us*), his multidisciplinary orientation embodied in the term Psychobiology anticipated today's mode by more than half a century. As Herrick himself made abundantly clear, both he and his lifelong friend Coghill were intellectually indebted to C. J.'s elder brother Clarence for their orientation. (As mentioned earlier, Clarence was the founder of the *Journal of Comparative Neurology*. Judson called it "the exponent of his [Clarence's] psychobiological interests." It is significant that the journal was originally called the *Journal of Comparative Neurology and Psychology*.)

Early on, Clarence envisioned a scientific meta-department of psychobiology, a holistic biological approach to the problem of behavior, meaning its anatomical, physiological, and psychological study from the mutual perspectives of phylogeny and ontogeny. Although Clarence published more than 150 papers and monographs between 1877 and 1910, it is through the labors of his younger brother, Coghill, and Adolf Meyer, the father of American psychiatry, that the concept of psychobiology comes down to us today. C. J. actualized the concept through his evolutionary reconstruction of the higher vertebrate brain by intensive anatomical analysis of fish and of amphibian material (especially the urodeles). Coghill actualized the ontogenetic aspect through his correlative neuroanatomical–behavioral studies of developing salamanders (urodeles).

In the best spirit of the psychological conception, C. Judson Herrick always had his eye on behavior when thinking about the structure and function of the nervous system. For example, in his classic *The Brain of the Tiger Salamander* he wrote:

What happens during the emergence of specific reflexes from the total reactions is, first, the development of an increasing number of collateral branches of the primary axons and the central linkage of sensory and motor pathways in ever more complicated patterns. Then, second, in the adjusting centers additional neurons are differentiated, the axons of which take longer or shorter courses, branching freely and participating in the formation of a nervous feltwork of extraordinary complexity. These neurons are not concerned primarily with specific reflexes but with the coordination and integration of all movements. Some parts of this intricate fabric, generally with thicker fibers, more or less well fasciculated, activate mass movements of primitive type, and other parts control local reflexes as these are individuated. But these systems of fibers are not segregated in completely insulated reflex arcs. They are interconnected by collateral branches with one another and with the interstitial neuropil. There are lines of preferential discharge, but whether any one of them is actually fired depends on numberless factors of peripheral stimulation and central excitatory state.

And when he turned his attention to matters of individual development, Herrick of course recognized the principle of motor primacy and the innappropriateness of applying a simple stimulus–response formula to even the earliest stages of behavioral activity in the most primitive of vertebrate embryos:

The stimulus–response formula has wide application and great usefulness as a basic concept in physiology and psychology, but its apparent simplicity is illusory and has tended to divert attention from essential features of even the simplest patterns of behavior....[Coghill's] researches have demonstrated beyond question that in this animal [salamander embryo] the neuromuscular system is so organized ... that, when first activated from the sensory zone, the resulting movement is a total response of all the musculature that is mature enough to respond to nervous excitation. These "total patterns" of activity are not disorderly, and they become progressively more complicated while the apparatus of local reflexes ("partial patterns") is slowly differentiated within the larger frame of the total pattern. The development of both the total pattern and the partial patterns is initiated centrally, and throughout life all of them are under some measure of unified central control ... The patterning of these orderly movements is determined by the intrinsic structure of the nervous system. This structural pattern is not built up during early development under the influence of sensory excitations, for in the embryo the motor and sensory systems attain functional capacity independently of each other; and when central connection between the sensory zone and the motor zone is made, the first motor responses to excitation exhibit an orderly sequence, the pattern of which is predetermined by the inherited organization then matured.... This early structural differentiation goes on independently of any stimulus–response type of activity, though the latter may modify the pattern of subsequent development.... The stimulus-response mechanism is not a primary factor in embryogenesis; it is a secondary acquisition.

Herrick was sensitive to evolutionary changes in early behavioral development in the vertebrate series:

It must be borne in mind that the development of the individual does not exactly recapitulate the phylogenetic development ... The pattern of the sequence of structural changes which take place during prefunctional stages of growth is determined by the organization of the germ plasm and the interaction of the genetic factors with one another. This organization, in turn, has been determined during preceding evolutionary history in adaptation to the environment and habitus of the species in question. In broad lines the history of ancestral development is repeated in the growth of the embryo, but cenogenetic modifications of it [i.e., new features] may appear in adaptation to changing conditions, as illustrated, for instance, by the appearance of some local reflexes earlier in mammals than in amphibians.

I have quoted Herrick's own words at some length not only to let him speak for himself, but to give the "flavor" of the man's intellectual range. Here he is writing about these grand matters in a context that in other hands might have merely provided the occasion for a highly local rendition of numerous histological facts about the brain of the lowly tiger salamander, and not only does it not seem out of place or pretentious, it seems entirely fitting and informative. Would that we all could place our empirical labors in such a broad context every now and then!

So we strive to honor C. Judson Herrick's memory with the volume at hand, which presents a developmental and evolutionary perspective on a single topic of neuroanatomy, neurophysiology, and behavior; we trust that he would have been pleased with our attempt at psychobiology.

STUDIES ON THE DEVELOPMENT OF
BEHAVIOR AND THE NERVOUS SYSTEM

Volume 3

NEURAL AND BEHAVIORAL SPECIFICITY

Section 1

HISTORICAL AND THEORETICAL ASPECTS

INTRODUCTION

As we are busy at work in the shock-mounted rooms in our laboratories, surrounded by copper shielding, stainless steel, digital counters, storage oscilloscopes, hydraulic microdrives, microelectrodes, stereotaxic devices, and other futuristic necessities for recording the activity of individual nerve cells, it is difficult to realize that we are painstakingly trying to answer questions which were put forth by philosophers several centuries ago. At the bottom of the nativism–empiricism controversy—the question of the extent to which knowledge is determined by innate and experiential factors—is the question of how those features of the brain develop which mediate perception, particularly their dependence or nondependence on experience. The empiricists emphasized sensory experience as the root of knowledge; the nativists emphasized the innate predilections which force us to process sensory experience in particular modes. At the neural level, these conceptions are precisely mirrored in our present-day concern with the degree of sharpness of tuning of neurons (functional specificity) and the degree of specificity of connections between neurons (anatomical specificity) in advance of sensory experience. At the behavioral level, especially with respect to perception, we are particularly eager to define "what is there" before sensory experience has begun to influence the system, or what features of perceptual processing remain uninfluenced in the face of severe experiential perturbations.

As pointed out by William Lippe in the first chapter in Section 1, we "moderns" can take credit for reformulating the nativism–empiricism controversy as a matter for developmental analysis, thus making it amenable to ever-increasing scientific study and potential resolution. The fact that the controversy is just as lively as it ever was, although in modern dress, is evident in all the chapters of this volume.

In an attempt to increase our analytic precision in coming to experimental and conceptual grips with this fascinating derivative of the more general nature–nurture problem, the author of the second chapter in the present

3

section has systematically delineated the *various* roles which experience might play in the development of behavior and the nervous system. Experience does not serve merely one function (i.e., to modify already developed behavior, neural structure, or function), but it can operate during the maturation process itself to sustain, facilitate, or, in certain instances, induce (determine) a particular course of development. By distinguishing between these different functions of experience, we can refine our understanding of its role in neural and behavioral development. On the other hand, it is recognized that not all aspects of neural (and even behavioral) specificity need be dependent upon experience for their development.

INNATE AND EXPERIENTIAL FACTORS IN THE DEVELOPMENT OF THE VISUAL SYSTEM: HISTORICAL BASIS OF CURRENT CONTROVERSY

WILLIAM R. LIPPE

Psychology Laboratory
Division of Research
North Carolina Department of Mental Health
Raleigh, North Carolina

I. Introduction

The ability of all organisms to survive in the complex and varied environments in which they live ultimately depends upon a variety of developmental processes that take place during both embryonic and postnatal life. Although the experimental study of these processes within the nervous system had its inception during the first half of this century with the pioneering work of such experimental neuroembryologists as Ross Harrison, Paul Weiss, Roger Sperry, and Viktor Hamburger, it has been only during the

5

last decade that neuroscientists in general have joined in this venture. Thus, neurobiologists and psychobiologists no longer view behavior and nervous system structure and function as finished products and ask questions only about how they work in adult organisms. They are now cogently aware that all neurobehavioral states have a complex epigenetic history, and they are actively investigating the developmental processes by which these states are attained.

To a large extent this interest in development on the part of students of behavior and the nervous system has its roots in the recognition of various sorts of specificities in both behavior and in nervous system function and organization. For example, ethological studies, especially of nonmammalian vertebrates, have provided numerous examples of striking behavioral specificities. Thus, many precocial forms of birds are known to be selectively responsive to the maternal call of their particular species (Gottlieb, 1971). An impression of the high degree of specificity of nervous system organization can easily be gleaned by observing the aggregation of cell bodies and their axons into distinct nuclear groups and fiber tracts, respectively. Numerous studies of the connections between central nervous system neurons and both muscles and peripheral receptors have provided classic examples of specificity in cell-to-cell connections (Gaze, 1970). Furthermore, it is now recognized that different types of afferent fibers may selectively innervate specific portions of a common target cell (Lynch, Matthews, Mosko, Parks, & Cotman, 1972; Lynch, Stanfield, & Cotman, 1973). The selective responsiveness of neurons in the different sensory systems to specific parameters of sensory stimulation provides excellent examples of functional specificities. For example, single cells in the mammalian visual cortex are selectively responsive to line stimuli having a particular orientation (Hubel and Wiesel, 1959), and cells in the somatosensory system respond only to certain submodalities of stimulation [e.g., pressure versus light touch (Mountcastle, 1961)]. Similarly, cells in the auditory system are responsive only to a restricted range of tonal stimuli (Katsuki, 1961), and some cells respond only to certain types of frequency- or amplitude-modulated sounds (Whitfield & Evans, 1965).

While these and other examples of neural and behavioral specificities provide intriguing challenges for developmental analysis, during the past decade the highly selective responsiveness of cells in the visual system has been a particular focus of experimentation. Working primarily with the cat, rabbit, and monkey, these studies have sought to determine whether the development and/or maintenance of the selective responsiveness of visual cells is dependent upon visual experience or whether their response specificity can develop and be maintained in the absence of such experience. In the following pages I will deal with selective aspects of this work. My purpose will not be to review the results of these studies since this has been adequately covered by other contributors to the present volume (see Daniels & Pettigrew; Grobstein & Chow; Tees). Rather, I will outline the historical roots within philosophy, psychology, and physiology from which this neurobiological line of research has evolved.

II. Modern Philosophy

The period of philosophy referred to here as "modern" begins in the 17th century with the writings of such philosophers as René Descartes, Francis Bacon, and John Locke and extends into the 18th and 19th centuries to include the works of George Berkeley, David Hume, and Immanuel Kant. The philosophy of this period is unique in its complete break with past tradition and its overriding interest in questions of epistemology; that is, questions of whether or not it is possible to obtain knowledge of reality, how reliable this knowledge is, and, in particular, how reliable knowledge can be obtained. In proposing answers to this latter question, individual philosophers typically emphasized either the importance of the innate structure of the mind or the importance of sensory experience, points of view that have since come to be denoted by the terms nativism and empiricism, respectively. As has recently been pointed out by Stent (1975), these two epistemological points of view have formed the basis upon which scientists in various disciplines have attempted to conceptualize their respective subject areas.

The actual development of modern philosophy during the 1600s was conditioned by two important events of the 16th and 17th centuries (Watson, 1963, pp. 121–136). The first of these events was the rise of the Renaissance (1450–1600). This marked a complete break with the reliance upon and subservience to dogma and authority which had characterized the prior period of the later Middle Ages (1150–1450). The new humanistic spirit of this age emphasized man's own critical powers of reasoning to reach truth, and this, in part, stimulated philosophers of the 17th century both to question traditional authority and to formulate new methods of inquiry by which they believed reliable knowledge could be obtained. The second and most significant event was the rise of modern science during the 17th century. Much of the scientific knowledge of the Middle Ages consisted of the teachings of ancient scholars that had been handed down and accepted for centuries. These teachings, in turn, were primarily based upon insight, intuition, and a process of argument from accepted first principles to what *should* be.

Beginning in the 17th century, however, the methods of empirical observation and mathematical deduction were introduced as procedures of scientific inquiry. Although the use of these methods led to epoch-making discoveries in both the physical and biological sciences, they also raised two epistemological issues that largely determined the course of modern philosophy (Lamprecht, 1955, pp. 219–221). The first of these issues concerned the relative utility of reason as opposed to sense experience in the acquisition of knowledge. Thus, some individuals argued that the evidence of the senses is trustworthy and can provide reliable knowledge, while others asserted that sense experience is subjective and unreliable and that reason is sufficient in itself for obtaining knowledge. The second issue concerned the relationship of sense experience to the realities of nature. Prior to the 17th century sensory experience had been regarded as being the direct presence of the realities of nature before the observer. In the 17th century, however, many scientists came to regard sensory experience as being subjective states that are caused by, but do not necessarily accurately represent, objective substances. Thus, although sense experience arises because of nature, it might not accurately reveal what nature is.

Seventeenth century philosophers considered it essential that these questions be answered in order that both the discoveries and methodological procedures of the new science have adequate and necessary epistemological justification. Consequently, modern philosophy became primarily concerned with the epistemological question of how trustworthy knowledge of the world can be obtained. In proposing answers to this question, individual philosophers typically adopted either a nativist or empiricist position. The nativist position holds that the mind possesses elements of knowledge that are not derived from sense experience or learning but are in some manner derivatives of an innate cognitive structure. On the other hand, the empiricist position holds that sense experience is the sole source of knowledge and rejects the possibility of innate or *a priori* knowledge.

A. Nativism

René Descartes (1596–1650), the founder and first major figure of modern philosophy, was a strong advocate and herald of the nativist point of view. In brief, Descartes sought to establish a comprehensive system of knowledge that would be universally valid for all men. He proceeded by first doubting the truth of all his ideas and beliefs and then sought to discover simple ideas that could unequivocally be known to be true without any possibility of doubt because of their clarity and distinctiveness. Starting with these simple "self-evident" truths, Descartes used reason and deduction to infer more complex and remote propositions, which he believed would constitute a universal knowledge possessing the certainty of mathematics.

Descartes termed these self-evident truths "innate ideas." These ideas do not arise from sense experience but are derived solely from the individual's capacity to think—they stem from the innate endowment of the mind. Furthermore, these ideas comprise universal and valid knowledge possessed by all men. Included among them are the ideas of the self as a thinking being, God, as well as certain geometric axioms and the concepts of space, time, and motion. Thus, Descartes seemed to be saying that the mind possesses certain innate perceptual capacities that enable individuals to recognize shapes of objects and correctly localize them in space and time. Descartes' nativism is also coupled with the belief that reason is the only means capable of attaining truth and obtaining knowledge of reality. Although sense experience might serve as an aid when used correctly, ideas derived from sense experience are subject to error since they do not possess the clarity and distinctiveness necessary to guarantee truth. Furthermore, since sensations are subjective states of mind, not qualities inherent in objects themselves, they cannot inform us about the true reality of matter.

The nativism and rationalism of Descartes drew sharp reactions, especially from British philosophers; and during the latter half of the 17th century and throughout most of the 18th century, the pendulum swung in the opposite direction, and empiricism became the dominant epistemology (see below). However, the nativist tradition was revitalized in the latter half of the 18th century through the writings of the German philosopher Immanuel Kant (1724–1804).

Kant's primary objective was to establish a solid philosophical basis for the conclusions of modern science. He asserted that certain types of knowledge or judgments are common to all sciences, and he felt that if the possibility of such judgments could be demonstrated, then mathematics and the physical sciences would be validated. Kant termed these judgments *a priori* synthetic judgments, and he included among them such propositions as "The shortest distance between two points is a straight line" and "Every event has a cause." *A priori* synthetic judgments, he asserted, are not derived from experience and observation but are necessary conditions that presuppose experiences and provide the context within which experience *must* be framed. As such, they constitute knowledge that is necessary, not merely probable, and is valid for all men at all times.

Kant sought to prove that *a priori* synthetic judgments are possible by analyzing man's cognitive structure and the intellectual processes by which knowledge is acquired. He maintained that the mind possesses two types of innate functions; that is, functions that are neither built up from nor influenced by experience. These functions impose an inevitable order upon both sensory experience and intelligible concepts. The first type of innate function is the *a priori* intuition of space and time. Kant argued that objects and events are not in themselves related in space and time, but that the mind imposes these types of order upon all experiences. The fact that we experience events and objects as having spatial and temporal relationships is a psychological necessity having its basis in the mind's innate structure.

The categories of the understanding constitute the second type of innate cognitive function. These are unifying activities of the mind by which we organize and think about sense data. As with the intuitions of space and time, we are obliged to think about sense data in terms of these categories, not because of anything intrinsic to the objects of experience themselves, but because the innate structure of the mind necessitates that sense data be organized under these categories. It is because of these activities of the understanding that our experiences are unified and coherent and are not a number of chaotic, unrelated sensations. For example, the tendency to perceive events in terms of cause-and-effect relationships rather than as independent occurrences having no necessary connection to each other derives from the category of causality.

In summary, Kant viewed the mind as being partially constitutive of experience and not a mere passive receiver of sense impressions. Implicit in this position is the view that our perceptions are not gradually built up over time by the association of initially unrelated sensations. Rather, our perceptions as we first experience them are already unified because of the necessary conditions for experience imposed by the mind. As will become apparent later, the Kantian notion that the mind actively organizes sense experience was incorporated into Gestalt psychology and has also proved to be consistent with what we now know about mechanisms of sensory processing.

B. Empiricism

Empiricism was primarily formulated in the writings of 18th and 19th century British philosophers, most notably by John Locke, George Berkeley, and David Hume. However, it should be briefly noted that the empiricist position actually has its roots in the earlier writings of Francis Bacon (1561–1626) and Thomas Hobbes (1588–1679). Bacon was distrustful of past authority and considered it essential to formulate a method of inquiry wherein reliable knowledge could be obtained. However, unlike Descartes, who a decade later would emphasize the use of reason and deduction as means of obtaining truth, Bacon formulated an inductive method of scientific inquiry based upon empirical observation. It is in his emphasis upon empirical observation versus reason that Bacon heralded the empiricist tradition. Hobbes, although primarily a political philosopher, belongs to the empiricist tradition because he was the first to state the empiricist position that all knowledge is derived from sense experience. Neither Bacon nor Hobbes, however, fully appreciated the epistemological implications of the empiricist position, and it is John Locke (1632–1704) who is typically credited with presenting empiricism in its classic form.

Locke strongly rejected the proposition that men possess innate ideas and in doing so was, in part, reacting against the theory of innate ideas which had been previously advanced by Descartes. Instead he maintained that at birth the mind is a "white paper" and that all knowledge and ideas are subsequently derived from experience.[1] He further went on to argue that experience is of both external and internal things and events, and he denoted these two types of experience by the terms sensation and reflection, respectively. Sensation supplies us with ideas of the sensory qualities of objects such as color, taste, and temperature, while reflection upon or observation of the operations of one's mind upon the ideas derived from sensation give rise to ideas such as those of perception and thinking. Locke termed the ideas derived from sensation and reflection simple ideas since they cannot be further analyzed into simpler ideas or elements. The mind was pictured as playing a passive role in receiving these ideas. However, Locke also stressed that the mind can play an active role in combining, contrasting, and abstracting simple ideas to form more complex ideas. For example, the idea of gold is really a complex ideas compounded out of the simple ideas yellow, a certain weight, a certain hardness and so on, while the abstract idea of man as a general class concept is arrived at by comparing and contrasting perceptions of individual men.

Locke's basic propositions that man does not possess any innate or *a priori* knowledge and that all ideas and knowledge are derived solely from experience became the basic tenets of the empiricist epistemologies of such 18th and 19th century philosophers as George Berkeley (1685–1753) and David Hume (1711–1776). These philosophers did not modify these basic assumptions but concerned themselves with working out the logical implications of a distinction which Locke had made between the primary and secondary qualities of objects. This critical line of inquiry need not concern us. How-

[1] Both Hobbes and Locke stated that men possess certain characteristics that are part of their original nature and are not acquired by experience. For example, Hobbes stated that "Of appetites and aversions, some are born with men ..." while "The rest, which are of particular things, proceed from experience ..." (Hobbes, 1946, p. 32). Similarly, Locke stated that "God has stamped certain characteristics upon men's mind, which ... may perhaps be a little mended, but can hardly be totally altered and transformed into the contrary" (Locke, 1947, p. 247). Thus, while they asserted that all *knowledge* is acquired by experience, they also seemed to be suggesting that man's actions and capacity to acquire knowledge are, in part, determined or constrained by his original nature.

ever, Locke's notion of the compounding of simple into complex ideas did lead directly to the development of British associationism, which, because of its importance to subsequent developments in psychology, will be briefly outlined here.

Locke's notion that experience gives rise to simple ideas which are then compounded into more complex ideas implied a type of atomistic conception of the mind; that is, a conception that the mind is composed of elementary units that are combined in various ways. This conception made explicit the possibility of an association psychology wherein it would merely be necessary to define the laws governing the association of elementary ideas in order to understand the various aspects of mental life, such as the origin of perceptions as well as the lawful manner in which certain sequences of thoughts occur together. A number of 18th and 19th century philosophers had enumerated various laws of association, but it is David Hartley (1705–1757) who is usually credited with establishing associationism as a formal doctrine and psychological system (Boring, 1950, pp. 193–199; Murphy, 1932, pp. 24–26).

The doctrine of associationism as first formalized by David Hartley, and later rigorously systematized by James Mill (1773–1836), maintains that all ideas, thoughts, and perceptions are composed of simple elements that have been combined according to laws of association. The mind is pictured as being a blank slate at birth. Complex thoughts and perceptions are thought to be gradually acquired by a process in which simple ideas resulting from sense experience are passively linked together. Thus, sensations A, B, and C are pictured as giving rise to perceptible effects or ideas, a, b, and c. If these sensations frequently occur together, then the occurrence of any single sensation will give rise to a complex of all three ideas. For example, one's perception of a tree—which seems to be immediate and unitary—has actually developed over a period of time from the association of simple ideas of color, extension, smell, and so on. In a similar manner, all mental states have been built from, and can be analyzed into, elementary units.

In summary, two alternative conceptions of how knowledge is acquired developed within philosophy between the 17th and 19th centuries. The nativist point of view emphasized the innate cognitive structure of the mind and its active role in imposing an inevitable organization upon sensory experience. The empiricist point of view emphasized that all knowledge is derived from experience and viewed the mind as the passive receptor of elementary bits of sense data. This point of view then gave rise to the associationist doctrine that all aspects of mental life are explicable in terms of the association of simple ideas into complex thoughts, ideas, and perceptions. As we shall now see, the nativist and empiricist points of view were carried over into psychology, although in a somewhat different form.

III. Psychology

The founding of experimental psychology as an independent science during the middle of the 19th century actually represented the synthesis of specific problems and approaches that had hitherto been the province of either philosophy or physiology (Boring, 1950). Thus, it is not surprising that the nativist and empiricist points of view which had arisen in philosophy were carried over into various systems or schools of psychology that developed during the 19th and 20th centuries. The epistemological question of how reliable knowledge of the world is obtained was transformed into the psychological question of how we perceive the world and, in particular, whether the abilities to perceive various spatial aspects of the environment such as shape, size, and depth are present at birth ("innate") or whether such perceptions are built up through learning and experience. These alternative points of view can be best illustrated by comparing two systems of psychology that took opposing positions on this issue: introspectionism and Gestalt psychology. [The reader should see Heidbreder (1933) and Köhler (1947) for a discussion and contrast of the introspectionist and Gestaltist points of view. Hochberg (1962) provides an excellent summary of the history of nativism and empiricism in perception.]

A. Introspectionism

Introspectionism was the first systematic position or school of thought in experimental psychology and, as described below, emphasized the contributions that experience and learning make to the manner in which the environment is perceived. The introspectionist position was first formalized by the German psychologist Wilhelm Wundt in 1879 and was further systematized by Bradford Titchener, Wundt's student and the main proponent of the introspectionist position in the United States. The basic tenet of introspectionism, as formulated by Wundt, was that all complex states of consciousness such as perceptions, emotions, and thoughts are not unitary but are built up from the association of unitary processes of sensations and feelings. The goal of psychology was conceived to be the identification of these elementary processes and the determination of how, and according to what laws, they are associated. This was to be achieved by the *introspection of immediate conscious experience*. For example, a subject would be shown a book in the laboratory under controlled conditions and be requested to report his *immediate experience* of hues, brightnesses, and shapes and not merely that he was observing a book. In the latter case the subject would be describing the object itself, that is, his basic elementary conscious processes as they had been associated and imbued with meaning by learning and experience, rather than his immediate conscious experiences themselves.

The introspectionist psychologists asserted that one's perceptions of the environment are not unitary and immediate but are built up by experience and learning. They distinguished between sensations (bare sensory experiences revealed by introspection) and perceptions (the world of objects as normally experienced), and they argued that sensations are the primary elements of experience from which perceptions are constructed. For example, a pencil lying on top of a table is perceived to be an independent unit segregated from the background because we have learned through past experience that the variety of sensations aroused by this object move together and change in a similar manner when the conditions of illumination are changed. The pencil and table stimulate a mosaic of retinal points and central connections that are functionally independent so that our perception of the pencil as a unitary object segregated from the table cannot be attributed to any intrinsic property of nervous system structure or function. It is only through learning and experience that our perception of a unitary object segregated from the background is achieved. The perception of motion was thought to arise from the association of successive visual sensations and eye movements as the image of an object moved across the retina, and the perception of depth was explained by an individual's learning to use cues such as size, linear perspective, and the kinesthetic feedback from ocular muscles which occurs during convergence and accommodation. Similarly, the phenomena of size and shape constancy were explained by learning.

B. Gestalt Psychology

The school of Gestalt psychology was founded around 1912 by the German psychologists Max Wertheimer, Kurt Koffka, and Wolfgang Köhler and arose in large part as a revolt against the introspectionist doctrine that perceptions of objects are built up from the association of elementary sensations. The Gestaltists asserted that elementary associations are artificial constructs since they are not apparent in normal perceptual experience but are revealed only by the artificial method of analytic introspection. Thus, they started with perceptual experience as it normally occurs to the "naive" observer as their primary datum and found it to be characterized by its singleness and wholeness. Objects are immediately sensed as being unified wholes segregated from their background rather than as being composites of independent sensation units. Perceptual experience is characterized by its Gestalt quality—its tendency to be "formed." These aspects of perceptual organization are spontaneous and immediate and do not occur as the result of learning and experience. Rather, they are the inevitable consequences of the organization which the brain *actively imposes* upon sensory input according to its inherent principles of operation. These include the principles of similarity (similar parts are seen together as a group), contiguity (parts contiguous in space or time are seen together as a group), and closure (gaps tend to be filled in).

In order to demonstrate the operation of these intrinsic principles of brain function, Gestaltists frequently selected "neutral" stimuli (stimuli free of any associated meaning) such as dots and showed how they were structured in the perceptual field. For example, three dots in close proximity to each other are perceived as being grouped together rather than as three independent and unrelated elements. Similarly, if two points of light are projected onto the retina some distance apart and flashed on and off in quick succession, then the individual experiences movement between the two points. Since this occurs in the absence of a succession of sensations between the two retinal points, the Gestaltists maintained that the perception of movement is immediate and not built up from the association of successive sensations.

In summary, the introspectionists asserted that the ability to perceive spatial aspects of the environment such as form, size, and depth must be learned, and they tended to view the nervous system as the passive transmitter of local and mutually independent events. In contrast, Gestaltists asserted that the ability to perceive spatial aspects of the environment is inborn and viewed the brain as a dynamically interactive system that actively organizes sensory input. It might also be noted here that the empiricism/nativism issue was not peculiar to philosophy and psychology; early sensory physiologists such as Müller (1801–1885), Helmholtz (1821–1894), and Hering (1834–1913) also tended to divide themselves along these lines on particular questions of visual perception. For example, Hering proposed that each retinal point possesses a local sign for depth, and that the perception of depth derives from the algebraic summation of all retinal local signs stimulated by an object. On the other hand, Helmholtz asserted that the perception of depth depends upon learned cues such as size and linear perspective and kinesthetic feedback from ocular muscles associated with convergence and accommodation (Hochberg, 1962, pp. 282–288).

C. The Organization of Behavior

A major stimulus to the experimental study of the role that learning and experience play in the development of perception occurred in 1949 with the publication of *The Organization of Behavior* by the Canadian psychologist Donald Hebb. In this classic work Hebb attempted to bridge the conceptual gap that existed between psychology and neurology, and he formulated the first general theory of behavior to be based upon the known anatomy and physiology of the nervous system. Within the context of the present discussion, that aspect of his theory dealing with perception is of particular importance for a number of reasons. First, Hebb provided a synthesis of the nativist and empiricist traditions by suggesting that perception has a partially innate and partially learned organization.[2] Second, he explicitly defined the question of whether perception depends upon innate or experiential factors to be a *developmental* issue. This is not to imply that prior investigators had been unaware of developmental considerations; however, Hebb was the first to clearly operationalize the question to be one of what perceptual abilities and neural organization and function the organism is provided with at birth, what perceptual abilities and neural organization the organism possesses as an adult, and what dynamic processes occur in between. Third, he provided the conceptual framework that directly led to the *experimental* study of the role of experiential factors is perceptual development.

Hebb proposed that at birth we possess a basic neural circuitry which mediates very simple perceptual processes. For example, he asserted that the perception of figure/ground relationships is a direct product of the inherited structural and functional characteristics of the nervous system and is both present at birth and immediate and inevitable in any perception as the Gestaltists had maintained. On the other hand, these innate structural and functional characteristics of the nervous system are not able to mediate more complex perceptual abilities such as shape and form perception. These latter abilities are only gradually acquired through learning and experience and are said to develop by a complex neurological process in which nerve cells present at birth become functionally associated into multiunit cell assemblies.

Hebb drew support for his theory from two sources of evidence. First, Austin Riesen (1947) had reported that chimpanzees reared in total darkness until the time that they normally make effective use of vision only exhibit rudimentary visual abilities, such as pupillary responses and pursuit of a moving light. The acquisition of visually mediated responses such as object recognition occurred very slowly and required visual experience with objects. Second, von Senden (1949) had reported that individuals given sight by surgical means after having been blind since birth as the result of congenital cataracts were able to perceive figure/ground relationship upon the first occurrence of vision, but they were apparently unable to perceive pattern and shape. For example, these individuals were unable to see a

[2] It is important to note that Hebb used the term "innate" to mean "present at birth" and recognized that "innate" functions might be "learned," that is, "established in utero as a result of ... neural activity itself" (Hebb, 1949, p. 121).

triangle as such at a single glance but had to slowly seek out corners and lines. The ability to perceive objects as distinctive wholes at a single glance was acquired very gradually.

The publication of Hebb's book stimulated numerous investigators to test experimentally the theory that experiential factors play an important role in the development of perceptual functions. Since the typical method of training animals to differentially respond to visual stimuli in order to test their perceptual abilities cannot be easily used with newborn mammals, investigators made use of the deprivation experiment. It was assumed that by depriving a newborn animal of visual experience its perceptual development could be delayed until it was old enough to be trained (Fantz, 1965). The effects of visual experience on the development of perceptual functions could then be assessed by comparing visually naive and visually experienced animals of the same age. It soon became apparent that visual deprivation does not simply retard perceptual development (Chow, Riesen, & Newell, 1957), and that visually deprived animals are not simply older animals with "newborn" perceptual abilities. Nevertheless, these early studies did demonstrate that, in some species, the absence of visual experience during early development leads to the impairment of certain perceptual abilities such as form and depth discrimination in the adult organism (Beach & Jaynes, 1954; Riesen, 1966; Tees, this volume). These results were thus consistent with the notion that early visual experience is necessary for the normal development of certain perceptual abilities.

IV. Sensory Physiology

Although the early studies of visual deprivation and restricted rearing suggested that visual experience during early development plays an important role in the ontogeny of certain perceptual functions, the logical extension of this line of investigation to the analysis of the role that visual experience plays in the development of the physiological mechanisms of visual system coding did not occur until the early 1960s. This is in large part due to the fact that, up until around 1960, the study of sensory system coding was in many respects still in its infancy, and visual physiologists had little knowledge of how neurons within the visual system of the adult organism coded or represented various features of the external environment. To be sure there had been some progress at both the conceptual and empirical levels. For example, it was shown that retinal ganglion cells in the cat are particularly responsive to specific features of visual stimuli such as changes in stimulation and spatial contrasts in illuminance (Barlow, 1972; Kuffler, 1953). Such findings clearly demonstrated that the function of individual neurons is not simply to signal the presence and intensity of light at a particular point in the visual field, and that the visual system does not merely transmit a high fidelity copy of the distribution of light falling on the retina. However, these findings were inadequate to explain how features such as shape, pattern, and spatial localization might be encoded by neural activity.

In 1959, a major conceptual and empirical breakthrough occurred in the understanding of the mechanisms of sensory coding. Two independent groups of investigators, Lettvin, Maturana, McCulloch, and Pitts (1959), and Hubel and Wiesel (1959), discovered that single neurons within the visual systems of frogs and cats, respectively, were selectively responsive to specific spatiotemporal patterns of visual stimuli. Lettvin *et al.* discovered four classes of optic nerve fibers in the frog which differed on the basis of their selective responsiveness to different stimulus patterns. These included "sustained contrast detectors," which responded to a simple difference in brightness; "edge detectors," which responded to moving edges; "net convexity detectors," which responded to small moving spots; and "dimness detectors," which responded to a dimming of the visual field. Similarly, Hubel and Wiesel found that single neurons within the visual cortex of the cat were poorly driven by overall retinal illumination or by diffuse spots of light. Vigorous responses were evoked only by slitlike stimuli, such as light or dark bars located within a neuron's receptive field, and typically the orientation and direction of movement of the stimulus were found to be critical for evoking responses. Individual cells were most effectively driven by a line or bar stimulus oriented in a horizontal, vertical, or oblique position, and the cell's response was abolished when the stimulus was positioned orthogonal to its preferred orientation. Similarly, movement of a stimulus in a certain direction was frequently found to be particularly effective in driving a neuron. After these early observations that cells within the visual cortex of the cat are both orientation and direction specific, it was discovered that most of these cells are also binocularly driven and can be excited by stimulation of either eye (Hubel & Wiesel, 1962). Furthermore, it has now been shown that the response of binocular cells is specific to a certain angular or retinal disparity (Barlow, Blakemore, & Pettigrew, 1967). Thus, when the eyes of a cat are converged to a focal point, a binocular stimulus must be positioned at a certain distance from the eyes to evoke a maximum response. The optimal disparity varies from cell to cell, and it has been argued that this disparity specificity constitutes the code for binocular depth perception.

It might be well to digress a moment to point out that the original studies of both Lettvin *et al.* and Hubel and Wiesel established a new research strategy in sensory physiology and led to a new concept of the role of single neurons in sensory coding. Prior to 1959 the belief that the primary function of individual neurons was to register the distribution of light on the retina had led visual physiologists to use simple flashes of light in their neuro-physiological experiments. However, the observations of Lettvin *et al.* and Hubel and Wiesel made it clear that individual neurons perform tasks far more complex than the simple registration of light. They detect or encode specific spatial and temporal features of visual stimuli which are of particular biological significance and thus possess high information content for the organism. This new conception of sensory neurons as pattern or feature detectors, in turn, shifted sensory physiologists away from the sole use of static stimuli such as light flashes and simple tone bursts in their neuro-physiological experiments. During the last decade, the stimulus paradigms utilized by sensory physiologists have broadened to include dynamic stimuli, such as moving lines and frequency-modulated sounds, whose spatial and temporal structure more closely resemble the types of stimuli normally encountered by organisms.

The discovery of some of the functional properties of single neurons within the visual cortex of the adult cat provided the normative data upon which the developmental analysis of visual system functioning could be based. Furthermore, the possibility that visual experience might play an important role in the development of these functional properties was raised by the findings that the absence of visual experience during early develop-ment leads to subsequent deficits in visually guided behavior. Thus, begin-ning in the early 1960s, the origin of the selective responsiveness of visual cortical neurons was subjected to experimental analysis. These initial studies reported two primary findings. First, it was reported that neurons with adult-type specificities (binocularity, orientation, and direction specificity) are present in the visual cortex of visually naive kittens (Hubel & Wiesel, 1963). Second, it was reported that abnormal early visual experience resulted in a population of functionally abnormal cortical neurons. In particular, im-balances and incongruities of early binocular experience were found to produce a population of cortical cells that could only be monocularly excited (Hubel & Wiesel, 1965; Wiesel & Hubel, 1963, 1965). On the basis of these findings it was concluded that many of the specific properties of visual cortical neurons are genetically or innately determined and develop *fully* in the absence of visual experience. Visual experience was viewed as merely serving to *maintain* already developed functional characteristics (Wiesel & Hubel, 1974).

More recent experiments have come however, to different conclusions regarding the relative importance of genetic and postnatal experiental factors in determining the selectivity of cortical neurons (Barlow & Pettigrew, 1971; Pettigrew, 1974). These studies have reexamined the response pro-perties of cortical neurons in visually naive kittens and have reported that such neurons are not *as selectively responsive* to all stimulus dimensions as are neurons in adult cats. In particular, neurons in kittens were found to respond over a much broader range of stimulus orientations and retinal disparities than cells in adult cats, and it was concluded that visual experience is responsible for the developmental sharpening of responsiveness to these stimulus dimensions. Thus, some workers have concluded that visual experience is, in fact, *necessary for the full development* of certain adult-type response properties, and that experience does not merely serve to maintain already developed functional characteristics (Pettigrew, 1974; see Daniels & Pettigrew; Grobstein & Chow, this volume).

The question regarding the role that visual experience plays in the functional development of the visual system has raised the related question of how visual experience and the genome contribute to the development of the specific neural connections which underlie these functional properties. It is generally agreed that much of the neural circuitry in the visual system is genetically determined; that is, it is established before visual experience can be effective or subsequently develops in the absence of visual experience (Pettigrew, 1974; Wiesel & Hubel, 1974). Presently, the chemoaffinity theory of neuronal specificity would appear to provide the best explanation of how such specific connections are established in the absence of visual experience (Sperry, 1945, 1965; see Keating; Meyer & Sperry, this volume). This theory, originally proposed to account for the prefunctional organization of neural connections in lower vertebrates, proposes that the precise patterning of connections between individual neurons is based upon the operation of highly selective cytochemical affinities. It is suggested that individual neurons acquire unique biochemical labels under genetic control early in development, and that neurons with similar labels subsequently establish preferential connections with each other.

On the other hand, some workers have asserted that the genome is incapable of prespecifying or programming all neural connections within the visual system and that the elaboration of some connections depends, in part, upon individual visual experience. In particular, it has been suggested that visual experience contributes to the elaboration of the pattern of cortical connections which subserves binocular disparity (Pettigrew, 1974; Shlaer, 1971; see Daniels & Pettigrew; Grobstein & Chow, this volume). There are a number of possible mechanisms whereby visual experience might participate in the establishment of refinement or neural connections. For example, visual experience might be responsible for the establishment of certain connections *de novo*, or it might serve to selectively maintain particular connections as a function of specific patterns of synaptic use and disuse (see Daniels & Pettigrew; Gottlieb; Grobstein & Chow, this volume, for a fuller discussion of this issue). However, irrespective of the particular mechanism or mechanisms involved, this latter point of view stands in sharp contrast to the notion that certain functionally adaptive patterns of neural connections develop *in toto* in the absence of individual visual experience.

There now exists an extensive literature dealing with the role that post-natal visual experience plays in the development of the visual system in a variety of species (see Daniels & Pettigrew; Grobstein & Chow; Tees, this volume). This literature clearly demonstrates that, in some species, different types of abnormal visual experience early in development result in sub-sequent abnormalities in visual system anatomy and physiology. Thus, it is clear that both anatomical and physiological processes can be affected by early visual experience. Nonetheless, at the moment, there does not appear to be a simple solution to the question of whether visual experience, in fact, normally contributes to the functional and/or anatomical development of the visual system (Wiesel & Hubel, 1974).

V. Summary and Conclusions

In the preceding sections I have traced the evolution of the modern neurobiological study of the role that individual visual experience plays in the functional development of the visual system from its roots in philosophy, psychology, and physiology. To briefly summarize, the historical roots of this issue can be traced back to the beginning of modern philosophy and the formulation of two alternative positions of how reliable knowledge of the world is acquired. The nativist position held that certain elements of knowledge are derived from the innate structure of the mind while the empiricist point of view asserted that sense experience is the sole source of knowledge. With the founding of experimental psychology in the middle of the 19th century, the *epistemological* question of how reliable knowledge of the world is obtained was transformed into the *psychological* question of how we perceive the world. The nativism–empiricism question then became one of whether the abilities to perceive various spatial aspects of the environment such as depth and shape are innate (present at birth) or whether such perceptions are gradually built up through learning and experience. Although various 19th and 20th century psychologists and physiologists took opposing positions on this issue, it was the publication of *The Organization of Behavior* by Donald Hebb in 1949 which directly led to the experimental study of the role that learning and experience play in the development of perceptual abilities. Hebb clearly defined the question of whether perception depends upon innate or experiential factors to be a developmental issue, and he formulated a theory of perceptual development which proposed that the development of particular perceptual abilities depends, in part, upon early visual experience. The results of subsequent studies were consistent with this hypothesis: animals deprived of visual experience early in development were found to be impaired in various perceptual abilities later in life. These findings, in turn, raised the possibility that early visual experience might normally contribute to the functional development of the visual system. However, up until around 1960 little was known of how various features of the external environment were encoded by neural activity, and the absence of these normative data precluded the study of the functional development of the visual system. The pioneering studies of Hubel and Wiesel in the late 1950s and early 1960s on the response properties of single neurons within the visual cortex of the adult cat provided some of these normative data. These data, in turn, provided the empirical basis for the initial studies of the functional development of the visual system, which soon followed.

During the last decade and a half, the visual systems of both mammals and lower vertebrates alike have continued to serve as particularly useful models for the analysis of the role which experiential and genetic factors play in the development of both neural and behavioral specificities. This is well reflected in the contributions to the present volume. The chapters by Grobstein and Chow and by Daniels and Pettigrew both provide a cross-species analysis of the role which early visual experience plays in the development of both the structural and functional properties of the visual system. These chapters are nicely complemented by Tees' review of the role which visual experience plays in the development of a variety of perceptual behaviors in mammals. Two common themes run through these chapters: (1) The effect or lack of effect of early experiential manipulations is commonly taken to indicate whether a particular experience or source of stimulation is normally incorporated into the development of a specific phenotype. However, it is important to distinguish between what such studies reveal about the role that experience *normally* plays in *development* versus what they tell about neural and behavioral *plasticity* in the more general sense of the term. (2) It is important to determine not only *whether* but also *how* early experience plays a role in development. It is now apparent that early experience can play a number of different roles in the development of both neural and behavioral properties. These two important issues are dealt with in Gottlieb's first chapter. In his second chapter, Gottlieb addresses the question of what role auditory experience during embryonic development plays in the ontogeny of species-specific auditory perception in birds.

The chapters by Grobstein and Chow, Daniels and Pettigrew, Tees, and Gottlieb provide evidence that experiential factors *do* play important roles in the development of both neural and behavioral specificities. Nonetheless, the nervous system is not a "tabula rasa" before experiential factors become capable of influencing neural structure and function. There is a high degree of order and specificity in the patterning of neural connections which is established *prefunctionally*. To account for the development of these selective connections, Roger Sperry first proposed in the 1940s that individual neurons acquire unique biochemical labels early in development under genetic control, and that cells with similar labels subsequently establish selective connections with each other through the operation of cytochemical affinities. This chemoaffinity theory of neuronal specificity has since generated an enormous amount of research, much of which has recently been interpreted as being inconsistent with the theory as originally proposed. The chapters by Meyer and Sperry and by Keating review much of this controversial literature.

In closing, I would like to point out that, from the developmental point of view, the question is not one of genes versus experience. To rule out the possible contribution of a given experience to the development of a particular phenotype is not to say that structure, function, or behavior is encoded in the genome. Nor does the demonstration that experience is necessary for the development of a particular phenotype imply that genes are unimportant or play a relatively minor role. The goal of developmental analysis is to characterize the variety of events at each stage of development which ultimately give rise to a given phenotype.

References

Barlow, H. B. Single units and sensation: A doctrine for perceptual psychology? *Perception*, 1972, **1**, 371–394.

Barlow, H. B., & Pettigrew, J. D. Lack of specificity of neurones in the visual cortex of young kittens. *Journal of Physiology (London)*, 1971, **218**, 98–100P.

Barlow, H. B., Blakemore, C., & Pettigrew, J. D. The neural mechanism of binocular depth discrimination. *Journal of Physiology (London)*, 1967, **193**, 327–342.

Beach, F. A., & Jaynes, J. Effects of early experience upon the behavior of animals. *Psychological Bulletin*, 1954, **51**, 239–263.

Boring, E. G. *A history of experimental psychology*. New York: Appleton, 1950.

Chow, K. L., Riesen, A. H., & Newell, F. W. Degeneration of retinal ganglion cells in infant chimpanzees reared in darkness. *Journal of Comparative Neurology*, 1957, **107**, 27–42.

Fantz, R. L. Ontogeny of perception. In A. M. Schrier, H. F. Harlow, & F. Stollnitz (Eds.), *Behavior of nonhuman primates* (Vol. 2). New York: Academic Press, 1965, Pp. 365–403.

Gaze, R. M. The formation of nerve connections. New York: Academic Press, 1970.

Gottlieb, G. *Development of species identification in birds. An inquiry into the prenatal determinants of perception*. Chicago, Ill.: The University of Chicago Press, 1971.

Hebb, D. O. *Organization of behavior*. New York: Wiley, 1949.

Heidbreder, E. *Seven psychologies*. New York: Appleton, 1933.

Hobbes, T. *Leviathan*. Oxford: Blackwell, 1946.

Hochberg, J. E. Nativism and empiricism in perception. In L. Postman (Ed.), *Psychology in the making*. New York: Knopf, 1962. Pp. 255–330.

Hubel, D. H., & Wiesel, T. N. Receptive fields of single neurones in the cat's striate cortex. *Journal of Physiology (London)*, 1959, **148**, 574–591.

Hubel, D. H., & Wiesel, T. N. Receptive fields, binocular interaction and functional architecture in the cat's visual cortex. *Journal of Physiology (London)*, 1962, **160**, 106–154.

Hubel, D. H., & Wiesel, T. N. Receptive fields of cells in striate cortex of very young, visually inexperienced kittens. *Journal of Neurophysiology*, 1963, **26**, 994–1002.

Hubel, D. H., & Wiesel, T. N. Binocular interaction in striate cortex of kittens reared with artificial squint. *Journal of Neurophysiology*, 1965, **28**, 1041–1059.

Katsuki, Y. Neural mechanism of auditory sensation in cats. In W. A. Rosenblith (Ed.), *Sensory communication*. Cambridge, Mass.: M.I.T. Press, 1961. Pp. 561–583.

Köhler, W. *Gestalt psychology*. New York: New American Library, 1947.

Kuffler, S. W. Discharge patterns and functional organization of mammalian retina. *Journal of Neurophysiology*, 1953 **16**, 37–68.

Lamprecht, S. P. *Our philosophical traditions. A brief history of philosophy in western civilization*. New York: Appleton, 1955.

Lettvin, J. Y., Maturana, H. R., McCulloch, W. S., & Pitts, W. H. What the frog's eye tells the frog's brain. *Proceedings of the Institute of Radio Engineers*, 1959, **47**, 1940–1951.

Locke, J. *On politics and education*. Roslyn, N.Y.: Walter J. Black, 1947.

Lynch, G., Matthews, D. A., Mosko, S., Parks, T., & Cotman, C. Induced acetylcholinesterase-rich layer in rat dentate gyrus following entorhinal lesions. *Brain Research*, 1972, **42**, 311–318.

Lynch, G., Stanfield, B., & Cotman, C. Developmental differences in post-lesion axonal growth in the hippocampus. *Brain Research*, 1973, **59**, 155–168.

Mountcastle, V. B. Some functional properties of the somatic afferent system. In W. A. Rosenblith (Ed.), *Sensory communication*. Cambridge, Mass.: M.I.T. Press, 1961. Pp 403–436.

Murphy, G. *An historical introduction to modern psychology*. New York: Harcourt, 1932.

Pettigrew, J. D. The effect of visual experience on the development of stimulus specificity by kitten cortical neurons. *Journal of Physiology (London)*, 1974, **237**, 49–74.

Riesen, A. H. The development of perception in man and the chimpanzee. *Science*, 1947, **106**, 107–108.

Riesen, A. H. Sensory deprivation. In E. Stellar & J. M. Sprague (Eds.), *Progress in physiological psychology* (Vol. 1). New York: Academic Press, 1966. Pp. 117–147.

Shlaer, R. Shift in binocular disparity causes compensatory change in the cortical structure of kittens. *Science*, 1971, **173**, 638–641.

Sperry, R. W. The problem of central nervous system reorganization after nerve regeneration and muscle transposition. *Quarterly Review of Biology*, 1945, **20**, 311–369.

Sperry, R. W. Embryogenesis of behavioral nerve nets. In R. L. DeHaan & H. Ursprung (Eds.), *Organogenesis*. New York: Holt, 1965. Pp. 161–186.

Stent, G. S. Limits to the scientific understanding of man. *Science*, 1975, **187**, 1052–1057.

von Senden, M. *Raum—und Gestaltauffassung bei operierten Blindgeborenen vor und nach Operation*. As cited in Hebb, D. O. *Organization of behavior*. New York: Wiley, 1949.

Watson, R. I. *The great psychologists. From Aristotle to Freud*. Philadelphia, Penn.: Lippincott, 1963.

Whitfield, I. C., & Evans, E. F. Responses of auditory cortical neurons to stimuli of changing frequency. *Journal of Neurophysiology*, 1965, **28**, 655–672.

Wiesel, T. N., & Hubel, D. H. Single cell responses in striate cortex of kittens deprived of vision in one eye. *Journal of Neurophysiology*, 1963, **26**, 1003–1017.

Wiesel, T. N., & Hubel, D. H. Comparison of the effects of unilateral and bilateral eye closure on cortical unit responses in kittens. *Journal of Neurophysiology*, 1965, **28**, 1029–1040.

Wiesel, T. N., & Hubel, D. H. Ordered arrangement of orientation columns in monkeys lacking visual experience. *Journal of Comparative Neurology*, 1974, **158**, 307–318.

THE ROLES OF EXPERIENCE IN THE DEVELOPMENT OF BEHAVIOR AND THE NERVOUS SYSTEM

GILBERT GOTTLIEB

Psychology Laboratory, Division of Research
North Carolina Department of Mental Health
Raleigh, North Carolina

I. Introduction

The nature–nurture question is neither trivial nor simple (nor dead); it has ensnared, teased, and persistently occupied some of the best scientific minds of the century [see, for example, the reviews by Kuo (1921, 1967), Lehrman (1953, 1970), Lorenz (1965, 1970), and Schneirla (1956, 1966)]. The recent recognition of boundaries and constraints on learning (Hinde & Stevenson-Hinde, 1973; Seligman & Hager, 1972) is an important conceptual step forward in our understanding of the interplay of organismic and environmental factors in the determination of species-typical behavior. Another conceptual issue that stands in need of clarification is the various roles that early experience can play in the development of species-specific or species-typical behavior. (The terms *species-specific* and *species-typical* are used in a normative, descriptive sense throughout this essay.) The present article is devoted to that task, especially dealing with the interrelationship between maturation and experience in development. Although the focus is on behavior, I think the present notions are also applicable to the development of the nervous system, as I shall try to indicate. In undertaking this analysis, I am quite conscious of standing on the shoulders of Z.-Y. Kuo, T. C. Schneirla, and D. S. Lehrman in particular. Through their collective writings it has become clear that "innate," "instinctive," species-specific, or species-typical behavior has a developmental background that is worthy of theoretical interest and experimental analysis, particularly from the standpoint of discovering entirely unanticipated dependencies of species-typical behavior on prior experience, sometimes extending even into the prenatal sphere (Gottlieb, 1973). Although the analysis of the roles of experience in the development of species-typical behavior is the topic of this essay, this should not be construed to mean that the author believes that experience (as narrowly defined below) is necessarily involved in all aspects of behavioral development—in fact, I present some evidence on this very point myself later in this volume. The present analysis is addressed to clarifying the various ways experience can be involved in development, and, to the extent it is successful, such an analysis sheds light on what is meant when we say experience is *not* involved in development.

II. Experience

Although Schneirla's (1956, 1966) original definitions of experience were of enormous value in focusing attention on the necessity and prospects of developmental analysis, I think it is now necessary to sharpen his statements in order to delineate the different ways in which experience can contribute to the development of behavior. Schneirla defined experience in a rather global way:

... "experience," defined as *the effects of extrinsic stimulation upon development and behavior*. [Schneirla, 1956, p. 405; italics in original]

... *experience* ... defined as the contributions to development of the effects of stimulation from all available sources (external and internal), including their functional trace effects surviving from the earlier development.... [Schneirla, 1966, p. 288, italics in original]

In light of his knowledge of the fundamental tenets of developmental biology, Schneirla attempted to call attention to the possibilities for interactions at all levels and stages of epigenetic development by putting forth an all-embracing definition of experience. Schneirla also defined experience in this general way in order to transcend the more restricted usage and understanding of the term, which makes it synonymous with known instances of learning, the point being that during development many experiences (described below) can have very potent physiological, anatomical, and behavioral effects that are distinct from existing notions of conditioning or learning. (The term experience includes instances of conditioning and learning, but it is not restricted to these phenomena.) By using the term in this general sense, Schneirla, among others, was able to prepare the way for an acceptance of the principle of bidirectional (reciprocal) effects of maturation and experience in the development of behavior (Gottlieb, 1970), which, to the extent it continues to be clarified and validated, can be a useful integrative conception of the relationship between "nature" and "nurture" in ontogeny. The need in developmental theory for the term experience (and the need to define it more precisely) has been recognized by several writers. For example, Moltz has written:

Admittedly, the term experience is difficult to define precisely, but some such term is evidently needed to designate instances . . . in which involvement with the ontogenetic milieu operates to structure behavior through channels which do not appear to depend on learning as currently conceived [Moltz, 1965, p. 40].

To sharpen the basis of the discussion, I would like to narrow Schneirla's original definitions of experience to refer to the spontaneous or evoked activity of exteroceptive, interoceptive, and proprioceptive sensory systems (i.e., the activity of sensory organs, fiber tracts, projection and association areas), as well as the exercise of the motor (neuromusculoskeletal) side, thus including both sensory and motor neural (bioelectric) activity as well as overt behavioral activity. In a word, experience involves sensory or motor *function*, whether evoked or spontaneous.[1] The inclusion of neural activity is called for not only because we now have electrophysiological monitoring techniques that can put us in touch with these events on the most microscopic developmental basis (e.g., Provine, 1973), but because *spontaneous* (as well as evoked) neural activity may play an important role in neural maturation and behavioral development (Berger, 1969; Gottlieb, 1970, 1973;

---

[1] This definition of experience is still rather broad but it is more specific, and also narrower, than Schneirla's. I think clarity is served by these restrictions. While one cannot help but agree with Schneirla that everything that happens inside and outside the organism is potentially important and thus fodder for developmental analysis, I do not think that it is any longer necessary to subsume all such events under the term experience in order to assure that their possible bearing on development will not escape notice. Although I am sympathetic to criticisms that I have heard of the overinclusive nature of Schneirla's definition of experience, I feel that the original overinclusiveness served an important purpose in drawing attention to the need for the classical ethologist, among others, to define "not-experience," a challenge that I think has never been taken up very explicitly. (See Bateson, 1975, for an exceptionally keen analysis of that problem.) I hope the present essay also contributes something on that score.

Hamburger, 1973; Oppenheim, 1974; Roffwarg, Muzio, & Dement, 1966). Although the present definition of experience is couched largely in neural terms, it is entirely appropriate for the behaviorist and others to continue to specify experiential manipulations exclusively by reference to operations performed "outside" of the animal (i.e., by a description of procedures for creating sensory deprivation or enhancement, motor immobility, etc.). Outside of some possible gain in precision, the main advantage of a neurally biased definition is that it allows for the inclusion of spontaneous activity as an experiential variable.

III. Roles of Experience in Development

In the present article I would like to propose that experience can play at least three roles in the development of behavior and the nervous system; it can *maintain* (sustain, preserve) ongoing developmental states or particular end points, it can *facilitate* development, and it can *induce* (channel, determine) development. I think it is of prime theoretical and practical importance to distinguish clearly between these alternatives, not only to avoid what have been persistent terminological and semantic problems in the history and theory of instinctive behavior (e.g., Lehrman, 1970), but also to clarify some conceptual difficulties in the neurobiological literature concerning the role of experience in the development of "specificity" in the nervous system, especially the relationship between maturation and experience. (For the present purpose maturation is defined as the proliferation, migration, growth, and differentiation of neural cells and their axonal and dendritic processes.)

A. Maintenance

The lowest level or weakest effect of function (experience) on the development of behavior or the maturation of the nervous system concerns the necessity of function merely to preserve an already developed state or end point, regardless of how the state or end point itself was achieved. Maintenance (maintaining experience) can also be required to keep an immature system intact, going, and functional so that it is able to reach its full development at a later stage; in this sense, maintenance serves to-be-achieved end points. (A novel example of such an experiential effect in the development of innate behavior is described at length in my later chapter in this volume.)

A blatant example of maintenance can be seen in extreme instances of sensory deprivation which cause adult humans to behave inefficiently and perhaps even to undergo "psychotic" experience of hallucinations or delusions when their usual sensory input is so drastically reduced (e.g.,

Bexton, Heron, & Scott, 1954). Here the ordinary, everyday effects of activity or function seem to be necessary to maintain routine behavioral efficiency and, in some individuals at least, to preserve nonpsychotic perceptual and thought content.

At a developmental level, long-term sensory deprivation during early neonatal development can lead to atrophy and disintegration of neural tissue in the sensory system deprived of stimulation, as the earliest studies in this area amply demonstrated (e.g., Chow, Riesen, & Newell, 1957).

On the motor side, preventing overt movement in chick embryos for one to two days during embryonic development results in muscular atrophy and immobility of the joints of the extremities (Drachman & Sokoloff, 1966). The movements being prevented in this case were very likely spontaneously occurring ones, not sensory-instigated, reflexive activities (Hamburger, 1971). Although the appropriate experiment has not yet been done, such short-term immobilization at later, postnatal stages (when the muscles and joints are not in such a formative stage of differentiation and growth) would very probably not result in such severe atrophy and ankylosis of the joints.

At a more advanced level of behavioral complexity, involving perception, it would appear that if young domestic chicks are deprived of hearing the maternal call of their species for several days after hatching, they become relatively unresponsive to it (Graves, 1973; Spalding, 1873). In a similar vein, Dawkins (1968) attributes the persistence and ultimate specificity of the young chick's preference for pecking at solid hemispheres to the dual effects of rewarding experiences which maintain that preference and unrewarding experiences which extinguish the proclivity to peck at flat objects. These results would seem to be prime examples of *functional validation* at the behavioral level (see resumé of M. Jacobson's theory of neural specificity below).

In the "higher" realms of learned behavior (fear conditioning in this case), Campbell and Jaynes' (1966) notion of *reinstatement* as an important developmental phenomenon is strictly of a maintenance character, involving as it does the periodic partial repetition of an earlier experience which is effective when the animal has had a specific earlier experience but relatively ineffective (i.e., does not induce learning) in the absence of the early experience. Campbell and Jaynes posit reinstatement as the means whereby the effects of certain earlier experiences persist into adulthood; in the absence of reinstatement, they contend that the early experiences would not influence adult behavior.

As an aside, it bears mention that much of the operant conditioning literature is concerned with the effectiveness of different reinforcement schedules on the maintenance of behavior, although there is unfortunately relatively little research emphasis on how the behaviors in question developed initially.

The possibility of maintaining certain kinds of vocal behavior in young infants via operant social reinforcement has been demonstrated by Rheingold, Gewirtz, and Ross (1959), for example. An operant framework is currently being applied to the development of species-specific song in birds by Stevenson (1969). From her early results, it is virtually certain that maintenance is involved (in certain species, at least) in the "shaping" of the final song. (The extent to which auditory experience may also have facilitating and even inductive effects on the achievement of song is discussed below.)

Finally, although many electrophysiological investigators studying the development of neural specificities in sensory systems have not been clear on whether they are studying the maintenance, facilitative, or inductive effects of experience, at least one theory is quite clear on this point. This is M. Jacobson's (1974) theory of *functional validation*, which views experience or function as preserving specific neural connectivities or specific "feature detectors," while the absence of functional activation through sensory deprivation leads to the degeneration of other connectivities and detectors. Thus, according to this theory, the specificity of neural connections and neural functions is clearly viewed as a consequence of the selective experiential maintenance of end points achieved by prior neural maturation processes. Because Jacobson is concerned primarily with explaining specificity in the visual system, no mention is made of the motor side as such. Also, this theory restricts itself to the late-maturing type II neurons of Cajal [also called *microneurons* (Altman, 1967)], which, in direct contrast to type I, or *macroneurons*, have short axons with profuse and highly local interconnection exclusively within the *central* nervous system. I see no reason why, in principle, the maintenance point of view (effect of exercise) could not hold for macroneurons or for the motor side, especially in light of the many species of higher vertebrates (birds and mammals) in which motility begins early in embryonic or fetal development (Gottlieb, 1973; Hamburger, 1973; Oppenheim, 1974).

In conclusion, much of behavior and neural circuitry which is considered innate, in the sense that it appears to develop and perfect itself in the absence of experience, could be nonetheless dependent on experience for its maintenance. This important distinction, i.e., whether experience plays a contributory role in the maturation of the nervous system and in the development of the behavior or merely in their maintenance, is all too often not observed in discussions bearing on the nature–nurture problem and the neural specificity literature, even though it is an experimentally resolvable issue depending only on the use of appropriate developmental research strategies as, for example, outlined by Solomon and Lessac (1968). The research strategies that allow one to distinguish the precise role of experience in the normal development of behavior and the nervous system are rather demanding and not always immediately obvious, so perhaps that is why so few studies, especially in the neural specificity literature, lend themselves to clear interpretation on this point (see, for example, the reviews by Grobstein & Chow and by Tees in this volume).

B. Facilitation

This represents a quantitative or regulative effect of experience on the development of behavior (or the nervous system). An important difference between the maintenance and facilitative effects of experience is that the latter quantitatively assist in the developmental achievement of certain states or end points, whereas the former operate to preserve already achieved states or end points. The difference between facilitative and *inductive* effects of experience, on the other hand, is that the former refer to instances where development of the behavior (or neural structure and function) will eventually occur even in the absence of the experience (though it may be subpar without experience), whereas in the absence of inductive experience behavior (or neural connectivity or activity) would take a different course and reach a different outcome. Facilitative experiences thus regulate maturation, hasten development, improve performance, increase perceptual differentiation, raise the animal's general perceptual and learning abilities, etc., whereas inductive experiences determine whether or not a given behavioral or neural aspect is present or not. Inductive (or determinative) experiences thus exert the strongest possible effect on development, maintenance the weakest, with facilitation intermediate and probably the most ubiquitous of the three.

Examples of "low-level" facilitative effects of *spontaneously* occurring experience (function) are the hypothesized effects of rapid-eye-movement (REM) sleep on the fetus and newborn. Roffwarg *et al.* (1966) have suggested that REM sleep facilitates neural structural differentiation and growth (i.e., maturation) of the central nervous system, and Berger (1969) theorizes that REM sleep provides the intrinsic mechanism necessary for the proper development of binocular oculomotor control which, he feels, initially at least, is independent of peripheral visual input during wakefulness. Another example of the facilitative effect of motor exercise comes from Zelazo, Zelazo, and Kolb (1972), who observed that deliberate and explicit prolongation of reflexive stepping in the human neonate between birth and 8 weeks of age resulted in an earlier onset of independent walking around one year of age. This kind of research, especially with humans, is never without important considerations of negative as well as positive side effects (Pontius, 1973), but the particular effect under discussion can nonetheless be described as facilitative in the specific sense that it involved earlier-than-usual onset of independent locomotion.

Instances of the rather fundamental facilitative influences of *evoked* sensory function would include the following. In the visual system, for example, the presence of appropriate sensory stimulation accelerates sensory functional (EEG) maturation (Paulson, 1965; Peters, Vonderahe, & Powers, 1956), and its absence decelerates functional (ERG) maturation (Zetterström, 1956). The same kind of quantitative changes are observed at the structural level. As shown by Parnavelas, Globus, and Kaups (1973), there is an increase of about 8% in the number of dendritic spines in the visual cortex of albino rats which have been reared under constant illumination instead of cycles of light and dark (but see O'Steen & Anderson, 1971). Apparently, the cortical dendritic spines increase their number in response to a wide range of sensory stimulation (Schapiro & Vukovich, 1970). These results are of particular importance because each additional dendritic spine signifies another synaptic contact. To complicate matters, other studies indicate that sensory stimulation may cause an increase in the *size* of synapses with a concomitant decrease in *number* of synapses, depending on the nature of the synapse and its location in the cortex (upper or lower half) (Cragg, 1968). [A very informed review of this complicated field has recently appeared (Globus, 1975).]

The same sort of quantitative effects also holds true for thresholds, be they behavioral or physiological. For example, when duck embryos are deprived of normally occurring auditory stimulation, fewer of them are behaviorally responsive to the maternal call of their species after hatching, and those that do respond show a longer latency than nondeprived ducklings (Gottlieb, 1971). Paulson (1965) found that 24 hours of prior light exposure decreased the latency of the *a*-wave of the ERG as well as the evoked response in the optic lobe of duck embryos so exposed. If chick embryos are exposed to light during the course of incubation, they hatch sooner than dark-incubated embryos (heat being carefully controlled) (Lauber & Shutze, 1964). Exposure to certain sounds can either accelerate or decelerate hatching time in quail embryos (Vince, 1973). Prior exposure to light facilitates the young chick's behavioral approach to a flickering light, whereas prior exposure to sound delays the approach to a source of visual flicker (Bateson & Seaburne-May, 1973). Prior exposure to light also facilitates the visual imprinting (learning) process (Bateson & Wainwright, 1972).

Examples of the facilitative effects of experience operating at a higher level of biopsychological complexity are represented by the well-known physiological, anatomical, and behavioral effects of early (prenatal and postnatal) handling in rodents (Ader & Grota, 1973; Denenberg & Zarrow, 1971; Levine, 1970). [The question has been raised whether these effects are always beneficial and whether experimental handling so greatly transcends the normal experience of wild rodents as not to be a useful experimental procedure for understanding normal development (Daly, 1973), but for the present purpose these important questions are momentarily suspended merely for the sake of pointing to diverse examples of the facilitating effects of experience. The problem of the role of experience in normal development is a key one, and it is discussed at length below.] One would like to be able also to include here the negative adaptive effects of early experiential deprivation (e.g., in dogs; Fuller, 1967), but, as with the case of the design of most deprivation studies, it is necessary to point out that one cannot be sure whether the effects of the absence of social experience represent a failure of maintenance or an absence of facilitation. [The research methodology of Lessac & Solomon (1969) speaks to this point: the results of their demonstration study with beagles suggest that both maintenance and facilitation may be involved, depending on which psychological or behavioral functions are later examined.] The investigators involved with the early environmental enrichment studies in rats have become aware of these interpretative difficulties and they are now trying to design their studies in such a way that maintenance and facilitative effects can be distinguished (e.g., Rosenzweig, 1971). The point is that the cerebral and behavioral effects of these studies are at most a quantitative (facilitative) effect—they do not seem to fit in the category of inductive (determinative) effects of experience, in the sense that the control or deprived animals do develop a cerebral cortex, etc., and they are able to solve problems, but their cortices are thinner and their problem-solving abilities are quantitatively inferior to those of the experimental or enriched animals. [It bears mention that these particular enrichment studies may not be portraying strictly developmental phenomena—apparently the same results can be achieved with adult rats (Riege, 1971).]

The paradigm of perceptual learning, as it applies to development, represents a facilitative effect of experience, whether one conceives of the specific effect as leading to an enrichment of perceptual abilities (Hebb, 1949) or as a differentiation of perception (Gibson, 1969). Either outcome represents a quantitative improvement which transcends that which would be present in the absence of the particular experience or set of experiences. There has been an unfortunate tendency in the imprinting literature not to distinguish clearly between the facilitative effects of perceptual learning and the inductive effects of the imprinting experience. For example, both Sluckin (1965) and Gibson (1969) seem to view imprinting as an instance of perceptual learning. By lumping imprinting and perceptual learning, one fails to appreciate two distinct investigative problems: experiences that lead to improvements in perceptual *discrimination* versus experiences that lead to the induction of a positive perceptual *preference* for a given object (i.e., a determinative effect of experience). In imprinting, the latter is logically prior to the former, and it is the more fundamental of the two problems; perceptual learning accrues on the basis of the preference (and other related sensory-perceptual experiences), whereas the preference itself is a result of the imprinting experience. Perceptual learning would allow the imprinted animal to make ever finer discrimination of the preferred object over similar ones in simultaneous choice tests where both objects are present. There may be a tendency to confuse imprinting and perceptual learning because *exposure* to the object (or some feature of the object) is necessary for either phenomenon to occur and thus is common to both. (The role of perceptual learning in the development of species identification is discussed still further in a later chapter by the author.)

A paradigmatic study of the probable role of perceptual learning in the development of depth perception is that by Tees (1974 and this volume). In Tees' study, neonatal rats were either allowed visual experience (light-reared) or denied visual experience (dark-reared) for various times after birth and then tested for the fineness of their depth discrimination in a visual-cliff apparatus. Each group was tested at one age only in a design that allowed the discrimination of facilitative from maintenance effects of experience. Tees' results indicate that depth perception in rats develops *and improves* in the absence of visual experience; the rate at which it improves is slower than in light-reared rats, however, and, most important, the ability of visually deprived rats to make fine discriminations never reaches the level of the visually experienced rats, thereby implicating the visual experience as facilitative. In addition, after an even longer period of deprivation, rather than showing further improvement in their depth perception, the performance of light-deprived rats eventually begins to deteriorate in the continued absence of visual experience, thereby showing the maintenance aspect of visual stimulation. Thus, in this study, visual experience can clearly be said to play a facilitative role in the development of fine depth perception, possibly as a consequence of perceptual learning. (If the improvement and ultimate keenness of depth perception could be shown to be a consequence of sheer exposure of the eyes to nonpatterned light independent of the necessity for visual depth experiences, then it would not be correct to call this an instance of perceptual learning although it would still be appropriate to label the effect of light as facilitative.) Tees' results are depicted in Fig. 1.

Another area of research where there has been a persistent problem in separating the maintenance from the facilitative effects of early experience concerns the many developmental studies of stimulus generalization. These studies usually employ complete sensory deprivation and testing at a single

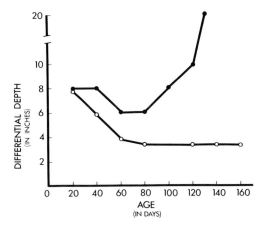

Fig. 1. When the depth of the visually deep side of a "visual cliff" is systematically varied to determine the fineness of depth discrimination in animals which always prefer to descend to the shallowest side, visually inexperienced (dark-reared, ●) rats do not develop the fine differential depth discrimination of visually experienced (light-reared, ○) rats. From Tees (1974).

age [see, for example, the review by Ganz (1968)], so when a deficit is observed, i.e., a shallower generalization gradient in the deprived than in the control group, it is not possible to infer whether the deficiency stems from the lack of facilitating (here, perceptual sharpening) effects of experience or merely the maintenance aspect. Further, to correctly interpret the precise nature of the facilitating effects of experience in the development of stimulus generalization, it is necessary to know whether specific experience with certain perceptual dimensions is requisite to the sharpening of discrimination and therefore to a steeper generalization gradient, or whether the experiential requirement is relatively nonspecific; one must realize, of course, that experience may play different roles in the development of different perceptual dimensions.

In summary, there are three main ways in which experience can facilitate behavioral, physiological, and anatomical development. As shown in Fig. 2, experience can (1) accelerate development, (2) boost terminal achievement, and (3) accelerate development *and* boost terminal achievement. To illustrate (1), in which there is merely an acceleration of development but no change in terminal level of achievement, it will be recalled that exposure to light causes chick embryos to hatch earlier than nonexposed embryos, but the latter do hatch. Similarly, in my own behavioral work (Gottlieb, 1971), devocalized, aurally isolated Peking ducklings are delayed in their ability to discriminate their species maternal call from the wood duck maternal

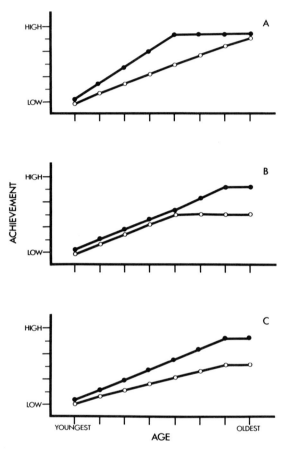

FIG. 2. Three modes of facilitation: experience causes accelerated development (A); boost in terminal level of achievement (B); and a combination of accelerated development and an elevated terminal level of achievement (C). See text for examples of each mode at the behavioral, physiological, and anatomical levels of analysis. ● —— ●, with experience; ○ —— ○, without experience.

call—they could not do that until 48 hours after hatching, whereas vocal, communally incubated Peking ducklings are able to make that discrimination by 24 hours after hatching. At the physiological level, Paulson (1965) found an earlier evoked visual response in visually experienced as compared to inexperienced duck embryos. At the anatomical level, the diameters of cell nuclei and the volume of internuclear material per nucleus in the visual cortex reach their peak at earlier ages in visually experienced as opposed to visually inexperienced mice. While such growth in the visual cortex is accelerated by visual stimulation, the visual cortex of the dark-reared control animals eventually reaches a comparable level on these same parameters, even though the animals remain in the dark (Gyllensten, Malmfors, & Norrlin, 1965).

With reference to the second mode (2), in contrast to the first one, there is actually an enduring quantitative difference in the level of ultimate achievement caused by the presence or the absence of experience. For an example at the behavioral level we have Tees' dark-reared rats, which, although they can discriminate the shallow from the deep side of a visual cliff, do not ever reach the level of fine depth perception exhibited by light-reared rats. At the physiological level, if the tuning of orientation-specific visual cells, or, for example, the frequency sensitivity of auditory neurons, were not to reach the degree of sharpness in the absence of experience which they do with experience, then that would be an example of the second mode of facilitation. At the anatomical level we have the aforementioned example from the research of Parnavelas et al. (1973), in which albino rats reared under constant illumination attain a larger number of dendritic spines in their visual cortex than rats reared in light–dark cycles.

The third mode in which facilitation can operate represents a combination of the first two modes, referring to instances where accelerated development results in a terminal level of achievement above that of the experience-deprived animal.

In conclusion, the foregoing makes clear the methodological necessity of recurrently sampling from the experience-deprived control group at various ages in order to be able to distinguish the facilitative effects of experience that result merely in acceleration from effects that result in a persistent difference in ultimate level of attainment. These important distinctions are so often overlooked in the developmental literature that we have very few conclusive examples of the persistence of early advantages (or disadvantages) relative to the numerous instances of acceleration (or deceleration) as such.

C. Induction

This is the most dramatic effect of experience, one that students of development find most significant and interesting: instances in which the presence or the absence of a particular experience (or set or sequence of experiences) completely determines whether or not a given species-typical neural feature or behavioral activity, whether sensory-perceptual or motor-behavioral, will manifest itself later on in development. While such "canalizing" effects are well known in embryology and developmental endocrinology where, for example, the presence or the absence of certain gonadal hormones in the prenatal period determines whether the genitalia will be of the male or female type upon maturity (e.g., Goy, Bridgson, & Young, 1964; Willier,

Gallagher, & Koch, 1937), there are very few clear-cut examples of the inductive experiential effects in the neural and behavioral literature when one seeks for them in the context of supplying the normal developmental underpinning for species-typical behavior or neural structure or function. While the determinative effects of induction clearly involve the notion of "plasticity," many experiments committed in the name of plasticity have unfortunately little to contribute to our understanding of experiential mechanisms underlying normal (i.e., species-typical) development, as will be discussed in more detail later in this section. Imprinting would represent an inductive phenomenon *par excellence* in those instances where the early experience brings about a normal (usually occurring) later state of affairs which would not occur but for the early experience. Defined in this restrictive way, there are actually few examples of imprinting, the early experiential basis of mating preferences and song-learning in certain species of birds being perhaps the best known candidates (see below). One has the impression that there may be many such examples in normal or species-typical development, but they occur within such a complex web of biopsychological *constraints* that we have not yet been able to clearly grasp and appreciate them—imprinting does not really represent a "blank slate" model of development, although that model may be the one which most readily comes to mind in thinking about inductive influences in development.

A paradigmatic study of the inductive effects of experience in the normal development of behavior is that by Wiens (1970), involving an analysis of substrate preferences in red-legged frogs (*Rana aurora*). The usual habitat of of these creatures is a shallow pond or overflow area, characterized by slender, emergent willow branches, cattails, submerged weeds stems and grasses—all essentially linear structures that would cast more or less linear shadows on the muddy substrate. In the laboratory, Wiens reared red-legged larvae in one of three "habitats" and tested them pre- and postmetamorphically for their "habitat" preference. He reared one group in white pan with parallel black stripes on its floor and walls, a second group in a white pan with black squares on its floor and walls, and a third group in a "featureless" white pan. The larvae were tested for their substrate ("habitat") preference by placing them in a chamber, half of which was covered by the striped pattern and half by the black squares. Each tadpole's preference was recorded by the amount of time it spent in each half of the test chamber during a 3-minute test period. When tested premetamorphically (Stages 35–40 in Fig. 3), the stripe-reared larvae showed a statistically significant preference for the striped side of the test compartment, whereas the square-reared group showed a slight but insignificant preference for the side with the square pattern. When tested postmetamorphically, the stripe-reared group continued to show a strong preference for the striped side and the square-reared group showed a slight increase in their bias toward the

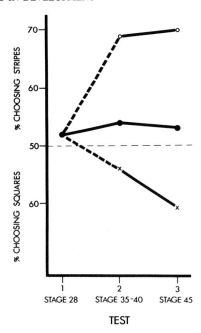

FIG. 3.   Red-legged frogs' choice of substrate ("habitat") pattern as a function of their larval rearing environment. The larvae were raised in a "featureless" white pan (control condition) until they had passed Stage 28, at which time they were placed in a striped pan or one with squares on its floor and walls. As indicated by the test results at Stage 28, the larvae manifested no preference for the striped or squared substrate before being transferred from the control to the experimental conditions. Subsequently, they were given further choice tests premetamorphically (Stages 35–40) and postmetamorphically (Stage 45) to determine whether the rearing environment determined their substrate preference. The strip-reared larvae (O) developed a significant preference for their substrate pattern, but the square-reared larvae (X) did not. ●, Control. Based on Wiens (1970).

side with squares, but this was still a statistically nonsignificant preference. Most important, as shown in Fig. 3, the group reared in the featureless pan continued not to show a preference for either of the two substrate patterns at any of the ages, thus allowing an unequivocal diagnosis of the experiential effect as an inductive one. Thus, the rearing environment of red-legged frog tadpoles determines their later choice of substrate pattern, and this determinative influence operates within perceptual constraints so a preference for certain types of patterns is more readily induced than others.[2]

[2] Experiments by Wiens and others on other species of *Rana* suggest that the positive inductive effects described for *Rana aurora* may be a special case. O'Hara (1974), for example, has found that certain early exposure circumstances can lead to an *avoidance* of the familiar pattern in later preference tests in *Rana clamitans*. Wiens' study with *R. aurora* nonetheless provides a paradigm for the demonstration of an inductive effect of experience on the development of species-specific behavior.

Whereas the example above is exclusively perceptual in character, the one to be described now is perceptual–motor in character. This has to do with the rather complicated developmental background to visually guided reaching or placing in the kitten, as analyzed by Held and Hein and their associates (Hein & Diamond, 1972; Held & Hein, 1963). In order for the kitten to be able to move its limbs and body in space in an adept, species-typical way, the kitten must attain a body-centered visual spatial framework. In order to attain this framework, the kitten must not only have certain visual and motor experiences, but it must have these experiences in a particular *sequence*.

In order to develop skillful visually guided reaching, the young kitten must first fully experience itself moving its body in a visually defined space (e.g., a room with objects in it). The movement must be self-produced: if the kittens are passively moved about by carrying them, they do not achieve a proper body-centered visual spatial framework. In addition, to do well in the reaching test, they must be able to perceive their limbs as they locomote about the room. Kittens which locomote about the room with an Elizabethan collar around their neck (so that they cannot see their forelegs) do not develop skillful reaching—they must have the visual feedback of seeing their forelimbs move in space. Finally, if visually naive kittens are permitted to see their foreleg as they move about in an otherwise dark room (applying a special luminescent to the leg makes it visually perceptible in the dark), this is insufficient to establish skillful visually guided reaching with that fore-leg. This experience is effective only if the kittens have first been allowed to establish a body-centered visual spatial framework by locomoting in a lighted room, even wearing the Elizabethan collar. If they are then allowed to view that foreleg in an otherwise dark surround, their visually guided reaching behavior becomes perfected. In other words, the development of visually guided reaching with a forelimb takes place only in the context of an already acquired "locomotory space."

Kittens that have not been allowed to locomote about the room under their own power do not achieve a body-centered visual spatial framework, as shown by the fact that they collide with obstacles in a test enclosure that has only narrow channels of passage. They need not have previous experience seeing their forelimbs move to achieve a body-centered framework: kittens allowed to locomote in a lighted room wearing Elizabethan collars later perform well in the obstacle course. A further point of interest, attesting to the specificity of the experiential effects, is that the visually guided reaching which is perfected when the kittens are now allowed to see their luminescent forelimb in an otherwise dark surround is restricted to the forelimb viewed! Hein and his collaborators also performed the reciprocal experiment of covering one eye and allowing the kittens to see both their forelimbs as they locomoted in a lighted room. In that case visually guided placing or reaching (with either forelimb) was normal with the "experienced" eye but deficient with the other eye.

These investigations of visual–motor coordination indicate not only (1) the inductive effects of experience but (2) the nature of the requisite experiences. This represents a significant advance in the developmental analysis of behavior. All too few developmental studies attempt to deal with both of these aspects of development.

The question could be quite properly raised why the results of the present analysis of the development of visual–motor coordination are classed as inductive rather than merely facilitative effects of experience. First, there is what could be called a qualitative difference between the behavior of the appropriately and inappropriately experienced animals in the obstacle course:

The experimental animals moved very slowly when placed in the obstacle course. They repeatedly walked directly into the blocks and showed frequent startle responses to this contact. Normally reared kittens of the same age quickly thread their way between the obstacles with a sinuous motion. They avoid contact with the blocks and startle responses are absent [Hein and Diamond, 1972, p. 396].

Second, with respect to the development of visually guided reaching or placing, it is only those animals that had previously developed guided locomotion (a body-centered framework) that display it. The animals that had not previously developed guided locomotion do not display visually guided reaching. Thus, it is not a matter of both groups displaying the behavior and one group merely being better at it (which would be a facilitative effect). It is not until the kittens achieve a body-centered visual framework that they are able to perform the behavior; otherwise they perform at a chance level.

Finally, it is important to note that there are two separable components to visual–motor coordination of the forelimbs in the kitten. One of these is visually triggered limb extension, the other is visually guided placement of the limb. The former requires only rearing in diffuse light for its development (Hein, Gower, & Diamond, 1970), whereas the latter requires the rather more specific background experience described above. In sum, maintenance is necessary to visually triggered limb extension, whereas induction is necessary to visually guided placing.

I would like now to turn to imprinting for the final few (and much more problematical) examples of the inductive effects of experience in the normal development of behavior. The concept of imprinting was originally introduced to describe the various aspects of the early learning of species identification in those avian species which ". . . do not recognize their own species 'instinctively'" (Lorenz, 1937, pp. 262–263). In the ensuing welter of laboratory research with young birds, there has been a tendency to disregard the original problem (the developmental basis of species identification) in favor of showing how "plastic" young birds are, and especially to show how easily their identification (social preferences) can be misdirected to other species via surrogate-rearing or cross-fostering, the implication being that the latter process (interspecific imprinting) tells us how the former (intraspecific imprinting) occurs. Because of this orientation, and the corollary (and, I think, erroneous) assumption that if a young bird's species identification can be misdirected, it must not be selectively perceptive of members of its own species to begin with, there has been a widespread failure to adopt the proper control procedure of presenting the parentally naive bird with species-specific auditory and visual stimuli to actually determine whether the parentally inexperienced bird is indifferent to species-specific patterns of stimulation in advance of contact with its parents and/or siblings. Interestingly, in all cases where some form of this control procedure has been used, the "naive" young birds have been shown to be biased to species-specific parental (or sibling) auditory and/or visual stimuli in advance of parental contact, the selectivity of the auditory aspect usually, but not always, being more evident than the visual (for example, in chicks and ducklings: Gottlieb, 1965, 1971; in chicks: Griswold, 1971; in quail: Heaton, Miller, & Goodwin, 1975; in pheasants: Heinz, 1973; in finches: Immelmann, 1972).

These findings must make us chary of interpreting the role of experience in the development of intraspecific identification as an inductive one, although one might readily conclude that induction *is* a major feature of interspecific imprinting. In other words, there may very well be two separate processes here rather than a single one. There is the developmental process entailed in the animal's becoming selectively responsive to other members of its own species in advance of contact with them, and a second process that *modifies* this original preference by way of making the animal responsive to members of another species. The second process almost certainly involves induction, in the sense of requiring exposure to the alien species—the first one may or may not involve induction (e.g., the young animal may be directed to members of its own species by experiencing its own sensory and perceptual attributes during earlier development).

Perhaps an example of the two processes will help. Ichneumonid wasps normally parasitize the caterpillar *Ephestia*. That is, apparently guided by the sense of smell, they selectively lay their eggs on the larva of *Ephestia*. Reasoning that the rearing experience was influencing their subsequent choice of parasite, Thorpe (1938; Thorpe & Jones, 1937) reared developing ichneumonid wasps on the larvae of a different caterpillar (*Meliphora*) to determine whether this rearing experience would shift the olfactory preferences of the wasps in adulthood. Testing the adults in a two-choice olfactometer, Thorpe found that 66% of the *Meliphora*-reared larvae responded positively to the odor of *Meliphora* larvae, whereas the control group showed no such preference. (The *Meliphora* odor emanated from one arm of the olfactometer, and uncontaminated air from the other.) So a positive preference for the alien species was induced by rearing on the alien larvae. But when these same insects were given a simultaneous choice between *Meliphora* odor and *Ephestia* odor, 65% chose the *Ephestia* odor in preference to the *Meliphora* odor. And, when these same insects, either before or after testing with *Meliphora*, were given a choice between the *Ephestia* odor and a noncontaminated airstream, 85% responded positively to the *Ephestia* odor. The fact that these insects, which were not reared on *Ephestia* larvae, manifested the usual preference for *Ephestia* signifies that the experiment cannot explain the development of the normal, species-specific preference of ichneumonids to selectively parasitize *Ephestia*. The results do speak to induction and plasticity. they do involve creating a preference where none existed, but they do not tell us how the normal process of development results in the usual, species-typical outcome.[3]

Perhaps a single dramatic example of the same sort of problem from the avian imprinting literature will suffice. F. Schutz (1965) was among the first to demonstrate the long-range effects of imprinting. He reared mallard duck males with other duck species for the first 8–10 weeks of life and observed that about two-thirds of these males chose to mate with members of the species they were reared with upon maturity a number of months later. The control group consisted of mallard males, each of which ". . . was reared in its own pen in individual acoustic and optical isolation until they were able to fly at nine weeks of age" [translated from Schutz (1965) p. 84]. All these ducks subsequently paired and mated with members of their own species. Thus, so-called sexual imprinting in mallards has relevance to their establishment of social bonds with other species, not with mallards. It seems to me that the relevance of the behavior of the control group to the problem of the development of intraspecific identification has never really been fully appreciated, and I would not be surprised to find that some students believe sexual imprinting is responsible and necessary for correct intraspecific mat-

---

[3] The experiments reviewed above entail possible methodological complications that have not been discussed because I wanted primarily to use the experimental results to illustrate the conceptual problems. Recently, Manning (1967) has taken quite a different approach to the problem in a study of olfactory preferences in fruit flies, and his results suggest that habituation to originally noxious odors may be involved as well as (or instead of?) the induction of a positive preference based on early exposure. It is far from clear, but there may be two separate empirical problems here, one associated with establishing positive preferences for certain naturally occurring odors (the work on ichneumonids) and the other associated with diminishing the aversive nature of abnormally high concentrations of certain odors (the work on fruit flies).

ing choices in adulthood, whereas it represents nothing more than another instance, albeit striking, of a kind of plasticity which has questionable relevance to problems of species-specific development. Immelmann (1972) seems to be one of the few researchers on long-term imprinting who appreciates the possible differences in developmental processes underlying extra-specific and species-specific preferences.

The above distinctions have been blurred not only in research on imprinting but also in many studies of the role of experience in the development of neural specificity, where there have been many more demonstrations of plasticity in modification-type experiments than in normal developmental processes. For example, after more than a decade of fascinating neurophysiological research on the effects of sensory deprivation and stimulus substitution on the function of cells in the visual cortex of the kitten, it is only this past year that a normative study was published describing the development of binocular disparity, motion and orientation "detectors" in the kitten's visual cortex (Pettigrew, 1974)![4] While I really do not wish to minimize the importance of determining the existence of plasticity in neural and behavioral development, I do wish to call attention to how little we know about the role and importance of inductive processes in species-typical behavior, relative to how much we seem to know about plasticity in development generally.

To close this section on a more positive note, there are some clear indications of inductive influences in some areas of normal development, one of which is the development of bird-song. Nicolai (1959), working with young bullfinches, and Immelmann (1969), with zebra finches, have shown that the young male learns the song of its father (or foster father, be it human or canary or another species of finch), and the youngster passes this song along to its male offspring in the same manner. The social bond is especially important in these particular species, as shown by the fact that the offspring of a hand-reared bullfinch selectively learn an abnormal song from their father even though normal bullfinch singing is to be heard in the vicinity. The same kind of socially canalized selectivity has been observed by Immelmann with his finches.

---

[4] According to Pettigrew (1974), the earlier, groundbreaking studies of Hubel and Wiesel (1963) did not distinguish between motion and orientation specificity in their normative observations, and they also may have reached an erroneous conclusion on the sharpness of orientation selectivity in immature and inexperienced cortical cells. Hubel and Wiesel found orientation-specific cells to be very sharply tuned in advance of experience, possibly because they used centrally depressing anesthetics which, as pointed out by Pettigrew (1974), tend to sharpen an otherwise broad responsiveness. In support of Pettigrew's point, Blakemore and Mitchell (1973) did not find sharply tuned cells in inexperienced cortex, and they did not use depressant anesthetics.

The presumptive importance of an inductive model in the development of species-typical song is further suggested by the fact that species such as chaffinches, white-crowned sparrows, and Arizona juncos, when placed in social isolation early, do not produce species-typical song in adulthood. If they are exposed to playbacks of a model early in development they do produce normal song, but, unfortunately, it is not entirely clear whether this is the way they usually acquire their song because members of a *group* of "social isolates" of the same age do apparently stimulate each other sufficiently to eventually produce normal or near normal song (reviewed by Marler and Mundinger, 1971), which is suggestive of facilitation rather than induction. It has been clearly demonstrated in this work that the song-learning from models takes place during a species-typical, demarcated period (100 days in some species, shorter in others) and that the learning is constrained by what would appear to be vocal and acoustic similarities, with own species' characteristics representing the high point in the gradient and the slope falling off with more distantly related species. Naturally, to take a properly analytic view of song-learning, it is necessary to examine the various constituents of the final product because only certain specific features of the full song may require induction, as, for example, in the case of the terminal flourish in chaffinch song. Still other features may require facilitation, some features no auditory experience, and so on.

Finally, it has been suggested that natural food preferences are possibly induced by the first feeding experience in snapping turtles (Burghardt & Hess, 1966), and again there are constraints which make certain food more effective than others (Burghardt, 1967). There is also evidence which indicates that the initial dietary preferences of weanling rats are very strictly determined by the mother's diet as the pups experience characteristic smells and tastes upon ingesting her milk (Galef & Henderson, 1972). This would appear to be a transitory inductive effect, however—at least in the laboratory.

As far as the nervous system is concerned, I do not think an inductive effect of experience (or function) has as yet been unambiguously demonstrated in the context of normal development. For example, the neurons in the kitten's visual cortex which are selectively responsive to visual stimuli presented at particular orientations appear to be somewhat (i.e., slightly) biased in advance of visual experience (Blakemore & Mitchell, 1973; Pettigrew, 1974; Daniels & Pettigrew, this volume), so the effect of experience in "fine tuning" or sharpening these preexisting preferences may be facilitative rather than inductive. On the other hand, the prism-induced shifts in binocular disparity found by Shlaer (1971) suggest that binocular disparity could be an inductive consequence of experience under normal conditions of development.

The problem of deciding whether to classify these shifts as inductive or facilitative presents a clear and instructive example of the key issues, so it may be useful to describe the problem more fully. If normal, fully mature binocular disparities are present in kittens that have never experienced visual stimulation, then prism-induced shifts merely speak to plasticity, not to how the disparities develop under normal conditions. The normal development of disparity would not be an inductive phenomenon, though it could require experience for maintenance and it might even be facilitated by experience. Pettigrew (1974) finds that immature and inexperienced cortical neurons "tolerate" a wider range of disparities than visually experienced cells. He says the selectivity of binocular disparity (as well as orientation specificity) is narrowed down by maturation and by experience. Thus, this would appear to be a facilitative effect of experience, at least from the physiological point of view. At the anatomical level, however, Pettigrew hypothesizes that experience is essential to the appearance of a certain kind of synaptic terminal (F-type) which causes the sharpening of disparity and orientation specificity by an inhibitory function.

To the extent that the actual growth and differentiation of F-type terminals is strictly a consequence of experience, this would represent an inductive effect at the anatomical level of analysis. It is not contradictory to have an inductive effect at the anatomical level reflected as a facilitative effect at the physiological level; the logic of the nervous system allows one to envisage several instances where this might happen besides in the sharpening of visual "tuning curves." (The same could hold true for the tuning of the frequency response of neurons in the auditory system, for example.) This sort of incongruity—which might also sometimes be present in the relationship between behavior and physiology or behavior and anatomy (Hamburger, 1973)—underscores the necessity of keeping the levels of analysis (anatomy, physiology, behavior) quite distinct in conceptualizing the effects of experience on the development.[5]

To return to the discussion of inductive experiential effects on neural development, if the "laws" of neuronal maturation postulated by Bok (1915)

---

[5] A nagging problem, which is very difficult to resolve, is the apparent absence of an "objective" basis to decide whether the initial physiological orientation specificities described by Blakemore and Mitchell (1973) and by Pettigrew (1974) are really biased sufficiently in the visually inexperienced kitten such that the experiential effect should be described as facilitative rather than inductive. If the "very vague" initial bias is taken to be insignificant (as it is in Wiens' inexperienced, control tadpoles in Fig. 3), then the experiential effect could be described as inductive at the physiological level. I do not see an immediate solution to this problem, but perhaps statistical tests, such as those used to show the presence or the absence of perceptual preferences in the behavioral literature, might also be applicable to the physiological orientation specificities. Please see footnote 3.

and by Ariëns Kappers (Ariëns Kappers, Huber, & Crosby, 1936, pp. 73–85)—*stimulogenous fibrillation* and *neurobiotaxis*—were correct, which they seem not to be, they would be excellent examples of the inductive effects of neural function on neuroanatomical maturation. Bok's notion of stimulogenous fibrillation held that a growing bundle of nerve fibers activates less mature neuroblasts, such that the axon of the newly developing nerve cell grows in the same direction taken by the electrical current that radiates from the growing bundle. Ariëns Kappers' conception of neurobiotaxis referred to dendritic growth, holding that the maturing dendrites of the nerve cell grow *toward* the nerve bundles from which they receive the greatest amount of electrical stimulation. These two laws of axonal and dendritic growth, therefore, would account for the development of particular pathways in the nervous system entirely by function, and thus, if the laws were correct, they would represent an explanation of neuroanatomical specificity by inductive functional means.

Not only do present-day developmental neurobiologists no longer believe in the validity of stimulogenous fibrillation and neurobiotaxis, my impression is that very few of them would counsel inductive experiential mechanisms in species-typical neural development at all, particularly at the anatomical level. This is not to say that developmental neurobiologists are, by and large, of such a conservative turn of mind that they do not believe that experience can alter the nervous system—by now almost everyone knows of the outcome of the trailblazing experiments by Hirsch and Spinelli (1971) and by Blakemore and Cooper (1970), in which the prolonged exposure of kittens to horizontal or vertical stripes has been shown to lead to a disproportionate ratio of cortical cells responding to these stimuli subsequently—it is just that those experiments can be looked upon as showing evidence of a certain kind of neural modifiability or plasticity at the physiological level, not necessarily explicating "how a developing brain *normally* gets itself wired for adaptive function" in the usual course of development (Sperry, 1971; also see Meyer & Sperry, this volume).

If these modification experiments are taken to reflect something about the role of experience at the anatomical level in normal developmental processes, they are usually interpreted as showing the importance of *maintenance* (e.g., Jacobson, 1974). In that view, the disproportionately high ratio of cells responding to vertical or horizontal visual stimuli stems from the fact that the preexisting neural connections responsible for the response to other stimuli (e.g., oblique and diagonal lines) were not preserved in the face of the (abnormal) rearing experience (i.e., these connections would not have atrophied in the face of usual experience). Thus, the anatomical "modification" in this instance is viewed as an outcome of experience operating in the sense of maintenance rather than induction, as it would be if Pettigrew's hypothesis about the F-type synapses turns out to be correct. The argument Blakemore (1973, pp. 67–68) uses against the maintenance interpretation is that he finds no regions of "silent" cortex and no decrease in neuron density in the kittens reared in the restricted (horizontal or vertical stripe) environments. I think quantification could make these results very compelling for facilitation or even induction (modification), depending on what the quantitative assessment revealed about initial orientation specificity, relative amount of "silent" area, and neuron density or, even better, synaptic density in the restricted versus normally reared kittens. In the absence of quantitative comparison—which may pose a very difficult problem because of sampling and other difficulties—I do not see how the matter can be resolved properly.

In actuality, then, it is not possible to precisely delineate the role of experience in the restricted rearing experiments because of an absence of quantitative information on the distribution of cell types in the normal course of development. If it were possible to perform an experiment in which it could be shown that restricted rearing results in absolutely more cells responding to a particular orientation than in normally reared kittens, then this would clearly be an instance of an inductive modification at the physiological level. Whether or not this outcome would reflect an inductive experiential effect at the neuroanatomical level is still another question, of course, but it would seem to imply such a mechanism. Finally, as with the extraspecific imprinting studies, it would be important to try to show whether the inductive modification tells us about the usual course development, or whether these modifications speak only to plasticity as such.

IV. Summary and Conclusions

In this essay I have tried to specify the various ways in which experience can play a role in behavioral, physiological, and anatomical development. If one is interested in a simple yes-or-no answer to the question, Does experience affect the development of behavior and the nervous system?, the different ways in which experience does affect development (*when* it does) are all too often ignored. A related problem is the banality of recurrent demonstrations of experiential modification or experiential modifiability, when these demonstrations are attended by a failure to relate the significance of such modifications to the normal (usual) route or outcome of species-typical development. (The modifications are often done without the benefit of normal developmental baseline information.) In the literature on this topic, there seems to be the tacit assumption that, if a given feature of neural or behavioral development can be shown to be susceptible to the influence of experience, then experience must normally play a part in its ontogeny. As one proceeds through this volume, it will become abundantly clear that there are reasons for doubting this assumption. Consequently, it behooves those of us who are committed to showing the importance of experience in neural and behavioral development to do so in ways which are clearly relevant to an understanding of the normal conditions of development.

In an attempt to delineate and clarify the various ways in which experience could play a role in neural and behavioral development, in the present essay I have narrowed T. C. Schneirla's definition of experience to refer specifically to the spontaneous or evoked activity of exteroceptive, interoceptive, and proprioceptive sensory systems, and the exercise of the motor side, thus including both sensory and motor neural activity as well as overt behavioral activity. Under this definition, experience involves sensory and motor *function*, whether spontaneous or evoked. Although this definition is couched largely in neural terms, it is entirely appropriate for the behaviorist and others to continue to specify experiential manipulations exclusively by reference to operations performed "outside" the animal (i.e., by describing the experimental procedures for creating sensory deprivation or enhancement, motor immobility, and so on). Besides some gain in precision, the other advantage of a neurally biased definition is that it explicitly allows for the inclusion of spontaneous activity as an experiential variable, a trend that is in keeping with several current theories of neural and behavioral development.

I have proposed that experience, thus defined, can play at least three roles in the development of behavior and the nervous system: It can *maintain* (sustain, preserve) ongoing developmental states or particular end points, it can *facilitate* development, and it can *induce* (channel, determine) development. In my opinion, a large part of the controversy in the history and theory of instinctive behavior has been occasioned by a failure to make these elementary conceptual distinctions, and the same fate has sometimes seemed to threaten the current literature on neural specificity. It is hoped that the present essay, and the volume as a whole, will make a positive contribution in these particular respects.

In addition to failing to make what will have seemed to some to be essential qualifications here and there throughout the essay, I have also failed to indicate in any important way the indirect and remote means by which experience may sometimes achieve its ultimate effects on neural and behavioral development. In all too many cases I have written as though sensory stimulation merely affects the sensory system under consideration, and the same for motor activity, whereas *other* systems (sensory, motor, cardiovascular, endocrine) are also capable of being affected by these experiences; and, in fact, in some (or many?) cases, it may be the latter in particular (cardiovascular, endocrine) which have an important role in mediating the consequent changes in behavior and neural structure and function. The main aim of this essay has been to designate as clearly as possible the three rather different ways in which experience can operate during development, and in so doing I have deliberately avoided heaping complication upon complication. Since the involvement of systems other than the sensory and motor is a reality of neural and behavioral development, these complications will ultimately have to be included in any account of developmental biopsychology which pretends to be complete.

Acknowledgments

The author wishes especially to thank P. P. G. Bateson, Robert B. Cairns, William R. Lippe, and Ronald W. Oppenheim for their constructive comments on a preliminary draft of this article, as well as for many hours of helpful talk on developmental problems in general.

This review was written in connection with research supported by the North Carolina Department of Mental Health and Research Grant HD-00878 from the National Institute of Child Health and Human Development.

References

Ader, R., & Grota, L. J. Adrenocortical mediation of the effects of early life experiences. *Progress in Brain Research*, 1973, **39**, 395–405.

Altman, J. Postnatal growth and differentiation of the mammalian brain, with implications for a morphological theory of memory. In G. Quarton, T. Melnechuk, & F. O. Schmitt (Eds.), *The neurosciences: A study program*. New York: Rockefeller University Press, 1967. Pp. 723–743.

Ariëns Kappers, C. U., Huber, G. C., & Crosby, E. C. *The comparative anatomy of the nervous system of vertebrates, including man* (Vol. 1). New York: Hafner, 1960. (Originally published, 1936.)

Bateson, P. P. G. Specificity and the origins of behavior. In J. S. Rosenblatt, R. A. Hinde, E. Shaw, & C. Beer (Eds.), *Advances in the study of behavior* (Vol. 6). New York: Academic Press, 1976. Pp. 1–20.

Bateson, P. P. G., & Seaburne-May, G. Effects of prior exposure to light on chicks' behaviour in the imprinting situation. *Animal Behaviour*, 1973, **21**, 720–725.

Bateson, P. P. G., & Wainwright, A. A. P. The effects of prior exposure to light on the imprinting process in domestic chicks. *Behaviour*, 1972, **42**, 279–290.

Berger, R. Oculomotor control: A possible function of REM sleep. *Psychological Review*, 1969, **76**, 144–164.

Bexton, W. H., Heron, W., & Scott, T. H. Effects of decreased variation in the environment. *Canadian Journal of Psychology*, 1954, **8**, 70–76.

Blakemore, C. Environmental constraints on development in the visual system. In R. A. Hinde (Ed.), *Constraints on learning*. New York: Academic Press, 1973. Pp. 51–73.

Blakemore, C., & Cooper, G. Development of the brain depends on the visual environment. *Nature (London)*, 1970, **228**, 477–478.

Blakemore, C., & Mitchell, D. E. Environmental modification of the visual cortex and the neural basis of learning and memory. *Nature (London)*, 1973, **241**, 467–468.

Bok, S. T. Stimulogenous fibrillation as the cause of the structure of the nervous system. *Psychiatrie en Neurologie*, 1915, **19**, 393–408.

Burghardt, G. M. The primacy effect of the first feeding experience in the snapping turtle. *Psychonomic Science*, 1967, **7**, 383–384.

Burghardt, G. M., & Hess, E. H. Food imprinting in the snapping turtle, *Chelydra serpentina*. *Science*, 1966, **151**, 108–109.

Campbell, B. A., & Jaynes, J. Reinstatement. *Psychological Review*, 1966, **73**, 478–480.

Chow, K. L., Riesen, A. H., & Newell, F. W. Degeneration of retinal ganglion cells in infant chimpanzees reared in darkness. *Journal of Comparative Neurology*, 1957, **107**, 27–42.

Cragg, B. G. Are there structural alterations in synapses related to functioning? *Proceedings of the Royal Society, Series B*, 1968, **171**, 319–323.

Daly, N. Early stimulation of rodents: A critical review of present interpretations. *British Journal of Psychology*, 1973, **64**, 435–460.

Dawkins, R. The ontogeny of a pecking preference in domestic chicks. *Behaviour*, 1968, **25**, 170–186.

Denenberg, V. H., & Zarrow, M. X. Effects of handling in infancy upon adult behavior and adrenocortical activity: Suggestions for a neuroendocrine mechanism. In D. H. Walcher & D. L. Peters (Eds.), *Development of self-regulatory mechanisms*. New York: Academic Press, 1971. Pp. 39–71.

Drachman, D. B., & Sokoloff, L. The role of movement in embryonic joint development. *Developmental Biology*, 1966, **14**, 401–420.

Fuller, J. L. Experiential deprivation and later behavior. *Science*, 1967, **158**, 1645–1652.

Galef, B. G., Jr., & Henderson, P. W. Mother's milk: A determinant of the feeding preferences of wean[1]ing rat pups. *Journal of Comparative and Physiological Psychology*, 1972, **78**, 213–219.

Ganz, L. An analysis of generalization behavior in the stimulus-deprived organism. In G. Newton & S. Levine (Eds.), *Early experience and behavior*. Springfield, Ill.: Thomas, 1968. Pp. 365–411.

Gibson, E. J. *Principles of perceptual learning and development*. New York: Appleton, 1969.

Globus, A. Brain morphology as a function of presynaptic morphology and activity. In A. H. Riesen (Ed.), *The developmental neuropsychology of sensory deprivation*. New York: Academic Press, 1975. Pp. 9–91.

Gottlieb, G. Imprinting in relation to parental and species identification by avian neonates. *Journal of Comparative and Physiological Psychology*, 1965, **59**, 345–356.

Gottlieb, G. Conceptions of prenatal behavior. In L. R. Aronson, E. Tobach, D. S. Lehrman, & J. S. Rosenblatt (Eds.), *Development and evolution of behavior*. San Francisco, Cal.: Freeman, 1970. Pp. 111–137.

Gottlieb, G. *Development of species identification in birds*. Chicago, Ill.: University of Chicago Press, 1971.

Gottlieb, G. (Ed.). *Behavioral embryology*. New York: Academic Press, 1973.

Goy, R. W., Bridgson, W. E., & Young, W. C. Period of maximal susceptibility of the prenatal female guinea pig to masculinizing actions of testosterone propionate. *Journal of Comparative and Physiological Psychology*, 1964, **57**, 166–174.

Graves, H. B. Early social responses in *Gallus*: A functional analysis. *Science*, 1973, **182**, 937–938.

Griswold, J. G. *Initial perceptual status of chicks with respect to parental objects and changes of status with increasing age*. Unpublished doctoral dissertation, Pennsylvania State University, 1971.

Gyllensten, L., Malmfors, T., & Norrlin, M.-L. Effect of visual deprivation on the optic centers of growing and adult mice. *Journal of Comparative Neurology*, 1965, **124**, 149–160.

52   GILBERT GOTTLIEB

Hamburger, V. Development of embryonic motility. In E. Tobach, L. R. Aronson, & E. Shaw (Eds.), *The biopsychology of development*. New York: Academic Press, 1971. Pp. 45–66.
Hamburger, V. Anatomical and physiological basis of embryonic motility in birds and mammals. In G. Gottlieb (Ed.), *Behavioral embryology*. New York: Academic Press, 1973. Pp. 51–76.
Heaton, M. B., Miller, D. B., & Goodwin, D. G. Species-specific auditory discrimination in bobwhite quail neonates. 1975, unpublished manuscript.
Hebb, D. O. *The organization of behavior*. New York: Wiley, 1949.
Hein, A., & Diamond, R. M. Locomotory space as a prerequisite for acquiring visually guided reaching in kittens. *Journal of Comparative and Physiological Psychology*, 1972, **81**, 394–398.
Hein, A., Gower, E., & Diamond, R. M. Exposure requirements for developing the triggered component of the visual-placing response. *Journal of Comparative and Physiological Psychology*, 1970, **73**, 188–192.
Heinz, G. Responses of ring-necked pheasant chicks (*Phasianus colchinchus*) to conspecific calls. *Animal Behaviour*, 1973, **21**, 1–9.
Held, R., & Hein, A. Movement-produced stimulation in the development of visually guided behavior. *Journal of Comparative and Physiological Psychology*, 1963, **56**, 872–876.
Hinde, R. A., & Stevenson-Hinde, J. G. (Eds.). *Constraints on learning*. New York: Academic Press, 1973.
Hirsch, H. V. B., & Spinelli, D. N. Modification of the distribution of receptive field orientation in cats by selective visual exposure during development. *Experimental Brain Research*, 1971, **13**, 509–527.
Hubel, D. H., & Wiesel, T. N. Receptive fields of cells in striate cortex of very young, visually inexperienced kittens. *Journal of Neurophysiology*, 1963, **26**, 994–1002.
Immelmann, K. Song development in the zebra finch and other Estrildid finches. In R. A. Hinde (Ed.), *Bird vocalizations*. London: Cambridge University Press, 1969. Pp. 61–74.
Immelmann, K. Sexual and other long-term aspects of imprinting in birds and other species. In D. S. Lehrman, R. A. Hinde, & E. Shaw (Eds.), *Advances in the study of behavior* (Vol. 4). New York: Academic Press, 1972. Pp. 147–174.
Jacobson, M. A plenitude of neurons. In G. Gottlieb (Ed.), *Aspects of neurogenesis*. New York: Academic Press, 1974. Pp. 151–166.
Kuo, Z.-Y. Giving up instincts in psychology. *Journal of Philosophy*, 1921, **18**, 645–664.
Kuo, Z.-Y. *The dynamics of behavior development*. New York: Random House, 1967.
Lauber, J. K., & Shutze, J. V. Accelerated growth of embryo chicks under the influence of light. *Growth*, 1964, **28**, 179–190.
Lehrman, D. S. A critique of Konrad Lorenz's theory of instinctive behavior. *Quarterly Review of Biology*, 1953, **28**, 337–363.
Lehrman, D. S. Semantic and conceptual issues in the nature-nurture problem. In L. R. Aronson, E. Tobach, D. S. Lehrman, & J. S. Rosenblatt (Eds.), *Development and evolution of behavior*. San Francisco, Cal.: Freeman, 1970. Pp. 17–52.
Lessac, M. S., & Solomon, R. L. Effects of early isolation on the later adaptive behavior of beagles: A methodological demonstration. *Developmental Psychology*, 1969, **1**, 14–25.
Levine, S. The pituitary-adrenal system and the developing brain. *Progress in Brain Research*, 1970, **32**, 79–85.
Lorenz, K. The companion in the bird's world. *Auk*, 1937, **54**, 245–273.
Lorenz, K. *Evolution and modification of behavior*. Chicago, Ill.: University of Chicago Press, 1965.
Lorenz, K. [A consideration of methods of identification of species-specific instinctive behavior patterns in birds.] In K. Lorenz (R. D. Martin, trans.), *Studies in animal and human behavior* (Vol. 1). Cambridge, Mass.: Harvard University Press, 1970. (Originally published, 1932.) Pp. 57–100.

Manning, A. "Pre-imaginal conditioning" in *Drosophila*. *Nature (London)*, 1967, **216**, 338–340.
Marler, P., & Mundinger, P. Vocal learning in birds. In H. Moltz (Ed.), *The ontogeny of vertebrate behavior*. New York: Academic Press, 1971. Pp. 389–450.
Moltz, H. Contemporary instinct theory. *Psychological Review*, 1965, **72**, 27–47.
Nicolai, J. Familientradition in der Gesangsentwicklung des Gimpels (*Pyrrhula phyrrula* L.). *Journal für Ornithologie*, 1959, **100**, 39–46.
O'Hara, R. K. Effects of developmental stage and prior experience on habitat selection in three species of anuran larvae. Unpublished M. S. thesis, Michigan State University (East Lansing), 1974.
Oppenheim, R. W. The ontogeny of behavior in the chick embryo. In D. S. Lehrman, J. S. Rosenblatt, R. A. Hinde, & E. Shaw (Eds.), *Advances in the study of behavior* (Vol. 5). New York: Academic Press, 1974. Pp. 133–172.
O'Steen, W. K., & Anderson, K. V. Photically evoked responses in the visual system of rats exposed to continuous light. *Experimental Neurology*, 1971, **30**, 525–534.
Parnavelas, J. G., Globus, A., & Kaups, P. Continuous illumination from birth affects spine density of neurons in the visual cortex of the rat. *Experimental Neurology*, 1973, **40**, 742–747.
Paulson, G. W. Maturation of evoked responses in the duckling. *Experimental Neurology*, 1965, **11**, 324–333.
Peters, J. J., Vonderahe, A. R., & Powers, T. H. The functional chronology in developing chick nervous system. *Journal of Experimental Zoology*, 1956, **133**, 505–518.
Pettigrew, J. D. The effect of visual experience on the development of stimulus specificity by kitten cortical neurones. *Journal of Physiology (London)*, 1974, **237**, 49–74.
Pontius, A. A. Neuro-ethics of "walking" in the newborn. *Perceptual and Motor Skills*, 1973, **37**, 235–245.
Provine, R. R. Neurophysiological aspects of behavior development in the chick embryo. In G. Gottlieb (Ed.), *Behavioral embryology*. New York: Academic Press, 1973. Pp. 77–102.
Rheingold, H. L., Gewirtz, J. L., & Ross, H. W. Social conditioning of vocalizations in the infant. *Journal of Comparative and Physiological Psychology*, 1959, **52**, 68–73.
Riege, W. H. Environmental influences on brain and behavior of year-old rats. *Developmental Psychobiology*, 1971, **4**, 157–167.
Roffwarg, H. P., Muzio, J. N., & Dement, W. C. Ontogenetic development of the human sleep-dream cycle. *Science*, 1966, **152**, 604–619.
Rosenzweig, M. S. Effects of environment on development of brain and of behavior. In E. Tobach, L. R. Aronson, & E. Shaw (Eds.). *The biopsychology of development*. New York: Academic Press, 1971. Pp. 303–342.
Schapiro, S., & Vukovich, K. R. Early experience effects upon cortical dendrites: A proposed model for development. *Science*, 1970, **167**, 292–294.
Schneirla, T. C. Interrelationships of the "innate" and the "acquired" in instinctive behavior. In P. P. Grassé (Ed.), *L'Instinct dans le comportement des animaux et l'homme*. Paris: Masson, 1956. Pp. 387–452.
Schneirla, T. C. Behavioral development and comparative psychology. *Quarterly Review of Biology*, 1966, **41**, 283–302.
Schutz, F. Sexuelle Prägung bei Anatiden. *Zeitschrift für Tierpsychologie*, 1965, **22**, 50–103.
Seligman, M. E. P., & Hager, J. L. (Eds.). *Biological boundaries of learning*. New York: Appleton, 1972.
Shaler, R. Shift in binocular disparity causes compensatory change in the cortical structure of kittens. *Science*, 1971, **173**, 638–641.
Sluckin, W. *Imprinting and early learning*. Chicago: Aldine, 1965.
Solomon, R. L., & Lessac, M. S. A control group design for experimental studies of developmental processes. *Psychological Bulletin*, 1968, **70**, 145–150.

Spalding, D. A. Instinct: With original observations on young animals. *MacMillan's Magazine*, 1873, **27**, 282–293.

Sperry, R. W. How a developing brain gets itself properly wired for adaptive function. In E. Tobach, L. R. Aronson, & E. Shaw (Eds.), *The biopsychology of development*. New York: Academic Press, 1971. Pp. 27–44.

Stevenson, J. G. Song as a reinforcer. In R. A. Hinde (Ed.), *Bird vocalizations*. London: Cambridge University Press, 1969. Pp. 49–60.

Tees, R. C. Effect of visual deprivation on development of depth perception in the rat. *Journal of Comparative and Physiological Psychology*, 1974, **86**, 300–308.

Thorpe, W. H. Further experiments on olfactory conditioning in a parasitic insect. The nature of the conditioning process. *Proceedings of the Royal Society, Series B*, 1938, **126**, 370–397.

Thorpe, W. H., & Jones, F. G. W. Olfactory conditioning and its relation to the problem of host selection. *Proceedings of the Royal Society, Series B*, 1937, **124**, 56–81.

Vince, M. A. Some environmental effects on the activity and development of the avian embryo. In G. Gottlieb (Ed.), *Behavioral embryology*. New York: Academic Press, 1973. Pp. 285–323.

Wiens, J. A. Effects of early experience on substrate pattern selection in *Rana aurora* tadpoles. *Copeia*, 1970, No. 3, 543–548.

Willier, B. H., Gallagher, T. F., & Koch, F. C. The modification of sex development in the chick embryo by male and female sex hormones. *Physiological Zoology*, 1937, **10**, 101–122.

Zelazo, P. R., Zelazo, N. A., & Kolb, S. "Walking" in the newborn. *Science*, 1972, **176**, 314–315.

Zetterström, B. The effect of light on the appearance and development of the electro-retinogram in newborn kittens. *Acta Physiologica Scandanavica*, 1956, **35**, 272–279.

Section 2

NEUROSPECIFICITY: CHEMOAFFINITY THEORY

INTRODUCTION

Although there is a good bit of controversy concerning the precise roles experience plays in the development of neural specificity, and thus perhaps an undue conceptual emphasis on experience, the earliest stages of neural aggregation and interconnection are most likely under strictly molecular and biochemical control (chemoaffinity theory). These early embryonic stages are most readily studied in species in which development takes place in externally laid eggs; consequently fish, amphibians, and, to a lesser extent, birds have most often been utilized for research on these early stages, perhaps giving rise to the erroneous notion that chemoaffinity plays a greater role in neural specificity in these organisms than it does in mammals. As is evident in the following two chapters by Keating and by Meyer and Sperry, experience must be conjured with in theorizing about the development of neural specificity in fish and amphibians, and chemoaffinity needs to be considered as a factor in mammals.

The basic notion of chemoaffinity theory is that the selective formation of synapses between nerve cells is based on a complementary fit in their cytochemical constitution or "label." Thus, it is on this (theoretical) basis, for example, that particular cells in the retina connect to particular cells in the next higher level of the visual system (tectum) with amazing regularity and precision. The orderliness of retinotectal connections in certain species of fish and frogs has received an enormous amount of well-deserved inquiry. All sensory systems in all vertebrates (that we know about) exhibit very orderly synaptic connections from the periphery to their more central way-stations, so unraveling the early basis of neural specificity in the so-called lower vertebrates may very well have application to mammals. Whether the later stages of neural specificity are less susceptible to (or less dependent on) the influence of experience in the lower vertebrates (fish, amphibians) than in the higher vertebrates (birds, mammals), as is usually held to be the case, is a moot question at the moment. Much more emphasis has been placed on *experiential* manipulations in mammals, while the strategy with the lower organisms has been *surgical* derangement or rearrangement. Thus, our current conclusions on the possibly greater developmental rigidity in fish and amphibians relative to the developmental plasticity of higher vertebrates may be partly a consequence of the experimental strategies employed with each vis-à-vis neural specificity. The behavioral evidence does not necessarily favor the view that amphibians are developmentally rigid (see section in immediately preceding chapter on inductive effects of experience, for example).

THE FORMATION OF VISUAL NEURONAL CONNECTIONS: AN APPRAISAL OF THE PRESENT STATUS OF THE THEORY OF "NEURONAL SPECIFICITY"

M. J. KEATING

Division of Developmental Biology
National Institute for Medical Research
London, England

I. Introduction

Two fields of biological endeavor stand out as most exciting at the present time: that involving the study of development and that investigating neural function and behavior. The excitement in these fields derives in part from the fact that, in both, much yet remains to be discovered on even the most general principles underlying the phenomena being observed and in part from the fact that, while limited, our knowledge in these fields is increasing at an unprecedented rate.

A conjunction and an overlap of these two fields occurs in those disciplines in which the development of the brain is studied. The aim of the developmental neurobiologist must be the unraveling of the mechanisms by which the organization and function of the adult brain is achieved. In acknowledging the dual parenthood of his discipline, he will naturally seek to marry the methodology and concepts of modern developmental biology to those of the neural sciences. In order that such a union be fertile, one must recognize those aspects of brain development that reflect events primarily of a developmental nature, those events peculiar to neural development, and those at the interface between the two.

The unique feature of the brain is the way in which the vast numbers of its constituent elements are selectively linked so that information from receptors is distributed differentially to particular subsets of the central cells; the latter again connect differentially with further components of higher integrative centers, and ultimately, a differential activation of selected motor elements is achieved. The processes responsible for the elaboration of the ordered synaptic connections that characterize the mature brain represent an example of those at the interface of developmental biology and neurobiology. They require, as a substrate, early ontogenetic events associated with the appearance of the neural plate and the neural tube. Further restriction of the developmental potencies of the primitive neural cells yields different populations of neurons of characteristic morphology and neurochemistry, while selective and controlled cellular migrations assure that the various populations achieve their correct relative positions. It is generally conceded that these early proliferative and differentiative events that produce clearly recognizable neuronal phenotypes represent neuronal examples of general developmental processes.

Selectivity of interneuronal connections is, however, much more precise than mere linkage of particular neuronal populations, such as retinal ganglion cells, and those of particular visual centers, such as optic tectum or lateral geniculate nucleus. Thus, developmental control of synaptogenesis extends to precise connections between particular cells of one group and particular cells of the target group. The extent to which these spatially ordered connections between neuronal populations are also the product of similar but much more precisely controlled developmental processes is the subject of this essay.

II. Development of the Chemoaffinity Theory

The investigation of the mechanisms of selective synaptogenesis requires a system of precisely organized connections that is accessible to experimental manipulation so that the response of the system to perturbation may be studied. The system that has proved to be most fruitful in this respect is that linking the retina to the contralateral optic tectum in fish and amphibians. The optic tectum is the main visual center in these animals, and it is responsible for the localization of visual stimuli in space and for organizing the appropriate orienting and striking behavior (Kicliter, 1974; Sperry, 1944). To perform this function it is necessary that there exist, in some sense, a "map" of the visual world in the tectum. There is now considerable anatomical (see Lázár, 1971), electrophysiological (Gaze, 1958a; Jacobson, 1968a; Maturana, Lettvin, McCulloch, & Pitts, 1959; Schwassman, 1968), and behavioral (Schwassman & Krag, 1970; Sperry, 1944) evidence that this map is produced by the orderly distribution of optic nerve fiber terminal arborizations across the surface of the optic tectum. A spatial replication of the retina, and hence of the visual field of the contralateral eye, thus exists on the tectum (Fig. 1), with the nasal field (temporal retina) projecting to rostral tectum, temporal field (nasal retina) to caudal tectum, superior field (ventral retina) to medial tectum, and inferior field (dorsal retina) to lateral tectum. A diagrammatic representation of the pattern of connections from the retina to the tectum that underlies this contralateral visuotectal projection is shown in Fig. 2a.

Here, then, exists an orderly pattern of synaptic connections generated during development. What particularly commended this system for study as a model of selective synaptogenesis was the ability of the optic nerve fibers in the adult animal to regenerate after section. Matthey (1925, 1926) described the return of accurate visual behavior after optic nerve section or after homoplastic eye transplantation in *Triturus cristatus*. The restoration of visual function after transplantation of the eye in amphibians was subsequently documented exhaustively by Stone and his co-workers (Stone, 1930; Stone & Cole, 1931; Stone & Usher, 1927).

Thus far, optic nerve regeneration had been viewed largely as an interesting regenerative phenomenon. It was Sperry who realized the opportunities that the phenomenon of regeneration offered to those interested in the mechanisms controlling the formation of specific nerve connections. During the process of nerve regeneration the connections between the retina and the tectum are established in an orderly fashion. In this time the system may be experimentally perturbed and the effects of this interference may be

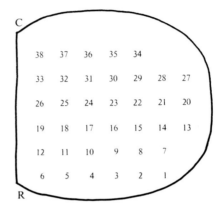

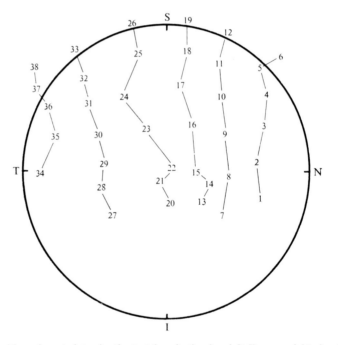

FIG. 1. Normal contralateral retinotectal projection in adult *Xenopus*, right visual field to left tectum. The upper diagram represents the tectum seen from above. The midline is to the left, rostral (R) in front and caudal (C) behind. The numbers on the diagram represent electrode positions. The lower diagram is a chart of the right visual field extending from the center of the field out to 100°. N, Nasal; T, temporal; S, superior; I, inferior. The numbers on the field chart indicate the optimal response positions for the corresponding electrode positions on the tectum. From Straznicky, Gaze, & Keating (1974). A detailed account of the techniques by which such maps are obtained, and of the limitations on interpretations based on such maps, may be found in Hunt & Jacobson (1974a).

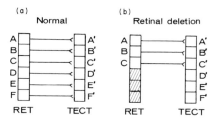

FIG. 2. (a)   Diagrammatic representation of the retinotectal projection. The retina (RET) consists theoretically of an array of labeled cells projecting to the tectum (TECT), the cells in which are thought to possess complementary labels. (b) Representation of the results of Attardi & Sperry (1963).

observed. The second necessary condition for experimental analysis is thus present.

The problem to be explained is the differential behavior of retinal ganglion cells. Why do nasal retinal ganglion cells behave differently from temporal retinal ganglion cells in the manner in which they connect with tectal cells? Sperry argued that this differential behavior could reflect either differential extraneous influences acting upon an essentially homogeneous population of retinal ganglion cells or, alternatively, intrinsic differences between the ganglion cells themselves.

Of the possible extraneous influences that could operate on a homogeneous set of retinal ganglion cells to produce the normal pattern of retinotectal connections, two in particular enjoyed favor at the time of the early 1940s when Sperry began his studies. The first of these derived from the concept of "contact guidance" emphasized by Weiss (1934, 1941). Nerve processes do not grow freely into a totally fluid medium (Harrison, 1910), but on the contrary require some structural interface along which to move. The microenvironment in which the growing nerve fiber extends contains many fibrous elements, which may serve as such a substrate. If these structural microchannels between the retina and the tectum were arranged in such a fashion that optic fibers growing out from the temporal pole of the retina were guided inevitably to the rostral pole of the tectum, while fibers growing out from the nasal pole of the retina were delivered to the caudal tectum and fibers from intermediate retinal positions were distributed to intermediate tectal positions, then selective retinotectal connections would result. It would be unnecessary then to ascribe intrinsic differential properties to the retinal ganglion cells themselves.

The second possible extrinsic mechanism popular at that time with behavioral scientists—and lucidly expressed, albeit in a somewhat extreme form, by Holt (1931)—emphasized the role of "functionally adaptive value" in the persistence of neuronal connections. Theories of this general nature viewed the initial process of synaptogenesis as diffuse and random; those connections which produced behavior that was functionally adaptive were preserved while the other connections were lost or at least rendered functionless. Again, on this view, no intrinsic differences were attributed to the retinal ganglion cells themselves.

Sperry realized that the role of such extrinsic influences could be examined in an experimental situation in which the normal geometrical relation between the eye and the tectum was disturbed as, for example, by eye rotation. Sperry (1942, 1943), therefore, rotated one eye in a newt and cut the optic nerve. The nerve regenerated with the eye in a rotated position and Sperry was able to deduce from behavioral observations the type of visuotectal projection that was produced after optic nerve regeneration. If either of the above extrinsic mechanisms were the determining factors, the resultant visuotectal projections should have been normal. If microchannels guide fibers from the temporal retinal pole to rostral tectum and fibers from the nasal retinal pole to caudal tectum, the normal topographic pattern of retinotectal connections should be restored. A similar result should occur if the functionally adaptive value of a connection is the determining principle. In that case the initial connections would be diffuse and random, but only those that produced normal visuomotor behavior should persist.

In fact Sperry observed very different results. Visuomotor reactions were systematically inverted and reversed in animals in which the eye had been rotated by 180°. These functionally maladaptive responses remained totally uncorrected until the death of the animal and indicated that whatever factors govern the formation of visual synaptic connections after regeneration of the optic nerve, functionally adaptive values is not one of them. What appeared to be happening was that fibers from a given retinal locus were reestablishing functional contact with the same areas of the optic tectum to which they had originally projected, even though the retinal loci had been rotated to a new topographic position within the orbit of the eye. Thus, temporal retinal ganglion cells normally project to rostral tectum, and these same cells still did so, even though the cells had been transported to a nasal position within the orbit. Similarly the translocated nasal retinal cells still projected to caudal tectum.

Comparable results were obtained from similar experiments on anuran amphibians (Sperry, 1944) and teleost fish (Sperry, 1948). Electrophysiological confirmation of Sperry's deduction that following eye rotation the optic fibers regenerate to their normal tectal sites was provided by Gaze (1959). Stone (1944) and Sperry (1945) transplanted an eye from one orbit to the opposite orbit such that one of the two primary retinal axes remained in normal orientation while the other axis was reversed. In such animals the visuomotor behavior was correctly oriented in the one visual axis but consistently inverted in the other. Again the result is that which would be predicted if the regenerated retinal fibers regained their previous tectal target.

On the basis of these observations, Sperry (1951, 1963) formulated a hypothesis to account for the formation of retinotectal connections either during regeneration of the optic nerve or during normal development. Since the differential behavior of the retinal ganglion cells was not due to extrinsic influences that had seemed reasonable candidates for such a role, Sperry postulated that the differential behavior reflected intrinsic differences between the ganglion cells. The neurons of the retinal ganglion cell population are thus different one from another—each neuron is specific. The term "neuronal specificity" has hence been attached to this hypothesis. Since these differences are intrinsic, they must be viewed as terminal differentiative events in the sequence of neuronal maturation. As such, the differences would be acquired early in neuronal life, and the precise differentiative event would depend upon the position the neuron (or its precursor) occupied at a critical period of early development.

Sperry suggested that the manifestation of this differentiation was the synthesis of a cytochemical label unique to that particular neuron. A parallel specification process was postulated for the tectal cells. The final element of the hypothesis consisted of the suggestion that selective neuronal connections formed on the basis of a unique chemoaffinity between an axon terminal containing a cytochemical label and the tectal element that contained a matching/complementary label. This version of the theory of neuronal specificity is thus known as the "chemoaffinity theory" (see Meyer & Sperry, this volume).

This hypothesis possesses several excellent features. It was, of course, compatible with the data from which it derived; it accorded with general embryological principles of position-dependent pattern formation, and it linked classical embryology to the peculiarly neural process of selective synaptic formation. The overriding virtue of the theory was, however, its apparent testability. It has prompted experimental investigation and thus the generation of large amounts of data over the succeeding 30 years. The fact that, by general consensus, the theory has accounted adequately for most, if not all, of these data is a tribute to the theory's vigor.

Any theory successful on such a scale faces two types of danger. The first is that a hypothesis that is compatible with the data and, therefore, provides an adequate conceptual framework within which such data may be described and discussed, gradually transmutes into dogma, regardless of whether the newer data justify such a transition. The second danger is of the opposite type, described by Hunt and Jacobson (1974a): "When a venerable scientific concept is perceived to be less than completely correct, there is frequently an over-zealous reaction against it" (p. 203). In attempting to steer a course between such a Scylla and Charybdis, it is necessary to delineate various components of the theory and to consider to which of these components any experimental question is directed.

This essay is, therefore, an attempt to consider the present status of the chemoaffinity theory. I shall examine the individual components of the theory with a view to determining whether the more recent data compel one to accept that component, whether it remains a plausible hypothesis but no more, or whether in fact the data suggest that some modification of this component is required. For this purpose it is useful to divide the theory into four components: (1) Neurons are intrinsically different. (2) These differences, which are position-dependent, are acquired very early in neuronal life by the classical embryological processes of determination and of differentiation. (3) The differences are cytochemical in nature. (4) The "rule of connection" linking cytochemically labeled neuronal arrays is a selective and exclusive one whereby a labeled axon seeks out only its normal target, ignoring other less appropriately labeled targets. I shall consider the hypothesis in terms of the particular neuronal population on which it was based, the retinal ganglion cells; but it must be realized that the power of the theory is that it may be generalized to account for all systems of spatially ordered neuronal connections (Sperry, 1963, 1965, 1971), and my comments are also intended to be applicable to these more general cases.

III. That Retinal Ganglion Cells Are Intrinsically Different from Each Other

The core postulate of the theory of neuronal specificity is the suggestion that processes of differentiation render each neuron different from its fellows. The manifestation of that differentiation could take one of several forms (see Section X), but in this section of the essay I will examine the extent to which acceptance of the postulate is forced by data presently available.

The hypothesis that the differential behavior of retinal ganglion cells is a product of the separate terminal differentiative pathways followed by individual retinal ganglion cells was, and is, a very reasonable suggestion. In questioning it, I do not wish to create the impression that I consider it to be incorrect. It will argue, however, that one is warranted in maintaining a degree of reservation about the proposition that "neuronal specificity" is a demonstrated fact, at least, in the sense defined here (i.e., as referring to intrinsic individual differences in the cytochemical constitution of neurons).

The point of tracing the historical evolution of the theory in the previous section was to emphasize that the hypothesis—that differentiation has produced gene-dependent intrinsic differences between retinal ganglion cells—was entertained only after the exclusion of some possible extrinsic influences. Indeed, apart from directly measuring the unknown component that constitutes the postulated difference, the hypothesis can be sustained only in a negative sense. The hypothesis could be demonstrated as fact only if all *possible* extrinsic influences were excluded, and this, of course, cannot be done. One might ask whether all *reasonable* candidates for the role of differential extrinsic influence had been eliminated, in which case the most reasonable hypothesis to hold would be that of neuronal specificity. This question may be rephrased by asking whether it is easy to construct feasible models in which the differential behavior of retinal ganglion cells reflects differences which are extrinsically imposed rather than the product of intrinsic ganglion cell differentiation. Keating and Kennard (1975) have argued that such models, compatible with present data, are quite possible and, by way of illustration, offered one such model. This model proposed that a spatially ordered difference in retinal ganglion cell labels was not due to differential gene activity of ganglion cells, but was rather the effect of a spatially ordered difference in an extrinsically produced substance, which itself alters ganglion cell labels without altering the pattern of gene activity within the ganglion cells. Keating and Kennard suggested that the source of such extrinsic material might be the retinal pigment epithelium. The end result, on this model, is the same as that of the chemoaffinity theory, namely, that retinal ganglion cells are differently labeled; the mechanism by which such labels are produced is, however, quite different. An experimental situation in which one might be able to distinguish between the intrinsic model and the extrinsic model would involve rotation of the neural retina without rotation of the underlying pigment epithelium. If this rotation were performed after the period of retinal polarization (see Section IV), then any neuronal specificity theory would predict a rotated map of the visual world on the tectum. The suggested extrinsic model predicts a normal map. There are, unfortunately, considerable technical difficulties involved in such an experiment.

One reason for dwelling on this point is that further research in this field might well involve looking for differences between retinal ganglion cells maintained in tissue culture. The rational basis for this experimental ploy would be the assumption that any proposed differences are stable under culture conditions. While such an assumption is not unreasonable if one believes the differences to be the product of the differentiated state, it is not necessarily valid if one views the retinal ganglion cells as an essentially homogeneous population in which differences exist only as the result of ongoing interactions *in vivo* with substances deriving from a source external to the ganglion cells.

The data presently available do not compel the view that retinal ganglion cells undergo a "fieldlike differentiation" which causes their subsequent differential behavior. It is quite possible to construct models to explain the connections formed by different retinal ganglion cells, which differ from that involved in the chemoaffinity theory in a much more radical manner than the one outlined here (see, for example, Chung, 1974; Keating & Kennard, 1975). Similarly, none of the published experimental findings conclusively localize the source of the postulated tectal markers with reference to which the incoming optic axons are believed to orient. It is, thus, not yet necessary to accept that such markers exist on tectal neurons.

The constituent of the chemoaffinity theory which asserts that each neuronal element of an array is rendered different from the other elements by processes of intrinsic differentiation, while still the most plausible view, probably best merits at the present time that peculiarly Scottish judicial verdict "not proven."

IV. Acquisition of Retinal Polarity

If, for the moment, we put aside the reservations expressed in the preceding section as to whether the evidence yet compels the view that retinal ganglion cells are, themselves, intrinsically specified, then we may review, in their own terms, an extensive group of experiments in which this reservation was not made. This group of experiments was concerned with analyzing those events occurring early in development that appear to be critical in determining the pattern of the subsequently appearing retinotectal connections.

If retinal ganglion cells acquire unique properties as a result of their position in the developing retina, then the time at which this property is acquired may be revealed by observing the effects of eye rotation at various developmental stages. If, after the eye inversion, the resultant map is rotated, this implies that the critical events have already occurred, whereas, if the map is normal, it is reasonable to conclude that the critical process occurred after the eye inversion. Early experiments by Stone (1944) on *Ambystoma punctatum* and by Székely (1954a) on *Triturus vulgaris* used behavioral criteria to assess the normal or reversed nature of the visuomotor map, and they showed that in these urodeles the important events occurred very early in life before retinal differentiation was complete. Jacobson (1968a) rotated the developing eyecup in larval *Xenopus laevis* and, using electrophysiological methods, mapped the contralateral visuotectal projection in postmetamorphic animals. He found rotated maps after the initial rotation had been carried out on animals at Stage 31 or later (Nieuwkoop & Faber, 1967), whereas normal maps were obtained if the eye rotations were performed before Stage 29. This period again correlates with that of retinal differentiation.

Experiments designed to study the acquisition of axial polarity in amphibian limb buds (Harrison, 1918, 1921) had shown that the anteroposterior axis is acquired before the dorsoventral. Sperry (1945), realizing that the adequate specification of the position of a retinal ganglion cell must occur along at least two axes, predicted that in retinal differentiation, as in the limb, the anteroposterior (nasotemporal) axis might be determined before the dorsoventral. If this were the case, then 180° rotation early in the critical period should produce retinotectal maps inverted in the anteroposterior (nasotemporal) axis but normally oriented in the dorsoventral axis, while rotation later in the critical period would produce inversion about both axes. Székely (1954a) transplanted a right eye of *Triturus* to the left orbit of a carrier animal with inversion of either the anteroposterior or the dorsoventral axis and was able to demonstrate that the anteroposterior axis was indeed determined before the dorsoventral axis. Jacobson (1968a) described a similar sequence in *Xenopus*. There thus does indeed appear to be a temporal separation of those events determining the anteroposterior and dorsoventral axes of the retina.

In an important and very elegant series of papers, Hunt and Jacobson have recently sought to characterize some of the features of what they called "the specification of positional information in retinal ganglion cells" in *Xenopus* (reviewed in Hunt, 1975a). Since such a process involves some form of interaction between the developing eye and extraocular tissues, Hunt and Jacobson (1972a) asked whether this inducing ability was restricted to periorbital tissues or was more widely distributed in the body of the embryo. They were able to show that the latter possibility was the correct one. Developing eyes at Stage 28 were transplanted to body flank, where they remained during the normal period in which they would have acquired "specificities," and then were transplanted to a final carrier at Stages 32–34. The carriers developed through metamorphosis and their contralateral visuotectal projections when mapped were such as to indicate that the retinal ganglion cells had acquired positional information by reference to the tissues of the body flank. The axial information required to establish retinal positional information is thus widely distributed throughout the embryo.

Once acquired, the positional information in the retinal ganglion cells is stable in that neither back-transplantations of a specified eye to a Stage 28 host, nor maintenance of a newly specified eye in tissue culture for 10 days, alter the axial polarity of the growing eye (Hunt & Jacobson, 1972b). There is, however, an earlier period in development during which the developing eye does possess axially distributed positional information which is not stable. Earlier views that prior to the critical period the eye was "unspecified" and acquired positional information only during Stages 29–30 were shown to be incorrect by Hunt and Jacobson (1973), who removed developing eyes from embryos as early as Stage 22 (at which time the developing eye is present merely as the proencephalic bulge of the forebrain) and grew the eyes in tissue culture. Under such conditions the eyes underwent normal cytodifferentiation, and when they showed the morphological and histological characteristics of eyes from Stage 37/38 larvae, Hunt and Jacobson transplanted the cultured eyes in various orientations, into the orbits of carrier animals. These subsequently generated retinotectal maps which were ordered in such a fashion as to indicate that the very young eyes contained an axial polarity and that the maps produced were organized according to these reference axes.

In a second experiment designed to illustrate the same principle, eyes were transplanted prior to Stage 28 from the orbit to the ventral midline of the embryo, permitted to differentiate there to Stage 39/40, and then transplanted to the orbit of a Stage 39/40 carrier animal. The results indicated that no axial information was acquired by the eyes transplanted to the ventral midline (in contrast to those eyes transplanted to lateral situations on body flank) and that the maps that such eyes generated subsequently reflected axial information possessed by the eye prior to Stage 28. Similar conclusions had earlier been reached by Feldman and Gaze (unpublished results), who had transplanted eyes prior to Stage 28 to the body flank where, for various reasons not yet entirely clear, the eyes did not acquire positional information from this site. When transplanted again to an orbit these eyes formed retinotectal connections which showed a pattern appropriate to the original orientation of the eye prior to Stage 28.

The events of Stage 28/31 do not then involve the initial establishment of ocular axes because such exist earlier. Prior to Stage 28, however, these axes are reversible whereas at Stage 28/31 the axes are "locked-in" with reference to the general body axes of the embryo. The time required to produce the reversal of the retinal axes in the pre-Stage 28 embryonic *Xenopus* eyes was shown to be between 2 and 6 hours (Hunt & Jacobson, 1974b).

The "critical period" which irreversibly determines the retinal axes lasts some 5 hours from Stages 28–31 in *Xenopus* embryos and could reflect the onset of a necessary maturational state of either the eye or of the extra-ocular tissues or, indeed, of both. Hunt and Jacobson (1974c) transplanted eyes from one stage of embryonic life into hosts of another stage (hetero-chronic transplantations) to assess from which structure the control trigger comes for the irreversible step. They concluded that the time of "specifica-tion" correlates with the developmental stage of the eye primordium rather than that of the extraocular milieu. They inferred, therefore, that the control trigger for the critical process resides within some structure of the developing eye.

The terminology used to describe these early processes has varied from investigating group to investigating group, and within groups it has changed with time. Thus, Stone (1944, 1948, 1960) referred to the "functional polar-ization" of the retina, but most other workers have referred to this period as that of retinal "specification," although there have been significant dif-ferences of view as to exactly what was being specified. While Székely (1954a) termed the process "functional specification" of the retina, more recently the terms "specification of retinal central connections" (Jacobson, 1968b, 1969; Sharma & Hollyfield, 1974) and "specification of retinal ganglion cells" (Jacobson, 1967, 1968a) have been used. Both of these latter terms, which are usually used in an equivalent sense, imply the acceptance of two postulates of the chemoaffinity theory, namely that it is the ganglion cells themselves that are specified and that as a result "the position at which each retinal ganglion cell connects in the tectum is already fully specified at Stage 31" (Jacobson, 1968a). Gaze and Keating (1972) criticized this termin-ology on two grounds. First, they pointed out that the two terms are not strictly synonymous in that the embryonic location of a retinal ganglion cell at Stage 31 does not, of itself, completely determine the tectal con-nections that cell will form (see Section VI). Second, at that stage only a small fraction of the final population of ganglion cells are present; the great majority of ganglion cells appear much later. It is surely inappropriate, therefore, to refer to this very early process as one that specifies retinal ganglion cells.

The general title given by Hunt and Jacobson to their series of papers discussed above was "specification of positional information in retinal ganglion cells," but throughout the series there is a conceptual transition as to exactly what is being specified. Thus, early in the series it is positional information *in* retinal ganglion cells that is being "specified" during Stages 28–31. This gradually changes first to "specification of positional informa-tion that each ganglion cell *will act upon*" and then to specification of positional information in the retina. Later, the events of Stages 28–32 are said to be establishing a "developmental program for spatial organization of the entire set of retinal locus specificities," while in the final paper (paper IV) of the series, "specification" refers not to the initial establishment of the developmental program, but to the "locking in" process whereby "permanent retinal axes" are established.

Given the multiplicity of meanings that have been attributed to "specification" in this context, it is probably a term to be avoided. It is perhaps more accurate to return to the terminology of Stone and to recognize the events occurring early in retinal life as those that establish an axial polarity of the retina across two dimensions, with the evidence indicating that these early axes are orthogonally distributed. Neither the nature of this polarity, nor indeed the retinal structure that is polarized, is known. What is now known of this early developmental process, which profoundly influences the subsequent behavior of the retinal ganglion cells, may be summarized as follows:

1. The position-dependent behavior of retinal ganglion cells requires the establishment very early in development of retinal axes about which positional information is distributed.

2. Events very early in neurogenesis establish such axes in those structures that will untimately differentiate into retina. The axes may exist at neural plate stages and are certainly present in *Xenopus* by Stage 22.

3. These early putative axes may be altered by cues external to the developing eye rudiment, but in the absence of such cues these early axes will transform into permanent retinal axes.

4. The time necessary for external cues to modify the putative axes is 2–6 hours.

5. At Stages 28–31 in *Xenopus*, the previously existing axes are "locked-in" with reference to the axes of the embryo by cues distributed along the body of the embryo. This "locking-in" process occurs first along the anteroposterior axis and then along the dorsoventral axis. After this time, in the intact eye, the retinal axes are not modifiable.

6. The trigger for the "locking-in" comes from a structure within the eye.

The search for intraocular events temporally correlated with the establishment of permanent retinal axes has produced two interesting pieces of information. Jacobson (1968b) showed that ganglion cell precursor neuroblasts in the center of the retina undergo their final DNA synthesis at Stage 28/29, just prior to the final "locking-in" events at Stage 29/30. Jacobson pointed out that in many developing systems DNA replication and differentiation are mutually exclusive events. Holtzer (1963, 1968, 1970) has suggested that differentiation requires a particular type of preceding cell cycle. The "quantal" cell cycle is one in which two daughter cells are produced, each with synthetic machinery different from that operating in the mother cell. The view has been developed that terminal differentiative events in all cell types require DNA synthesis and nuclear division (Holtzer, 1970; Holtzer & Sanger, 1972). Supporting evidence for this concept from studies of myogenesis, chondrogenesis, and erythrogenesis, is discussed by Holtzer, Weintraub, Mayne, and Mochan (1972).

It would seem, then, that the trigger for the "locking-in" of the retinal reference axes could come from the ganglionic precursor cells at the center of the developing retina. Experimental support for this proposition would be provided by the demonstration that factors which delayed the differentiation of retinal ganglion cells also delayed the "locking-in" process. Bergey, Hunt, and Holtzer (1973) found that exposure of *Xenopus* embryos to 5-bromodeoxyuridine (BUdR) delayed the terminal differentiation of retinal neurons. The application of BUdR at different developmental stages selectively blocked the differentiation of particular retinal neuronal populations. Treatment at a stage that delayed differentiation of the ganglion cells also delayed the final axial polarization of the retina. Treatment at a later stage, which permitted retinal ganglion cell differentiation but blocked the maturation of the other retinal neuronal populations, did not delay the final axial polarization (Hunt, Bergey, & Holtzer, 1975).

Dixon and Cronly-Dillon (1972) described a second feature of ocular development in *Xenopus* which undergoes a change at the time of irreversible axial polarization. They examined the ultrastructure of the developing retina and observed the presence of intercellular gap junctions that could be found throughout the retina until Stage 30/31. These gap junctions between cells of the neural retina disappeared from the central retinal areas at this time, persisting only at the peripheral retinal margin, these latter being sites of retinal growth (Straznicky & Gaze, 1971). This central disappearance of gap junctions thus correlated with the time of irreversible polarization of the retina.

Loewenstein (1973) has reviewed the evidence that intercellular communication through low-resistance junctions, which permit the passage of ions and smaller molecules, may play an important role in the control of cellular differentiation. Such junctions could be the relays through which may be transferred positional information that will determine the course of cellular differentiation. This positional information may be transmitted only to cells coupled by gap junctions and is, perhaps, effective only after the final DNA synthesis of the ganglion cell precursor.

The temporal correlations discussed between certain features of retinal ganglion cell differentiation in the center of the retina and irreversible axial polarization of the retina have been taken to mean that "axial specification was a programmed component of ganglion cell differentiation" (Hunt, 1975b). This is a position comparable with the view that axial polarization involves the specification of positional information in retinal ganglion cells, and it might be felt that the BUdR experiments and gap junction data provide compelling data in support of such a concept. If such data are indeed compelling, then surely the reservations expressed at the end of the preceding section, in which doubt was entertained that the retinal ganglion cells are themselves the site of intrinsic differentiation, must be withdrawn.

Although the view taken above is both plausible and, possibly, the most likely explanation of the data, it is true to say that the evidence supporting the model is not definitive. Temporal correlation is not itself sufficient to demonstrate causation. Thus, the cessation of DNA synthesis and the disappearance of gap junctions may be associated merely with the process that differentiates retinal ganglion cells from other retinal neuronal elements, rather than the process that is postulated to differentiate each retinal ganglion cell from its fellows. It must be pointed out that Holtzer's concept of a "quantal" cell cycle critical to the process of differentiation derived from studies on cells whose final stages of differentiation involved a qualitative change in new protein synthesis. Thus, new proteins characteristic of the differentiated state are synthesized, and the differentiative controls operate, presumably, at the level of the genome itself, i.e., at transcriptional levels.

The exquisite degree of chemodifferentiation of retinal ganglion cells which is envisaged in the chemoaffinity theory may also involve the synthesis of qualitatively different molecular labels by each individual ganglion cell. This type of control would, however, be very expensive in genetic terms. Most workers, from the early suggestions of Sperry, have felt that the postulated chemical differences might well involve quantitative differences of one species of macromolecule (see Section X). If the latter were the case, then the controls involved may well operate at a posttranscriptional level, and Holtzer's concepts may not apply to such a mechanism. We may again, for the sake of argument, consider the possible role of nonneural retinal elements in this process of retinal polarization. Perhaps significant parameters of axial polarization involve the cessation of DNA synthesis in central retinal pigment cells. I have no information on this matter, nor on the effects of BUdR administration on the differentiation of retinal pigment cells. Dixon and Cronly-Dillon (1974) have recently reported, however, that gap junctions are present between pigment epithelial cells of central retina until Stage 32, but that subsequently such gap junctions disappear.

The suggestion that pigment epithelial cells may contain the necessary positional information to constitute an aspect of retinal polarity which is manifest by the behavior of retinal ganglion cells is not as unreasonable as might first appear. It has been known for many years that a normal retina may be regenerated with appropriate axial polarity from the pigment epithelium (Stone, 1960). Levine and Cronly-Dillon (1974) showed that pigment cells from the center of the adult newt retina were able to impart axial polarity to the whole of the regenerating retina. Thus, the pigment cell population contains the necessary information to develop retinal polarity.

Further evidence that retinal pigment cells might be involved in determining the patterns of synaptic connections formed by optic nerve fibers is considered in Section VIII.

Recent experiments have thus provided considerable information about the process by which axial polarity is imposed on the developing retina. These experiments, however, neither definitively identify the process as one involving primarily the retinal ganglion cell population nor, of themselves, demonstrate that the ganglion cells acquire cytochemical labels as a result of differentiative events. Such interpretations must be viewed as speculation compatible with, but going beyond, the data presently available, not as conclusions inevitably forced from the results obtained.

V. Acquisition of Tectal Polarity

The nature of the spatial information present in the tectum, with reference to which the optic fibers arrange themselves in an orderly fashion across the surface of the optic tectum, is not known. A minimal view, which would allocate no role to tectal positional markers, is one in which retinotectal connections are the product of a precise temporal matching of the arrival of optic fibers under the maturation of tectal postsynaptic sites. This timing hypothesis, considered by Sperry (1951) and by Jacobson (1960), would involve a very closely controlled sequential arrival of optic fibers from different retinal areas, so that the only vacant newly developed tectal postsynaptic sites at the time of arrival of a given small group of optic fibers are those sites appropriate to those optic fibers. Although such timing mechanisms may operate in the development of connections in other systems such as the mammalian hippocampus (Gottlieb & Cowan, 1972), they do not appear adequate to account for the formation of the retinotectal map, since disruption of the normal temporal sequence of retinal fiber input to the tectum, in *Xenopus*, does not prevent the development of a normal retinotectal projection (Feldman, Gaze, & Keating, 1971; Hunt & Jacobson, 1972b).

Thus, it would seem that some form of positional information must exist at the tectal level to at least orient the incoming optic fibers. Although there now exists extensive information as to the time at which the spatial polarity is established for the distribution of positional information in the retina, no such information exists for the tectum[1] Crelin (1952) performed rotations of tectal tissue early in development of *Ambystoma* in an attempt

[1]Note added in proof: A seminal paper in this field has recently appeared by Chung & Cooke, *Nature*, 1975, **258**, 126.

to define that stage following which such rotations produced rotated visuo-motor behavior. His results were, however, somewhat ambiguous. If one accepts that the presence of an ordered retinotectal projection is evidence of the possession by tectal tissue of some form of polarity, then the presence of an ordered map at Stage 48 in *Xenopus laevis* tadpoles (Gaze, Keating, & Chung, 1974) indicates that, by this early stage, the tectum contains biaxially ordered spatial information.

Rotations of small portions of the tectum in adult goldfish (Yoon, 1973) and *Xenopus* (Levine & Jacobson, 1974) produced subsequent visual maps in which that part of the projection which had regenerated into the rotated reimplant was correspondingly rotated. These findings indicated that the positional markers existing in the tectum and governing the ordering of optic fibers are distributed locally throughout the tectum and do not consist, for example, of marker regions only at the most polar regions of the tectum. As Levine and Jacobson (1974) have emphasized, neither the "biochemical identity nor the cellular localization of the conjectured 'positional markers'" are known.

VI. Translation of Polarized Neuronal Arrays into Ordered Neuronal Connections

When developmental processes have generated polarized neuronal arrays, there still remains the problem of selectively linking corresponding elements in the arrays. To facilitate discussion in this section one may, despite the cautionary comments of the previous sections, accept that the most likely hypothesis on the mode of action of the developmental axes is the differential cytochemical labeling of the retinal ganglion cells and tectal neurons. Even if the developing program exerts its effects in some other manner, the production of selective synaptic associations will still require explanation.

Sperry (1951), when considering this problem in the elaboration of his chemoaffinity theory, put forward what he recognized as the simplest solution, namely that a retinal neuron with a given label would have a biochemical affinity for the tectal neuron with a corresponding label, but would experience a biochemical incompatibility when contacting tectal cells which possessed other than the appropriate label. Lasting synaptic connections would be established only between neurons of high affinity. Sperry (1951, 1963, 1965) thus postulated a rule-of-assembly of retinotectal connections in which was embodied the characteristics of selectivity, exclusivity, and invariance. After the acquisition early in development of stable labels, a retinal ganglion cell should form synapses only with tectal cells that possessed a matching label, and retinotectal synaptic relationships should be invariant (Fig. 2a).

This postulated "rule-of-assembly" possessed not only clarity and plausibility, but also the supreme value of readily lending itself to experimental investigation. The experimental strategy that has been widely used to analyze this rule of connection involves the creation of relative size disparities between the innervating and innervated structures, usually by removal of part of the retina or part of the tectum, sometimes by both. The rationale of this strategy lies in the opportunity it provides for abnormal retinotectal synaptic relationships to arise. If the selective and exclusive rule-of-assembly is the correct one, no abnormal relationship should form, connections persisting only between those elements that would have connected in normal development (Fig. 2b).

This experimental approach was pioneered by Attardi and Sperry (1963). Removal of part of the retina was combined with section of the optic nerve in adult goldfish. After regeneration of the optic nerve, the distribution in the tectum of the fibers from the remaining portions of the retina was examined by histological methods. Only those tectal areas that would normally have received fibers from the remaining retinal areas were found to be innervated. Tectal areas that would normally have received fibers from the absent portions of the retina received no optic innervation. Thus, even when offered the opportunity of large areas of available postsynaptic space, fibers from a given region of retina ignored innapropriate tectal areas and homed in on their predesignated target. Sperry's "rule-of-assembly" appeared to be the correct one.

Similar results were obtained by Jacobson and Gaze (1965) in adult goldfish. With electrophysiological techniques, these workers found that reinnervation of a tectum from only half a retina was restricted to the appropriate tectal half and, conversely, following ablation of the medial or lateral half of the tectum and section of the optic nerve, only that portion of the retina which normally innervated the remaining tectal areas was found after regeneration to project to these areas.

In embryonic chicks quadrantic retinal ablations at days 6–8 resulted in a quadrantic innervation defect in the corresponding tectal area, the residual three-fourths of the retina projecting only to the appropriate three-fourths of the tectum (De Long & Coulombre, 1965).

Considerable evidence thus existed to support the view that the "mapping function" relating retinal ganglion cells to tectal elements is a rigid one whereby every element of the retinal array has a unique element of the tectal array assigned to it. The term element here is not meant necessarily as a synonym for cell, since the tectal organization is such that one retinal ganglion cell contacts the processes of several tectal neurons, and, conversely, a tectal neuron receives contacts from several retinal ganglion cells. The use of elements in this context then means "cells at a given retinal (tectal) locus."

Given such a "mapping function" as this, then, the location of a retinal ganglion cell in the embryonic retinal field rigidly determines the tectal location of its axonal termination. In this case the process of retinal ganglion cell "specification" not only renders the cell different from its fellows, but also at the same time specifies the connections that cell may form. It would, therefore, be permissible to use the terms "retinal ganglion cell specification" and "specification of central connections" of retinal ganglion cells in an equivalent sense (Jacobson, 1967).

Until this time the invariant connectivity relations of the retinotectal system of lower vertebrates under a wide range of experimental conditions had been one of its most remarkable characteristics. Once the developmental processes leading to eye polarization have taken place, then eye rotations, contralateral eye transplantation, and the creation of size disparities had all failed to disturb the normal pattern of retinotectal connections. The pattern of the latter had indeed seemed immutable and the molecular interactions governing synaptic affinities could well have been viewed as of the "lock" and "key" variety—the key on each element of the retinal ganglion cell array seeking only its particular "lock" in the tectal array.

In the last 10 years, however, an increasing number of experimental situations have been produced in which it has been possible to modify retinotectal synaptic relationships.

The first such modifiability was observed in the retinotectal projections from surgically constructed "compound eyes" in *Xenopus laevis*. These eyes were created by uniting two nasal or two temporal half-eyecups at developmental Stage 32 (Nieuwkoop & Faber, 1967), that is, after the developmental axes of the eye are irreversibly fixed. One would have predicted that the optic innervation from these eyes would have been restricted to only half of the tectal surface—to the rostral half in the case of "double-temporal" eyes, and to the caudal half in the case of "double-nasal" eyes. The technique of compound eye construction had been introduced by Székely (1954b) in *Triturus*. On the basis of behavioral observations following rostral or caudal tectal lesions in these animals, Székely had indeed concluded that a double-temporal eye projected only to rostral tectum and that a double-nasal eye projected only to caudal tectum. Surprisingly, however, when such eyes were created in *Xenopus* and the retinotectal projections were mapped electrophysiologically (Gaze, Jacobson, & Székely, 1963, 1965), it was found that fibers from each half of the retina projected across the entire rostrocaudal

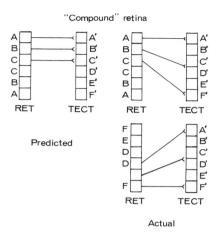

"Compound" retina

Predicted

Actual

FIG. 3. Representation of the predicted and actual projections from compound eyes in *Xenopus*. RET, retina; TECT, tectum.

extent of the optic tectum (Fig. 3). These authors pointed out that this result meant that one and the same part of the tectum is capable of forming appropriately organized connections with either temporal or nasal retina when such a retina forms part of a compound eye. Thus, retinal ganglion cells from the center of the embryonic eyecup, when they form part of a double-temporal eye, connect with the most caudal tectum, whereas similar cells, when they form part of a double-nasal eye, project to the most rostral tectum. The relationship between such central retinal cells and the tectum did not, in this experimental situation, appear to be immutable.

Sperry (1965), however, suggested that the spreading of connections from the half-retina of a compound eye over the entire rostrocaudal extent of the tectum in these cases might be more apparent than real, in that the tectum to which a compound eye projects may not represent a complete tectum. Since the differentiation and continued growth of the optic tectum is known to be dependent upon the optic fiber input (Kollros, 1953; Larsell, 1931; McMurray, 1954), it could be that as the tectum contralateral to a compound eye received fibers from only half a retina, then only the corresponding half of the tectum may go on developing. Because two similar hemiretinas supply it, this half of the tectum receives a double complement of fibers and may well hypertrophy until it comes to resemble in size and shape a normal tectum (Fig. 4). Thus, the "normal" tectum over which each half-retina of a compound eye spreads its connections may not be a normal tectum at all but an enlarged version of that half of the tectum to which the half-retina normally projects. If this were the case, then the pattern of retinotectal

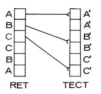

Tectal Hypertrophy

Fig. 4.   Explanation of the projection from compound eyes, based on the view that the corresponding half of the tectum has hypertrophied.

connections seen in *Xenopus* with "compound eyes" would be that predicted on the basis of the selective and exclusive rule-of-assembly, and the results could be readily incorporated into Sperry's chemoaffinity theory.

This suggestion was investigated by Straznicky, Gaze, and Keating (1971a), who examined the nature of the "suspect" tectum in *Xenopus* with one compound eye by causing it to be innervated directly by a normal eye. This was achieved by sectioning the optic chiasma in postmetamorphic animals and placing at the site of section a Millipore filter. Regenerating optic fibers attempting to reach the contralateral optic tectum meet this barrier and are deflected to innervate directly their ipsilateral optic tectum. The normal eye thus comes to innervate the tectum previously innervated by the compound eye, and the compound eye projects to the tectum previously receiving from the normal eye. If the suspect tectum were indeed a hypertrophied half-tectum, and if the linkage rule were the invariant "mapping function," then uncrossing the optic chiasma should have produced the following retinotectal projections: (1) from the normal eye to the "half-tectum," there should project only that half of the normal eye that corresponds in type to the components of the compound eye; (2) from the compound eye to the normal tectum, each half of the compound eye should project to only the appropriate half of the normal tectum. The results obtained by Straznicky *et al.* (1971a) did not support these predictions. The normal eye gave a normal projection to the suspect tectum, and each half of the compound eye projected across the entire extent of the normal tectum. The authors concluded that the tectum innervated by a compound eye is not an hypertrophied half-tectum, and that the problems presented by the apparent plasticity in retinotectal connections revealed by the compound eye projection still remained.

Such problems were, however, not confined to *Xenopus* with embryonic eye operations. Gaze and Sharma (1970), extending the earlier tectal ablation experiments of Jacobson and Gaze (1965) in adult goldfish, obtained a different type of result. Removal of the caudal half of the optic tectum led subsequently to the appearance of the displaced projection from the missing half-tectum on the residual rostral tectum. In those cases where the optic nerve had not been sectioned concomitantly with the partial tectal ablation, there was not a uniform compression of the whole visual field onto the surface of the remaining tectum. The most temporal retina projected most rostrally on the remaining tectum, the most caudal available tectum was occupied by fibers from most nasal retina, but between these areas there was frequently a dual retinal input, one from the retinal position "correct" for the tectal area and one from the nasal retina. Even in these tectal areas receiving dual retinal innervation, the projections from both retinal areas maintained their correct retinotopic order of polarity. In some of those animals in which the tectal ablation had been combined with optic nerve crush, an orderly compression of the entire visual field, and hence of the retina, across the residual rostral tectum was seen (Fig. 5). Gaze and Sharma (1970) suggested that the differences between their results and those of Jacobson and Gaze (1965) reflected some difference between the mechanisms ordering retinotectal connections in the rostrocaudal tectal axis as opposed to the mediolateral tectal axis.

Yoon (1971), however, was able to show that orderly field compression occurred across both axes of the retinotectal system after a range of tectal ablations. This compression of optic fibers from the whole retina into partial tectum occurred whether or not the optic nerve was cut at the time of tectal ablation. In a very elegant series of subsequent experiments Yoon (1972a) demonstrated that removal of tectal tissue was not necessary to produce field compression. The separation of rostral and caudal tectal areas by either thin pieces of tantalum foil or absorbable gelatin barriers could subsequently produce compression of the entire field across the rostral tectum in front of the barrier. Yoon was also able to show that this compression of the entire retinotectal input into half a tectum was reversible. Removal of the tantalum foil or resorption of the gelatin barrier was followed by the expansion of the retinal input to cover the entire tectum.

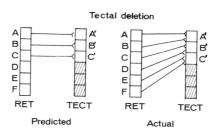

FIG. 5.   Representation from an eye to a partial tectum: (left) on the basis of the selective and exclusive rule of connection; (right) the observed result. RET, retina; TECT, tectum.

Sharma (1972a, 1972b) described, in goldfish, field compression onto the remaining tectal surface after removal of the rostral half-tectum and also after removal of strips of tectal tissue oriented either in the mediolateral tectal axis (1972a) or the rostrocaudal tectal axis (1972b). The converse size-disparity experiment on the adult goldfish has been performed by Horder (1971) and Yoon (1972b). Both these workers reported that, after removal of the temporal half of the retina, the remaining nasal half of the retina spreads its connections over the entire tectum. Yoon also reported the same phenomenon after removal of the nasal half of the retina, although Horder did not find such expansion of the temporal retinal projection after nasal retinal lesions.

The combination of temporal retinal removal and caudal tectal ablation was performed by Horder (1971) and Yoon (1972c). The end result of this procedure was that the projection from nasal hemiretina, which normally innervates caudal tectum, is transposed onto the foreign rostral tectum (Fig. 6).

Thus, after the early experiments, the results of which emphasized the invariant nature of retinotectal connections, a wide range of similar experiments on larval *Xenopus* and adult goldfish yielded results that demonstrated an apparent plasticity in retinotectal synaptic relationships. The early results had been interpreted as supporting the selective and exclusive rule of assembly of the retinotectal system. It is not unreasonable to conclude, therefore, that the much more extensive data, of an opposite sense, call this particular rule into question. Straznicky *et al.* (1971a) and Gaze and Keating (1972) have argued that these more recent data might be taken to indicate an alternative mapping function operating to link retinal and tectal elements. This function, given the descriptive term "systems matching," observed the polarity of the retinal and tectal systems (see Sections IV and V). Within this constraint, however, it was suggested that each retinal element did not have a unique image in the tectum as postulated by the selective and exclusive function, but rather that the mapping func-

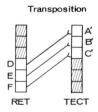

FIG. 6.   Representation of the result obtained when a nasal half-retina (RET) confronts the rostral half of the tectum (TECT).

tion was such that the most nasal retinal cells available connect with the most caudal tectal elements available, the most temporal retinal cells present connect with the most rostral tectal cells available, and intermediate retinal cells connect with proportionately intermediate tectal positions. The function would operate in a similar fashion linking dorsoventral retinal cells to the mediolateral tectal axis. It was realized that such a mapping function probably operated through mechanisms whereby labeled presynaptic axons would compete for postsynaptic space.

A conclusion along these lines is forced if the original assumptions underlying the experimental strategy are indeed valid. One of these assumptions was that the label marking the specificity of the neuron, once acquired, was stable. This view, firmly stated in the literature (Jacobson, 1967, 1970; Sperry, 1951) was questioned by Straznicky et al. (1971a). These authors recognized that since the operation to produce a "compound eye" in Xenopus laevis is performed at an early developmental state, the possibility existed that developmental processes might have reorganized whatever factors label a neuron so as to reconstitute within each half-retina the range of labels associated normally with a whole retina. Phenomena of this nature, whereby a developing system responds to deletion of a part of its substance by reconstituting a whole system, are termed in embryology "regulation." If each half-retina of a compound eye were to regulate so that the complete range of retinal ganglion cell labels was present in each half-retina, then the observed spreading of connections from the half-retina across the tectal surface would be entirely in accord with the selective and exclusive mapping function, and there would be no need to invoke an alternative function such as that of systems matching (Fig. 7).

Similar considerations may be applied to the experimental situation in

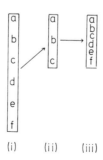

(i)   (ii)   (iii)

FIG. 7.   Representation of the postulated regulation of specificity labels in a neural structure after ablation of half that structure. (i) Distribution of labels a–f in a normal structure. (ii) Immediately after removal of half that structure. (iii) End result of the regulative process; the restoration of labels a–f.

which portions of tectal tissue are removed. It is conceivable that the remaining tectal tissue "regulates" so as to reconstitute the range of labels normally associated with a complete tectum.

Straznicky *et al.* (1971a) and Gaze and Keating (1972) considered the possibility that regulative interactions were relabeling partial retinas or partial tecta but concluded that this explanation, while conceptually possible, would require the persistence and operation of regulative phenomena in adult animals, whereas regulation, in the sense that this term was being used, is essentially an embryonic phenomenon. Yoon (1972a), however, favored the view that the readjustment in retinotectal synaptic relationships obtained after tectal lesions indicated the relabeling of the remaining cells and that, therefore, the apparent flexibility in retinotectal connections in animals with such lesions reflected the operation of the selective and exclusive mapping function proposed by Sperry.

Meyer and Sperry (1973, 1974) agreed with this latter interpretation. They presented the two conflicting arguments clearly. In those situations in which changed synaptic relationships have been observed, then either the rigid mapping function is operating and the cell labels are labile, or the cell labels are fixed and the mapping function is of a competitive or systems-matching nature. Meyer and Sperry (1973) felt that the adult anuran retinotectal system might provide a critical testing ground on which to examine the two hypotheses. They, therefore, produced partial tectal ablations in *Hyla regilla* and observed, subsequently, no compression of the whole visual field onto the remaining tectum. Such a result, earlier obtained after partial tectal ablations in larval *Xenopus* (Straznicky, Gaze, & Keating, 1971b) and in postmetamorphic *Xenopus* (Straznicky, 1973), stands in contrast with those obtained after partial tectal ablations in adult goldfish. These results on anurans, argued Meyer and Sperry, support the rule of connection originally formulated by Sperry and militate against the competitive variant proposed by Straznicky *et al.* (1971a) and Gaze and Keating (1972). Since the original rule of connection is correct, the argument proceeds, then the most parsimonious explanation of these situations in which it is apparently not observed in that regulation of the cell labels has occurred.

This position is seductive in its elegant coherence. It does, however, oversimplify the difficulties inherent in proposing that "field regulation" can occur in adult tissues. To propose, as do Meyer and Sperry (1973), that because a system is still growing, it is capable of field regulation, overlooks the fact that in most embryonic systems the regulative phase ceases before growth begins, and certainly in all such systems growth extends well beyond the time at which the system is regulative.

Operations on the developing eyecup in *Xenopus* embryos to construct compound eyes certainly take place at a time when regulative phenomena are possible. In fact, animals in which one half of the developing eyecup was removed, generated eyes from the remaining ocular tissue which gave normal retinotectal maps (Berman & Hunt, 1975; Feldman & Gaze, 1975). These results could well indicate that under such conditions regulation has occurred. Horder and Spitzer (1973) showed that when half an eyecup is removed at these stages, then after a slight delay cell division resumes at the cut edge. The residual half-eye thus regenerates a whole eye. In the case of double-nasal compound eyes, cell division does not resume at the opposed cut edges (Feldman & Gaze, 1972), and the two situations are not, therefore, totally comparable. It would be a mistake to believe that because half-eyes regulate, then necessarily each half of a compound eye must also do so. It must be admitted, however, that the possibility of regulative reconstitution of a complete range of labels in each half of a compound eye reduces the confidence with which the projections from such eyes may be said to support the systems-matching rule of interconnection. In other situations, however, in which retinal projections compress into partial tecta, or partial retinas expand over the whole tectum, evidence is now emerging which argues strongly against regulative interactions as the responsible mechanism. First, there were the findings of Sharma (1972a, 1972b), which showed that, after a strip lesion of the tectum, the retinotectal projection distributed itself on the remaining tectum as though the tectal gap was not there. It is of the essence of regulative fields that the tissues in the field are in close communication with each other. Such would certainly not be the case in tectal areas separated by a gap. Those favoring tectal regulation as the explanation of Sharma's results would be forced to postulate "partial" regulation of each tectal area, the degrees of "partial" regulation occurring in the separated tectal areas being exactly complementary. A regulative field possessing such properties would be most bizarre. Sharma himself interpreted his results as favoring the "systems-matching" mode of connection.

Cook and Horder (1974) and Meyer (1975), set out to investigate the properties of partial tectal fragments in goldfish. Both groups of workers reached the conclusion that the tectal remnant did not undergo regulation. Cook and Horder based their conclusion on the early pattern of retinotectal connections formed when the optic nerve regenerated into such a remnant, and Meyer on the basis of the way in which half-retinas projected to such half-tecta. The conclusion that regulation does not occur in goldfish half-tecta leads to the interpretation that the compression of the fibers from a whole retina onto such a partial tectum is the result of some form of competitive interaction between the incoming optic fibers for available post-synaptic space.

Finally, Feldman, Keating, and Gaze (1975) described, in *Xenopus*, the projection of fibers from half of the retina of a known normal eye, distributing in an orderly fashion across the whole tectal surface. In this case the half-retina cannot have regulated since it formed part of a normal eye, the whole of which projected across the surface of the other optic tectum. The elements of the half-retina projecting to both tecta thus sent their fibers to different sites on the two tecta. It seems that there are no terminal cues that uniquely match a fiber from a given retinal locus with a particular tectal site.

The size-disparity paradigm was introduced by Attardi and Sperry (1963), who obtained results compatible with the selective and exclusive chemo-affinity rule. Since that time the experimental design has been used extensively to study the rules under which neuronal arrays interconnect. The results from such experiments have shown, for the most part, a state of affairs differing in kind from that obtained by Attardi and Sperry. Before such results can be taken to invalidate the "selective and exclusive" rule, one must be reasonably sure that the assumptions implicit in the paradigm are fulfilled. Controversy at present centers on this issue. The protagonists of one view argue that synaptic labels are not stable under the experimental conditions being used and that, hence, no valid test of the chemoaffinity rule has been performed. The alternative argument is that the assumption of stable labels is likely to be correct and that, therefore, a different rule of connection is required. It is my opinion that, on balance, the latter position is the more valid at present. The control of selective synaptogenesis appears to reside in mechanisms operating on a competitive basis.

The present situation must, however, be viewed as a fluid one. Certain results are difficult to accommodate in such a scheme. These findings include the original Attardi and Sperry results, confirmed recently by Meyer (1975); those on partial tectal ablations in anurans (Meyer & Sperry, 1973; Straznicky, 1973; Straznicky et al., 1971b); and the observations by Sharma (1972a, 1972b) and by Cook and Horder (1974) to the effect that patterns of early regeneration to tectal remnants are those that would be predicted on the basis of a "selective and exclusive" rule. Until further explanations are found to account for these results, we may be sure that we have not yet reached a definitive statement adequately describing those mechanisms that control the formation of selective neuronal connections.

VII. Development of the Adult Pattern of Retinotectal Connections

The early experimental study of mechanisms controlling the formation of selective connections in the retinotectal system involved observations of patterns of regeneration of optic fibers after section of the optic nerve under a variety of circumstances (Gaze, 1959; Gaze & Jacobson, 1963; Sperry, 1943, 1944, 1945). More recent experiments have analyzed the effects of experimental manipulation of the retina or the tectum in the adult animal, with or without section of the optic nerve (see Section VI). The application of conclusions deriving from this latter type of study to the initial formation of connections in the normal animal involves at least two assumptions: (1), that factors governing regeneration and the reestablishment of neuronal connections are similar to those operating in normal development; (2) that perturbation of the system by experimental interference does not, of itself, disturb the normal operation of these controlling factors.

The necessity for these assumptions may be avoided by studying the normal animal in which no experimental perturbation has been introduced. It may be possible in this situation to examine the validity of earlier conclusions without invoking the above assumptions. For example, at the end of Section VI, the conclusion was advanced that early developmental events do not rigidly determine the synaptic relationships entertained by retinal ganglion cells. It was suggested that the synaptic patterns formed between polarized neuronal arrays may well be determined by the context in which the two extent neuronal populations are interconnecting.

The developing retinotectal projection offers a useful system in which to examine this proposition. In amphibians, such as *Xenopus*, the retina and the optic tectum continue to grow during larval life. During this period the system is readily accessible to observation. Also in these animals, the retina and the tectum display differential modes of growth the result of which is that, during larval life, the existing complements of differentiated retinal ganglion cells and differentiated tectal cells are not those that will interconnect in the adult animal. If these neuronal arrays do interconnect in order at these developmental stages, this would provide support for the contextual nature of the rules governing synaptic formation between polarized neuronal arrays.

In the tadpole retina, growth occurs by accretion of cells at the ciliary margin (Glucksmann, 1940; Hollyfield, 1971; Jacobson, 1968b; Straznicky & Gaze, 1971). New cells added at this marginal germinative zone differentiate into the elements of the various retinal layers. This continuous addition of new cells at the margin contributes to the gradual increase in retinal diameter that occurs with growth. Retinal growth thus occurs concentrically, with cells that comprised the entire retinal extent at early developmental stages being progressively displaced by the appearance of younger cells at the periphery, so that in the adult animal these older cells constitute central retina. This growth process continues throughout the larval period and into postmetamorphic life in *Xenopus* (Straznicky & Gaze, 1971).

Similar concentric modes of retinal growth have been described in fish (Hollyfield, 1972), chick (Fujita & Horii, 1963), and mouse (Sidman, 1961). The tectum, on the other hand, does not grow in this concentric fashion. Autoradiographic analysis (Straznicky & Gaze, 1972) revealed that in *Xenopus* the tectum forms from rostroventral to caudomedial by the serial addition of strips of cells that displace the preexisting tissue rostrolaterally. Kollros (1953) had earlier observed a rostrocaudal sequence of tectal developments in *Rana*, and a similar course of chick tectal growth has been described by Fujita (1964) and by LaVail and Cowan (1971), although in the case of the chick the whole process occurs much faster than in amphibians.

The differing modes of growth of the retina and the tectum pose an interesting topological problem in retinotectal synaptic relationships. One consequence of a concentrically growing retina is that in early to mid-larval stages the existing retina consists of those elements which in the adult will comprise central retina. These elements in the adult *Xenopus* will form synapses with central tectal areas. Because of the curvilinear nature of tectal growth, at the early to mid-larval stages the existing mature tectum consists of those elements which in the adult will occupy rostral tectum and receive synaptic input from temporal retinal fibers. It is of interest to know whether these complements of neurons, which in the adult are noncorresponding, will nevertheless form an orderly retinotectal projection during development.

Optic axons leave the *Xenopus* retina at Stage 31/32, are present in the optic chiasma by Stage 35, and reach the optic tectum by Stage 40. The nature of the retinotectal projection, as revealed by electrophysiological recording at various developmental stages, has been described by Gaze, Chung, and Keating (1972) and by Gaze, Keating, and Chung (1974).

Within a very short time of the arrival of optic fibers at the developing tectum, visually evoked unitary activity may be recorded through a microelectrode situated in the rostrolateral portion of the tectum. In the earlier stages, activity at any one electrode position could be evoked from large regions of the visual field; and over the small area of rostral tectum from which activity could be recorded, there was no obvious order in the visual projection.

Such order was first seen at Stage 48/49, and the order present was that seen in the adult; namely, nasal visual field projected rostrally, temporal visual field caudally, superior field medially, and inferior field laterally. During later larval stages the extent of tectum from which activity could be recorded increased, as more caudal areas become innervated, and by the end of larval life the tectal surface is completely covered. At all stages the entire visual field projected to the innervated tectal areas. Although the order (polarity) of visual field positions projecting to the tectum was normal in the larvae, the detailed arrangement is different from that in the adult. In the latter, equidistant steps of electrode position across the tectal surface produced equidistant changes in corresponding visual field position. In the tadpole, until just before metamorphic climax, this is not the case: disproportionately large areas of the innervated tectum are occupied by fibers from the nasal retina (temporal field).

Gaze *et al.* (1972, 1974) drew the following conclusions from their studies: First, tectal polarity exists by Stage 48 of larval life, regardless of whatever parameter of whichever tectal element constitutes this property, since the tectum at this stage is capable of organizing a set of incoming optic fibers into the correct order. Second, however, the results suggested that the detailed patterning of retinotectal connections in larval life is not the same as that existing in the adult animal. Thus, retinal cells, which in the adult will connect only with central tectum, connect in early larval stages with rostral tectal elements. Later these optic fibers are displaced caudally by newly arriving temporal retinal fibers, which now innervate the most rostral tectum, these latter fibers being in their turn displaced caudally by even newer temporal retinal fibers.

The conclusion that retinotectal synaptic connections change during development can be sustained only if there are indeed synapses formed between optic fibers and tectal cells from early larval stages. That such synapses are formed during larval life in *Xenopus* has been demonstrated histologically by Scott (1974), and that these optic synapses are functional from very early larval stages has been shown by Chung, Keating, and Bliss (1974).

Meyer (1974) has described a similar developmental shift in the retinotectal connections of juvenile goldfish. The existence, in both fish and amphibians, of ordered but transitory connections during development again leads one to the view that there are no unique cues between a given retinal fiber and a particular tectal locus. One must conclude either that the postulated cell labels are continuously changing during larval life or that retinotectal connections are determined by a rule that does not involve unique chemoaffinities.

VIII. Retinal Pigment Abnormalities and Anomalies of Visual Connections

Another approach to the mechanisms governing the formation of selective neuronal connections lies in the analysis of neural abnormalities associated with genetic mutations. Such mutations create conditions that cannot be mimicked by even the most delicate surgery, and a study of these unusual conditions may help unravel some of the underlying developmental processes.

In the last decade, interest has been generated by the discovery that animals with mutant genes of the albino allelomorphic series frequently have abnormal retinofugal pathways. In particular, the number of retinal fibers projecting to the ipsilateral side of the brain is reduced in albino rats (Lund, 1965), mice (Guillery, Scott, Cattenach, & Deol, 1973), guinea pigs (Giolli & Creel, 1973), ferrets (Guillery, 1971), rabbits (Sanderson, 1975), mink (Sanderson, Guillery, & Shackelford, 1974), cats (Guillery, 1969), and even the tiger (Guillery & Kaas, 1973). The topography of the visual projections has been studied in most detail in Siamese cats. Guillery (1969) noted an unusual laminar structure of, and an abnormal organization of the retinal input to, the lateral geniculate nucleus in such cats. Electrophysiological recordings by Guillery and Kaas (1971) and by Hubel and Wiesel (1971) showed that fibers from some 20° of the retina, temporal to the normal line of decussation, which in the normal animal project to lamina A1 of the ipsilateral geniculate, in the Siamese cat cross instead to the opposite lateral geniculate nucleus. In this contralateral geniculate nucleus, the aberrant fibers terminate retinotopically in that part of the nucleus that would have been occupied by fibers from the same 20° of the retina of the ipsilateral eye had these fibers not crossed to the opposite side of the brain. The pattern of termination of these aberrant fibers was that which would result if the lateral geniculate nucleus treated the fibers as though they had come from the ipsilateral rather than the contralateral eye. This arrangement led to the view that the basic anomaly in Siamese cats was one in which the retinal ganglion cells were appropriately specified for their retinal site of origin but incorrectly labeled for the path to follow at the optic chiasma. This conclusion, if correct, implies that there must be two "specifying" mechanisms in the retina, one labeling the ganglion cell according to its retinal position and the second, quite independently, determining the retinal equivalent of the line of decussation. This interpretation does depend upon the belief that the geniculate cells comprising the abnormal portion of lamina A1 are themselves normal, a view for which one has no independent evidence. Indeed the interlaminar zone between the abnormal A1 and lamina A is lost, but it is not known whether this defect is primary or secondary to the abnormal retinal input.

Sanderson, Guillery, and Shackelford (1974) have examined whether the defective visual pathways seen in albinos are associated only with the specific metabolic defect of this mutation, a defect in the enzyme tyrosinase, or whether it is associated with other defects of pigment metabolism. They investigated minks of several different genotypes and discovered that the abnormal decussation of retinogeniculate fibers is associated with defects in the retinal pigment epithelium, regardless of the gene defect or gene combination defect that produces the reduction in retinal pigment.

Wise (1975) studied the geniculate projections in rats of the King–Holtzman heterochromic hybrid variety. These animals have one red eye in which pigment granules are totally absent, and one black eye in which pigment exists in the iris and the choroid but is absent from the retinal pigment epithelium. The ipsilateral retinogeniculate pathway from both eyes was similar to that in albinos, and Wise concluded that pigmentation in the retinal pigment epithelium, rather than that of other ocular tissues, is the critical feature influencing the chiasmatic pathway followed by retinal fibers.

An ingenious experiment by Guillery *et al.* (1973) set out to define some of the characteristics of the process by which the pigment epithelium influences the behavior of the retinal ganglion cells. "Flecked" mice are animals that are homozygous for the albino gene at its normal locus but also possess one wild-type variant of the gene translocated to one of the X-chromosomes. Because, in the female, there is random inactivation of one of the X-chromosomes then in female flecked-mice those cells in which the wild-type gene is on the active X-chromosome are pigmented, whereas those in which the wild-type gene is on the inactive X-chromosome are albino. The pigment epithelium in such flecked mice is made up of patches of normally pigmented and albino tissue. If retinal ganglion cells were influenced primarily by retinal pigment epithelium in their immediate vicinity, then there should also be islands of normal and abnormally specified ganglion cells. If this were the case, then the abnormality found in flecked mice should be intermediate between normal and albino. Guillery *et al.* (1973) found no such intermediate reduction in the number of fibers projecting to the ipsilateral side of the brain in flecked mice. They concluded that some intercellular mechanism enabled the nonmutant cells to influence the function of mutant cells so as to mask the abnormal effects usually associated with such cells. It may be recalled that in Section IV attention was drawn to the temporal correlation between the disappearance of gap junctions between retinal pigment cells and the irreversible polarization of the retina in *Xenopus* (Dixon & Cronly-Dillon, 1974).

Less attention has been paid to the fate of the retinotectal projection in these mutant animals. Berman and Cynader (1972) described an increased tectal representation of the contralateral retina upon the superior colliculus of Siamese cats, with caudal displacement of the representation of the vertical meridian of the visual field. Such a result appeared analogous to the "compression" of the visual field onto partial tecta in goldfish. Gaze and Keating (1972) suggested that this result therefore argued for the existence of a similar "systems-matching" type of rule governing retinotectal connections in mammals.

It has, however, been claimed subsequently that in squirrels, tree shrews, and cats (Kaas, Harting, & Guillery, 1974; Lane, Kaas, & Allman, 1974) the entire retina projects to the contralateral optic tectum in the normal animal. One would not, therefore, expect the albino mutants to have abnormal retinotectal projections, and Lane *et al.* (1974) confirmed this prediction.

The finding that the entire retina projects to the contralateral tectum in normal mammals occasions considerable surprise since the accepted view of only partial decussation of optic fibers was believed to apply to all retinal fiber populations. If this recent finding is true it implies (1) that the mechanisms ordering retinogeniculate input are different from those ordering retinotectal connections; (2) that the mechanisms determining the "line of decussation" at the retinal level operate only on a subset of retinal ganglion cells; and (3) that further information as to the precise topography of the direct ipsilateral retinotectal input in these animals is required. It is perhaps relevant to mention that behavioral studies of tectal function in the normal cat imply that the visual function is restricted only to one hemifield, not to the whole retina (Sherman, 1974).

Recently, a further complication to this story has been provided by the findings of Lund, Lund, and Wise (1974) on retinal projections in pigmented and albino rats. These authors claim that the entire retina projects to the contralateral dorsal lateral geniculate nucleus in normal animals. In albino rats the projection from temporal retina is larger and the projection of the vertical meridian on the lateral geniculate nucleus is displaced, a result reminiscent of the Berman and Cynader (1972) finding in the optic tectum of Siamese cats.

It would appear that the present time is not the best at which to attempt a unified hypothesis to account for the anomalous visual projections in animals with abnormalities of the retinal pigment epithelium. It is sufficient to say that work on these mutants has provided a major approach to the study of mechanisms of neuronal specificity in the visual system of mammals, that it has drawn attention to the role of the retinal pigment epithelium in these matters, and that it is now implied that the mechanisms controlling the decussation or nondecussation of retinal fibers at the optic chaisma are even more complex than previously realized.

Studies of the way in which the abnormal input to the lateral geniculate nucleus is transferred to the visual cortex (Guillery, Casagrande, & Oberdorfer, 1974; Hubel & Wiesel, 1971; Kaas & Guillery, 1973) have yielded some extremely intriguing results. Any comprehensive theory attempting to account for the formation of functional connections must seek to accommodate these findings. Limitations of space preclude the consideration of these results here. The final pattern of functional geniculocortical connections appears, however, to reflect the interplay of functional and prefunctional mechanisms. (For further discussion of this point see Guillery *et al.*, 1974; Keating, 1975a.)

IX. Experimental Perturbations of the Mammalian Visual System

The development of surgical techniques that permit interference with the fetal or neonatal visual system at a time when synaptic connections are being formed has enabled experimental situations to be established in mammals, which are broadly similar to those that have been used extensively in studies of the lower vertebrate visual system.

The overall strategy adopted in these pioneering studies resembles those of the size-disparity paradigm, in which the ability of the neurons to form abnormal connections under experimental conditions is studied.

The removal of an eye in newborn rats deprives those visual centers which would usually receive from that eye, of their normal neuronal input. Lund (1972) and Lund, Cunningham, and Lund (1973) described an increased input from the remaining eye to these deprived centers, this input arising in part from retinal areas that project normally only to the contralateral visual centers. Lund and Lund (1975) produced a partial innervation defect in one optic tectum by a partial retinal lesion to the contralateral eye in neonatal rats. This defect was filled by an anomalous projection from the ipsilateral eye, but not necessarily from the homotopic part of the ipsilateral retina. Although Lund (1972) and Lund et al. (1973) claimed that such anomalies did not occur following lesions in older animals, Goodman, Bogdasarian, and Horel (1973) described axonal sprouting in adult rats following eye enucleation, but they found that it occurred only in those centers already receiving an input from the remaining ipsilateral eye.

Chow, Mathers, and Spear (1973) sounded a cautionary note about the significance of anomalous fiber projections demonstrated by anatomical techniques. They described axonal sprouting following enucleation of an eye in neonatal rabbits, the fibers spreading from the remaining eye into areas of the ipsilateral colliculus normally innervated only by the contralateral eye. Using electrophysiological techniques they could not find, however, any evidence that the anomalous projection was capable of driving collicular cells.

Schneider (1973) removed one superior colliculus in the neonatal hamster and described a whole range of abnormal retinal projections of those fibers denied their normal site of termination. The response of the mammalian retinotectal system to partial lesion of the tectum appears to involve the compression of the fibers from the whole retina into the remaining tectum in topographic order (Jhaveri & Schneider, 1974; Schneider & Jhaveri, 1974). Miller (1975) describes similar results following partial tectal lesions in neonatal rats.

The interpretation of these mammalian results is, of course, plagued with the same conceptual difficulties facing the lower vertebrate material (see Section VI). The basic problem is that there is no independent measure of that cellular property which influences the connections that the neuron will form. The broad similarity between some of these results and those obtained in parallel experimental situations in lower vertebrates does permit one to hope that mammalian visual neuronal connections are subject to the same general type of control mechanism that exists in lower vertebrates. It is also clear that the neuronal connections that do exist in the normal animal are not only ones that *can* exist. It does not seem that the normal pattern of connections is produced because such connections are the only ones possible between the neuronal populations being studied. Any theory of the formation of selective neuronal connections must thus explain not only why certain connections are formed but why other potentially possible connections are not formed.

X. Molecular Mechanisms Involved in Selective Synaptic Formation

It must be admitted at the outset of this section that nothing is known of the molecular moieties participating in the recognition processes that underlie the formation of synapses. Enough is known, however, to permit tentative speculations about the constraints under which such molecular interactions must operate.

Taking the retinotectal system as a model, there are three fundamental processes involved in the determination of the neuronal connections entertained by the system. First, the determination of the axes of the developing retina (and presumably, of the developing tectum); second, the conversion of this axial information into position-dependent cellular properties (the cytochemical "labels" of the chemoaffinity theory); and third, the interactions between such labeled cells that permit and maintain synapse formation.

The first of these is one of the classical problems of developmental biology, namely, the acquisition of spatially distributed pattern. Wolpert (1969) is responsible for organizing and clarifying the components of the concept of positional information, many of which were implicit in earlier work.

Our ignorance of the molecular nature of the substances, the distribution of which conveys the postulated positional information, is only thinly disguised by terming them "morphogens." Neither is it known whether positional information along one axis is the result of a monotonically distributed gradient of concentration of a single morphogen (Crick, 1970), or of two morphogens distributed with opposite polarity (Dalcq, 1938), or, indeed, if it is a spatially distributed gradient of morphogen at all. Thus, Goodwin and Cohen (1969) proposed a model for the specification of positional information that involved the propagation of two signals through the tissue at differing velocities. The phase angle or temporal delay between the two signals could convey positional information. Both Wolpert and Goodwin and Cohen recognized that the retinotectal projection provided an excellent system in which to apply their models. Recently Meinhardt and Gierer (1974) have considered the acquisition of polarity in the developing retina and its transition from a reversible to an irreversible state. Basing their speculations on an earlier model (Gierer & Meinhardt, 1972), they suggested that an initially very slight spatial asymmetry of material in a tissue might transform autocatalytically into a much more marked asymmetry, accounting in this way for the development of irreversible polarity in *Xenopus* eyes raised from Stage 22 to 38 in tissue culture (Hunt & Jacobson, 1973).

A slightly different model of positional information has been advanced by McMahon (1973) to account for the development of the slime mold (*Dictyostelium discoideum*). The reason for drawing attention to this model in a review on the lower vertebrate visual system is that the author emphasizes the role of intercellular contacts in the regulation of morphogenetic activity. Given the temporal correlation discussed earlier between cell coupling and retinal polarization, McMahon's ideas may well be of relevance to this system.

Having established, in some form, positional information to which a cell is exposed, there yet remains the problem of its interpretation by the cell so as to select that particular course of molecular differentiation which will endow the cell with the appropriate position-dependent properties. Models of the way in which positional information may interact with the genome to produce position-dependent differentiation have been considered by Babloyantz and Hiernaux (1974).

The problem in the retinotectal system is that the nature of the postulated molecular differentiation is unknown. Selective synaptic formation is viewed generally as an extremely precise manifestation of a more general phenomenon, that of intercellular recognition. Roth (1973) suggests as mediators of cell communication and cell–cell recognition the glycosyl transferases and their glycosyl acceptors, both of which are found on the cell surface. Barondes (1970) and Marchase, Barbera, and Roth (1975) have suggested that such molecules participate in the formation of retinotectal connections. Hughes (1975) pointed out, first, that the activity of such glycosyl transferases could be affected by "modifier" proteins from some other source and, second, that a spatially distributed gradient of concentration of these modifier proteins could produce an array of neurons with different glycoprotein labels.

That such surface molecules may manifest their presence by activities other than synapse formation was investigated by Barbera, Marchase, and Roth (1973). Building upon earlier work, which had demonstrated differences in adhesibility between cells from different tissues and from different brain regions, Barbera *et al.* decided to find out whether there was preferential adhesion between cells that would become neuronally linked as opposed to cells that do not neuronally link. In their assay system a ^{32}P-labeled cell suspension of either dorsal or ventral embryonic chick retina was placed in dishes containing both ventral and dorsal tectal halves. The authors showed that cells from the dorsal retina adhered preferentially to ventral tectum and cells from ventral retina adhered preferentially to dorsal tectum. This preferential adhesion is similar to the innervation pattern of the retinotectal system. This remarkable result has been interpreted with appropriate caution by the authors. Indeed, some care is warranted before it can be accepted that the cell surface recognition phenomenon being demonstrated here is the one involved in specific synaptogenesis. Nevertheless, such an assay system is a most promising advance in our attempts to understand the mechanisms of selective cell recognition.

At various places in this essay one has had to consider the possibility that changed patterns of synaptic connections are due to temporal changes in cell labels. I have usually implied that I felt such changes unlikely as the explanation of the data being considered. Without withdrawing from that position, it is only fair to point out the temporal changes in the cell surface behavior of retinal and tectal cells from the embryonic chick have been described (Gottlieb, Merrell, & Glaser, 1974). These changes were, however, in tissue-specific aggregation activity, and there is no evidence that the components being studied by Gottlieb *et al.* are involved in synaptic formation, nor that such temporal changes in cell label occur after the embryonic phase.

Most of those who have sought to model the molecular interactions underlying retinotectal synaptic connections have incorporated two assumptions of the chemoaffinity theory into their models. First, they accept that the manifestation of the specificity of the individual retinal ganglion cell lies in a surface cytochemical label; and second, it is tacitly assumed that such labels are the product solely of synthetic machinery deriving from the pattern of gene activity that constitutes the terminally differentiated state of the ganglion cell.

It is both legitimate and perfectly compatible with the data presently available to challenge both of these assumptions. Keating and Kennard (1975) (see Section III of this essay) extended the ideas of Hughes (1975) to suggest, for the sake of argument, that the pigment epithelium might be the cell population that is polarized and undergoes the position-dependent terminal differentiation. For example, pigment epithelium at different retinal loci light produce different quantities or different types of "modifier protein." This could influence the ganglion cells in the vicinity which, as a result, alter their surface glycosyl transferases. The end result is the same labeled ganglion cells, with the label reflecting the cell's position in the retina. In this case, however, the labeled mechanism is extrinsic to the ganglion cell, not intrinsic to it. If this were the mechanism by which ganglion cells acquire their labels, then ganglion cells maintained apart from pigment epithelium in tissue culture might well revert to a homogeneous population. It is of interest in this context to note that in the assay system of Barbera et al. (1973) the pigment cells from different retinal areas displayed the same preferential adhesion to tectal fragments as did the neural retinal cells from those areas. Thus pigment cells from dorsal retina adhered preferentially to ventral tectal fragments while those from ventral retina preferred dorsal tectal fragments.

It is true that it is difficult to conceive of mechanisms by which pre- and postsynaptic structures recognize each other which do not involve specific molecular structures (cytochemical labels). It is difficult, but it is not impossible. Lettvin (cited in Chung, 1974) has suggested that the position-dependent property of a retinal ganglion cell, instead of involving a specific cell label, could reside in the "spontaneous" *firing pattern* of the cell. If the events associated with retinal polarization established a mechanism which imposed some form of spatiotemporal order on the firing pattern of ganglion cells relative to their neighbors, then such a firing pattern would constitute "interpreted" positional information. What is necessary for this class of model is a means whereby the "spontaneous" firing of a neuron (perhaps the relationship between the firing patterns of neighboring axons) influences the synaptic connections that those axons form. This suggestion must be distinguished from the older views which proposed that selective functional relationships between neural systems and their effectors might be achieved by specific patterns of impulses rather than by selective neuronal connections (see Székely, 1974; Weiss, 1936). In the model being considered here the firing patterns are responsible for the *creation* of selective neuronal connections. Chung, Raymond, and Lettvin (1970) thus argued that the structure of a neuron might be changed by the functional firing patterns to which that neuron is subject. Chung, Gaze, and Stirling (1973) described changes in the patterning of connections in the contralateral retinotectal projection of adult *Xenopus* subjected to prolonged continuous stroboscopic illumination. The retinal receptive field properties changed markedly. While the two-dimensional map of the retina on the contralateral tectum was not disturbed, the characteristic depths of different optic fiber types in the optic tectum were completely disrupted in the strobe-reared animals. Chung et al. felt that such disturbances in synaptic relationships provided support for the view that the pattern of activity in a neuron might influence the synaptic contacts that the neuron will entertain.

I am not aware of models designed specifically to accommodate a competitive systems-matching rule of connections, but in many of the models the difference between ganglion cells is a quantitative difference of some particular molecular moiety rather than a qualitative difference between different moieties. Such quantitative labels may well lend themselves to competitive behavior. Sidman (1974), considering other systems of neuronal connections, also reached the conclusion that cell surface molecules mediating synaptic recognition must operate in a competitive mode since there is clear evidence that the number of realizable synaptic relationships is much greater than that actually achieved. Some interactions involve a much better fit than others, synaptic contact between cells of relatively poor molecular match being displaced by contact between cells of better match.

XI. Intertectal Neuronal Connections: The Role of Visual Experience in Their Formation, Maintenance, and Modification

The role of the environment in the moulding of the mature nervous system remains a matter of intense interest and considerable controversy. It is conceded by all that brain development requires an adequate external environment that permits the survival of the organism. Whether, however, the external environment plays a more determinative role in brain development and, if so, in which systems this role has an important part, remains to be elucidated, as also does the mode by which environmental experience modulates the structural and functional maturation of the brain (see Gottlieb, Section 1 of this volume).

In recent years there has been a rapid accumulation of evidence to the effect that manipulation of the sensory environment produces changes in the functional synaptic connections of the mammalian visual system (see Daniels & Pettigrew and Grobstein & Chow, in the next section of this volume). I would like to consider briefly some evidence that visual function and, in particular, binocular visual experience plays a part in the patterning of a system of neuronal connections pertaining to the representation of the binocular visual field in *Xenopus laevis*. This work has been reviewed in more detail elsewhere (Keating, 1974, 1975a).

The two optic tecta in anuran amphibians are linked by a system of neuronal connections that form the second stage of the projection of the binocular portion of the visual field through an eye to its ipsilateral optic tectum (Gaze, 1958b; Gaze & Jacobson, 1962). This system does not involve the main intertectal commissure but passes by way of the postoptic commissures (Keating & Gaze, 1970a). Each optic tectum receives two projections from the binocular visual field, one directly from the contralateral eye and one indirectly from the ipsilateral eye through the postoptic commissures. The pattern of connections in this intertectal system may be deduced by observing the transformation that occurs as the contralateral visuotectal projection through one eye is transferred through these connections from the contralateral tectum to the ipsilateral tectum to form the ipsilateral visuotectal projection from the same eye. In normal animals the intertectal connections are organized such that the two visuotectal projections at each optic tectum are in register. Any one point in binocular visual space projects through *both* eyes to the same tectal locus (Gaze & Jacobson, 1962; Keating & Gaze, 1970a).

Interest in this system centers on the claim that in *Xenopus* the pattern of intertectal connections can be changed by procedures that alter the normal binocular visual experience of the animal (Keating, 1968; Keating & Gaze, 1970b). If the contralateral visuotectal input was altered by surgical manipulation of an embryonic or larval eye, it was found that the intertectal connections changed so as to keep the two visuotectal inputs to each tectum in register. The ipsilateral visuotectal projection to a tectum, in other words, "followed" the normality or abnormality of the contralateral visuotectal projection to that tectum. Depending upon the precise abnormality imposed upon the developing eye, and the consequent abnormality in the contralateral visuotectal projection through that eye, a great variety of patterns of functional connectivity in the intertectal system have been produced (Gaze, Keating, Székely, & Beazley, 1970; Keating, Straznicky, & Gaze, in preparation).

That such intertectal plasticity might reflect a mechanism requiring binocular visual experience was proposed by Keating (1968) and by Gaze *et al.* (1970). Such a view was supported by the finding that binocular visual deprivation of animals with one abnormal eye prevented the appearance of an altered pattern of intertectal connections (Keating, 1974; Keating & Feldman, 1975). Monocular visual deprivation which, of course, disrupts normal binocular visual experience, also suffices to prevent the rearrangement of intertectal connections (Keating, in preparation). Binocular visual function is, therefore, clearly implicated in the plastic reordering of intertectal connections that may follow surgical manipulation of one eye in *Xenopus*.

Normal *Xenopus* that were dark-reared to prevent binocular visual experience, as well as larval animals with one eye rotated that were subsequently dark-reared, developed a normal pattern of intertectal connections (Keating & Feldman, 1975). This means that innate developmental processes, independent of visual experience, are capable of generating the normal pattern. The earlier suggestion (Gaze et al., 1970; Keating, 1968) that the development of intertectal connections, as well as their plastic remodeling, would require visual experience has not been sustained. Visual deprivation does, however, reduce the precision with which such connections form and it seems that normal visual experience might well perform a "fine tuning" of the innately produced pattern. (For similar effects in the mammalian visual system and the avian auditory system, see Daniels & Pettigrew and Gottlieb, respectively, later in this volume.) A quantitative study of the maturation of the intertectal connections in normal and visually deprived *Xenopus* is in progress.

Keating (1974) proposed that the normal developmental role of this functionally dependent tuning might well reside in the desirability of maintaining the two visual inputs at each tectum in register throughout postmetamorphic life. During this time the relative position of the two eyes changes, rapidly during metamorphosis, more slowly in juvenile life, and only very slowly in adult life. In order to maintain the registration of the binocular input through the two eyes while the interocular geometry is thus changing, the intertectal connections must change. It is this change which could be effected by binocular visual experience. The remodeling of intertectal connections following eye rotation would thus represent the exaggerated response, under experimental conditions, of the normal "tuning" mechanism. If the normal developmental role of the "tuning" is that suggested above, then one might expect the range of the mechanism to reduce with age, since the normal changes in interocular geometry occur more slowly as the animal gets older. (Grobstein & Chow, this volume, use essentially the same line of reasoning to account for the experience-dependency of binocular vision in the mammalian visual system.)

The capacity of the intertectal system in *Xenopus* to respond to experimentally induced changes in interocular geometry does, in fact, decrease with age (Keating, Beazley, Feldman, & Gaze, 1975; Keating & Feldman, in preparation), mirroring the postulated requirements of the system according to this hypothesis. Evidence for a small-scale plasticity of the intertectal system in the adult amphibian has also been presented (Keating, 1975b).

It is not known whether the changing pattern of intertectal connections represents the growth of new fiber processes and the establishment of new synaptic contacts, or whether it represents the selection of a new subset of effective synapses from a much wider set of morphologically extant but functionally ineffective synapses. The role of experience in effecting this change of pattern would presumably be viewed by Gottlieb (Section 1 of this volume) as inductive in the former case and facilitative in the latter case. Keating (1975c) rotated by 90° one eye in a Stage 63 *Xenopus* and determined the time necessary for the change in intertectal pattern to occur.

The time required was some 6–12 days, a time course that is compatible with either of the two suggested modes by which the pattern of functional intertectal connections might change.

Attempts to obtain a similar modification of intertectal connections following eye rotations in larval *Rana* have been unsuccessful (Jacobson, 1971; Jacobson & Hirsch, 1973; Skarf, 1973; Skarf & Jacobson, 1974). This is both surprising and disturbing since one would have expected similar mechanisms to operate in these two anurans. Some possible reasons for these different responses to similar experimental procedures are being investigated. The differences suggest that all the effective variables of the experimental situation have not yet been identified.

A functional pattern of intertectal connections in urodele amphibians, similar in organization to those of *Rana* and *Xenopus*, has recently been described (Brändle & Stirling, 1975; Keating & Stirling, 1975). It will be interesting to see whether these animals display the intertectal plasticity seen in *Xenopus*.

In vertebrates as far apart as amphibians and higher mammals, highly organized systems of connections subserving the neural replication of the binocular visual world appear to be susceptible to developmental modification by visual experience. It is to be hoped that those systems in which these effects have already been described may serve as models on which to study further the structural and functional effects of environmental manipulation. The relationship of such processes to those ongoing interactions between the environment and the brain that underlie phenomena such as learning and memory remains enigmatic but may, it is hoped, be clarified by such studies.

XII. Summary

That version of the theory of neuronal specificity known as the chemo-affinity theory was advanced by Sperry in the 1940s and has become, quite deservedly, the most widely accepted view of the mechanisms controlling the formation of selective neuronal connections. The components of this elegant and powerful theory constitute a hierarchy of postulates: first, that neurons are intrinsically different as a result of processes of differentiation; second, that the particular pathway of terminal differentiation upon which a neuron embarks depends upon positional information that neuron or its precursor receives; third, that the manifestation of this postulated terminal differentiation is an individual cytochemical label; and fourth, that the "rule of connection," whereby cytochemically labeled neuronal arrays link, is one involving selectivity and exclusivity.

Since its formulation the theory has prompted a considerable body of experimental work aimed at the elucidation of the mechanisms of selective synaptogenesis. This work has been reviewed in order that the current status of the chemoaffinity theory may be assessed.

The theory has been remarkably successful in accounting for most, if not all, of the recent findings. No comprehensive alternative theory has been advanced. Under such circumstances it is not surprising that many regard the theory as demonstrated fact. This essay is intended to sound a cautionary note. It is argued with respect to the first three postulates of the theory that, while they remain the most plausible of hypotheses, no data yet exist which compel the view that the postulates are correct. It is proposed that recent experiments require the modification of the fourth postulate, so that the concept of competition between a population of presynaptic axons for available postsynaptic space be incorporated into the "rule of connection."

It is to be hoped that newly emerging techniques may permit the identification and measurement of those cellular properties involved in selective synaptogenesis and, by so doing, settle many of those issues which are at present unresolved.

References

Attardi, D. G., & Sperry, R. W. Preferential selection of central pathways of regenerating optic fibers. *Experimental Neurology*, 1963, **7**, 46–64.

Babloyantz, A., & Hiernaux, J. Models for positional information and positional differentiation. *Proceedings of the National Academy of Sciences U.S.*, 1974, **71**, 1530–1533.

Barbera, A. J., Marchase, R. B., & Roth, S. Adhesive recognition and retinotectal specificity. *Proceedings of the National Academy of Sciences U.S.*, 1973, **70**, 2482–2486.

Barondes, S. H. Brain glycomacromolecules and interneural recognition. In F. O. Schmitt (Ed.), *The neurosciences: Second study program*. New York: Rockefeller University Press, 1970.

Bergey, G. K., Hunt, R. K., & Holtzer, H. Selective effects of bromodeoxyuridine on developing *Xenopus laevis* retina. *Anatomical Record*, 1973, **175**, 271.

Berman, N., & Cynader, M. Comparison of receptive-field organization of the superior colliculus in Siamese and normal cats, *Journal of Physiology (London)*, 1972, **224**, 363–389.

Berman, N., & Hunt, R. K. Visual projections to the optic tecta in *Xenopus* after partial extirpation of the embryonic eye. *Journal of Comparative Neurology*, 1975 **162**, 23–42.

Brändle, K., & Stirling, R. V. Development of the ipsilateral visual projection in axolotls treated with thyroxine. *Journal of Physiology (London)*, 1975, **250**, 28–29P.

Chow, K. L., Mathers, L. H., & Spear, P. D. Spreading of uncrossed retinal projection in superior colliculus of neonatally enucleated rabbits. *Journal of Comparative Neurology*, 1973, **151**, 307–322.

Chung, S. H. In search of the rules for nerve connections. *Cell*, 1974, **3**, 201–205.

Chung, S. H., Gaze, R. M., & Stirling, R. V. Abnormal visual function in *Xenopus* following stroboscopic illumination. *Nature (London)*, 1973, **246**, 186–189.

Chung, S. H., Keating, M. J., & Bliss, T. V. P. Functional synaptic relationships during the development of the retinotectal projection in amphibians. *Proceedings of the Royal Society, London, Series B,* 1974, **187**, 449–459.

Chung, S. H., Raymond, S. A., & Lettvin, J. Y. Multiple meaning in single units. *Brain, Behavior and Evolution,* 1970, **3**, 72–101.

Cook, J. E., & Horder, T. J. Interactions between optic fibers in their regeneration to specific sites in the goldfish tectum. *Journal of Physiology (London),* 1974, **241**, 89P–90P.

Crelin, E. S. Excision and rotation of the developing *Amblystoma* optic tectum and subsequent visual behavior. *Journal of Experimental Zoology,* 1952, **120**, 547–578.

Crick, F. Diffusion in embryogenesis. *Nature (London),* 1970, **225**, 420–422.

Dalcq, A. M. *Form and causality in early development.* London: Cambridge University Press, 1938.

De Long, R. G., & Coulombre, A. J. Development of the retinotectal projection in the chick embryo. *Experimental Neurology,* 1965, **13**, 351–363.

Dixon, J. S., & Cronly-Dillon, J. R. The fine structure of the developing retina in *Xenopus laevis. Journal of Embryology and Experimental Morphology,* 1972, **28**, 659–666.

Dixon, J. S., & Cronly-Dillon, J. R. Intercellular gap junctions in pigment epithelium cells during retinal specification in *Xenopus laevis. Nature (London),* 1974, **251**, 505.

Feldman, J. D., & Gaze, R. M. The growth of the retina in *Xenopus laevis*: II. Retinal growth in compound eyes. *Journal of Embryology and Experimental Morphology,* 1972, **27**, 381–387.

Feldman, J. D., & Gaze, R. M. The development of half-eyes in *Xenopus* tadpoles. *Journal of Comparative Neurology,* 1975 **162**, 13–22.

Feldman, J. D., Gaze, R. M., & Keating, M. J. Delayed innervation of the optic tectum during development in *Xenopus laevis. Experimental Brain Research,* 1971, **14**, 16–23.

Feldman, J. D., Keating, M. J., & Gaze, R. M. Retinotectal mismatch: A serendipitous result. *Nature (London),* 1975, **253**, 445–446.

Fujita, S. Analysis of neuron differentiation in the central nervous system by tritiated thymidine autoradiography. *Journal of Comparative Neurology,* 1964, **122**, 311–328.

Fujita, S., & Horii, M. Analysis of cytogenesis in chick retina by tritiated thymidine autoradiography. *Archivum Histologicum Japonicum,* 1963, **23**, 359–366.

Gaze, R. M. The representation of the retina on the optic lobe of the frog. *Quarterly Journal of Experimental Physiology and Cognate Medical Sciences,* 1958, **43**, 209–214. (a)

Gaze, R. M. Binocular vision in frogs. *Journal of Physiology (London),* 1958, **143**, 20P. (b)

Gaze, R. M. Regeneration of the optic nerve in *Xenopus laevis. Quarterly Journal of Experimental Physiology and Cognate Medical Sciences,* 1959, **44**, 290–308.

Gaze, R. M., & Keating, M. J. The visual system and 'neuronal specificity'. *Nature (London),* 1972, **237**, 375–378.

Gaze, R. M., & Jacobson, M. The projection of the binocular visual field on the optic tecta of the frog. *Quarterly Journal of Experimental Physiology and Cognate Medical Sciences,* 1962, **47**, 273–280.

Gaze, R. M., & Jacobson, M. A study of the retinotectal projection during regeneration of the optic nerve in the frog. *Proceedings of the Royal Society of London, Series B,* 1963, **157**, 420–448.

Gaze, R. M. & Sharma, S. C. Axial differences in the reinnervation of the goldfish optic tectum by regenerating optic nerve fibres. *Experimental Brain Research,* 1970, **10**, 171–181.

Gaze, R. M., Jacobson, M., & Székely, G. The retinotectal projection in *Xenopus* with compound eyes. *Journal of Physiology (London),* 1963, **165**, 484–499.

Gaze, R. M., Jacobson, M., & Székely, G. On the formation of connections by compound eyes in *Xenopus. Journal of Physiology (London),* 1965, **176**, 409–417.

Gaze, R. M., Chung, S. H., & Keating, M. J. Development of the retinotectal projection in *Xenopus. Nature (London)*, 1972. **236**, 133–135.

Gaze, R. M., Keating, M. J., & Chung, S. H. The evolution of the retinotectal map during development in *Xenopus. Proceedings of the Royal Society of London, Series B*, 1974, **185**, 301–330.

Gaze, R. M., Keating, M. J., Székely, G., & Beazley, L. Binocular interaction in the formation of specific intertectal neuronal connections. *Proceedings of the Royal Society of London, Series B*, 1970, **175**, 107–147.

Gierer, A., & Meinhardt, H. A theory of biological pattern formation. *Kybernetik*, 1972, **12**, 30–39.

Giolli, R. A., & Creel, D. J. The primary optic projections in pigmented and albino guinea pigs: An experimental degeneration study. *Brain Research*, 1973, **55**, 25–39.

Glucksmann, A. Development and differentiation of the tadpole eye. *British Journal of Ophthalmology*, 1940, **24**, 153–178.

Goodman, D. C., Bogdasarian, R. S., & Horel, J. A. Axonal sprouting of ipsilateral optic tract following opposite eye removal. *Brain, Behavior and Evolution*, 1973, **8**, 27–50.

Goodwin, B., & Cohen, M. H. A phase-shift model for the spatial and temporal organization of living systems. *Journal of Theoretical Biology*, 1969, **25**, 49–107.

Gottlieb, D., & Cowan, W. M. Evidence for a temporal factor in the occupation of available synaptic sites during development of the dentate gyrus. *Brain Research*, 1972, **41**, 452–456.

Gottlieb, D. I., Merrell, D., & Glaser, L. Temporal changes in embryonal cell surface recognition. *Proceedings of the National Academy of Sciences U.S.*, 1974, **71**, 1800–1802.

Guillery, R. W. An abnormal retinogeniculate projection in Siamese cats. *Brain Research*, 1969, **14**, 739–741.

Guillery, R. W. An abnormal retinogeniculate projection in the albino ferret (*Mustela furo*). *Brain Research*, 1971, **33**, 482–485.

Guillery, R. W., Casagrande, V. A., & Oberdorfer, M. D. Congenitally abnormal vision in Siamese cats. *Nature (London)*, 1974, **252**, 195–199.

Guillery, R. W., & Kaas, J. H. A study of normal and congenitally abnormal retinogeniculate projections in cats. *Journal of Comparative Neurology*, 1971, **143**, 73–100.

Guillery, R. W., & Kaas, J. H. Genetic abnormality of the visual pathways in a 'white' tiger. *Science*, 1973, **180**, 1287–1289.

Guillery, R. W., Scott, G. L., Cattenach, B. M., & Deol, M. S. Genetic mechanisms determining the central visual pathways of mice. *Science*, 1973, **179**, 1014–1016.

Harrison, R. G. The outgrowth of the nerve fiber as a mode of protoplasmic movement. *Journal of Experimental Zoology*, 1910, **9**, 787–948.

Harrison, R. G. Experiments on the development of the forelimb of Amblystoma, a self-differentiating, equipotential system. *Journal of Experimental Zoology*, 1918, **25**, 416–462.

Harrison, R. G. On relations of symmetry in transplanted limbs. *Journal of Experimental Zoology*, 1921, **32**, 1–136.

Hollyfield, J. G. Differential growth of the neural retina in *Xenopus laevis* larvae. *Developmental Biology*, 1971, **24**, 264–286.

Hollyfield, J. G. Histogenesis of the retina in the killifish, *Fundulus heteroclitus. Journal of Comparative Neurology*, 1972, **144**, 373–379.

Holt, E. B. *Animal drive and the learning process.* London: Williams and Noorgate, 1931.

Holtzer, H. Comments of induction during cell differentiation. *Colloquium Gesellschaft fuer Physiologische Chemie*, 1963, **13**, 171–176.

Holtzer, H. Induction of chondrogenesis: A concept in quest of mechanisms. In R. Fleischmajer & R. E. Billingham (Eds.), *Epithelial-mesenchymal interactions*. Baltimore, Md.: Williams and Wilkins, 1968.

Holtzer, H. Myogenesis. In O. Schjeide and J. de Villis (Eds.), *Cell differentiation*. Princeton, N.J.: Van Nostrand-Reinhold, 1970.

Holtzer, H., & Sanger, J. W. Myogenesis: Old views rethought. In B. Banker and R. Pryzbalski (Eds.), *Research in muscle development and the muscle spindle*. Amsterdam: Excerpta Medica, 1972.

Holtzer, H., Weintraub, H., Mayne, R., & Mochan, B. The cell cycle, cell lineages, and cell differentiation. *Current Topics in Developmental Biology*, 1972, **7**, 229–256.

Horder, T. J. Retention, by fish optic nerve fibers regenerating to new terminal sites in the tectum, of 'chemospecific' affinity for their original sites. *Journal of Physiology (London)*, 1971, **216**, 53P–55P.

Horder, T. J., & Spitzer, J. L. Absence of cell mobility across the retina in *Xenopus laevis* embryos. *Journal of Physiology (London)*, 1973, **233**, 33P–34P.

Hubel, D. H., & Wiesel, T. N. Aberrant visual projections in the Siamese cat. *Journal of Physiology (London)*, 1971, **218**, 33–62.

Hughes, R. C. *Membrane glycoproteins: A review of structure and function*. London: Butterworth, 1975.

Hunt, R. K. Developmental programming for retinotectal patterns. In *Cell patterning. Ciba Foundation Symposium 29* (new series). Amsterdam: Associated Scientific Publishers, 1975. (a).

Hunt, R. K. The cell cycle, cell lineage, and neuronal specificity. In H. Holtzer and J. Reinart (Eds.), *The cell cycle and cell differentiation*. Berlin: Springer-Verlag, 1975. (b)

Hunt, R. K., & Jacobson, M. Development and stability of positional information in *Xenopus* retinal ganglion cells. *Proceedings of the National Academy of Sciences U.S.*, 1972, **69**, 780–783. (a)

Hunt, R. K., & Jacobson, M. Specification of positional information in retinal ganglion cells in *Xenopus*: Stability of the specified state. *Proceedings of the National Academy of Sciences U.S.*, 1972, **69**, 2860–2864. (b)

Hunt, R. K., & Jacobson, M. Specification of positional information in retinal ganglion cells of *Xenopus*: Assay for analysis of the unspecified state. *Proceedings of the National Academy of Sciences U.S.*, 1973, **70**, 507–511.

Hunt, R. K., & Jacobson, M. Neuronal specificity revisited. *Current Topics in Developmental Biology*, 1974, **8**, 203–259. (a)

Hunt, R. K., & Jacobson, M. Rapid reversal of retinal axes in embryonic *Xenopus* eyes. *Journal of Physiology (London)*, 1974, **241**, 90P–91P. (b)

Hunt, R. K., & Jacobson, M. Specification of positional information in retinal ganglion cells of *Xenopus*: Intra-ocular control of the time of specification. *Proceedings of the National Academy of Sciences U.S.*, 1974, **71**, 3161–3620. (c)

Hunt, R. K., Bergey, G. K., & Holtzer, H. Bromodeoxyuridine: Localization of a developmental program in *Xenopus* optic cup. *Developmental Biology*, 1975 (in press).

Jacobson, M. *Studies in the organization of visual mechanisms in amphibians*. Unpublished doctoral dissertation, University of Edinburgh, 1960.

Jacobson, M. Starting points for research in the ontogeny of behavior. In M. Locke (Ed.), *Major problems in developmental biology*. New York: Academic Press. 1967.

Jacobson, M. Development of neuronal specificity in retinal ganglion cells of *Xenopus*. *Developmental Biology*, 1968, **17**, 202–218. (a)

Jacobson, M. Cessation of DNA synthesis in retinal ganglion cells correlated with the time of specification of their central connections. *Developmental Biology*, 1968, **17**, 219–232. (b)

Jacobson, M. Development of specific neuronal connections. *Science*, 1969, **163**, 543–547.

Jacobson, M. Development, specification and diversification of neuronal connections. In F. O. Schmitt (Ed.), *The neurosciences: Second study program*. New York: Rockefeller University Press, 1970.

Jacobson, M. Absence of adaptive modification in developing retinotectal connections in frogs after visual deprivation or disparate stimulation of the eyes. *Proceedings of the National Academy of Sciences U.S.*, 1971, **68**, 528–532.

Jacobson, M., & Gaze, R. M. Selection of appropriate tectal connections by regenerating optic fibers in adult goldfish. *Experimental Neurology*, 1965, **13**, 418–430.

Jacobson, M., & Hirsch, H. V. B. Development and maintenance of connectivity in the visual system of the frog. I. The effects of eye rotation and visual deprivation. *Brain Research*, 1973, **49**, 47–65.

Jhaveri, S. R., & Schneider, G. E. Retinal projections in Syrian hamsters: Normal topography, and alterations after partial tectum lesions at birth. *Anatomical Record*, 1974, **178**, 383.

Kaas, J. H., Harting, J. K., & Guillery, R. W. Representation of the complete retina to the contralateral superior colliculus of some mammals. *Brain Research*, 1974, **65**, 343–346.

Kaas, J. H., & Guillery, R. W. The transfer of abnormal visual field representations from the dorsal lateral geniculate nucleus to the visual cortex in Siamese cats. *Brain Research*, 1973, **59**, 61–95.

Keating, M. J. Functional interaction in the development of specific nerve connections. *Journal of Physiology* (*London*), 1968, **198**, 75P–77P.

Keating, M. J. The role of visual function in the patterning of binocular visual connections. *British Medical Bulletin*, 1974, **30**, 145–151.

Keating, M. J. Early visual experience and the development of the visual system. *Progress in Neurobiology*, 1975 (in press). (a)

Keating, M. J. Plasticity of intertectal connections in adult *Xenopus*. *Journal of Physiology* (*London*), 1975 **248**, 36–37P. (b)

Keating, M. J. The time-course of experience-dependent synaptic switching of visual connections in *Xenopus laevis*. *Proceedings of the Royal Society of London, Series B*, 1975 **189**, 603–610. (c)

Keating, M. J., & Feldman, J. D. Visual deprivation and intertectal neuronal connections in *Xenopus laevis*. *Proceedings of the Royal Society of London, Series B*, 1975, **191**, 467–474.

Keating, M. J., & Gaze, R. M. The ipsilateral retinotectal pathway in the frog. *Quarterly Journal of Experimental physiology and Cognate Medical Sciences*, 1970, **55**, 284–292. (a)

Keating, M. J., & Gaze, R. M. Rigidity and plasticity in the amphibian visual system. *Brain, Behavior and Evolution*, 1970, **3**, 102–120. (b)

Keating, M. J., & Kennard, C. The amphibian visual system as a model for developmental neurobiology. In K. Fite (Ed.), *The amphibian visual system: A multidisciplinary approach*. Springfield, Ill.: Thomas, 1975.

Keating, M. J., & Stirling, R. V. The presence of an organized ipsilateral visuotectal projection in a urodele. *Neuroscience Letters*, 1975 (in preparation).

Keating, M. J., Beazley, L., Feldman, J. D., & Gaze, R. M. Binocular interaction and intertectal neuronal connections in *Xenopus laevis*: Dependence upon developmental stage. *Proceedings of the Royal Society of London, Series B*, 1975, **191**, 445–466.

Kicliter, E. Flux, wavelength and movement discrimination in frogs: Forebrain and midbrain contributions. *Brain, Behavior and Evolution*, 1974, **8**, 340–365.

Kollros, J. J. The development of the optic lobes in the frog. *Journal of Experimental Zoology*, 1953, **123**, 153–187.

Lane, R. H., Kaas, J. H., & Allman, J. M. Visuotopic organization of the superior colliculus in normal and Siamese cats. *Brain Research*, 1974, **70**, 413–430.

Larsell, O. The effect of experimental excision of one eye on the development of the optic lobe and opticus layer in larvae of the tree frog (Hyla regilla). II. The effect on cell size and differentiation of cell processes. *Journal of Experimental Zoology*, 1931, **58**, 1–20.

LaVail, J. H., & Cowan, W. M. The development of the chick optic tectum. II. Autoradiographic studies. *Brain Research*, 1971, **28**, 421–441.

Lázár, G. The projection of the retinal quadrants on the optic centres in the frog. *Acta Physiologica Academiae Scientiarum Hungaricae*, 1971, **19**, 325–334.

Levine, R. L., & Cronly-Dillon, J. R. Specification of regenerating retinal ganglion cells in the adult newt, *Triturus cristatus*. *Brain Research*, 1974, **68**, 319–329.

Levine, R. L., & Jacobson, M. Deployment of optic nerve fibers is determined by positional markers in the frog's tectum. *Experimental Neurology*, 1974, **43**, 527–538.

Loewenstein, W. R. Membrane junctions in growth and differentiation. *Federation Proceedings*, 1973, **32**, 60–64.

Lund, R. D. Uncrossed visual pathways of hooded and albino rats. *Science*, 1965, **149**, 1506–1507.

Lund, R. D. Anatomic studies on the superior colliculus. *Investigative Ophthalmology*, 1972, **11**, 434–441.

Lund, R. D., & Lund, J. S. Spatially inappropriate retinotectal connections in rats. *Anatomical Record*, 1975, **181**, 416.

Lund, R. D., Cunningham, T. J., & Lund, J. S. Modified optic projections after unilateral eye removal in young rats. *Brain, Behavior and Evolution*, 1973, **8**, 51–72.

Lund, R. D., Lund, J. S., & Wise, R. P. The organization of the retinal projection to the dorsal lateral geniculate nucleus in pigmented and albino rats. *Journal of Comparative Neurology*, 1974, **158**, 383–404.

McMahon, D. A cell contact model for cellular position determination in development. *Proceedings of the National Academy of Sciences U.S.*, 1973, **70**, 2396–2400.

McMurray, V. M. The development of the optic lobes in *Xenopus laevis*. The effect of repeated crushing of the optic nerve. *Journal of Experimental Zoology*, 1954, **125**, 247–263.

Marchase, R. B., Barbera, A. J., & Roth, S. A molecular approach to retinotectal specificity. In *Cell patterning. Ciba Foundation Symposium 29* (new series). Amsterdam: Associated Scientific Publishers, 1975.

Matthey, R. Récuperation de la vue après résection des nerfs optiques chez le *Triton*. *Comptes Rendus des Séances de la Société de Biologie*, 1925, **93**, 904–906.

Matthey, R. Récuperation de la vue après greffe de l'œil chez le *Triton*. *Comptes Rendus des Séances de la Société de Biologie*, 1926, **94**, 4–5.

Maturana, H. R., Lettvin, J. Y., McCulloch, W. S., & Pitts, W. H. Evidence that cut optic nerve fibers in the frog regenerate to their proper places in the tectum. *Science*, 1959, **130**, 1709–1710.

Meinhardt, H., & Gierer, A. Applications of a theory of biological pattern formation based on lateral inhibition. *Journal of Cell Science*, 1974, **15**, 321–346.

Meyer, R. L. Growth of the retinotectal system in juvenile goldfish. *Caltech Annual Reports Biology*, 1974, 136–137.

Meyer, R. L. Tests for regulation in the goldfish retinotectal system. *Anatomical Record*, 1975, **181**, 426.

Meyer, R. L., & Sperry, R. W. Tests for neuroplasticity in the anuran retinotectal system. *Experimental Neurology*, 1973, **40**, 525–539.

Meyer, R. L., & Sperry, R. W. Explanatory models for neuroplasticity in retinotectal connections. In D. G. Stein, J. J. Rosen, & N. Butters (Eds.), *Plasticity and recovery of function in the central nervous system*. New York: Academic Press, 1974.

Miller, B. F. Effects of superior collicular lesions in fetal rats on the development of the retinotectal projection. *Anatomical Record*, 1975, **181**, 428.

Nieuwkoop, P. D., & Faber, J. *A normal table of Xenopus laevis (Daudin)*. Amsterdam: North-Holland, 1967.

Roth, S. A molecular model for cell interactions. *Quarterly Review of Biology*, 1973, **48**, 541–563.

Sanderson, K. J. Retinogeniculate projections in the rabbits of the albino allelomorphic series. *Journal of Comparative Neurology*, 1975, **159**, 15–27.
Sanderson, K. J., Guillery, R. W., & Shackelford, R. M. Congenitally abnormal visual pathways in mink (*Mustela vison*) with reduced retinal pigment. *Journal of Comparative Neurology*, 1974, **154**, 225–248.
Schneider, G. E. Early lesions of the superior colliculus: Factors affecting the formation of abnormal retinal projections. *Brain, Behavior and Evolution*, 1973, **8**, 73–109.
Schneider, G. E., & Jhaveri, S. R. Neuro-anatomical correlates of spared or altered function after brain lesions in the newborn hamster. In D. G. Stein, J. J. Rosen, & N. Butters (Eds.), *Plasticity and recovery of function in the central nervous system*. New York: Academic Press, 1974.
Schwassman, H. O. Visual projection upon the optic tectum in foveate marine teleosts. *Vision Research*, 1968, **8**, 1337–1348.
Schwassman, H. O., & Krag, H. M. The relation of visual field defects to retinotectal topography in teleost fish. *Vision Research*, 1970, **10**, 29–42.
Scott, T. M. The development of the retinotectal projection in *Xenopus laevis*: An autoradiographic and degeneration study. *Journal of Embryology and Experimental Morphology*, 1974, **31**, 409–414.
Sharma, S. C. Reformation of retinotectal projections after various tectal ablations in adult goldfish. *Experimental Neurology*, 1972, **34**, 171–182. (a)
Sharma, S. C. Redistribution of visual projections in altered optic tecta in adult goldfish. *Proceedings of the National Academy of Sciences U.S.*, 1972, **69**, 2637–2639. (b)
Sharma, S. C., & Hollyfield, J. G. Specification of retinal central connections in *Rana pipiens* before the first appearance of the first post-mitotic ganglion cell. *Journal of Comparative Neurology*, 1974, **155**, 395–408.
Sherman, S. M. Monocularly deprived cats: Improvement of the deprived eye's vision by visual decortication. *Science*, 1974, **186**, 267–269.
Sidman, R. L. Histogenesis of mouse retina studied with thymidine ^{3}H. In G. K. Smelser (Ed.), *Structure of the eye*. New York: Academic Press, 1961.
Sidman, R. L. Contact interaction among developing mammalian brain cells. In A. A. Moscona (Ed.), *The cell surface in development*. New York: Wiley, 1974.
Skarf, B. Development of binocular single units in the optic tectum of frogs raised with asymmetrical visual stimulation. *Brain Research*, 1973, **51**, 352–357.
Skarf, B., & Jacobson, M. Development of binocularly driven single units in frogs raised with asymmetrical visual stimulation. *Experimental Neurology*, 1974, **42**, 669–686.
Sperry, R. W. Reestablishment of visuomotor coordination by optic nerve regeneration. *Anatomical Record*, 1942, **84**, 470.
Sperry, R. W. Visuomotor coordination in the newt (*Triturus viridescens*) after regeneration of the optic nerve. *Journal of Comparative Neurology*, 1943, **79**, 33–55.
Sperry, R. W. Optic nerve regeneration with return of vision in anurans. *Journal of Neurophysiology*, 1944, **7**, 57–70.
Sperry, R. W. Restoration of vision after crossing of optic nerves and after contralateral transplantation of eye. *Journal of Neurophysiology*, 1945, **8**, 15–28.
Sperry, R. W. Patterning of central synapses in regeneration of the optic nerve in teleosts. *Physiological Zoology*, 1948, **21**, 351–361.
Sperry, R. W. Mechanisms of neural maturation. In S. S. Stevens (Ed.), *Handbook of experimental psychology*. New York: Wiley, 1951.
Sperry, R. W. Chemoaffinity in the orderly growth of nerve fiber patterns and connections. *Proceedings of the National Academy of Sciences U.S.*, 1963, **50**, 703–710.

Sperry, R. W. Embryogenesis of behavioral nerve nets. In R. L. De Haan & H. Ursprung (Eds.), *Organogenesis*. New York: Holt, 1965.

Sperry, R. W. How a developing brain gets itself properly wired for adaptive function. In E. Tobach, E. Shaw, & L. R. Aronson (Eds.), *Biopsychology of development*. New York: Academic Press, 1971.

Stone, L. S. Heteroplastic transplantation of eyes between the larvae of two species of *Amblystoma. Journal of Experimental Zoology*, 1930, **55**, 193–261.

Stone, L. S. Functional polarization in developing and regenerating retinae of rotated grafted eyes. *Proceedings of the Society for Experimental Biology and Medicine*, 1944, **57**, 13–14.

Stone, L. S. Functional polarization in developing and regenerating retinae of transplanted eyes. *Annals of the New York Academy of Sciences*, 1948, **49**, 856–865.

Stone, L. S. Polarization of the retina and development of vision. *Journal of Experimental Zoology*, 1960, **145**, 85–96.

Stone, L. S., & Cole, C. H. Grafting of larval and adult eyes in *Amblystoma punctatum. Proceedings of the Society for Experimental Biology and Medicine*, 1931, **29**, 176–178.

Stone, L. S., & Usher, N. T. Return of vision and other observations in replanted amphibian eyes. *Proceedings of the Society for Experimental Biology and Medicine*, 1927, **25**, 213–215.

Straznicky, K. The formation of the optic fiber projection after partial tectal removal in *Xenopus. Journal of Embryology and Experimental Morphology*, 1973, **29**, 397–409.

Straznicky, K., & Gaze, R. M. The growth of the retina in *Xenopus laevis*: An autoradiographic study. *Journal of Embryology and Experimental Morphology*, 1971, **26**, 67–79.

Straznicky, K., & Gaze, R. M. The development of the tectum in *Xenopus laevis*: An autoradiographic study. *Journal of Embryology and Experimental Morphology*, 1972, **28**, 87–115.

Straznicky, K., Gaze, R. M., & Keating, M. J. The retinotectal projections after uncrossing the optic chiasma in *Xenopus* with one compound eye. *Journal of Embryology and Experimental Morphology*, 1971, **26**, 523–542. (a)

Straznicky, K., Gaze, R. M., & Keating, M. J. The establishment of retinotectal projections after embryonic removal of rostral or caudal half of the optic tectum in *Xenopus laevis. Proceedings of the International Union of Physiological Sciences*, 1971, **9**, 540. (b)

Straznicky, K., Gaze, R. M., & Keating, M. J. The retinotectal projection from a double-ventral compound eye in *Xenopus laevis. Journal of Embryology and Experimental Morphology*, 1974, **31**, 123–137.

Székely, G. Zur Ausbildung der lokalen funktionellen Spezifität der Retina. *Acta Morphologica Academicae Scientiarum Hungaricae*, 1954, **5**, 157–167. (a)

Székely, G. Untersuchung der Entwicklung optischer Reflexmechanismen an Amphibien-larven. *Acta Physiologica Academicae Scientiarum Hungaricae*, 1954, **6**, Suppl. 18. (b)

Székely, G. Problems of neuronal specificity in the development of some behavioral patterns in amphibia. In G. Gottlieb (Ed.), *Aspects of neurogenesis*. New York: Academic Press, 1974.

Weiss, P. In vitro experiments on the factors determining the course of the outgrowing nerve fibre. *Journal of Experimental Zoology*, 1934, **68**, 393–448.

Weiss, P. Selectivity controlling the central-peripheral relations in the nervous system. *Biological Review*, 1936, **11**, 494–531.

Weiss, P. Nerve patterns: The mechanics of nerve growth. *Growth*, 1941, **5**, 163–203.

Wise, R. P. The visual system of heterochromic rats. *Anatomical Record*, 1975, **181**, 511.

Wolpert, L. Positional information and the spatial pattern of cellular differentiation. *Journal of Theoretical Biology*, 1969, **25**, 1–47.

Yoon, M. G. Reorganization of retinotectal projection following surgical operations on optic tectum of goldfish. *Experimental Neurology*, 1971, **33**, 395–411.

Yoon, M. G. Reversibility of the reorganization of retinotectal projections in goldfish. *Experimental Neurology*, 1972, **35**, 565–577. (a)

Yoon, M. G. Synaptic plasticities of the retina and of the optic tectum in goldfish. *American Zoologist*, 1972, **12**, 106. (b)

Yoon, M. G. Transposition of the visual projection from the nasal hemiretina onto the foreign rostral zone of the optic tectum in goldfish. *Experimental Neurology*, 1972, **37**, 451–462. (c)

Yoon, M. G. Retention of the original topographic polarity by the 180° rotated tectal reimplant in young adult goldfish. *Journal of Physiology* (*London*), 1973, **233**, 575–588.

RETINOTECTAL SPECIFICITY: CHEMOAFFINITY THEORY

RONALD L. MEYER AND R. W. SPERRY

Division of Biology
California Institute of Technology
Pasadena, California

I. Introduction

The early studies on retinotectal regeneration showed with behavioral tests that the functional properties mediating visual direction and involving the "local sign," or "positional" specificity in the retinal field are restored in accurate detail in regrowth of the optic nerve onto the midbrain tectum and that this orderly recovery occurs regardless of maladaptive behavioral effects (Sperry, 1943, 1944, 1945). By combining behavioral tests with selective tectal lesions, it was shown further that the orderly restitution of behavioral properties reflects an underlying order in the anatomical remapping

111

of fiber projections on the tectum. Anterior, dorsal, or posterior tectal ablations before and after optic nerve regeneration in five species from three genera of adult anurans confirmed a topographic plan in retinotectal projection in the normal state and also demonstrated its selective reestablishment in regeneration (Sperry, 1944). The tectal lesions after optic nerve regeneration produced differential blind areas or scotomata comparable in location and in size to those produced prior to optic nerve section.

From these and related findings (Sperry, 1951a) it was concluded that ganglion cells of each retinal locus are normally destined to grow connections with a corresponding complementary locus in the tectum. It was inferred that retinal and tectal neurons must acquire through developmental differentiation cell-unique specific cytochemical properties that serve to identify each cell and its optic fiber extensions in accordance with the position occupied by the cell body within the retinal or tectal field. For each locus in the retina there must exist a corresponding complementary or matching locus in the tectum for which the retinal fibers have preferential chemical affinity. Midbrain transection and regeneration of the tectospinal tracts combined with eye rotation in *Triturus* (Sperry, 1948) gave further evidence for the differentiation of locus specificity among the tectal neurons.

The required distribution of retinotectal specificities and affinities was thought to be achieved through a polarized, fieldlike, or gradient type of morphogenetic differentiation, first along the anteroposterior (i.e., rostrocaudal or nasotemporal) axis and then later on the dorsoventral axis of the developing retinal and tectal fields, these being conceived as subfields within the main axial gradients of the embryo (Sperry, 1944, 1965a). This means each neuron has its latitude and longitude, so to speak, encoded in its chemistry. Positional specificities in the tectum have certain properties complementary to those in the retina. Selective patterning of fiber aggregations and trajectories along the course of the optic nerve tracts and tectal radiations also were attributed to chemotactic guidance regulated by the same kinds of preferential cytochemical affinities (Attardi & Sperry, 1963; Sperry, 1963).

In addition to the locus specificities associated with retinal and tectal gradients and with directionality in visual space, it was possible to infer from behavioral tests after optic nerve regeneration the presence also of other dimensions of cell specificity, like those for mediation of learned color discrimination, luminosity, on–off, and off–on effects (Arora & Sperry, 1963; Sperry, 1965a). Each individual optic axon and even each microfilament of its growth tip was inferred to contain typically several modes of molecular specificity that help regulate chemotactic guidance to proper synaptic zones and selective reinnervation of correct target cells within the terminal synaptic zone.

It was not a precise cell-to-cell connectivity that was inferred, but rather cell-to-focal tectal area with extensive terminal overlap among neighboring fibers (Sperry, 1951b, 1958). The competitive interaction among overlapping terminal arbors for synaptic sites and appropriate density of innervation was conceived to involve preferential, graded affinities, not all-or-none select-ivity. Various other trophic, denervation, saturation, and related general factors were presumed to be operative (Sperry, 1951a). The preferential chemoaffinity effects were described as based on embryonic gradient and morphogenetic field systems, and other mechanisms of cell differentiation. Failure to include these developmental concepts and properties in the interpretation of neurospecificity theory has been a continuing source of confusion. These concepts do not exclude plasticity of developmental, experiential, or other sorts. Ideas that the resultant connectivity is necessar-ily rigid, prefixed, or exclusive have arisen mainly in reference to subsequent findings.

The appearance of this interpretation in the early 1940s directly reversed the prevailing doctrine of the time in which nerve growth was held to be diffuse and nonselective, with chemical and electrical theories ruled out in favor of mechanical guidance. It introduced a new order of complexity and refinement to concepts of cell differentiation and intercellular affinity in general that extended to the level of individual cells, paralleling functional differentiation throughout the sensorineuromotor system. Early objections that there were not enough distinct molecular species available subsided with advances in molecular biology.

Mainly the interpretation gave us a much needed explanatory scheme for the inheritance and prefunctional organization of the neural circuits for innate behavior, replacing concepts like "neurobiotaxis," "disuse atrophy," "equipotential nerve nets," and "resonance," and providing a credible neurogenetic basis for ethology. On these terms, function was conceived to play an important role in shaping innate behavioral traits, not during development, but indirectly over the span of generations acting as a selec-tion factor for differential preservation of genetic variations. These genetic factors control in turn neuronal specification, which determines fiber connection patterns. The scheme allows plenty of leeway for the added effects of learning and other forms of neural plasticity, including functional modulation and fine tuning of genetically determined neural structure during growth and development. The alternative suggestion that the funda-mental neural connectivity is wired up on the basis of impulse specificity in different neurons (Chung, Gaze, & Stirling, 1973; Keating, this volume) seems contraindicated by the evidence, as does the earlier proposal by Weiss (1931) along similar lines (Sperry, 1965b).

This general explanatory model has since been reinforced and refined by numerous electrophysiological, anatomical, and behavioral studies and has been found to apply equally well to other neuronal systems, such as the vestibular, cutaneous, oculomotor, and tectospinal pathways (Gaze, 1970; Jacobson, 1970; Sperry, 1951a, 1965a), and also to invertebrates (Baylor & Nicholls, 1971; Edwards & Palka, 1971). Further, a direct histological demonstration of the chemoaffinity hypothesis was obtained by combining nerve regeneration with retinal lesions in goldfish (Attardi & Sperry, 1963). This and similar subsequent experiments on both goldfish (Jacobson & Gaze, 1965; Roth, 1972; Westerman, 1965) and chick (Crossland, Cowan, Rogers, & Kelly, 1974; De Long & Coulombre, 1965) appear to confirm that the growing optic fibers show a selective preference for their correct tectal regions despite opportunities to terminate incorrectly in neighboring denervated areas.

Meanwhile, more recent studies have been interpreted as showing results inconsistent with the original hypothesis (Gaze, 1970). Compound eyes formed in frog embryos from two nasal or two temporal half-retinas were found to form their synaptic connections across the entire tectum (Gaze, Jacobson, & Székely, 1963, 1965). Also, in goldfish it was found that a remaining anterior half-tectum, after ablation of the posterior tectum, accepted orderly connections from the entire retina (Gaze & Sharma, 1970). In order for the whole retina to remap on the half-tectum, it appeared that the original synaptic connections in the intact half must break down and reform more anteriorly, while the optic fibers formerly connected to the excised tectum must form synapses with entirely new cells to which they normally never connect. To account for these and related findings, as described by Keating in the preceding article in this section, Gaze (1970) proposed a modified sliding scale or "systems matching" hypothesis whereby optic fibers form their terminals not at predestined targets but at correct relative positions along whatever fraction of tectal gradient is available. Later work by Yoon (1971, 1972a) and Sharma (1972a, 1972b) seemed to confirm the lack of predetermined connectivity. Yoon in particular reported further that the process of compression of the retinal projection map onto a half-tectum was reversible under conditions where the tectum was divided with a barrier of Gelfilm, which later resorbed. Other types of compound eyes, like nasal-ventral (Hunt & Jacobson, 1973a) or double-ventral eyes (Straznicky, Gaze, & Keating, 1974), have produced complex tectal projections that cannot be easily understood as the simple sum of the original retinal halves.

The interpretation is additionally complicated by apparent inconsistencies in the goldfish work and by lack of agreement between the electrophysiological data on which the evidence for plasticity has rested and correlated anatomical data. Yoon (1972b) and Horder (1971) both reported electrical evidence for uniform spreading of a surgically formed half-retina over an entire normal tectum. In contradiction, the original study of Attardi and Sperry (1963), using Bodian staining, and Roth's (1972) recent similar work showed that these same half-retinas preferentially terminated in the appropriate tectal region. Yoon (1972b) and Horder (1971) had further electrophysiological data apparently showing that if noncomplementary retinal and tectal halves were removed, the remaining retina spreads over the entire inappropriate half-tectum. Under these same conditions the anatomical evidence of Roth (1972) indicated that innervation was restricted to the region near the lesion, leading much of the tectum without optic fibers.

Further, the electrophysiological evidence has seemed in part self-contradictory. While Yoon (1972b) reported that both nasal and temporal hemiretinas showed plasticity, Horder (1971) had evidence that only a nasal half-retina expanded in this manner; and Jacobson and Gaze (1965) had data suggesting neither half did this. Although only a rough medio-lateral incision was sufficient to induce complete field compression onto the rostral tectum in Yoon's hands (1971), a similarly placed even larger lesion did not produce this result in Sharma's (1972b) experiment. Medial or lateral tectal ablations had been reported not to result in plastic remapping (Jacobson & Gaze, 1965), and the suggestion that this could be a consequence of interference with the medial optic tract was later supported in the results of Yoon (1971). Yet, according to Sharma (1972b), removal of the rostral tectum, causing comparable tract damage, did cause compression of visual field representation onto the caudal tectum. In the study of Gaze and Sharma (1970), simple removal of the caudal tectum regularly resulted in their finding rostral tectal loci from which two widely separated receptive fields could be recorded. Not one instance of this field duplication was found by Yoon (1971).

In neonatal rodents various alterations in retinal projection following different collicular and retinal lesions (Lund & Lund, 1973; Schneider & Jhaveri, 1974) raise questions about the role of chemoaffinity in the development of this system. In neonatal rats a mediolateral inversion of the retinal projection to ipsilateral colliculus formed after unilateral eye removal has been interpreted as contradicting chemoaffinity (Cunningham & Speas, 1975).

In the face of these mounting disparities and contradictions in the literature, it becomes increasingly difficult to see any uniform interpretation for the formation of retinotectal connections. The following is directed at some of the main discrepancies in the evidence and interpretations and includes new results of relevant recent experiments by the first author.

II. Compound-Eye Experiments

The projection maps obtained from experimentally formed compound eyes first raised serious questions about the chemoaffinity model. Compound eyes were formed surgically in amphibian embryos by removing the nasal or temporal half of the eye anlage and replacing it with a mirror half-eye from a donor. These double-nasal or double-temporal compound eyes eventually formed, in most cases, eyes of normal size and general appearance and developed functional retinotectal connections. The initial experiments were carried out by Székely (1954) in *Triturus*. He found visually guided behavior from such eyes to be abnormal. Although all animals reacted to stimuli over the entire field, the double-nasal animals acted as if the objects they saw were only in the temporal field, and the double-temporal animals localized all visual stimuli into the nasal field. Further, when the caudal half of the tectum was ablated, the double-nasal animals became blind, whereas the double-temporal animals were blinded by rostral tectal lesions. All these results were entirely in accord with the original chemoaffinity predictions.

Subsequent compound eye studies, however, by Gaze *et al.* (1963, 1965) using *Xenopus* and electrophysiological mapping methods gave different results. Each half of the compound eye was found to project topographically and in overlapping manner across the entire tectum with the nasotemporal orientation for each hemiretina reversed (Fig. 1). It was further shown by Straznicky, Gaze, and Keating (1971) that after metamorphosis,

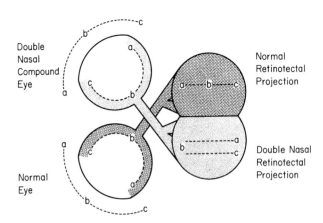

FIG. 1. Diagram of the visual field and retinotectal projection in an adult *Xenopus* with a double-nasal compound eye formed embryonically by surgically removing the temporal half of the eye vesicle and substituting from a donor a nasal half-vesicle mirror image to the nasal half left in the orbit.

when tectal development is largely completed, the fibers from the compound eye, after being sectioned and uncrossed at the chiasm, would regenerate ipsilaterally to again form a similar projection onto the ipsilateral tectum which had been normally innervated throughout development. This ruled out an interpretation suggested earlier (Sperry, 1965a) in terms of selective developmental hyperplasia of the appropriate innervated half-tectum, with hypoplasia of the uninnervated half, as had been obtained with surgically produced variations in eye size (Harrison, 1929; Stone, 1930).

The observed projection in *Xenopus* of each compound half-retina across the entire tectum in reverse orientation seemed to require a modified hypothesis in which it was proposed that the optic fibers, instead of finding pre-designated tectal sites, arrange themselves during growth in an orderly way as a competing system that fills up whatever gradient is available. This view retains the concept of cytochemical specificities arranged in gradient fashion, but the nerve connections are established on a flexible or sliding scale instead of one that is prefixed. This sliding scale or "football field" interpretation (Gaze, 1970) seemed to gain further reinforcement in later experiments demonstrating compression and expansion in the retinotectal system. This modified interpretation is incompatible with some of the early retinotectal data, as will be discussed more fully later, and particularly with recent findings on half-tectum frogs.

We have long favored a quite different explanation of the compound eye experiments (Meyer & Sperry, 1973, 1974; Sperry, 1965a) as follows: It is known that a morphogenetic field almost by definition (Weiss, 1939), if cut in half during early development, can be expected to undergo self-regulation to reorganize itself into a whole field. Such a reorganization of each half-retina would account for spread of the projection from each hemiretina over the entire tectum. We need merely suppose that each half-retina, when confronted with the reverse gradient forces of the other half, responds by forming a whole retinal field of its own, reduced in size and modified somewhat in shape to fit the existing confinements.

Thus, the compound eye in the *Xenopus* experiments may be thought of as having developed two full twin retinal fields, so far as the rostrocaudal gradient is concerned. These twin retinas are reduced in size and are set as mirror images joined near the vertical midline of the eye, with the rostro-caudal gradient of each twin reversed so that there is no abrupt break in cytochemistry in passing from one twin to the other. The resultant projection pattern on the tectum would be of the form obtained by Gaze *et al.* (1963, 1965). This kind of plastic reorganization of locus specificities involving morphogenetic regulation was always implicit in the chemoaffinity interpretation as evidenced in the prediction that the dorsoventral gradient might be reversed independently of the anteroposterior (Sperry, 1944) if the surgery were properly timed. The variables in the compound eye results, thus conceived, would no longer be a matter of the way in which nerve fibers grow and connect, but a question, rather, of the precursor developmental dynamics by which neurons acquire specificity. If the surgery is performed at a stage after the gradient properties and positional specificities have already become irreversibly fixed, the predicted tectal projection on these terms will be of the form obtained by Székely (1954), whereas there is no accounting for such results in the "sliding scale" hypothesis. The double-retina interpretation finds indirect support in the observation that a double lens is sometimes formed in the compound eye (Gaze, Keating, Székely, & Beazley, 1970). Also, it is known from the early work of Harrison (1921) that when the embryonic field of the developing limb bud is treated by analogous surgical procedures, the compound limb bud will frequently form two separate duplicate limbs oriented in mirror-image fashion, like the twin retinas.

The kind of retinal reorganization inferred for the compound eye does not involve a reversal of gradient polarity in either hemiretina, but only readjustments of scale in the preexisting gradients. There is an important difference between changing the direction of a gradient and merely altering its extent or range (Meyer & Sperry, 1973). The compound eye surgery was performed at a stage in which the retinal gradients are now known to be no longer plastic to reversal by eye rotation (Jacobson, 1968a), but this does not preclude the kind of plasticity involved in reorganizing a half-scale gradient into a whole-scale gradient.

The presence of regulative plasticity of the kind required is indicated in an early behavioral study of Székely (1957) on *Triturus*. He removed the nasal or temporal half of presumably "specified" eyes and rounded up the intact half into a small eye, which eventually developed into an eye of about half-normal size. Visual testing revealed only normal responses over the entire visual field with no indication of the directional distortions that would be expected had the halved retina not undergone reorganization into a whole-scale field. This same result was later confirmed by Gaze (1970) in *Xenopus* with electrical mapping, which showed a predominantly normal retinal projection across the entire tectum. Both results are most simply explained on the assumption that the remaining half-retina developed into a whole retina.

Further evidence for plasticity in these early retinal fields has been found recently by Hunt and Jacobson (1973a). Compound eyes in *Xenopus* made of nasal and ventral or nasal and contralateral temporal half-retinas were found to form projections in which each half-retina spread connections across the entire tectum. Even simple surgical bisection of the eye anlage resulted in mirror twinning of retinal projection (Hunt & Jacobson, 1973b). Sharma and Hollyfield (1974) obtained a similar compound type projection in one case in *Rana pipiens* simply by eye rotation. Both these findings are reminiscent of previous limb bud experiments showing mirror duplication after surgical splitting or rotation of a developing limb field (Harrison, 1921) and add to the growing support for the "mirror twinning" interpretation. Embryonic retinal regulation is also strongly indicated by the axial reversals found in the compound eyes of Hunt and Jacobson (1973a), by the distortions found to occur in the tectal projection from double ventral compound eyes (Straznicky et al., 1974), and by a variety of alterations recently found in other types of compound eyes (Hunt, 1975).

In other respects also the compound eye findings lend further support to chemoaffinity principles by furnishing new evidence against any simple mechanical or temporal scheduling in favor of guidance by prescribed affinities as follows: Compound eyes have been shown to grow in the same manner as normal eyes, largely by slow annular addition of cells at the margin (Feldman & Gaze, 1972). Central retinal cells differentiate and send out axons well in advance of the peripheral retinal cells. In contrast to normals, where central retinal cells project to the central tectum, the central cells in compound eyes project to the tectal margin, the rostral margin in the case of double-nasal eyes, and the caudal margin in the case of double-temporal eyes. This differential but orderly projection, under abnormal mismatch conditions, which occurs in spite of apparently identical timing and positional factors, is difficult to account for by other than some orderly intrinsic specificities in the ganglion cells with preferential affinities for particular central pathways and tectal terminations.

III. Determination of Positional Specificity

The prediction that specification of retinal ganglion cells involves differentiation on at least two separate axial gradients and occurs first on the anteroposterior (rostrocaudal or nasotemporal) axis and later on the dorsoventral axis, and that this could be demonstrated by surgical inversion of the eye at successively earlier stages (Sperry, 1944) was confirmed by Stone (1944), by Székely (1957), and by others since. Prior to a certain stage of development one expects surgical eye rotation to be readjusted by plastic embryonic processes that restore the conditions for normal retinotectal projection. As growth proceeds, the developmental capacities for such corrective readjustment are lost, and thereafter surgical rotation and other rearrangements produce corresponding distortions in retinotectal mapping and visual behavior (Fig. 2). During the critical period in which this changeover occurs, the cytochemical gradient properties of the intact eye become irreversibly determined and regardless of surgical rotation or heterotopic transplantation, they express thereafter their original chemoaffinities.

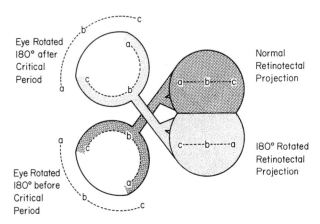

Fig. 2.   Diagram of the visual field and retinotectal projections of an adult amphibian after prior 180° rotation of the eye vesicle in the embryo before or after the critical period.

Experiments have been undertaken in and around the changeover period in an effort to find clues as to the nature of the specification process at the cellular and molecular level. Thus on the basis of thymidine labeling studies for DNA synthesis, Jacobson (1968b) suggested that neuronal specification occurs only after cessation of DNA synthesis, which was found to coincide with the end of the critical period. Prior to that (Stage 29 for *Xenopus*), the retinal ganglion cells were conceived to be "unspecified . . . did not know what their central connections should be, and received their information only after Stage 29" (Jacobson, 1970). In the original chemoaffinity interpretation the specification process was conceived somewhat differently. The eye, limb, and other organ fields were described as emerging in treelike fashion as subfields out of the main axial gradients of the embryo (Sperry, 1965a), in accordance with standard developmental doctrine. The specification process itself thus starts much earlier in this view and is traceable back to the initial polarization of the embryo as a whole. The finding that surgical inversion yields normal visual projection prior to Stage 29 and inverted vision afterward is taken to mean only that the specification process is no longer reversible after Stage 29. In these terms, the so-called critical period as revealed by grafting procedures is not when specification occurs, but only when the process reaches the stage of irreversibility (Meyer & Sperry, 1973).

The chemical differentiation underlying the specification process is conceived to start in simple form and to become increasingly complex and defined by stages involving multicellular interactions. Different phases and features of this complex biochemical process become fixed and irreversible at different times. For example, the positional specificities in a gradient may be irreversibly determined so far as reversal by eye rotation is concerned, but still remain plastic in regard to compression or expansion of the same gradient with its polarity unchanged (Meyer & Sperry, 1973). The critical stage for polarity reversal may be different also for different conditions, such as 180° rotation of the eye, inversion on one or the other axis only, or inversion of only one-half of a compound eye. From general developmental considerations intraretinal interactions can be expected to be of developmental consequence even after eye–body interactions have largely ceased. Such experiments tell us little about either the initiation or the completion of the specification process, only about its maturational stages and progressive loss of flexibility. On these terms the cessation of DNA synthesis in *Xenopus* might be a useful clue to the nature of the post-critical-period irreversibility, not necessarily the end product of specification. Possible significance of the observed correlation with DNA synthesis is dimmed by a recent failure to find it in *Rana pipiens* (Sharma & Hollyfield, 1974) and evidence that even in *Xenopus* most ganglion cells are formed after the critical period (Straznicky & Gaze, 1971).

The foregoing view of the specification process receives further experimental support from an important series of recent eye transplant experiments by Hunt and Jacobson (1973c). The eye vesicle in *Xenopus* embryos was removed at Stages 22–24, well before the critical period of Stages 28–32, and either transplanted to a neutral belly midline position in a carrier embryo or to cultures *in vitro* in which the eye developed to Stage 39/40. Subsequent reimplantation into the enucleated orbit of a Stage 39/40 host produced a retinotectal projection corresponding to the eye's original normal polarity, indicating that the developing eye even before the critical period possesses axial information and that the process of polarization can proceed *in vitro* independently of the embryo. In another series of inter-embryo transplants, systematic variation of the stages of both donor and host embryos showed that the final irreversible fixation of polarity was dependent primarily upon intrinsic factors within the eye (Hunt & Jacobson, 1974). Based on these and related results, Hunt and Jacobson (1973b, 1973c, 1974) have redefined their original use of "specification" (Hunt & Jacobson, 1972a, 1972b) to mean the irreversible fixation of axial polarity.

The precise timing and molecular mechanisms underlying the sequence of events in specification that ultimately lead to acquisition of cytochemical properties regulating selective fiber outgrowth and synapsis remain to be elucidated and presumably are closely tied to the basic mechanisms of cell differentiation. The recent demonstration that in *Xenopus* tadpoles there is a progressive caudal shift of the retinotopic projection across the growing tectum (Gaze, Keating, & Chung, 1974) does not contradict the idea of preferential terminations since it may only reflect developmental changes in the cytochemical properties of the enlarging retina or tectum. Even if one assumes a stable and final cytochemical differentiation, the presumably inappropriate retinal projection onto rostral tectum at early tadpole stages may be explained along lines similar to that proposed for plastic remapping of the retina into a surgically formed rostral half-tectum in goldfish (see Section IV on tectal lesions).

Caution is warranted, however, by recent questions about the nature, reality, and generality of the plasticity (Hunt & Jacobson, 1973b). It is not found apparently in chick embryos (Crossland et al., 1974; De Long & Coulombre, 1965) even though, like tadpoles, fiber ingrowth is at the rostral end of the tectum. In chicks there is also evidence for an early specification of retina. Dissociated retinal cells taken at stages before optic fibers grow across the tectum have been shown to adhere preferentially to the appropriate tectal half (Barbera, Marchase, & Roth, 1973). It may be noted that a similar result was obtained using pigment epithelial cells, thus lending credence to the suggestion (Sperry, 1944) that the specificity of the ganglion cells may derive in part from this epithelial tissue, not only when the retina is experimentally induced to regenerate from pigment epithelium, but also during normal development. The misdirected optic fiber growth seen in various albino mutants also suggests a similar link between epithelial and neural tissue (see Section VIII on plasticity in mammals).

IV. Tectal Lesion Experiments

Additional support for the sliding-scale interpretation came from experiments in goldfish (Fig. 3) in which it was found that surgical ablation of the caudal half-tectum led to an orderly compression of the whole retina onto the remaining rostral half-tectum (Gaze & Sharma, 1970). These results were generally confirmed and extended in electrophysiological studies in goldfish by Yoon (1971, 1972a) and Sharma (1972a, 1972b). Like the compound-eye experiments, these also were open to explanation on the grounds that a developing tectal field cut in half may undergo self-reorganization into a whole field. This would be expected without question in embryonic stages and might conceivably be possible in juvenile stages in goldfish in which the tectum and retina are still growing (Kirsche & Kirsche, 1961; Meyer, 1974). While such a late regulation would be surprising (Meyer & Sperry, 1973, 1974), to dismiss this possibility a priori (Gaze, 1974) is incautious, especially in view of the evidence on retinal specification in Amphibia indicating that these locus specificity properties can regulate well after many other cellular properties have ceased to be affected (see Hunt, 1975, and Section III on eye specification).

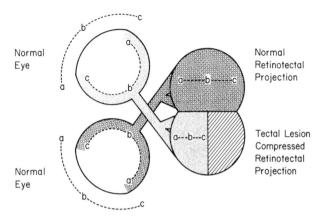

FIG. 3. Diagram of the visual field and retinotectal projection obtainable in a juvenile goldfish several months following either caudal tectal ablation, as indicated by the slashed region, or insertion of a mechanical barrier between rostral and caudal tectal halves.

Similar tectal ablations in adult tree frogs, *Hyla regilla* (in which tectal growth was complete), gave results consistent with an interpretation in terms of field regulation. Compression of the sort obtained in goldfish failed to occur (Meyer & Sperry, 1973). Electrophysiological mapping at various times after surgery showed little significant change in retinotectal projection even with combined section and regeneration of the optic nerve. Similar results have been reported also for *Xenopus* (Straznicky, 1973). Behavioral perimetry mapping in *H. regilla* demonstrated little or no recovery from the initial scotoma produced by the tectal ablations. Additional behavioral evidence indicated that optic fibers corresponding to the ablated tectum grew out of their usual course all the way to the appropriate symmetric synaptic zone of the contralateral tectum rather than terminating inappropriately in the rostral tectum. This growth to contralateral symmetric sites, however, was not responsible for the absence of compression, since compression also failed to occur after bilateral ablations (Meyer & Sperry, 1973). The results in adult tree frogs seemed to rule out the view that tectal terminations depend on relative positioning of fibers within available target areas in favor of tectal regulation.

Similar explanations involving reorganization of tectal specificities have also been advanced by other workers (Gaze, 1974; Hunt & Jacobson, 1973b; Yoon, 1971). However, several more recent studies designed to further test this interpretation indicate that tectal regulation may not be the principal answer (Meyer, 1975a, 1975b). Other explanations are now seen that can account for these plasticities in a manner compatible with chemoaffinity concepts. Before turning to these we need to consider certain gaps in the published evidence.

A. *Contradictions and Gaps in the Evidence*

The lack of compression originally reported by Jacobson and Gaze (1965) after full-length medial or lateral tectal ablation and optic nerve crush has not been satisfactorily reconciled with Yoon's (1971) demonstration of mediolateral compression after removal of only the caudal quadrant (see Introduction). Optic tract interference consequent to full length lesions has been invoked as an explanation but appears from autoradiographic evidence (Meyer, 1974) to be insufficient to prevent fibers from reaching the tectum. It remains possible, however, that the regenerating fibers initially reestablish an uncompressed projection and only slowly undergo compression over a period substantially longer than was allowed by Jacobson and Gaze. When 18 months were allowed for recovery after surgical ablation of medial tectum (Meyer, unpublished), electrophysiological mapping showed clear evidence of the predicted compression. A similar time-dependent plasticity for the rostrocaudal dimension suggested in other work was either considered inconclusive (Gaze & Sharma, 1970) or, involved a disruption of the normal optic pathways and a more complex double remnant preparation (Sharma, 1972b). Accordingly, a further study was undertaken, as described below.

A series of 5–11 cm fish sustaining caudal tectal ablations were studied electrophysiologically at 44–214 days after optic nerve interruption. A more accurate eye-in-water recording technique (Meyer, 1974) was employed after comparison with the eye-in-air method revealed several deficiencies: Eye alignment in air by retinal landmarks is much more difficult. The extreme myopia of some 50 diopters (Wartzok & Marks, 1973) results in receptive fields that are 5–10 times larger than normal (Cronly-Dillon, 1964; Jacobson & Gaze, 1965; Schwassman & Kruger, 1965; Yoon, 1971). In addition, an artifactual enlargement of the visual field representation was found that could mask field defects (Meyer, 1974).

Recordings taken at up to 2–3 months showed a relatively uncompressed visual field with a large posterior scotoma, while at longer periods the virtually complete compression previously reported (Gaze & Sharma, 1970; Yoon, 1971, 1972a) was confirmed. Thus, even in this plastic system, the evidence indicated the directive influence on fiber growth of specific position dependent affinities that must be accounted for in any comprehensive model.

Disagreement exists also on the effect of a surgical incision separating the rostral from the caudal tectum. Reversible full-field compression of the rostral half was found by Yoon (1971, 1972a) after simple transection or incision with insertion of Gelfilm. This compression was not found by Sharma (1972b, 1972c) after incisions even when combined with ablation of surrounding tissue. Contrary to Yoon and all available anatomical evidence, Sharma (1972b) further suggested that innervation of the caudal tectum may not be completely disrupted by such lesions. Arora (1973) found that these procedures did interrupt optic fibers, but, in contradition to both Yoon and Sharma, he reported that fibers once cut were unable to regrow across the tectal incision.

In an autoradiographic study (Meyer, 1974), transverse mediolateral incisions across even small regions of the dorsal tectum were found to disrupt virtually the entire innervation posterior to the lesion. After several months the posterior innervation became reestablished by fiber growth through the incision site. Even when a 500-μm-wide ablation was made between the rostral and caudal tectum, similar regrowth was eventually found penetrating the glia-filled scar.

In view of this ready growth across tectal incisions, Yoon's (1971) compression after incision seems surprising, but his sketches indicate the possibility of rather extensive tectal damage, which may have been sufficient to block fiber growth. In subsequent experiments more refined incisions did not produce compression (Yoon, personal communication), and insertion of a barrier was required (Yoon, 1972a). In this context the fine incisions of Sharma would not be expected to produce compression, and in those experiments involving midtectal ablations where compression was expected, the 5–11 months of postoperative recovery may have been long enough to permit the kind of reversal of compression found by Yoon (1972a).

In summary, the kind of tectal separation that has thus far produced compression involves a sustained interruption of tectal continuity and blockage of fiber growth. Since compression now appears not to be a consequence of an autonomous field-type regulation of tectal cytospecificities, the subsequent expansion of the projection following an incision-induced compression (Yoon, 1972a) could be a result of optic fiber regrowth across the incision to preferred sites of termination— the release of a forced and unstable condition. The autoradiographic data showed further a rather strong growth preference of the optic fibers to return to their correct laminae in the tectum within a few hundred micrometers after deflections in traversing the incision scar.

According to Yoon (1971, 1972a), posterior tectal ablation results in a uniform compression, whereas Gaze and Sharma (1970) and Sharma (1972b) found that part of the displaced map generally came to be superimposed on the remaining projection. This discrepancy remains unexplained. Until the relevant factors are understood, it may be more profitable to focus attention on the experiments involving optic nerve interrruption, which is probably more directly relevant for development.

The studies showing compression have relied almost exclusively on electrophysiological measurements presumed to come from the presynaptic terminal arbors of the optic fibers. This gives no direct evidence of functional synaptic connectivity. Recently Scott (1975) has succeeded in training hemitectal goldfish to discriminate visual stimuli presented to restricted regions of the visual field. Preliminary results indicate that vision is eventually restored within the original scotoma in an orderly progression that moves posteriorly from the anterior scotoma border. Her results suggest that the compression that has been mapped by electrophysiological recording from presynaptic optic terminals involves a correlated formation of tectal synapses and so represents a genuine reorganization in functional connectivity.

In contrast to previous results in *Hyla* (Meyer & Sperry, 1973) and *Xenopus* (Straznicky, 1973), significant, though apparently limited, compression of tectal projection has been recently found in *Rana* (Udin, personal communication). A consequent reinvestigation in *Hyla* with modified techniques indicates some possible signs of compression, but these seem to be much more limited than reported in *Rana* (Meyer, unpublished). Whether this represents a possible species difference or technical and procedural differences is not clear. It is worth noting, however, that interpreting small changes can be problematical. In frogs, terminal arbors of some fibers are several hundred micrometers long and the extent of dendritic arbors of some tectal cells is even greater (Maturana, Lettvin, McCulloch, & Pitts, 1960).

B. Latest Findings Countering Autonomous Field Regulation

In an autoradiographic study aimed at testing regulation (Meyer, 1975a), prior removal of a caudal half-tectum was combined with lesion of either a nasal or a temporal helf-retina and optic nerve crush. In the control, where a nasal half-retina grew onto the noncorresponding rostral half-tectum, a caudal bias of reinnervation, expected regardless of regulation, was found present up to 5 months after surgery. In fact, the caudalmost labeling was heavier than normal even spreading vertically beyond the usual confines of the normal terminal layers. At first sight this contrasts with similar electrophysiological studies (Horder, 1971; Yoon, 1972b) in which even topographic spreading was reported, but it is in line with Roth's (1972) Bodian study. Difficulty in electrically probing the downcurved rostral extreme of the tectum (Meyer, 1974) may help to mask the asymmetry of innervation as revealed by autoradiography.

According to the control findings, the innervation from a temporal hemiretina ought to be similarly biased toward the rostral end of the tectal remnant if tectal respecification occurs. If respecification does not occur, reinnervation ought to spread evenly across the entire tectal remnant. Autoradiography as late as 3–5 months after nerve crush gave little indication of any asymmetry in the distribution of terminals but rather showed evenly spread label across the entire rostrocaudal extent. The same result was also obtained in other cases following the same surgery when the optic nerve was recrushed after 5 months. These findings strongly discount the primacy of a developmental field type reorganization of tectal specificities in response to the lesion.

Preliminary electrophysiological evidence reported by Cook and Horder (1974) is also counterindicative of field regulation. They confirmed that the initial recordable projection which grows onto a half-tectum shows only limited compression, thus giving rise to a large posterior field scotoma. After allowing sufficient time for the completion of compression, the optic nerve was recrushed. Again, the initially regenerated map was found to lack a large part of the posterior visual field. Since a significant extent of initial fiber growth takes place in the optic nerve and tract and within the parallel layer of the tectum (Attardi & Sperry, 1963; Horder, 1974; Roth, 1972), the above result with electrical mapping taken alone might simply mean that the initial guidance of fiber growth is not subject to tectal regulative changes controlling termination in the plexiform layer. Taken together the auto-radiographic and electrophysiological evidence seems to contraindicate any automatic and stable lesion-induced respecification of the tectum.

C. Selective Deflection of Fascicles of the Optic Radiation

Chemoaffinity and other growth-regulating factors were implicated in an experimental series involving intertectal transplantation of fascicles of optic fibers (Meyer, 1974, 1975b). When selected fascicles of fibers (roughly 10–15% of the total tectal complement) were dissected free of the dorsal tectum and inserted into the contralateral tectum denervated by prior eye enucleation (Fig. 4), autoradiography and electrophysiology at up to 8 months indicated that these deflected fibers had spread over several times

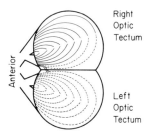

FIG. 4. Simplified diagrammatic representation of the course of optic fiber fascicles across superficial tectum. Select fascicles, such as those normally occupying the region indicated by the dashed lines on the right optic tectum, were cut free of surrounding tectum, deflected across the midline, and inserted into the anterior end of the opposite tectum, which in this case, was denervated by prior eye enucleation indicated by dashed lines on the left optic tectum.

more tectal area than normal, centered roughly on their appropriate territory. When a similar surgical deflection of fibers was carried out on a
normally innervated tectum, the transplanted fibers came to occupy, in
patchwork pattern, roughly the correct region of contralateral tectum.
Surprisingly, however, these tectal areas were often found to be exclusively
occupied by the deflected fibers, even though severed normal fibers with
presumably identical specificities were intermixed in the same regenerating
system. This segregation occurred regardless of whether these normal fibers
were left intact, suggesting active displacement of existing fiber terminals,
or whether they were temporarily disrupted by a transverse incision across
the rostral tectum. This latter exclusivity in occupation of local tectal
regions was confirmed by electrophysiological mapping. These recordings
additionally suggested that compression and other topographic distortions
may occur under these conditions, which would further indicate that tectal
regulation, ruled out in these experiments, is not necessary to explain these
kinds of plasticities. A place preference was simultaneously evidenced by
the tendency for these transplanted fibers to grow toward appropriate
regions even when inserted into inappropriate tectal areas. In addition to
chemoaffinity attraction between retinal and tectal elements, other factors
are indicated, such as interfiber competition for available terminal territory.

   In the above fiber deflection studies, there was some suggestion that inter-
mixing of fibers can be promoted by manipulating the order and timing of
ingrowing fibers or by misrouting fibers at the chiasm instead of at the rostral
tectum (Meyer, unpublished). Differences in these experimental variables
may possibly explain why segregation was not reported in previous lower
vertebrate work involving dual optic input onto one tectum (Arora, 1966;
Gaze & Keating, 1970; Sharma, 1973; Straznicky *et al.*, 1971). However, the
possibility that this could have been simply missed is supported by results of
a replication of Sharma's (1973) goldfish experiment, where, after unilateral
tectal removal, optic fibers miscrossing to the opposite tectum appeared by
autoradiography to displace, in places, the existing normal optic innervation (Meyer, unpublished). In a recent fiber deflection study Cronly-Dillon
and Glaizner (1974) also found electrophysiological evidence suggestive
of such displacement of normal innervation. However, the low success rate
(2 of 23 fish), the possibility of optic nerve damage during retinal surgery,
and the minimal effect indicated by their published map make interpretation
difficult.

D. Interpretation of Retinotectal Compression

Taken together, the preceding experiments argue against field regulation
(Meyer & Sperry, 1973), or any similar intrinsic reorganization of tectal
gradient specificities (Gaze, 1974; Hunt & Jacobson, 1973b; Yoon, 1973)

as the main cause of topographic compression or decompression. Some initial forced mismatching of presumably specified retinal and tectal elements would seem to be necessarily involved. In addition to mechanical and other chemical effects universal to nerve growth and connection, influential operative factors must presumably include a general terminal-junction-seeking growth pressure of unconnected optic fibers; homeostatic denervation and synaptic saturation effects; chemoaffinity interactions, including those among retinal fibers as well as between retinal and tectal elements; and competitive effects between normally overlapping fibers with preferential affinities. The picture of terminal patterning that emerges from the available evidence suggests preferential but not obligatory affinities for appropriate tectal elements, the fibers in their home territory being more effective competitors than more foreign fibers.

Recent electrophysiological, anatomical, and autoradiographic observations on half-tectum goldfish at successive stages of compression (Meyer, 1974) indicate a progressive abnormal thickening around the outer plexiform layer (main termination layer) that starts along the lesion border and then extends rostrally throughout the remnant half-tectum and is correlated with electrophysiological and behavioral evidence of compressed remapping (Scott, 1975). This evidence for a gradual caudorostral progression of compression across the tectum, along with other data, suggests an explanation along the following lines: After tectal ablation, say of the caudal half, and crush of the optic nerve, fibers from temporal retina tend to regrow by chemoaffinity guidance along proper pathways to their appropriate normal terminal zones on the rostral remnant, where they begin to form terminal arborizations and synaptic connections. Axons from the nasal retina, deprived of their preferred termination, on the other hand, continue a pressured exploratory growth, piling up near the caudal edge of the intact half-tectum. As the temporal fibers continue to arborize rostrally, forming a relatively uncompressed projection, the deprived exploratory nasal fibers tend to be increasingly excluded from rostral regions by the reduction in available terminal sites and in the stimulating effect of denervated tissue. These nasal fibers would thus be generally pressured toward the caudal border, their nearest chemoaffinity match and most competitive position. The nasal axons that normally terminate just caudal to the lesion border, however, would be nearly as competitive in chemical gradient terms as the nasal fibers just rostral to the lesion, and in addition would have extra competitive growth potency by virtue of their lack of other target cells. Since the number of synaptic sites is limited, the foregoing effect would pressure the adjacent temporal fibers to be displaced further rostrally, which in turn would displace fibers rostral to them, in domino fashion. Subsequently, with ever more nasal fibers filling in from the caudal edge, this sequence would continue until a fully compressed projection is achieved. At this point the driving force for compression, deprived fibers seeking terminal sites, is mitigated, with the retinal fibers having made what might be thought of as the best available matchings.

Chemoaffinity attractions between fibers from the same retinal regions may also contribute importantly to this topographic ordering (Meyer, 1974, 1975b). This interfiber affinity is conceived to operate not only between the growth cones and shafts of fibers growing down the nerve and transversing through the parallel layer of the tectum, but also between the growing terminals and terminal arbors of fibers within the plexiform layer where termination occurs. The increase of fiber surface area resulting from these terminal arborizations would be reasonably expected to increase such interfiber interactions. The tendency of fiber endings to aggregate near like fibers would work in itself to preserve and refine the topography with some independence of the precise position of fibers on the tectum. Retinotectal affinities would, of course, still be required for overall topography and general orientation of the projection.

The progressive remapping process may include a further important factor, namely, a modulatory shift in tectal cell specificity dependent upon, and maintained by, chemical influences from the regenerated retinal fibers. It has been generally presumed that the tectal cell specificity determining preferential affinity for synapse depends on the combined effect of intrinsic and extrinsic factors coming, respectively, from the cell's own chemical synthesis on the one hand and from different chemical inputs from surrounding cells on the other. It is possible that the latter extrinsic factors may include chemical products transmitted from the retinal fiber terminals or related contact-mediated changes, like those recently postulated to occur during development (McMahon, 1974). Accordingly the extra growth pressure for synapse along the lesion border in target-deprived axons that causes these fibers to synapse on near-match cells, as described above, would result in the transmission of slightly off-match extrinsic specificity products. These can be conceived to shift slightly thereby the overall specificity properties of the tectal border cells involved. This slight caudal shift of specificity (with a posterior lesion) would allow adjacent, even more caudal, unconnected fibers to synapse on the affected tectal cells, which in turn would further shift the cell's specificity in the caudal direction and permit acceptance of still more remote caudal retinal fibers. Logically this process would continue progressively until eventually fibers even from the far distant border of the lesion are accepted at the lesion edge, and the successive progressive shifts rostrally across the remaining intact tectum reach a stable equilibrium. It may be noted that this model for the shifting of fiber projections does not involve a functional breakdown. The shift from one set of afferents to another on each cell is accomplished gradually through progressive intermediate stages.

This interpretation suggests further that the scotoma would not become functional in a random or chaotic manner, nor in a general overall return first of faint, then stronger, vision throughout the missing half-field. On the above terms vision should return first along the anterior margin of the scotoma and then spread progressively backward toward the posterior periphery. This latter pattern of visual return is what seems to be demonstrated in the early data of Scott (1975) on behavioral mapping of compression by conditioning techniques with the optic nerve intact. The molecular machinery of each cell along a developing gradient must logically synthesize an intermediate average of the extrinsic chemical inputs received from adjacent cells on opposite sides. Any input specificity transmitted through afferent terminals as proposed here would presumably be weighted also in the established averaging process of these mature neurons or in its end products, in order to change the effective chemospecificity of the cell. Such considerations become important in setting the requirements and limitations for molecular models.

The foregoing represents the best interpretation for retinotectal compression we can see at present with existing evidence. Obvious uncertainties remain. It assumes that the individual optic fibers and tectal neurons are chemically specified according to the field position of their respective cell bodies, that orderly preferential contact affinities exist between the optic fibers and the tectal neurons, that these may be shifted by abnormal growth pressures, that the selective preferences for topographic mapping have their genesis in developmental field gradients and are gradient-structured, and that related axial gradient specificities exist throughout the brain and entire body which help determine the afferent pathways of fiber growth as well as central synaptic termination. It has never been claimed that these cytochemical affinities are exclusive or rigid or are the *only* factors regulating nerve growth and connection, and it has repeatedly been emphasized that the exact way in which they are expressed can be expected to vary in detail in different systems, different species, growth stages, and under different pathological and experimental conditions. It seems rather improbable that the mechanisms for topographic compression evolved to cope with such gross nervous system damage as produced in these experiments, and more likely that they are a secondary effect of certain demands of development.

In sum, the plastic reorganizations that follow tectal lesions are not only compatible with chemoaffinity concepts, but some of the observed effects, such as the initial specificity exhibited by optic fibers growing onto a half-tectum and the asymmetry of reinnervation following noncorresponding retinal and tectal lesions, directly support the idea of matching retinotectal preferences. These remapping phenomena, however, do bring to light the presence of additional competitive-type factors that importantly determine fiber growth and connectivity.

V. Retinal Lesions

Perhaps the most convincing and direct evidence for the chemoaffinity model has come from the retinal eye lesion experiments. With a modified Bodian stain selective for regenerating fibers, Attardi and Sperry (1963) showed in goldfish that different sectors of retinal field regenerate different and appropriate tectal projection patterns when the rest of the retina is removed (Fig. 5). The selective tectal termination was shown also with electrophysiological methods in a gross evoked potential study of tectal innervation following large retinal ablations (Westerman, 1965) and by a microelectrode recording experiment using a hemisected optic nerve preparation (Jacobson & Gaze, 1965). Similar selective tectal innervation has been demonstrated also in chick embryos by eye ablations prior to optic nerve outgrowth with a variety of anatomical techniques (Crossland et al., 1974; De Long & Coulombre, 1965).

More recent work on goldfish, however, seems to introduce some complications and discrepancies into this simple picture. A Bodian study by Roth (1972), though showing hemiretina innervation to be predominantly selective, suggested that this innervation may extend somewhat into inappropriate regions. A more serious discrepancy is found in Horder's report (1971)

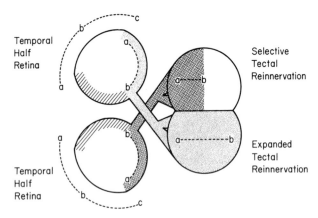

FIG. 5. Diagram of the visual field and retinotectal hypothetical projections in juvenile goldfish showing an example of rigidly selective innervation on one tectum or completely expanded reinnervation on the other tectum following optic nerve crush and lesion of nasal half-retina as represented by the slashed region.

that an isolated nasal retina spreads electrophysiologically across the entire tectum, although the tectal projection from temporal, dorsal, and ventral hemiretinas under the same conditions remained restricted selectively to the appropriate half-tectum. Even more plasticity was found in Yoon's unit-recording study (1972b), where both a nasal and a temporal half-retina were reported to have spread over the entire tectum (Fig. 5).

However, some important methodological differences between these apparently conflicting studies precluded definite conclusions. The findings showing substantial plasticity were based on relatively long postoperative survival periods, leaving the possibility that the optic fibers may have first grown to their appropriate regions and only later spread into other adjacent areas. This would be analogous to the changes in the regenerated optic projection seen after removal of the caudal half-tectum. Expected optic aberrations in the ocular system caused by the eye surgery may have produced measurement errors, and the discrepancy between these electrophysiological studies might be accounted for in these terms. Additionally, almost no systematic histology has been done in any of the above work to verify the size of lesion or the possibility of retinal regeneration, which was found to be quite extensive in the original Attardi and Sperry (1963) study.

Some of these potential complications were taken into account in a recent autoradiographic study (Meyer, 1975a, 1975b). At various periods after combined optic nerve crush and nasal or temporal retinal lesions made by several procedures, complete serial sections of both retina and tectum were taken. In general the resulting innervation was found to be preferentially but not rigidly selective (Fig. 6). There was some indication that the spread into

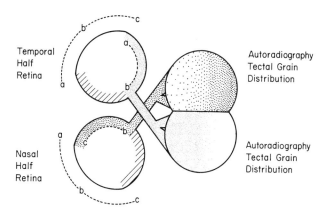

FIG. 6. Diagram of the initial selective tectal reinnervation indicated by the autoradiography studies on goldfish in which optic nerve crush was combined with lesions of either nasal or temporal half-retina as indicated by the slashed region.

foreign regions was greater with longer survival times, which may partially explain the differences in previous studies. While some of this apparent spreading may only reflect retinal regeneration that was quite significant in some cases, especially at long survival periods, terminal spread was evident in many animals where retinal regrowth was minimal or absent.

Reinnervation was most selective following nasal lesions, after which the appropriate rostral tectum was densely innervated and the caudalmost tectum hardly innervated at all. However, instead of the abrupt drop-off at the margin seen in controls, a gradientwise decrease in labeling was found to extend well into the caudal tectum. This attenuated spread that was evident in autoradiography may simply have gone undetected in previous studies which relied on electrophysiology or less sensitive anatomical methods, though some indication of spread was seen in Roth's (1972) Bodian study. The results do not conform with the electrophysiological evidence of Yoon (1972b) showing complete uniform expansions of a temporal half-retina. However, use of Yoon's lesion method, transcleral electrocoagulation, was found in the autoradiography studies to produce not only somewhat variable retinal destruction, but also extensive damage to the outer layers of the eye, resulting in gross morphological changes in eye structure and optics. Consequent measurement errors and the possibility that the recordings were from postsynaptic tectal cells (Yoon, personal communication) raise doubts about the exact retinal origin and tectal disposition of optic terminals in his study. Thus, it appears safe to conclude that fibers from the temporal half-retina exhibit strong, though not rigid, preference for the appropriate tectal half. This conclusion presumably applies as well to a dorsal or ventral half-retina, on which the literature is in reasonable agreement.

In the case of the nasal half-retina, the autoradiography indicated a lesser degree of selectivity. When more than 35–40% of the temporal retina was destroyed, the appropriate caudal regions of the tectum were more heavily innervated than the rostral area, but substantial rostral spread of labeling even to the extreme pole was often evident. When temporal eye lesions were smaller than about 35%, no difference between rostral and caudal grain densities were discernible several weeks after initial fiber ingrowth. Again, this contrasted with controls labeled immediately after eye lesions, where only light labeling of fibers of passage was seen in the rostral tectum. Thus, the view we get of the retinal lesion effects from the present evidence is an intermediate one supporting marked selectivity, but not as strict in goldfish as initially appeared.

An impressive high degree of selectivity has been demonstrated recently in Bodian stain (De Long & Coulombre, 1965) and autoradiographic studies (Crossland et al., 1974) on developing retinotectal projection in the chick following embryonic eye lesions. Some slight spreading may be indicated in the 300–500 μm transition zone from heavy labeling to background, which appears wider than might be expected for the normal projection. In the chick experiments fibers were clearly seen to bypass uninnervated foreign tissue en route to their appropriate sites, but as in goldfish, there was some suggestion that spreading was greater under these conditions. Since the retinal ablations preceded optic nerve outgrowth in these chick studies, the selectivity cannot be attributed to the presence of previous optic fibers. The suggestion that remnants of prior fiber channels confound the goldfish work (Jacobson, 1970) appears contraindicated by the chick data and also by the fairly rapid terminal and axon degeneration seen to follow nerve section in goldfish (Roth, 1972).

The evidence from juvenile goldfish points against the presence of embryonic field regulation of retinal remnants (Meyer & Sperry, 1973) or other postulated respecifications of retinal elements (Gaze, 1974; Hunt & Jacobson, 1974; Yoon, 1973). While conceivably some kind of complex partial regulation could explain the kind of expansion observed from a goldfish nasal hemiretina, such regulation is incompatible with the selectivity of innervation from temporal, dorsal, and ventral hemiretinas. These data, like those from half-tectum experiments, seem better explained in terms of chemoaffinity operating in combination with other general growth factors, e.g., a tendency for regenerating fibers to make use of available space and the biochemically stimulating effect of denervated tissue.

VI. Pathway Patterning

While the distribution of optic terminals on the tectum has been the subject of much experimentation, factors affecting the growth and structure of the optic pathways leading to the site of termination have received relatively little attention, perhaps partly because the usual behavioral and electrophysiological methods rarely give this information. In an anatomical study on goldfish, Attardi and Sperry (1963) first demonstrated by Bodian staining that fibers regenerating from retinal remnants preferentially select appropriate afferent routes through the optic tract and across the tectum to terminal tectal sites. They accordingly extended the chemoaffinity theory to include patterning of central fiber tracts, and proposed that the chemotatic patterning is regulated by biochemical specificities similar to those governing synapsis. These findings have been in part confirmed by Roth (1972) and extended recently to the optic nerve itself where, after disrupting nerve crush, the intricate retinotopic organization was found by both light (Roth, 1974) and electron microscopy degeneration techniques (Horder, 1974) to be reformed by the selective regrowth of optic fibers. In chicks, pathway selectivity through the tectum has also been observed in eye lesion experiments (Crossland et al., 1974; De Long & Coulombre, 1965). More direct evidence that this organization involves an active preferential selection of pathways comes from experiments in which the medial and lateral brachia of the optic tract have been surgically crossed (Arora & Sperry, 1962). Abruptly redirected fiber growth toward the appropriate pathway resulted.

While pathway patterning undoubtedly contributes to the formation of topographical termination, it alone is insufficient and, in some cases, not even necessary for orderly innervation. The fan-shaped spreading of optic fibers across the tectum from peripheral entry points means not only that most fibers must grow past inappropriate tectal sites but also that different fibers growing in virtually identical paths terminate in different regions. In the optic nerve of *Rana*, fibers appear to be randomly distributed (Maturana et al., 1960), and perhaps partially as a consequence, the initially regenerated retinotectal map is quite disorganized (Gaze & Jacobson, 1963; Gaze & Keating, 1970). Despite this, good retinotopic order is eventually restored (Gaze, 1959; Maturana, Lettvin, McCulloch, & Pitts, 1959). Even when fibers are surgically forced into abnormal paths, such as through the oculomotor nerve root (Gaze, 1959; Hibbard, 1967) or through dorsal cranium (Hibbard, 1959; Sharma, 1972d), appropriate termination tends to be achieved.

In goldfish there has been some suggestion from early behavioral (Sperry, 1951a) and anatomical work (Roth, 1972) that fiber guidance during regeneration is imperfect. Further recent evidence indicates that regenerating optic fibers may find their correct terminal sites in the dorsal tectum via quite abnormal routes outside even the medial brachium (Horder, 1974; Meyer, 1974). It should be emphasized, however, that most fibers in these studies, unless surgically prevented, did grow along or near their normal routes in accordance with previous evidence (Attardi & Sperry, 1963; Horder, 1974; Roth, 1972, 1974). Even in the anatomical studies where incorrect routes were surgically forced, a tendency of fibers to reestablish their appropriate pathways could be observed (Arora & Sperry, 1962; Hibbard, 1959, 1967). This orderly growth can be explained by chemoaffinity attraction between optic fibers and the cytochemically tagged elements, neural and nonneural, distributed along the optic pathway (Sperry, 1965a). It is inferred (Sperry, 1965a) that the cell surface membranes throughout the developing embryo, in all tissues, acquire cytochemical specificity labels. Selective affinities between optic fibers from contiguous retinal loci might also contribute to topographical order, but this interfiber interaction alone cannot explain the orientation of the topography relative to the rest of the nervous system. There is some suggestion that regenerating fibers have a tendency to grow into inappropriate neighboring routes after retinal lesions (Roth, 1972). This may be analogous to the expansion seen in the tectal innervation and suggests that the same kinds of factors may also operate in route selection.

VII. Tectal Gradients and Polarity

The inferred cytochemical polarization of the optic tectum and its postulated role in regulating the topography of retinal projection has not gone unquestioned and untested (Crelin, 1952; Jacobson, 1970; Levine & Jacobson, 1974; Sharma & Gaze, 1971; Stone, 1960; Yoon, 1973). The logical necessity for such has long been evident in view of a substantial array of experimental observations that seem to be accountable only on these terms. Crelin (1952) performed surgical rotations of the tectum of *Ambystoma* at different stages of development and later tested the resultant orienting responses. These were normal after early rotations but with late rotations became so confused as to be difficult to interpret. In more recent experiments on adult goldfish (Sharma & Gaze, 1971; Yoon, 1973) and postmetamorphic froglets (Levine & Jacobson, 1974), a rectangular piece of tectum comprising 10–20% of the total tectum was excised and reimplanted in rotated positions, breaking all optic connections in the process. In most instances where reinnervation of the implant was successful, its projection pattern was found to be correspondingly rotated (Fig. 7) with respect to the normal surrounding area. A substantial histological gap between the

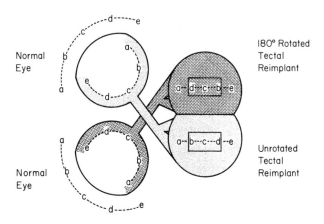

Fig. 7. Diagram of the kind of visual field and retinotectal projections in goldfish several months after excision of the indicated piece of central tectum and reimplantation in 0° or 180° rotated position (Levine & Jacobson, 1974; Sharma & Gaze, 1971; Yoon, 1973).

rotated tectal implants and the surrounding tectum has been shown both histologically and electrophysiologically that tends to isolate and insulate the reimplants and probably helps to preserve their intrinsic polarity, especially in goldfish. In the frog, this discontinuity eventually comes to be much less evident, but a significant gap may be present during the initial reinnervation of the implant. The absence of insulating reactions around tectal implants may account for the exceptional normal, unrotated projection onto rotated implants as observed in several frogs of Levine and Jacobson (1974). While the results further affirm the presence of cytochemical polarity and its importance in chemotactic guidance of fiber growth and termination, to argue that the extensive previous evidence has been ambiguous (Levine & Jacobson, 1974) seems unwarranted. The suggestion that the polarity of the tectum may be imposed initially during development by the ingrowing optic fibers (Jacobson, 1970) appears incompatible with the early eye rotation and other related observations.

VIII. Plasticity in Mammals

In the development of the retinogeniculate system in higher mammals, the requisites for cytochemical specificity and interneuron affinity in patterning of nerve pathways and connections appear to reach a peak in refinement, complexity, and precision, particularly in man, where close to one million optic fibers connect to about one million geniculate neurons in what appears to approximate a cell-to-cell relation (Polyak, 1957). Developing optic fibers advancing into the primate lateral geniculate nucleus must presumably carry cell-specific chemical labels to select for the latitude and longitude of specific target cells, not only in one central geniculate map, but among six separate maps arranged in laminar fashion, each map in register with the others. After finding the correct terminal locus in the correct one of the six layers, the invading retinal fibers must then make further selections among the types of neurons present, according to their specifications for color discrimination and other differential functions involved in feature detection, on–off, off–on, and luminosity effects. Most or all of these various selectivities expressed in geniculate synapses must also be extended and preserved among the system of geniculostriate synapses in the visual cortex.

There is much to suggest that chemoaffinity mechanisms similar to those indicated for lower vertebrates are responsible also for the developmental organization of the more elaborate visual pathways of mammals. However, the experimental conditions are more complex, and the developmental stages at which mammalian experiments are feasible and the kinds of surgical intervention are, of course, much more restricted. Because of the limited regenerative capacity in mammals, work on mature individuals has been largely confined to analyses of preterminal and collateral sprouting. Virtually nothing has been done on initial specification since eye development and optic nerve outgrowth are already far advanced in the neonatal placental animals that have been used to date.

This difficulty is circumvented in part in studies of genetic alterations of the visual system, as in albinos and particularly in Siamese cats. In the latter, for example, correlated with their cross-eye characteristic, a large section of temporal retinal fibers cross at the chiasm instead of growing to their usual ipsilateral geniculate layers (Guillery, 1969). Despite this abnormal path, the contralateral geniculate termination of these aberrant fibers is in the temporal fiber layer and in the order that would be expected from a chemoaffinity matching scheme for the retinogeniculate system (see Sperry, 1965). Contrary to a previous report (Berman & Cynader, 1972), the retino-collicular projection now also appears to be in accord with this kind of scheme (Lane, Kaas, & Allman, 1974). Although the geniculocortical topography seen by Kaas and Guillery (1973) similarly conforms with such a matching scheme, that recorded by Hubel and Weisel (1971) in another strain of Siamese cat (Kaas & Guillery, 1973) appears to present differences, and further evidence is needed before these disparities can be resolved.

Other relevant studies have involved various visual system lesions in neonatal animals where at least some optic axons are still capable of substantial growth. Lund and Lund (1973), for example, made small eye lesions in rat pups and found anatomical evidence in the mature animals that the projection of the lesioned eye to the superior colliculus contained a small correspondingly placed denervation zone. Surrounding fibers apparently failed to invade these areas, but fibers from the other eye, tentatively presumed to be homotopic to those destroyed, sprouted or changed course at the chiasm to find the denervated loci. However, the precise retinal origin and organization of this abnormal ipsilateral projection requires further elucidation.

In a series of experiments on newborn hamsters, unilateral removal of the superficial gray layer of superior colliculus (the site of the optic projection) has been found to result in hyperinnervation of the dorsal terminal nucleus of the accessory optic tract of the same side by optic fibers presumably destined for the missing collicular site. Many more fibers, however, grow across the lesioned colliculus to terminate in the opposite superior colliculus (Schneider, 1973). These aberrant fibers apparently select bisymmetric mirror target sites as shown behaviorally in the same kind of left–right reversal of visual responses that appear after crossed tectal innervation in amphibians (Sperry, 1945, 1951a). Excluding for the moment areas directly damaged or denervated, the displaced optic fibers innervate only those regions where optic fibers normally terminate. If the collicular lesion is restricted to the rostral half, compression onto the caudal remnant is indicated by recent Fink–Heimer studies (Schneider & Jhaveri, 1974). Provided subsequent electrophysiological studies confirm that an orderly compression is acquired, this would appear analogous to the goldfish half-tectum experiments and similar arguments would apply.

Behavioral tests on hamsters give tentative indications that the retinotopic order of aberrant crossed optic fibers is not as refined as normal (Schneider, 1973). However, in neonatal mammals only a few weeks of significant fiber elongation appear available for corrective growth after surgical intrusion (Kalil, 1973; Lund, Cunningham, & Lund, 1973). By contrast, in goldfish several months of regeneration seem to be required for stabilization of the retinotectal projection following simple nerve crush (Meyer, 1974; see above). The minor growth errors seen after collicular ablation in hamsters may in part reflect limitations in the quality and duration of plastic optic fiber growth in these animals.

Another approach has involved surgical denervation of areas contiguous to retinal projection sites. One of the simplest experimental designs consists of removal of one eye at various periods after birth (Kalil, 1973; Lund & Lund, 1971; Mathers & Chow, 1973). Resultant central denervation is most marked contralateral to the enucleation. Substantial abnormal invasion of the denervated areas can be seen to result anatomically in the lateral geniculate and in superior collicular regions normally occupied by the absent contralateral fibers. To interpret this in terms mainly of distal sprouting and expansion of the normal ipsilateral innervation may be premature. Subsequent work in rats indicates that chiasmal sprouting by fibers of the remaining eye may result in an extensive projection to the wrong (denervated) side of the brain (Cunningham & Freeman, 1974; Lund et al., 1973). Until a similar possibility has been ruled out in the other relevant studies, it is somewhat idle to invest in possible explanations for any violation of chemoaffinity-determined connectivity.

An important possible exception to the foregoing is found in an anomalous ipsilateral collicular projection in the rat following unilateral enucleation, which appears to be a polar mediolateral inversion of that expected from chemoaffinity matching (Cunnigham & Speas, 1975). However, this finding is somewhat at odds with previous work indicating only a limited anomalous projection (Lund et al., 1973; Lund & Lund, personal communication). Even if confirmed, some kind of chemoaffinity "flip-flop" or mechanical inversion of fiber growth path remains possible. In view of the indicated collicular pathology under these conditions and the presence of an appropriate organization along the rostrocaudal axis (Lund & Lund,

1971; Tsang, 1937), the conclusion that innervation is here determined independently of the tectum is hardly warranted (Cunningham & Speas, 1975).

Growth of optic fibers into centers where optic termination does not normally occur is almost entirely confined to areas that have been denervated or damaged simultaneously with extensive elimination of the normal terminal nuclei of the optic fibers, either by direct lesioning, as in the collicular experiments (Schneider, 1973), or by retrograde and possibly trans-neuronal effects, such as those produced in the lateral geniculate nucleus after striate cortex removal (Cunningham, 1972; Goodman & Horel, 1966). Under such conditions, with their normal terminal station removed, optic fibers are forced to seek alternative sites and may be supposed to invade first those that are pathologically attractive or stimulating as a consequence of the reaction to extensive denervation. It is an old observation that denervated tissue stimulates nerve fiber ingrowth and connections. The importance of denervation is indicated by observations on hamsters sustaining neonatal superior collicular lesions where, owing to variability in the lesioning technique, the inferior collicular projection to the medial geniculate body was differentially disrupted (Schneider, 1973). When this medial geniculate denervation was virtually complete, there was limited invasion by optic fibers. If only a small inferior collicular projection remained, however, little or no ingrowth was seen. This lack of invasion under the latter condition seems hardly attributable to an absence of synaptic space, but may be better accounted for by the absence of denervation pathology.

The evidence indicates generally that normal fibers are much better competitors for their appropriate termination sites than are foreign ones. Only a small fraction of normal fibers seems to be able to inhibit invasion by foreign fibers. Experiments in the septal nuclei of adult rats show this kind of inhibition of sprouting (Moore, Björkland, & Stenevi, 1971), and early studies on oculomotor reinnervation suggest that the original fibers can even displace foreign innervation after it is already established (Sperry & Arora, 1965; Marotte & Mark, 1970). The fact that optic neurons are physically capable of growing into the medial geniculate and other inappropriate but accessible areas but do not do so, even if some terminal space apparently remains available, argues for the operation in mammalian neurogenesis of selective chemoaffinity influences.

Further support for the notion that some of these novel connections in mammals are forced and are, in fact, second-order choices (not the preferred termination) comes from the above hamster studies of Schneider (1973), where, in addition to unilateral collicular lesioning, the optic innervation of the normal colliculus was eliminated by enucleation of the corresponding eye. Under these conditions the remaining optic fibers cross over to innervate extensively the unlesioned denervated colliculus. Simultaneously the inappropriate terminations in the lateral posterior nucleus, found only after a collicular lesion, are reduced. Apparently an increase in the number of appropriate cells available for innervation acts to decrease termination in less appropriate areas.

More complete answers are hindered by serious gaps in our knowledge of even the normal, much less the altered, innervation of these systems. Whether different retinal ganglion cells project to different nuclei or whether the same cells send separate collaterals to the different areas is far from clear, and much less so the temporal sequence of the innervation process. The Fink–Heimer method, applied in normals, appears to show areas of variable projection (Lund et al., 1973; Schneider, 1973), and one has to wonder whether the stain or other experimental factor may not be the variable. One of these "variable" areas is the lateral posterior nucleus of the hamster, a so-called "novel" projection area seen after collicular lesions. It is not entirely ruled out that this and perhaps even other "novel" projections might then be thought of as an amplification of a weak normal projection. Clearly, more evidence is needed before firm conclusions can be drawn.

Although the findings in lower vertebrates indicate a predominate lack of functional molding and modulation, the concept of chemoaffinity in synaptic patterning has never excluded additional effects of learning and other forms of functional plasticity. Observations on the effects of experience in shaping the visual system of mammals seem to indicate a significant functional influence in some species even in the primary visual cortex. The most dramatic examples have come from kitten-rearing experiments in which a surgically induced strabismus, or merely a few days of monocular deprivation during the fourth postnatal week, effectively disrupts the binocularity of cortical neurons (Hubel & Wiesel, 1970); or the exposure of otherwise dark-reared cats to a visual input consisting only of vertical or horizontal lines for even as little as 1 hour causes a pronounced corresponding bias in the orientation of cortical line-detecting cells (Blakemore & Cooper, 1970; Blakemore & Mitchell, 1973; Hirsch & Spinelli, 1970, 1971). Similar changes have been described following presentation for only a day of a moving vertical grating to an anesthetized paralyzed kitten deprived of prior visual experience (Pettigrew & Garey, 1974; see also Pettigrew, Olson, & Barlow, 1973).

Some of the accounts of these findings seem to take us back toward the position of more than 35 years ago, when it was believed that the animal builds its visual system mainly on the basis of environmental exposure and experience. Recent failures to confirm both the long-term (Maffei & Fiorentini, 1974) and short-term orientational effects (Stryker, 1974), plus disagreement on the extent to which line detectors develop without visual experience (Hubel & Wiesel, 1963; Pettigrew, 1974), now complicate the picture.

In any case it appears that in mammals, as in lower forms, the great bulk of the visual system is patterned prefunctionally by the growth process itself. This applies even at the cortical level where a great wealth of structure, including the basic cytoarchitecture and retinotopic projection, binocularity, motion detection circuity, and some orientation selective cells and their basic functional relations can be shown to develop without visual experience. That line detectors of all orientation can be found even if kittens are reared seeing only vertical lines, provided this visual experience is not during the "critical period" (Blakemore, 1974), seems to argue against the fundamental wiring being determined by input. It has long been emphasized (Sperry, 1951a) that the role of function in preserving, reinforcing, or evoking what already is innately prepared and organized in development must be distinguished from that of adding new connections; but also underscored has been the increasing difficulty of keeping such distinctions meaningful as one progresses more deeply into the association centers of the brain (Sperry, 1965a). In general, environmental modification seems best conceived in terms of fine tuning or alignment processes, such as for stereopsis. This is suggested also in the apparent collective changes in receptive field position following small prism-induced disparities (Shlaer, 1971; see chapters in this volume by Grobstein & Chow and by Daniels & Pettigrew for full description).

Thus much of the literature on neural development in mammals directly supports the notion of chemospecificity. The various plasticities that stand out against this background of specificity of connections not only can be readily interpreted within the chemoaffinity framework, but on close examination much of the data would appear even to support it. At the same time these plasticities point up the role in neuronal development of function and of growth factors other than chemoaffinity.

IX. Conclusion

The literature on the formation of retinotectal connections, particularly in the last decade, appears to present numerous confusing discrepancies and contradictions that seem at first sight to defy any consistent interpretation. Further examination, however, along with some recent experimental findings, indicates that the great bulk of the available evidence can probably still be explained in terms of the original chemoaffinity theory only slightly modified by a few conceptual additions and refinements that emerge from the recent disparity and lesion studies.

Acknowledgments

Supported by the F. P. Hixon Fund of the California Institute of Technology and U.S. Public Health Service Grant No. MH-03372.

References

Arora, H. L. Regeneration and selective reconnection of optic nerve fibers following contra-lateral cross in the tectum of the goldfish. *Anatomical Record*, 1966, **154**, 311.

Arora, H. L. Fate of regenerating optic fibers following brain lesions in goldfish. *Anatomical Record*, 1973, **175**, 266.

Arora, H. L., & Sperry, R. W. Optic nerve regeneration after surgical crossunion of medial and lateral optic tracts. *American Zoologist*, 1962, **2**, 389.

Arora, H. L., & Sperry, R. W. Color discrimination after optic nerve regeneration in the fish *Astronotus ocellatus*. *Developmental Biology*, 1963, **7**, 234–243.

Attardi, D. G. & Sperry, R. W. Preferential selection of central pathways by regenerating optic fibers. *Experimental Neurology*, 1963, **7**, 46–64.

Barbera, A. J., Marchase, R. B., & Roth, S. Adhesive recognition and retinotectal specificity. *Proceedings of the National Academy of Sciences, U.S.*, 1973, **70**, 2482–2486.

Baylor, D. A., & Nicholls, J. G. Patterns of regeneration between individual nerve cells in the central nervous system of the leech. *Nature (London) New Biology*, 1971, **232**, 268–270.

Berman, N., & Cynader, M. Comparison of receptive-field organization of the superior colliculus in Siamese and normal cats. *Journal of Physiology (London)*, 1972, **224**, 363–389.

Blakemore, C. Development of functional connexions in the mammalian visual system. *British Medical Bulletin*, 1974, **30**, 152–157.

Blakemore, C., & Cooper, G. F. Development of the brain depends on visual environment. *Nature (London)*, 1970, **228**, 477–478.

Blakemore, C., & Mitchell, D. E. Environmental modification of the visual cortex and the neural basis of learning and memory. *Nature (London)*, 1973, **241**, 467–468.

Chung, S. H., Gaze, R. M., & Stirling, R. V. Abnormal visual function in *Xenopus* following stroboscopic illumination. *Nature (London), New Biology*, 1973, **246**, 186–189.

Cook, J. E., & Horder, T. J. Interactions between optic fibers in their regeneration to specific sites in the goldfish tectum. *Journal of Physiology (London)*, 1974, **241**, 89P–90P.

Crelin, E. S. Excision and rotation of the developing *Amblystoma* optic tectum and subsequent visual recovery. *Journal of Experimental Zoology*, 1952, **120**, 547–578.

Cronly-Dillon, J. R. Units sensitive to direction of movement in the goldfish optic tectum. *Nature (London)*, 1964, **203**, 214–215.

Cronly-Dillon, J. R., & Glaizner, B. Specificity of regenerating optic fibers for left and right optic tecta in goldfish. *Nature (London)*, 1974, **251**, 505–507.

Crossland, W. J., Cowan, W. M., Rogers, L. A., & Kelly, J. P. The specification of the retino-tectal projection in the chick. *Journal of Comparative Neurology*, 1974, **155**, 127–164.

Cunningham, T. J. Sprouting of the optic projection after cortical lesions. *Anatomical Record*, 1972, **172**, 298.

Cunningham, T. J., & Freeman, J. A. Bilateral branching of single ganglion cells. *Society for Neuroscience, 4th Annual Meeting, St. Louis, Mo.*, 1974, Abstract, P. 183.

Cunningham, T. J., & Speas, G. Inversion of anomalous uncrossed projections along the mediolateral axis of the superior colliculus: Implications for retinocollicular specificity. *Brain Research*, 1975, **88**, 73–79.

De Long, R. G., & Coulombre, A. J. Development of the retinotectal topographic projection in the chick embryo. *Experimental Neurology*, 1965, **13**, 351–363.

Edwards, J. S., & Palka, J. Neural regeneration: Delayed formation of central contacts by insect sensory cells. *Science*, 1971, **172**, 591–594.

Feldman, J. D., & Gaze, R. M. The growth of the retina in *Xenopus laevis*: an autoradiographic study II. Retinal growth in compound eyes. *Journal of Embryology and Experimental Morphology*, 1972, **27**, 381–387.

Gaze, R. M. Regeneration of the optic nerve in *Xenopus laevis*. *Quarterly Journal of Experimental Physiology*, 1959, **44**, 290–308.

Gaze, R. M. *The formation of nerve connections*. New York: Academic Press, 1970.

Gaze, R. M. Neuronal specificity. *British Medical Bulletin*, 1974, **30**, 116–121.

Gaze, R. M., & Jacobson, M. A study of the retinotectal projection during regeneration of the optic nerve in the frog. *Proceedings of the Royal Society of London, Ser. B*, 1963, **157**, 420–448.

Gaze, R. M., & Keating, M. J. Further studies on the restoration of the contralateral retinotectal projection following regeneration of the optic nerve in the frog. *Brain Research*, 1970, **21**, 183–195.

Gaze, R. M., Jacobson, M., & Székely, G. The retinotectal projection in *Xenopus* with compound eyes. *Journal of Physiology (London)*, 1963, **165**, 484–499.

Gaze, R. M., Jacobson, M., & Székely, G. On the formation of connexions by compound eyes in *Xenopus*. *Journal of Physiology (London)*, 1965, **176**, 409–417.

Gaze, R. M., & Sharma, S. C. Axial differences in the reinnervation of the goldfish optic tectum by regenerating optic nerve fibers. *Experimental Brain Research*, 1970, **10**, 171–181.

Gaze, R. M., Keating, M. J., Székely, G., & Beazley, L. Binocular interaction in the formation of specific intertectal neuronal connections. *Proceedings of the Royal Society of London, Ser. B*, 1970, **175**, 107–147.

Gaze, R. M., Keating, M. J., & Chung, S. H. The evolution of the retinotectal map during development in *Xenopus*. *Proceedings of the Royal Society of London, Ser. B*, 1974, **185**, 301–330.

Goodman, D. C., & Horel, J. A. Sprouting of optic tract projections in the brain stem of the rat. *Journal of Comparative Neurology*, 1966, **127**, 71–88.

Guillery, R. W. An abnormal retinogeniculate projection in Siamese cats. *Brain Research*, 1969, **14**, 739–741.

Harrison, R. G. On relations of symmetry in transplanted limbs. *Journal of Experimental Zoology*, 1921, **32**, 1–126.

Harrison, R. G. Correlation in the development and growth of the eye studied by means of heteroplastic transplantation. *Archiv für Entwicklungsmechanik Organismen*, 1929, **120**, 1–55.

Hibbard, E. Central integration of developing nerve tracts from supernumary grafted eyes and brain in frog. *Journal of Experimental Zoology*, 1959, **141**, 323–352.

Hibbard, E. Visual recovery following regeneration of the optic nerve through the oculomotor nerve root in *Xenopus*. *Experimental Neurology*, 1967, **19**, 350–356.

Hirsch, H. V. B., & Spinelli, D. N. Visual experience modifies distribution of horizontally and vertically oriented receptive fields in cats. *Science*, 1970, **168**, 869–871.

Hirsch, H. V. B., & Spinelli, D. N. Modification of the distribution of receptive field orientation in cats by selective visual exposure during development. *Experimental Brain Research*, 1971, **13**, 509–527.

Horder, T. J. Retention, by fish optic nerve fibers regenerating to new terminal sites in the tectum, of "chemospecific" affinity for their original sites. *Journal of Physiology (London)*, 1971, **216**, 53P–55P.

Horder, T. J. Electron microscopic evidence in goldfish that different optic nerve fibers regenerate selectively through specific routes into the tectum. *Journal of Physiology (London)*, 1974, **241**, 84P–85P.

Hubel, D. H., & Wiesel, T. N. Receptive fields of cells in striate cortex of very young, visually inexperienced kittens. *Journal of Neurophysiology*, 1963, **26**, 994–1002.

Hubel, D. H., & Wiesel, T. N. The period of susceptibility to the physiological effects of unilateral eye closure in kittens. *Journal of Physiology (London)*, 1970, **206**, 419–436.

Hubel, D. H., & Wiesel, T. N. A study of normal and congenitally abnormal retinogeniculate projections in cats. *Journal of Comparative Neurology*, 1971, **143**, 73–100.

Hunt, R. K. Developmental programming for retinotectal patterns. *Ciba Foundation Symposium*, 1975, **29**, 129–157.

Hunt, R. K., & Jacobson, M. Development and stability of positional information in *Xenopus* retinal ganglion cell. *Proceedings of the National Academy of Sciences U.S.*, 1972, **69**, 780–783. (a)

Hunt, R. K., & Jacobson, M. Specifications of positional information in retinal ganglion cells of *Xenopus*: Stability of the specified state. *Proceedings of the National Academy of Sciences U.S.*, 1972, **69**, 2860–2864. (b)

Hunt, R. K., & Jacobson, M. Neuronal locus specificity: Altered pattern of spatial deployment in fused fragments of embryonic *Xenopus* eyes. *Science*, 1973, **180**, 509–511. (a)

Hunt, R. K., & Jacobson, M. Neuronal specificity revisited. *Current Topics in Developmental Biology*, 1973, **8**, 203–259. (b)

Hunt, R. K., & Jacobson, M. Specification of positional information in retinal ganglion cells of *Xenopus*: Assays for analysis of the unspecified state. *Proceedings of the National Academy of Sciences U.S.*, 1973, **70**, 507–511. (c)

Hunt, R. K., & Jacobson, M. Specification of positional information in retinal ganglion cells of *Xenopus laevis*: Intraocular control of the time of specification. *Proceedings of the National Academy of Sciences U.S.*, 1974, **71**, 3616–3620.

Jacobson, M. Development of neuronal specificity in retinal ganglion cells of *Xenopus*. *Developmental Biology*, 1968, **17**, 202–218. (a)

Jacobson, M. Cessation of DNA synthesis in retinal ganglion cells correlated with the time of specification of their central connections. *Developmental Biology*, 1968, **17**, 219–232. (b)

Jacobson, M. *Developmental neurobiology*. New York: Holt, 1970.

Jacobson, M., & Gaze, R. M. Selection of appropriate tectal connections by regenerating optic nerve fibers in adult goldfish. *Experimental Biology*, 1965, **13**, 418–430.

Kaas, J. H., & Guillery, R. W. The transfer of abnormal visual field representations from the dorsal lateral geniculate nucleus to the visual cortex in Siamese cats. *Brain Research*, 1973, **59**, 61–95.

Kalil, R. E. Formation of new retino-geniculate connections in kittens: Effects of age and visual experience. *Anatomical Record*, 1973, **175**, 353(A).

Kirsche, W., & Kirsche, K. Experimentelle Untersuchungen zur Frage Regeneration und Funktion des Tectum opticum von *Carassius carassius* L. *Zeitschift für mikroskopisch-anatomische Forschung*, 1961, **67**, 140–182.

Lane, R. H., Kaas, J. H., & Allman, J. M. Visuotopic organization of the superior colliculus in normal and Siamese cats. *Brain Research*, 1974. **70**, 413–430.

Levine, R. L., & Jacobson, M. Deployment of optic nerve fibers is determined by positional makers in the frog's tectum. *Experimental Neurology*, 1974, **43**, 527–538.

Lund, R. D., & Lund, J. S. Synaptic adjustment after deafferentation of the superior colliculus of the rat. *Science*, 1971, **171**, 804–807.

Lund, R. D., & Lund, J. S. Reorganization of the retinotectal pathway in rats after neonatal retinal lesions. *Experimental Neurology*, 1973, **40**, 377–390.

Lund, R. D., Cunningham, T. J., & Lund, J. S. Modified optic projections after unilateral eye removal in young rats. *Brain, Behavior and Evolution*, 1973, **8**, 51–72.

Maffei, L., & Fiorentini, A. Geniculate neural plasticity in kittens after exposure to periodic gratings. *Science*, 1974, **186**, 447–449.

Marotte, L. R., & Mark, R. F. The mechanism of selective reinnervation of fish eye muscle: I. Evidence from muscle function during recovery. *Brain Research*, 1970, **19**, 41–51.

Mathers, L. H., & Chow, K. L. Anatomical and electrophysiological studies of axonal sprouting in the rabbit visual system. *Anatomical Record*, 1973, **175**, 385(A).

Maturana, H. R., Lettvin, J. Y., McCulloch, W. S., & Pitts, W. H. Evidence the cut optic nerve fibers in a frog regenerate to their proper places in the tectum. *Science*, 1959, **130**, 1709–1710.

Maturana, H. R., Lettvin, J. Y., McCulloch, W. S., & Pitts, W. H. Anatomy and physiology of vision in the frog (*Rana pipiens*). *Journal of Neurophysiology*, 1960, **43**, 129–175.

McMahon, D. Chemical messengers in development: A hypothesis. *Science*, 1974, **185**, 1012–1021.

Meyer, R. L. Factors affecting regeneration of the retinotectal projection. (Doctoral dissertation, California Institute of Technology, 1974). *Dissertation Abstracts International*, 1975, **35**, 1510B. (Ann Arbor, Mich., University Microfilms No. 74–21603.)

Meyer, R. L. Tests for regulation in the goldfish retinotectal system. *Anatomical Record*, 1975, **181**, 427. (a)

Meyer, R. L. Tests for field regulation in the retinotectal system of goldfish. In D. McMahon & C. F. Fox (Eds.), *Developmental biology: Pattern formation and gene regulation*. New York: Benjamin, 1975, in press. (b)

Meyer, R. L., & Sperry, R. W. Tests for neuroplasticity in the anuran retinotectal system. *Experimental Neurology*, 1973, **40**, 525–539.

Meyer, R. L., & Sperry, R. W. Explanatory models for neuroplasticity in retinotectal connections. In D. G. Stein, J. J. Rosen, & N. Butters (Eds.), *Plasticity and recovery of function in the central nervous system*. New York: Academic Press, 1974, Pp. 45–63.

Moore, R. Y., Björklund, A., & Stenevi, U. Plastic changes in the adrenergic innervation of the rat septal area in response to denervation. *Brain Research*, 1971, **33**, 13–35.

Pettigrew, J. D. The effect of visual experience on the development stimulus specificity by kitten cortical neurones. *Journal of Physiology (London)*, 1974, **237**, 49–74.

Pettigrew, J. D., & Garey, L. J. Selective modification of single neuron properties in the visual cortex of kittens. *Brain Research*, 1974, **66**, 160–164.

Pettigrew, J. D., Olson, C., & Barlow, H. B. Kitten visual cortex: Short-term, stimulus-induced changes in connectivity. *Science*, 1973, **180**, 1202–1203.

Polyak, S. L. *The vertebrate visual system*. Chicago, Ill.: University of Chicago Press, 1957.

Roth, R. L. Normal and regenerated retino-tectal projections in the goldfish. (Doctoral dissertation, Case Western Reserve University, 1972). *Dissertation Abstracts International*, 1972, **33**, 4085B–4086B. (Ann Arbor, Mich., University Microfilms No. 73–6335.)

Roth, R. L. Retinotopic organization of goldfish optic nerve and tract. *Anatomical Record*, 1974, **178**, 453.

Schneider, G. E. Early lesions of superior colliculus: Factors affecting the formation of abnormal retinal projections. *Brain, Behavior and Evolution*, 1973, **8**, 73–109.

Schneider, G. E., & Jhaveri, S. R. Neuroanatomical correlates of spared or altered function after brain lesion in the new born hamster. In D. G. Stein, J. J. Rosen, & N. Butters (Eds.), *Plasticity and recovery of function in the central nervous system*. New York: Academic Press, 1974. Pp. 65–109.

Schwassman, H. O., & Kruger, L. Organization of the visual projection upon the optic tectum of some fresh water fish. *Journal of Comparative Neurology*, 1965, **124**, 113–126.

Scott, M. Y. Functional capacity of compressed retinotectal projection in goldfish. *Anatomical Record*, 1975, **181**, 474.

Sharma, S. C. Redistribution of visual projections in altered optic tecta of adult goldfish. *Proceedings of the National Academy of Sciences U.S.*, 1972, **69**, 2637–2639. (a)

Sharma, S. C. Reformation of retinotectal projections after various tectal ablations in adult goldfish. *Experimental Neurology*, 1972, **34**, 171–182. (b)

Sharma, S. C. Restoration of the visual projection following tectal lesions in goldfish. *Experimental Neurology*, 1972, **35**, 358–365. (c)

Sharma, S. C. Retinotectal connexions of a heterotopic eye. *Nature (London), New Biology*, 1972, **238**, 286–287. (d)

Sharma, S. C. Anomalous retinal projection after removal of contralateral optic tectum in adult goldfish. *Experimental Neurology*, 1973, **41**, 661–669.

Sharma, S. C., & Gaze, R. M. The retinotopic organization of visual responses from tectal reimplants in adult goldfish. *Archives Italiennes de Biologie*, 1971, **109**, 357–366.

Sharma, S. C., & Hollyfield, J. G. Specification of retinal central connections in *Rana pipiens* before the appearance of the first postmitotic ganglion cells. *Journal of Comparative Neurology*, 1974, **155**, 395–307.

Shlaer, R. Shift in binocular disparity causes compensating change in the cortical structure of kittens. *Science*, 1971, **173**, 638–641.

Sperry, R. W. Visuomotor coordination in the newt (*Triturus viridescens*) after regeneration of the optic nerve. *Journal of Comparative Neurology*, 1943, **79**, 33–55.

Sperry, R. W. Optic nerve regeneration with return of vision in anurans. *Journal of Neurophysiology*, 1944, **7**, 57–69.

Sperry, R. W. Restoration of vision after crossing of optic nerves and after contralateral transposition of the eye. *Journal of Neurophysiology*, 1945, **8**, 15–28.

Sperry, R. W. Orderly patterning of synaptic associations in regeneration of intracentral fiber tracts mediating visuomotor coordination. *Anatomical Record*, 1948, **102**, 63–76.

Sperry, R. W. Mechanisms of neural maturation. In S. S. Stevens (Ed.), *Handbook of experimental psychology*. New York: Wiley, 1951. Pp. 236–280. (a)

Sperry, R. W. Regulative factors in the orderly growth of neural circuits. *Growth (Symposium)*, 1951, **10**, 63–87. (b)

Sperry, R. W. Developmental basis of behavior. In A. Roe & G. G. Simpson (Eds.), *Behavior and evolution*. New Haven, Conn.: Yale University Press, 1958. Pp. 128–139.

Sperry, R. W. Chemoaffinity in the orderly growth of nerve fiber patterns and connections. *Proceedings of the National Academy of Sciences U.S.*, 1963, **50**, 703–710.

Sperry, R. W. Embryogenesis of behavioral nerve nets. In R. L. Dehaan & H. Ursprung (Eds.), *Organogenesis*. New York; Holt, 1965a. Pp. 161–186.

Sperry, R. W. Selective communication in nerve nets: impulse specificity vs. connection specificity., *Neurosciences Research Program Bulletin* 1965b, 3(5), 37–43.

Sperry, R. W., & Arora, H. L. Selectivity in regeneration of the oculomotor nerve in the cichlid fish, *Astronotus ocellatus*. *Journal of Embryology and Experimental Morphology*, 1965, **14**, 307–317.

Stone, L. S. Heteroplastic transplantation of eyes between the larvae of two species of *Amblystoma*. *Journal of Experimental Zoology*, 1930, **55**, 193–261.

Stone, L. S. Functional polarization in retinal development and its reestablishment in regenerating retinae of rotated grafted eyes. *Proceedings of the Society for Experimental Biology and Medicine*, 1944, **57**, 13–14.

Stone, L. S. Polarization of the retina and development of vision. *Journal of Experimental Zoology*, 1960, **145**, 85–96.

Straznicky, K. The formation of the optic fibre projection after partial tectal removal in *Xenopus*. *Journal of Embryology and Experimental Morphology*, 1973, **29**, 397–409.

Straznicky, K., & Gaze, R. M. The growth of the retina in *Xenopus laevis*: An autoradiographic study. *Journal of Embryology and Experimental Morphology*, 1971, **26**, 67–79.

Straznicky, K., Gaze, R. M., & Keating, M. J. The retinotectal projections after uncrossing the optic chiasma in *Xenopus* with one compound eye. *Journal of Embryology and Experimental Morphology*, 1971, **26**, 523–542.

Straznicky, K., Gaze, R. M., & Keating, M. J. The retinotectal projection from double-ventral compound eye in *Xenopus laevis*. *Journal of Embryology and Experimental Morphology*, 1974, **31**, 123–137.

Stryker, M. P. Selective exposure does not quickly modify orientation selectivity of visual cortex in paralyzed anesthetized kittens. *Society for Neuroscience, 4th Annual Meeting*, St. Louis, Mo. 1974, Abstract, P. 443.

Székely, G. Untersuchung der Entwicklung optischer Reflex mechanismem an Amphibien larven. *Acta Physiologica Academiae Scientiarum Hungaricae*, 1954, **6**, Suppl. 18.

Székely, G. Regulationstendenzer in der Ausbildung der "Funktionellen Spezifität" der Retinoanlage bei *Triturus vulgaris*. *Archiv für Entwicklungsmechanik der Organismen*, 1957, **150**, 48–60.

Tsang, Y. Visual centers in blinded rats. *Journal of Comparative Neurology*, 1937, **66**, 211–261.

Wartzok, D., & Marks, W. B. Directionally selective visual units recorded in optic tectum of the goldfish. *Journal of Neurophysiology*, 1973, **36**, 588–604.

Weiss, P. Das Resonanzprinzip der Nerventätigkeit. *Wiener Klinische Wochenschrift*, 1931, **39**, 1–17.

Weiss, P. *Principles of development*. New York: Holt, 1939.

Westerman, R. S. Specificity in regeneration of optic and olfactory pathways in teleost fish. D. R. Curtis & A. K. McIntyre (Eds.), *Studies in physiology*. Berlin: Springer, 1965. Pp. 263–269.

Yoon, M. Reorganization of retinotectal projection following surgical operations on the optic tectum in goldfish. *Experimental Neurology*, 1971, **33**, 395–411.

Yoon, M. Reversibility of the reorganization of retinotectal projection in goldfish. *Experimental Neurology*, 1972, **35**, 565–577. (a)

Yoon, M. Transposition of the visual projection from the nasal hemiretina onto the foreign rostral zone of the optic tectum in goldfish. *Experimental Neurology*, 1972, **37**, 451–462. (b)

Yoon, M. Retention of the original topographic polarity by the 180° rotated tectal reimplant in young adult goldfish. *Journal of Physiology (London)*, 1973, **233**, 575–588.

Section 3

NEUROSPECIFICITY: EXPERIENCE

INTRODUCTION

The present section covers visual specificity in mammals, principally rabbits and cats. As mentioned in the introduction to the preceding section, research on the development of neural specificity in the mammalian visual system has concerned later (postnatal) stages than that on amphibians and fish. There has also been a concomitantly greater emphasis on the role of experience in mammalian development. These two trends are "accidental," and they should not obscure the probable importance of molecular and biochemical factors at early stages of neurogenesis in mammals.

It is the cortex that has received the greatest amount of attention relative to other parts of the visual pathway. There are four basic kinds of functional specificities which have been examined to date. (1) *Orientation specificity*: defined as that angle of a slit of light which produces the most marked electrical response in a particular cell (analogous to the narrowness of a frequency "tuning" curve in an auditory neuron). These angles can be broad or narrow, depending on the experiential and maturational history of the animal. The trend in development is for more cells to become orientation specific and for oriented cells to become more specific in their orientation. There is disagreement on whether experience is essential to perfect the orientation specificity of cortical cells, especially in kittens (Daniels & Pettigrew in this section). (2) *Motion or direction specificity*: the particular direction of movement of light which produces the most marked response in a particular cell. Directional selectivity may develop earlier than orientation selectivity, but that is not yet certain. (3) *Binocularity*: simply defined as whether a cell is activated by one or both eyes. Most cortical cells are normally capable of being excited by either eye and are thus "binocular." Monocular rearing experience reduces the number of binocular cells relative to the normally reared kitten or to *total* visual deprivation. Binocularity is particularly interesting because it shows the effects of abnormal experience (monocular rearing) but not total deprivation. (4) *Binocular fusion (disparity)*: binocular cells are maximally responsive to stimulation impinging simultaneously on particular points of the two retinas (corresponding to stereo-scopic vision and our appreciation of depth). The development of binocular disparity is a function of experience—it is the sole neural specificity on which there is no disagreement on its experience-dependence.

One of the recurrent conceptual themes in the present volume is the view that a demonstration of experiential modification of neural structure or function does not necessarily signify that such experience plays a role in the normal (species-typical) maturation of said structure or function. This theme is epitomized in the first chapter in this section by Grobstein and Chow. These authors make a clear division between experiential effects that demonstrate the plasticity of neuronal function ("experience-sensitive pro-cesses") and those that demonstrate that experience is required for neuronal function to attain the normal specificity of the mature state ("experience-dependent processes"). An important consequence of this viewpoint is the appreciation of the fact that experience can normally play a role in develop-ment (facilitative, let's say), but it may not be necessary for the function (or structure) in question to eventually reach its characteristic level of specif-icity. It is within this conceptual framework that these authors are able to raise the possibility that the neural specificities which develop in the rabbit *without experience* are no different from those same specificities which deve-lop in the cat *with experience*. In the latter case, Grobstein and Chow suggest, experience may merely hasten a process that is capable of self-differen-tiation (i.e., via intrinsic dynamics of neural functional interaction).

An investigative question of some moment is whether the rabbit is con-siderably less plastic than the kitten, or whether the former's precocious sensorimotor maturation makes it appear less sensitive to the influence of experience, while the kitten's less precocious development makes it ap-pear more susceptible to experience. Both Grobstein and Chow, whose review emphasizes the rabbit, and Daniels and Pettigrew, who exphasize the kitten, address themselves to this question. The latter also address them-selves to the specificities at the lower relay stations of the mammalian visual system (retinal ganglion cells and lateral geniculate body, as well as the superior colliculus). Rabbits and cats process ("analyze") visual stimulation at subcortical levels differently, the former relying more on subcortical (particularly retinal) analysis than the latter. Since that is true, one wonders whether the rabbit may show more plasticity than the cat at lower levels of the visual system or whether our assumption of greater plasticity at the cor-tical level continues to be correct even when analytic functions differ. The findings thus far do not suggest developmental plasticity at the retinal level in the rabbit.

RECEPTIVE FIELD ORGANIZATION IN THE MAMMALIAN VISUAL CORTEX: THE ROLE OF INDIVIDUAL EXPERIENCE IN DEVELOPMENT

PAUL GROBSTEIN AND KAO LIANG CHOW

Department of Pharmacological and Physiological Sciences
University of Chicago
Chicago, Illinois, and *Department of Neurology*
Stanford University School of Medicine
Stanford, California

I. Introduction

Western scientific tradition recognizes two sources for the adaptiveness characteristic of living organisms. On the one hand, there is the genome, which can be thought of as a summary of many generations of previous experience in dealing with the environment. On the other hand, there is the individual experience of an organism, information acquired within his own lifetime. These two information sources—the genetic and the ontogenetic—interact during the development of the organism.

In practice, modern investigators of nervous system development are inclined to grant a fair measure of primacy to genetic information in the determination of patterns of neuronal connections. This has not always been the case. In the early part of this century, there was a strong feeling that neuronal connectivity was too complex to be based solely on genetic information. Since the necessary connections are those which produce adaptive behavior, it seemed reasonable that, during development, neuronal processes might grow with little intrinsic control, leaving it to individual experience to select those connections which produce functionally appropriate behavior.

This proposition was explicitly tested and rejected by Roger Sperry and his colleagues, who showed, in a number of different experimental paradigms, that connections producing nonadaptive behavior persist indefinitely, rather than being corrected [see Sperry (1965) for review of his own studies as well as the historical context]. Subsequent work has documented the enormous order present in the developing nervous system long before individual experience—in terms of information from the environment processed by the nervous system—can possibly play a role. The upshot is a greatly diminished concern as to whether genetic information is adequate to create rich patterns of specific interconnectivity, though it must be admitted, no great improvement in our understanding of how it does so.

Recently, however, interest in the possibility that ontogenetic information is incorporated into the developing nervous system has been reawakened by single-unit studies in the mammalian visual system. The fundamental observation is that the receptive field organization of neurons sampled from the striate cortex of different individuals may vary markedly, depending on the animal's early visual experience. Given two assumptions—that the samples are representative of the striate cortical population and that differences in receptive field organization indicate differences in neuronal connections—this observation indicates that neuronal connectivity can be affected by individual experience. We will term this "experience-sensitivity."

The importance of the first assumption may not be immediately obvious. It derives from an intrinsic limitation in the single-unit techniques used in most of the studies reviewed here: the inability to monitor the effects of visual experience on a single neuron. Instead, samples of the neuronal population of the striate cortex are made, and these samples are compared for animals with different visual experience. When the samples differ with respect to some parameter, the inference is made that visual experience has modified the behavior of single neurons. As will become clear, this inference is not always defensible; depending on the care which is taken, differences in samples may actually reflect changes in the detectability of neurons, rather than changes in the behavior of individual neurons. Evaluation of the second assumption, that receptive field organization reflects the pattern of connections, is somewhat outside the scope of this review and will, for the most part, be accepted as given.

The demonstration of experience-sensitivity, though providing *prima facie* evidence, is not, however, equivalent to the demonstration that ontogenetic information is incorporated during normal development. An alternative possibility is that experience is necessary to maintain a connection pattern which is elaborated solely on the basis of genetic information. The fundamental question is whether the functional appropriateness of neuronal connections depends on visual experience. Only in cases where the answer to this question is "yes" will we refer to the underlying process as experience *dependent*.

In general, this may be an exceedingly difficult answer to come by. In the simplest case, where the adaptive value of a particular set of connections is known, it is necessary to demonstrate, first, that such connections are not made in lieu of some critical piece of ontogenetic information, and second, that the connections are made differently and appropriately in animals with different experiences. The real problem comes when the functional significance of connections is not known, since one has no idea of what the critical piece of information might be nor whether the varying connections are appropriate to the varying experiences.

In this chapter, we will review single-unit studies on the role of visual experience in the development of the mammalian striate cortex, with particular attention to whether they demonstrate incorporation of ontogenetic information into the developing nervous system. In Section II we summarize the initial evidence indicating that visual experience affects striate receptive field organization. This evidence falls into the *prima facie* category, an early challenge being that the development of the striate cortex is essentially complete before visual experience is available to the developing organism. The legitimacy of this challenge is evaluated in Section III where we consider studies of the visually naive animal. Our conclusion in that section—that the development of receptive field organization is not complete, at least in some species, when visual experience first becomes available during normal development—permits, but does not of course compel, the conclusion that ontogenetic information is incorporated into the developing nervous system.

In Section III we also consider studies comparing receptive field development in animals receiving normal visual experience and those which are prevented from acquiring visual experience. These studies are important in providing a base line against which to evaluate the effects of more refined forms of abnormal visual experience and in evaluating whether experimental samples are adequately representative of the striate neuronal population. They are also concordant with the studies discussed in Section II in that the two aspects of receptive field organization which can be affected by abnormal visual experience—binocular specificity and orientation specificity—also normally develop after visual experience becomes available in some animals, and in these animals development of both can be delayed by delaying the onset of visual experience.

In Section IV we discuss the effects of abnormal visual experience on the development of these two aspects of receptive field organization and consider whether any other aspects are experience sensitive. A fundamental question is whether the sampling problem referred to previously can account for the observed effects or whether they actually represent cases of modified receptive field organization. For binocularity, the evidence is quite strong that abnormal visual experience produces modified receptive field organization. The evidence is less strong for orientation specificity; however, the time course of the development of orientation specificity is clearly affected by abnormal visual experience in some animals.

Whether the experience-*sensitivity* of the development of binocular and orientation specificity indicates experience-*dependence*, in the sense already described, is evaluated in Section V. In that section we also propose a general principle of experience-dependent development: that it is found where genetic information has some intrinsic limitation in assuring functionally appropriate connections and therefore leaves open a range of possibilities from which individual experience realizes one. This notion of ontogenetic factors operating within the constraints of a genetic plan is of course one of the recognized principles of development. Section VI is devoted to a survey of information relating to the mechanisms of experience-dependent development. It includes a brief description of anatomical work which supports one of our initial assumptions, namely, that differences in receptive field organization indicate differences in neuronal connections.

II. Initial Evidence

Hubel and Wiesel, shortly after their classical description of the receptive field characteristics of cat cortical cells, explicitly investigated the possibility that connections responsible for these characteristics were formed under the influence of visual experience. The possibility was made real by abundant behavioral evidence that animals deprived of visual experience early in life showed subsequent significant visual deficits (Riesen, 1966; see chapter by Tees). Hubel and Wiesel attacked the problem in two ways. They asked, first, whether neurons in the kitten before eye-opening, i.e., before visual experience, displayed adult properties and, second, whether animals raised with various forms of abnormal visual experience exhibited neurons with normal adult properties. These two approaches gave somewhat conflicting answers to the broad question of the involvement of visual experience in the development of the visual system. In brief, the answer to the first seemed to be "yes," neurons are present with typical adult properties before eye-opening (Hubel & Wiesel, 1963). The answer to the second was "no," animals raised with abnormal visual experience do not have normal distributions of adult properties (Wiesel & Hubel, 1963b).

This quandary, on the one hand that cortical neurons seem to have their functional connections before visual experience begins, and on the other hand, that subsequent visual experience seems to change the connections, has been a touchstone for much of subsequent work in the field, since it leaves unresolved the question of whether sensory input participates in patterning connections during normal development. Hubel and Wiesel interpreted their data as indicating that it does not. The basis for this was twofold. The first was the already mentioned evidence from animals assayed before visual experience. Since the naive state is already fully developed, they argued that there is no normal role for visual experience to play. The second point was the nature of the receptive field organization abnormalities produced by abnormal visual experience. Hubel and Wiesel focused on the binocularity of striate cortical neurons, their ability to be excited through either eye. Animals raised with various kinds of imbalances of visual experience generally have only monocular neurons. It seemed relatively straightforward to interpret this as a destruction of connections already present in the visually naive state.

This interpretation, despite the lack of an explanation for the undisputed sensitivity to abnormal experience, was generally accepted until Hirsch and Spinelli (1970) and Blakemore and Cooper (1970) independently reported that a second property of striate cortical receptive fields—their orientation specificity—was strongly influenced by visual experience. Kittens raised in environments consisting solely of vertical or of horizontal stripes subsequently exhibit an absence of neurons responsive to orientations greatly different from those experienced. Hubel and Wiesel (1963) had already suggested that orientation specificity, like binocularity, was present in the naive animal. To imagine changes in orientation specificity as resulting from a destruction of connections from a normally wired state is much less straightforward than to imagine shifts from binocular to monocular. Whether the mechanism is destructive or not, the effect seemed to be less maladaptive in a functional sense, since the outcome was one that "mirrored" the environment.

Still, the question of whether visual experience plays a role in normal development could not be regarded as fully settled. While the orientation effect seemed to be a response in agreement with the environmental stimuli, it nonetheless was destructive in that it left the cortex in an impoverished state with respect to a normal cortex, and, accepting Hubel and Wiesel, with respect to a visually naive cortex. This dramatizes the serious possibility (which must be considered for binocularity as well) that the effect of abnormal visual experience is not to alter patterns of connections but to bias the sample of neurons detected by a microelectrode, i.e., that there has not been a change in properties of individual neurons but rather that missing receptive field properties are characteristic of neurons that are not being sampled by the microelectrode.

In summary, by the end of 1970, there was strongly suggestive evidence that the striate cortical receptive field organization of the cat could be influenced by early visual experience. Two aspects of receptive field organization were implicated: binocularity and orientation specificity. In the former, though not so clearly in the latter, sampling bias seemed not to be an issue. Both effects, however, in light of Hubel and Wiesel's observations on the visually naive kittens, were interpretable as deteriorations of an initially fully developed system. If this interpretation was accepted, one would be left with a sensitivity of the system to destructive influence of sensory input but, by default, no role for sensory input to play in its normal formation. In what follows, we take up first the question of whether development of receptive field organization is complete before visual experience begins, and then the question of whether experience-dependent processes exist. We follow this order because studies on the visually naive animal provide significant insights into the effects of abnormal visual experience. More important, if development is normally completed before the onset of visual experience, then it seems unlikely that experience-dependent processes participate.

III. The Visually Naive Animal

There is now in the literature compelling evidence for both cat and rabbit that the visual pathways are not fully developed when the animal first opens its eyes, as judged by single-unit behavior in striate cortex. Before discussing this, it is worth noting the restricted character of the opposing claim of Hubel and Wiesel (1963). The original paper concluded, "many of the connections responsible for the highly organized behavior of cells . . . must be present at birth or within a few days of it." The cautious conclusion was appropriate for two reasons. On the one hand, the possibility always exists that new experiments will reveal new response properties of cortical cells. Hubel and Wiesel concentrated on binocularity and selectivity to the direction of movement of lines moving perpendicular to their long axis. Such properties are present in visually naive neurons. Subsequent work, discussed below, suggests that other properties, also typical of adult neurons, are not.

The second reason for the cautious conclusion may be more fundamental. While some neurons displayed the adult properties assayed for, not all did. In comparison with a normal adult, in the naive animal many fewer cells were recorded in a penetration, some of those recorded displayed less specificity, and there was some tendency to reduced effectiveness of the ipsilateral eye. In short, Hubel and Wiesel appropriately emphasized that single cells could display highly organized behavior without prior visual experience, but, considering cells in the striate cortex as a population, the evidence is not sufficient to insist it is fully developed before visual experience begins.

A population approach to the development of cortical receptive field organization was undertaken in the rabbit. These studies (Grobstein, Chow, Spear, & Mathers, 1973; Mathers, Chow, Spear, & Grobstein, 1974) showed that the striate cortex of a rabbit pup just before eye-opening differs from that of an adult (Chow, Masland, & Stewarts 1971; Hughes, 1971) in three ways: (1) of cells encountered in the pup, somewhat fewer are responsive to visual stimulation; (2) of those responsive to visual stimulation, a higher percentage are imprecise or indefinable in terms of their stimulus requirements, these cells are termed "indefinite;" and (3) no cells are found that prefer oriented bars or are selective for direction of stimulus movement. Directional cells and cells preferring oriented stimuli first appear after eye-opening, coincident with a decline in the percentage of indefinite cells. The time courses of these changes were followed up to about 2 weeks after eye-opening, but in fact continue somewhat beyond that time, and are illustrated in Fig. 1.

More recently, the dependence on patterned visual experience of the developmental transitions that normally follow eye-opening have been studied in the rabbit (Grobstein, Chow, & Fox, 1975). In these studies, one eye of rabbit pups was prevented from opening at the normal time by lid suture. Since the visual pathways in rabbit are almost entirely crossed, this provided a control, normally experienced cortex (contralateral to the normally opening eye) and an experimental, deprived cortex (contralateral to the sutured eye) in one animal. Both cortices were sampled in a number of animals about 2 weeks after eye-opening, a time when much of the transitions described previously has occurred in normal animals. The expected transitions did indeed occur in the control cortices of the monocularly deprived animals (open circles in Fig. 1). The deprived cortices of the same

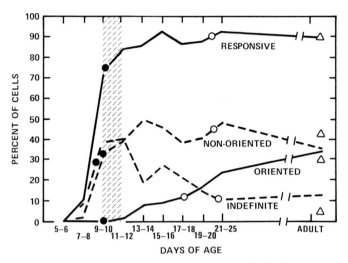

FIG. 1.   Time course of receptive field development in rabbit visual cortex and effects of delayed eye-opening. The upper solid curve shows the percentage of units encountered that were responsive to any form of visual stimulation at the ages indicated on the abscissa in normally reared rabbits. The age of which the eyes open is indicated by the shading. One interrupted curve ("indefinite") shows the percentage of units which though responsive could not be placed in a receptive field category. The other two curves show the percentages of units that fell into receptive field categories characteristically lacking, and having, orientation specificity (Grobstein *et al.*, 1973; Mathers *et al.*, 1974). Data for adults are taken from Chow *et al.*, 1971. Directionally selective neurons are not included in this figure.

Open circles show the percentage of units falling into these same four categories in the experienced cortices of monocularly deprived rabbits of 20–25 days of age. Filled circles show the percentages for the deprived cortices of the same animals (Grobstein *et al.*, 1975). These symbols have been placed on the curves of normal development according to the values they represent. Their clustering around 20 days for experienced, and around 10 days for deprived, cortices illustrates retardation of development in the latter. Triangles show the percentages for animals deprived for 3 months or longer (Chow & Spear, 1974).

animals, however, did not undergo the transitions expected from their age. In fact, in terms of percentage of nonresponsive cells and of indefinite cells and in terms of a total lack of cells preferring oriented stimuli, the deprived cortices were essentially indistinguishable from those of a normal animal sampled just before eye-opening (filled circles in Fig. 1). The only difference from such animals was the appearance of directional cells.

These studies represent an attempt to deal with the cortical population as a whole in the developing animal, both normal and deprived. An implicit assumption is that the percentages of cells falling into the various categories are a rough measure of the actual proportions of such cells in the cortex and, consequently, that changes in these percentages are indicative of transitions in the response characteristics of existing cells. While not directly testable, the assumption provides the most parsimonious interpretation of the available data. Explanations involving atrophy of particular cell types or changes in their detectability by microelectrodes require complicated and *ad hoc* assumptions of correlated adjustments in several classes of receptive field types to account for the evidence. Whatever the ambiguity related to detectability, there is a significant reduction in sampling bias associated with the inclusion of indefinite and nonresponsive neurons in the reported data.

Substantially similar results have recently been reported for the cat (Barlow & Pettigrew, 1971; Pettigrew, 1974). In addition to orientation and direction specificity, the specificity of binocular fusion was investigated. In these studies attempts were made to distinguish orientation from direction selectivity by comparing selectivity to spots and bars. Previous workers had not made such a distinction. At the time of eye-opening, kitten cortical neurons display poor specificity with respect to all three parameters: direction, orientational, and fusional selectivity. Directional selectivity develops fairly quickly after eye-opening and orientation selectivity some 2 weeks later, at the same time as fusional specificity. With respect to these parameters, animals 2–6 weeks old who had been deprived of visual experience by lid suture looked essentially like animals just before eye-opening, except for an increased percentage of cells showing directional selectivity.

The parallels between rabbit and cat data are obvious. Cells in the kitten lacking any specificity presumably correspond to the indefinite cells in the rabbit. Their acquisition of specificity following eye-opening may correspond to the transition from indefinite to oriented receptive field types hypothesized in rabbit. This transition, with respect to orientation, but not direction specificity, can be prevented from occurring at the normal time by preventing eye-opening. Explicit information is not available on the percentage of nonresponsive cells in neonatal kitten cortex but such cells are characteristic of deprived animals and, as already noted, many fewer cells are recorded in a pass through neonatal, as opposed to adult, cortex. This suggests that an increase of responsive cells following eye-opening, an increase which is sensitive to deprivation as described in rabbit, may well be the case in cat as well. Fusional specificity, characteristic of the predominantly binocular visual system of the cat, has no counterpart in the predominantly monocular rabbit visual system.

Two conclusions are clear from the cat and rabbit work. The first is that, as judged by single-unit response properties in visual cortex, the visual system is not fully developed before visual experience begins. Some cells seem to be not yet responsive, and many of those which are responsive are poorly specific along several stimulus parameters. The second conclusion is that the development of specificity along some of these parameters normally follows eye-opening and can be delayed by delaying eye-opening. The deprivation effects seen in rabbits 20–25 days old represent a failure to continue normal development, not a destruction of connections.

There is a third tentative conclusion about the visually naive animal which has been most explicitly documented for the rabbit, but which we suspect may apply to cat as well. While preventing an eye from opening prevents the correlated receptive field transitions from occurring at the normal time, it does not absolutely prevent their occurrence. Chow and Spear (1974) have reported that after 3 months or more of either monocular or binocular lid suture, the receptive field organization of the rabbit is indistinguishable from that of a normally experienced animal. This is indicated by triangular symbols in Fig. 1. It seems that the system can eventually catch up, and it is interesting to note that such "normalization" has been described anatomically in the visual cortex of the deprived mouse (Gyllenstein, Malmfors, & Norrlin, 1965). Whether prolonged deprivation will eventually lead to a subsequent degenerative process is an open question.

In the cat, the situation is less clear. The relative insensitivity of the appearance of directional sensitivity to deprivation in cat, as in rabbit, has already been noted. Pettigrew (1974) reports an occasional orientation selective cell in binocularly deprived 2–6-week-old kittens, though no disparity-specific cells. Blakemore and Van Sluyters (1974) note some cells with an "oriented bias" in a single 8-week-old binocularly deprived kitten. Disparity specificity was not evaluated in the earlier literature, and orientation and direction specificity were not clearly distinguished. However, Wiesel and Hubel (1965a) reported 41% "normal" cells in binocularly deprived $2\frac{1}{2}$–$4\frac{1}{2}$-month kittens. They also reported 32% "abnormal but responsive," meaning responsive over a wide range of directions of movement of a bar as well as a tendency to fatigue, and 27% nonresponsive. Ganz, Fitch, and Satterberg (1968) reported 12% nonresponsive in a small sample of cells from binocularly deprived 12–18-month-old animals. All the remaining cells were responsive to only one or two of the four tested directions of movement.

The point of this discussion is to raise the possibility that binocular deprivation in the cat has the same effect as does monocular deprivation on the deprived cortex of the rabbit; that is, it slows but does not stop transitions from nonresponsive to responsive and from nonoriented ("indefinite") to oriented. If one accepts the "normal" cell of Wiesel and Hubel (1965a) and the cells with restricted directional sensitivity of Ganz et al. (1968) as oriented, then there is a clear increase of oriented cells in older visually naive animals. Similarly, there is a decrease in nonoriented or "indefinite" cells. There is insufficient evidence in the literature to say what percentage of cells in the neonatal cat are nonresponsive, but allowing for the small sample, that percentage may decline between $2\frac{1}{4}$–$4\frac{1}{2}$ months and 12–18 months. If this interpretation is correct, the retardation of development brought about by deprivation in the cat is much more extreme than in the rabbit, in the sense that "normalization" under continued deprivation occurs over a much larger time course.

The finding of abnormally responsive and nonresponsive cells in binocularly deprived cats has been interpreted as a deterioration of preexisting connections. The present interpretation offers a major revision in that it proposes that these cells have not yet formed connections due to deprivation-caused delayed development, rather than that they have lost them. The reconsideration seems warranted in view of the rabbit studies, which show that deprivation causes a continuance of the preexperience status quo, rather than a deterioration. While we wish to draw attention to the possibility of delayed development in cat, we explicitly do not rule out the possibility that continued deprivation may lead to a subsequent destructive process.

The issue of nonresponsive and indefinite cells is crucial to interpreting the effects of abnormal visual experience. As noted in the Introduction, the inference that abnormal distributions of receptive field properties in a sample of neurons indicate that visual experience affects their connections requires the assumption that the sample is an adequate representation of a stable population of neurons. In the case of the results of selective orientation rearing, the *a priori* possibility exists that neurons responsive to nonexperienced orientations are not detectable because they have atrophied or because they have either lost or failed to develop their connections. Similar possibilities apply for abnormal binocular experience. If one of these possibilities is correct, then the effect of abnormal visual experience has not been to influence the connectivity of detectable neurons, but rather to make some detectable and others not. In general, atrophy on the scale necessary seems not to accompany abnormal visual experience. However, in many cases indefinite and nonresponsive neurons are present. These must be considered in determining whether a sampling problem, rather than modification of connections, accounts for abnormal distributions of receptive field properties following various abnormal visual experience regimes.

Wiesel and Hubel (1974) have quite recently reported results from a study of the visually naive macaque monkey. They recorded from one monkey at 2 days of age and from three subjected to binocular deprivation from 2 to up to 38 days. In addition, they recorded from one 21-day normally reared animal and one animal binocularly deprived from 21 to 49 days. Normal binocularity and orientation specificity were observed in the 2-day and 21-day normal animals. Of the 23 neurons in the former animal, none were nonresponsive or poorly orientation specific. The binocularly deprived animals exhibited some loss of binocularity, as well as some poorly driven and poorly specific neurons. Wiesel and Hubel concluded, much as they had earlier for the cat, that cortical circuitry is well developed in advance of visual experience and that the effect of deprivation is to cause the deterioration of the previously formed connections. This interpretation is opposed on both counts to the situation in rabbit and probably in cat. There is obviously no *a priori* reason why different developmental phenomena cannot exist in these different animals, particularly given the relatively mature state of the visual system in the monkey. There is apparently a genuine difference in the degree of orientation specificity in the neonatal monkey cortex as opposed to that in cat or rabbit.

In part, though, the differences are ones of interpretation. In the interest of clarifying the issues, we offer here an alternative interpretation of the monkey data. With respect to binocularity, there is no conflict with Barlow and Pettigrew (1971) and Pettigrew (1974) in the cat, since Wiesel and Hubel (1974) did not attempt to assay fusional specificity with the requisite precision. With respect to orientation specificity, the issue is not whether, in the neonate, some cells display it, but rather whether the same fraction of the population displays it as in a normally experienced animal. In essence, the issue turns on the presence of poorly specific and nonresponsive neurons in the binocularly deprived monkeys and their absence in the 2-day-old animal.

In rabbit, the evidence is quite compelling that nonresponsive and poorly specific neurons normally become specifically responsive following initiation of visual experience. Deprivation delays this transition; the presence of nonresponsive and poorly specific neurons represents therefore the retention of a neonatal state rather than destruction of existing connections. The sample reported by Wiesel and Hubel (1974) from their 2-day animal is not large enough to be certain that nonresponsive and poorly specific neurons are not a significant component of the neonatal monkey cortex. The presence of nonresponsive neurons is particularly difficult to evaluate since detection depends on the presence of spontaneous activity. If spontaneous activity is low or absent, a significant reservoir of neurons may be missed by microelectrode sampling. Were this to be the case in the neonatal monkey, sampling bias would favor responsive neurons. Subsequently, as spontaneous activity increased [as is characteristic of cortical maturation (cf. Mathers *et al.*, 1974)], nonresponsive neurons would become detectable. A later sample would then show a higher percentage of nonresponsive neurons, as observed in the binocularly deprived animals.

For this reason, it seems to us that the issue of the development of orientation specificity in the monkey is not settled. What does seem clear is that some neurons are orientation specific without significant visual experience; this is also true of deprived rabbit and probably of cat. Whether the time course of development of orientation specificity of any neurons in the monkey can be affected by delaying the onset of visual experience is unclear.

In summary, there is strong evidence for the rabbit and strongly suggestive evidence in the cat that the visual cortex is not wired and waiting for the eyes to open, but rather that there is an ongoing developmental process which spans the time when patterned visual experience first becomes available. The process includes transitions from poorly specific to more specific receptive field organization and probably from visually nonresponsive to visually responsive. Several of the developmental events which normally follow eye-opening can be affected, at least in their time course, by preventing the animal from receiving the normal visual experience. Visual experience, then, in the terms used by Gottlieb in the introduction to this volume, has at least a facilitatory effect on receptive field development. The connections subserving orientation specificity in the rabbit and those subserving orientation as well as fusional specificity in the cat seem to be sensitive. In the cat it is not known for certain whether either will develop despite continuous long-term deprivation. Finally, it is worth noting explicitly what Hubel and Wiesel properly stressed: much of cortical responsiveness *is* established prior to visual experience. This is perhaps most clearly demonstrated in the rabbit, which, in the normal adult, has several nonoriented but well-defined receptive field types (concentric, motion, uniform); these, unlike the oriented types, are clearly present before eye-opening. In the cat, which has predominantly oriented receptive field types, a correspondingly larger fraction of the neurons may be expected to be nonresponsive or indefinite at the time of eye-opening.

IV. Effects of Abnormal Visual Experience

If there has been some controversy about the first of Hubel and Wiesel's observations, i.e., that the naive cortex is fully developed, there has been none about the second: abnormal early visual experience produces dramatic effects on striate receptive field organization. Their elegant experiments on the effects of imbalances and incongruities of input to the two eyes in the kitten have been repeatedly confirmed and have led to an outpouring of experiments by others exploring new animals and new ways of influencing receptive field organization by early visual experience. Our feeling is that this work warrants the conclusion that there are in mammalian visual system development at least two independent processes that normally are sensitive to sensory input. These processes are revealed by the abnormalities in binocular fusion originally described by Wiesel and Hubel (1963b) and Hubel and Wiesel (1965), and those in orientation specificity described independently by Hirsch and Spinelli (1970) and Blakemore and Cooper (1970). We will discuss, first, effects on binocularity, then the effects on orientation specificity, and finally, consider some other parameters of receptive field organization.

A. Abnormalities in Binocular Experience

The effects of early abnormal visual input on binocularity of striate cortical cells represent the best analysis available of an experience-sensitive process. Not only has the process been investigated by a variety of abnormal experience regimes and in a number of animals, but a morphological correlate has been investigated. Discussion of the latter is postponed to Section V.

Wiesel and Hubel (1963b, 1965a, 1965b) provided the original evidence that binocular properties of cat striate cortex could be influenced by abnormal visual experience. They raised animals deprived of vision in one eye by either lid suture or coverage by a translucent occluder. In five animals recorded from at 8–14 weeks of age, 181 of 199 cells could be driven only by the experienced eye. Fifteen cells could not be driven at all, and the vast majority of the remaining cells, which were influenced by the deprived eye, had poor response selectivity. This was compared to a normal adult animal, in which the vast majority of neurons can be influenced by both eyes. Ganz et al. (1968) also found reduced numbers of binocular neurons in animals deprived for 1–6 months, but did not find any dominance of the experienced eye. Following reverse suture a slight increase in the ability of the deprived eye to drive cortical cells, accompanied by some decrease in nonresponsive cells, has been reported (Wiesel & Hubel, 1965b); this was confirmed by Chow and Stewart (1972).

An important additional observation made by Wiesel and Hubel (1963b) was that the severity of the deprivation effect depended markedly on the time at which deprivation was initiated. Normal visual experience for 1–2 months significantly reduced the deprivation effect, and in adult cats 3 months of deprivation had no effect at all. A more complete study (Hubel & Wiesel, 1970) indicated that monocular deprivation is particularly effective between 4 and 8 weeks. This clearly indicates that sensitivity to visual deprivation is a developmental effect, restricted to a particular stage. What remains unresolved is whether the stage is defined by chronological age or amount of prior visual experience.

Much the most interesting aspect of this monocular deprivation effect is the interdependence it reveals between the two eyes in the cat. The ability of one deprived eye to activate cortical neurons is significantly greater if the other eye is also deprived than if it is left open (Wiesel & Hubel, 1965a). This has given rise to the notion that there may be competition between afferents representing the two eyes for synaptic targets in the cortex.

These monocular deprivation experiments, like those with binocular deprivation, have been interpreted as revealing a deterioration of previously existing connections from the deprived eye. A reinterpretation, as in the binocular case, is worth considering. If it is correct that there are a large number of connections yet to be made in the kitten at the time of eye-opening, then those from the deprived eye might be expected to be made on a slower time course than those from the experienced eye. Particularly given the possibility of large numbers of initially nonresponsive cells, the shift in the ocular dominance histogram under monocular deprivation may represent a more rapid formation of connections by the experienced eye, with no destruction of connections from the deprived eye at all.

Two additional forms of abnormal visual experience leading to a reduction in binocularly activated cells, as compared to normal adults, were reported by Hubel and Wiesel (1965). Kittens were raised either with alternating occlusion, in which one eye was covered one day and the other the next, or with a surgically induced strabismus, produced by cutting one extraocular muscle. In both cases, each eye drove approximately equal numbers of cortical cells, but there was a great reduction (somewhat larger in the former case) in numbers of cells activated by both eyes. These animals seemed not to have the nonresponsive or indefinite cells characteristic of monocularly and binocularly deprived animals.

In summary, it appears that normal binocularity in the cat cortex will be absent in the face of either nonsimultaneous or asynchronous patterned visual input to the two eyes. By the latter is meant that the two eyes must be looking at the same thing. Hirsch and Spinelli (1971) reported a particularly dramatic instance of this: cats raised with goggles presenting different stimuli to the two eyes lacked binocularly activated cells.

We have, to some extent, offered an interpretation of the effects on binocularity consistent with the delayed development picture described in rabbit and suggested from binocularly deprived cat. It should be stressed, however, that the interaction between the two eyes produces a qualitatively different situation. The evidence suggests quite strongly that most neurons which would, in the normal course of development, have received inputs from both eyes are in the experiments described here receiving them from only one. We say this because there is no evidence for nonresponsive cells in the animals raised with strabismus or alternating occlusion. Indeed, Hubel and Wiesel (1965) report an unusual richness of activity in these animals. Blakemore and Van Sluyters (1974) provide additional evidence in their finding that the effects of monocular deprivation can be completely reversed by reverse deprivation within the critical period.

The slow versus fast time course of development could account for the inability of the deprived eye to activate cortical neurons in monocularly deprived animals. It does *not*, however, account for the results of non-synchronous or nonsimultaneous rearing. This, it seems to us, requires an additional factor, as clearly noted by Hubel and Wiesel (1965). Inputs from the two eyes are not functionally corresponding in these experiments, either because the eyes are not stimulated at the same time (alternating occlusion) or by the same visual space (strabismus). As a result, while all cells are activated and exhibit proper selectivity, they exhibit less than normal binocular convergence. This, it seems to us, is indicative of an input-sensitive process related to binocularity per se, isolated in relatively pure form. The monocular deprivation experiments probably represent the effects of abnormal visual input both on the input-sensitive process common to cat and rabbit, and on this binocular process.

A particularly elegant and imaginative demonstration of the binocular input-sensitivity was reported by Shlaer (1971), who raised kittens with prisms over their eyes so that the visual world was displaced 4° vertically on one retina with respect to the other. In normal animals, cortical cells tend to receive inputs from exactly corresponding retinal positions, as measured from retinal landmarks such as the optic discs. In prism-reared animals, cells tended to receive inputs from noncorresponding retinal positions. The non-correspondence reported was in a direction such as to compensate for the displacement produced by the prisms. A full account of this work has not been published, the numbers of cells reported are small, and there is some question whether there was sufficiently rigorous control for eye position. However, it receives support from the work of Pettigrew to be discussed next (also see Daniels & Pettigrew, this volume). Moreover, we believe it offers major insight into the functional role of the binocular input-sensitivity.

Barlow and Pettigrew (1971) and Pettigrew (1974) have looked at the precision with which retinal inputs are brought together on cortical cells in neonatal kittens and in older kittens, both normally experienced and binocularly deprived. They report that in neonatal animals the size of the field on the nondominant retina which, when stimulated simultaneously with the dominant retina gives an increased response, is quite large (a radius of 3°). With time the size of this field decreases and a peak response position begins to appear. Finally there is an active suppression by nondominant eye stimulation except for a small (0.5°) zone. This development of binocular specificity normally occurs over the first 6 weeks and has not occurred by that time in binocularly deprived animals.

This evidence suggests very strongly that the high degree of precision with which retinal points are brought together on striate cortical cells is dependent on visual experience. A similar process has been hypothesized for the anuran tectum (see the chapter by Keating). The situation appears to be one in which cortical cells initially receive excitatory input from afferents representing wider areas of retina than those over which the cells will finally respond. Many of these connections are ultimately reduced in their relative effectiveness leaving, presumably, those connections representing retinal points actually simultaneously stimulated by single points in visual space. In lieu of such simultaneously stimulated points, as in the alternating occlusion or strabismus experiments, the afferents representing one eye or the other dominate. This would appear to represent a breakdown of the system in attempting to cope with a greater noncorrespondence of retinal images than it is intended to handle. Such an interpretation could be confirmed directly by repeating Shlaer's experiments with a range of prism powers. A particularly compelling result would be to show that the range of prism-induced disparities which can be compensated corresponds to the size of the fields over which binocular facilitation occurs in visually naive animals.

Cortical single-unit studies on binocularity exist for only two other mammals. Baker, Grigg, and Von Noorden (1974) have recorded from macaque monkeys following monocular deprivation by lid suture or surgically induced strabismus. Much as in cats, monocular deprivation led to reduced numbers of cells driven by the deprived eye, and strabismatic animals exhibited a reduction in binocular cells with, except in one case no significant reduction of connections from either eye.

It has already been mentioned that 3 months of monocular deprivation in the rabbit does not lead to a reduction of connections from the deprived eye (Chow & Spear, 1974). In view of the fact that most of rabbit cortex represents space visible only through the contralateral eye and that, correspondingly, these cells are normally monocularly activated, this is consistent with the observation that much of the monocular deprivation effect in cats is the result of interaction between the two eyes.

Van Sluyters and Stewart (1974b) concentrated attention on the small cortical area which does receive binocular input in the rabbit. Somewhat surprisingly, in monocularly deprived animals there was no reduction in numbers of cells driven by the deprived eye, though there was some tendency to a reduced effectiveness of the deprived eye. There was also an apparent shift in directional sensitivity, which will be discussed in the subsequent section.

The explanation for the results of Van Sluyters and Stewart (1974b) may be that the rabbit visual system is not attempting a high precision of fusion even in the small area of binocular overlap and therefore does not possess a process of binocular experience-sensitivity like the cat. In the binocular areas of normal rabbit cortex, 50% of the binocular cells do not have fields through the two eyes that represent the same area of visual space [Van

Sluyters and Stewart (1974a)]. The observation that a greater percentage of binocular cells in the monocularly deprived than in the normal animal have nonidentical receptive fields through the two eyes, may, however, indicate some attempt to fuse inputs.

B. Abnormalities in Orientation Experience

The sensitivity of the orientation specificity of cortical neurons to abnormal visual experience was originally reported in the cat by Hirsch and Spinelli (1970) and Blakemore and Cooper (1970). Blakemore and Cooper (1970) raised kittens in such a way as to restrict their visual experience to either binocularly viewed horizontal or binocularly viewed vertical stripes. Such animals subsequently showed an absence of cortical neurons with orientation selectivities greatly different from those experienced. This is in contrast to normal cats, in which all orientations are equally represented. Hirsch and Spinelli (1970) raised kittens whose only visual experience was through goggles that allowed one eye a view of three horizontal lines and the other a view of three vertical lines. This led to a loss of binocularly activated neurons. In general, cells were activated only by one eye and had receptive field orientations corresponding to the visual experience of the eye through which they were activated.

As previously noted, there was some reluctance to accept this evidence as support for a normal role of visual experience in development, specifically, as indicating that orientation selectivity was influenced by visual experience. Hubel and Wiesel's (1963) characterization of the neonatal kitten made such a process unnecessary. On the other hand, the more recent evidence distinguishing orientation from direction selectivity and describing the sensitivity of the development of orientation selectivity to delayed eye-opening has already been discussed.

Additionally there existed the possibility that the reported effects represented simply a disuse atrophy of the connections of cortical cells pre-wired for orientations other than those experienced. There was some support for this interpretation. Hirsch and Spinelli (1970, 1971) reported large "silent areas" during electrode penetrations which might correspond to cells having lost their connectivity. Blakemore and Cooper (1970), however, explicitly noted an absence of such "silent areas."

It seems likely that goggle-reared animals were exhibiting more complicated effects than those having binocular single-orientation experience. Not only did they appear to have silent areas, but two restudies of the same animals after 1–3 years of normal visual experience (Pettigrew, Olson, & Hirsch, 1973; Spinelli, Hirsch, Phelps, & Metzler, 1972) both reported the appearance of binocularly activated, but in general, poorly orientation-specific cells. This may reflect the catching-up of a developmental process retarded by restrictive visual experience permitted by goggles. Alternatively, it may be analogous to the moderate "recapture" seen when monocularly deprived animals are forced to use their deprived eye (Chow & Stewart, 1972).

It is regrettable that there has been no full report as yet of the experiments by Blakemore and his colleagues, for their abnormal visual experience paradigm seems to represent a pure form of manipulation of an input-sensitive orientation-specificity process, just as strabismus and prism-reared animals seem to affect, in relatively isolated form, the input-sensitive binocular-specificity process. By this we mean that there is no evidence for nonresponsive or poorly responsive neurons. The available information suggests a critical period for the orientation process substantially the same as for monocular deprivation. Moreover, a relatively few hours of visual experience at the height of the critical period are sufficient to produce the effect (Blakemore & Mitchell, 1973).

The only other animal for which information is available on the sensitivity of cortical neurons to early visual experience restricted to single orientations is the rabbit. Mize and Murphy (1973) raised rabbits under conditions similar to those used by Blakemore and Cooper (1970) for cats. Animals were recorded from between 60 and 100 days of age. Those raised in horizontal stripes and those raised in vertical stripes appeared indistinguishable with respect to directional and orientational selectivity, and Mize and Murphy concluded that the plasticity present in cat was absent in rabbit. A weak effect may, however, have been present in their data. In the normal rabbit, 2 of 35 simple cells were found to be aligned with the roughly horizontal visual streak of the retina (Chow et al., 1971). Of 13 simple cells reported by Mize and Murphy from rabbits reared in a vertical environment, 3 had near-vertical orientations.

The negative conclusion of Mize and Murphy is puzzling in view of the rabbit's similarity to the cat in development of orientation selectivity and the response of this development to delayed eye-opening. The possibility always exists with negative findings that exactly the right manipulation was not found. However, a more intriguing explanation also exists. The initial appearance of orientation selectivity occurs somewhat later in cat than in rabbit, and the hypothesized retarded development of such selectivity under deprivation occurs over a much longer time course. The possibility thus exists that selectivity to orientations other than those experienced may be delayed in development in both rabbit and cat, but much longer in the latter. Mize and Murphy (1973) recorded from rabbits at 60–100 days of age. A direct test of this hypothesis can be made by recording from similarly reared animals at 20–25 days.

Van Sluyters and Stewart (1974b) provided some indirect evidence of an effect of visual experience on orientation selectivity in rabbit, at least in binocular areas of striate cortex. They reported evidence on direction selectivity, but it appears that they include many orientation-specific cells in this grouping. Cells in normal rabbits tend to favor horizontal or vertical directions. This clustering was reduced in cells driven by the deprived eye in monocularly deprived animals of 5–7 months of age.

We find this evidence on the response of cortical receptive fields to selective orientation rearing less easy to put together meaningfully than that on perturbation of binocular experience. The principal difficulty is whether the failure in cats to find cells selective for nonexperienced orientations indicates that (1) such cells have physically disappeared, (2) such cells are present but inactive, or (3) all cells have become selective for the experienced orientation.

There is no strong evidence for (1) and some indirect contrary evidence. The interdigitation of clusters of binocularly activated neurons between groups of monocularly activated neurons in cats given normal experience after goggle rearing (Pettigrew et al. 1973b; Spinelli et al., 1972) suggests that such clusters may correspond to the "silent areas" of the original investigations of these animals (Hirsch & Spinelli, 1971). If so, these cells did not physically disappear but simply became inactive.

This same set of observations gives some support to alternative (2): that cells are present but inactive. This alternative would fit rather easily with the picture that emerges from the developmental studies in the cat; i.e., that rate of development of orientation specificity depends on visual experience. Cells specific for experienced orientations might therefore develop more rapidly than those which are specific for other orientations. As already noted, an explanation can than be offered for the failure to obtain a selective rearing effect in rabbits, based on time-course differences. Indeed there is some support for this in the finding of Pettigrew et al. (1973b) that the binocular cells, perhaps newly responsive, do not show a pronounced vertical or horizontal orientation preference. Such animals, of course, have had considerable visual experience not restricted to single orientations. One would still like to know whether cats after prolonged (one year or more) restricted orientation experience ultimately develop cells having all orientation selectivities.

It has already been argued, however, that the goggle-reared animals may be exhibiting a deprivation as well as a selective-rearing effect. The silent cells and their recovery may relate to the former, rather than to the latter. Alternative (2) was explicitly rejected by Blakemore and Cooper (1970) in their purer form of restricted orientation rearing. If their interpretation is accepted, then it seems clear that a given cortical neuron can take up any of a range of orientation selectivities. In this case, one might be able to measure the range of potential selectivities of a cortical neuron by noting the nearest to the nonexperienced orientation in a large sample of neurons. These cells probably represent the extreme of their modifiable range.

To summarize, the *development* of orientation specificity clearly falls into the category of an experience-*sensitive* process. As judged by the single-unit properties, formation of the underlying connections can be delayed by delaying the onset of visual experience in both cat and rabbit. This result has been particularly clearly demonstrated in the rabbit under circumstances where poor optics or a general retardation of development have been ruled out as explanations. As we have already described, the situation is less clear in the monkey. On the other hand, the question of whether the orientation for which particular neurons come to be specific can be influenced by visual experience has not been satisfactorily resolved. A careful population analysis of tube-reared cats with particular attention to the existence of nonresponsive and of poorly orientation-specific neurons is needed to rule out the possibility of a more rapid rate of development of neurons intrinsically favoring experienced orientations.

Regardless of the outcome of this analysis, it seems unlikely that orientation specificity per se is a product of visual experience; that is, that cells tend to be orientation specific because the environment consists of straight lines. The principal reason for our skepticism is that rabbits certainly, and cats probably, develop orientation-specific neurons despite continued deprivation. Monkeys apparently have them before visual experience begins. Nor are we persuaded that the proportions of neurons with particular sensitivities is matched to the environment by visual experience. Our reasons for the skepticism are both theoretical and experimental. We will postpone discussion of the former and note here only that Blakemore (1974) has made an important observation that visual experience restricted to a particular orientation but given outside the critical period leads to development of orientation selectivities *not* favoring the experienced. It is our suspicion that the experience-sensitive process revealed by the selective orientation rearing has a functional consequence not yet clear from available experiments, and that the lining-up of orientation selectivities in cat may be an epiphenomenon.

C. Other Forms of Abnormal Visual Experience

The sensitivity of cortical receptive field organization to restricted experience regimes other than those aimed at binocular and orientational specificity have been explored in a few studies using exclusively the cat. A principal question is whether there are aspects of receptive field organization other than those already noted whose development is sensitive to visual experience. Whether the results reviewed indicate a third experience-sensitive process cannot be clearly answered, since the answer requires a fairly complete understanding of the response characteristics of visually naive cells and the mechanisms of their transformation to the adult state.

In an attempt to influence directional specificity, Cynader, Berman, and Hein (1973) recorded from two 6-month-old cats whose visual experience was restricted to 9-msec strobe flashes every 2 seconds. Of 98 units, 39% exhibited directional selectivity and 15% exhibited orientation selectivity. This was compared to levels of 62% and 85%, respectively, in normally reared cats. In addition, 13 units in strobe-reared animals were found to be responsive only to the strobe flash, whereas none were found in normally reared animals, and, in total, 53% of cells in strobe-reared animals responded to the strobe flashes, as opposed to only 10% in normal animals.

Low levels of orientation specificity, a reduction in highly specific directional units, and higher levels of strobe responsiveness were also found by Olson and Pettigrew (1974) in an independent study of strobe-reared cats at a younger age (6 weeks). Olson and Pettigrew noted further in strobe-reared cats a tendency to more sluggish responsiveness and a slightly larger average receptive field size. In addition, there was a higher percentage of monocular cells and a correlated misalignment of the eyes.

It seems likely that many of these results reflect simply a retention of the neonatal state as a result of insufficient visual stimulation, a conclusion reached by Olson and Pettigrew (1974). Because of the short exposure time, the total amount of visual experience in fact resembles that of binocularly deprived animals. The observed reduction in binocularly activated neurons indicates a small effect analogous to that in strabismic animals. The increased responsiveness to strobe illumination as opposed to control animals cannot be accepted as a response to selective stimulation without knowing whether neonatal animals also show high levels of strobe responsiveness. The same applies to directional selectivity, which is further complicated by different defining characteristics used by different investigators.

Pettigrew and Freeman (1973) and Van Sluyters and Blakemore (1973) have both reported results from animals whose sole visual experience was with spots; that is, these kittens never saw the linear contours which are the normal preferred stimulus for adult cortical neurons. The rearing circumstances were slightly different, but both reports indicate reduced percentages of orientation selectivity as compared to control animals of the same age. Van Sluyters and Blakemore (1973) report that one animal reared with large spots had higher levels of orientation selectivity than the other raised with small spots; both had significant levels of nonresponsive cells.

These results again are more indicative of a retention of the neonatal state than of a response of visual experience. Pettigrew and Freeman (1973) characterize one-third of their cells as "spot-detectors," in that they seem to prefer small moving spots to larger ones. As with strobe-responsiveness, it is difficult to evaluate this without information in respect the proportion of cells in the neonatal cortex that display similar properties.

Hirsch and Spinelli (1971) reported some evidence in their goggle-reared animals that receptive field shape could be influenced by visual experience. Fourteen of 93 units displayed double, parallel excitatory regions whose separation was similar to that of the three stripes to which the animal was exposed. Four cells displayed three excitatory regions. An abstract (Spinelli & Hirsch, 1971) reports that animals exposed solely to circular contours by goggle-rearing display receptive fields with circular configurations. None of these results have yet been described in sufficient detail to allow specula-tion as to their functional significance.

V. Experience-Dependent Processes and Their Functional Significance

In this review, we have attempted to focus attention on whether the evidence supports the conclusion that there is an experience-dependent aspect to receptive field development in striatal cortical cells and, if so, how many such processes there are and what the functional significance of each is. Up to this point we have been concerned with experience-*sensitivity*, i.e., whether the response characteristics of individual neurons can be influenced by visual experience. We now want to turn to the problem of experience-*dependence*, i.e., whether there are critical pieces of ontogenetic information that are provided by experience during normal development.

In general, the question is whether some or all striate cortical neurons retain a degree of multipotency with respect to some receptive field pro-perties into the time when visual experience begins and subsequently, as a consequence of normal visual experience, acquire properties that are a functionally meaningful reflection of that experience. The demonstration that animals raised with abnormal visual experience display a different spectrum of receptive field properties than normally reared controls, even of the same age, is not sufficient to establish an experience-dependent process. We have already noted two reservations in regard to such demon-strations: the possibility that what is found in abnormally reared animals is a retention of the neonatal state and the possibility of differential matura-tional rates and a resulting differential detectability of particular cell types. These are specific cases of the more general reservation we want to call attention to here: the finding of unusual receptive field properties in abnormally reared animals suggests the existence of an input-dependent process; it cannot, however, be assumed that the specific properties brought about are those that the process normally brings about.

An example of this is the loss of the ability of a deprived eye to activate cortical neurons in monocularly deprived animals. The example is a particularly appropriate one, since it was the progenitor of the entire body of work reviewed here. That observation, we believe, provided *prima facie* evidence that some input-dependent process exists. Taken at face value, the outcome made no functional sense. It is now possible, largely because of the imaginative experiment of Shlaer (1971) and the correlative evidence of Pettigrew (1974), to view the original observation as the consequence of an experience-dependent mechanism (normally accomplishing binocular fusion) which has been pushed beyond its limits.

More generally, so long as it was believed to be the case that the striate cortex was fully developed in advance of visual experience, it was difficult to accept that any process revealed by experiments involving abnormal visual experience could operate during normal development. It is for this reason that the research on the visually naive animal has played such a central role in our discussion. It is worth noting, however, purely as a theoretical point at the present time, that multipotency of neurons does not necessarily require that their response properties be nonspecific (see, for example, Gottlieb's discussion of the constraints of experiential input on behavioral and neural development elsewhere in this volume).

The theoretical point aside, the fact is that the available evidence on receptive field organization in visually naive animals is concordant with the evidence from animals raised with abnormal visual experience. In cats, orientation specificity and binocular specificity both seem to be lacking in most or all cortical neurons at the time of eye-opening; both can be at least delayed in their normal developmental time course by preventing the eyes from opening at the normal time; and both can be dramatically manipulated by abnormal visual experience. The same is true for the development of orientation specificity in rabbits; for monkeys the story is less clear.

This implies to us that there is indeed an experience-sensitive aspect to receptive field development of cortical cells. In fact, we are inclined to believe that there are a minimum of two independent experience-sensitive processes, one related to binocular specificity and one related to orientation specificity. These are independent processes, at least in the sense that orientation specificity will develop without binocular specificity, as in goggle-reared animals and strabismic animals. Whether binocular specificity can be produced without orientation specificity is less clear. This would require a technique for measuring binocular specificity with other than bar stimuli and its application to neonatal and, for example, spot-reared animals. A second reason for suspecting that the two processes are independent is that one of them—that related to orientation specificity—seems to be present in the rabbit. Since the other process, binocular specificity, is significant only for binocular visual processing, the finding of an experience-sensitive process common to cat and rabbit, the latter having predominantly monocular vision, suggests that it is related to something other than binocularity.

The input-*sensitive* process related to binocular specificity seems to us to qualify as an experience-*dependent* process, though, as we have earlier noted, verification of the failure of binocular specificity to develop during long-term deprivation is still lacking. The important point is that we believe we understand the functional significance of the underlying connections; they act to bring together on single neurons the retinal regions which are simultaneously stimulated by a single point in visual space. It is thus possible to modify the critical piece of ontogenetic information—which pairs of retinal region are in fact simultaneously stimulated. The evidence suggests that within a limited range a functionally appropriate modification of connections results.

This, it seems to us, may point to a general principle about the function of experience-dependent processes. The two eyes have independent developmental histories; their optics, positions, shapes all develop independently. In these circumstances, it may not be possible to say, in advance, exactly which regions on the two retinas will be seeing the same region in visual space. If this is true, it is not the case that the necessary connections are too complex or too specific for genetic information to determine. It is rather the case that genetic information alone is intrinsically inadequate to create the correct connections, for the correct connections, those which 'work," can only be identified once the system has begun to function.

A further consideration might be added on the basis of the experiments on binocular specificity. The entire process is not left to visual experience to perform. Rather the genetic information is such as to provide a wider range of excitatory connections than is ultimately used. The final subset which represents the specific case is selected on the basis of visual experience. The practical importance of this is that the naive state—roughly correctly wired—may appear to have the attributes of the fully developed state.

We have already indicated a degree of dissatisfaction with our understanding of what we have called an orientation-specific, experience-sensitive process. This dissatisfaction stems largely from our uncertainty as to the adaptive function of this sensitivity. In terms of the general proposition described above, it does not make sense for either line-detection or the favoring of certain orientations prevalent in the environment to depend on visual experience. The visual world has simply not been sufficiently variable over evolutionary time to make such a process useful.

Two other interpretations of the functional significance of orientation experience-sensitivity fit better with a concept of genetic inadequacy. Blakemore and Van Sluyters (1974) suggest that it represents simply another aspect of the process of ensuring precise fusion of inputs from the two retinas. This is a serious possibility, though experimentally unsupported. The explanation, however, does not account very well for the situation in binocular areas of rabbit cortex, nor at all for results in the predominantly monocular areas of rabbit cortex. Binocular specificity is poor in binocular areas of normally reared rabbit, both with respect to field position and orientation through the two eyes. Monocular deprivation does not make it impressively worse. In monocular areas, where binocular specificity cannot be an issue, there is the already described retardation of orientation selectivity in visually deprived rabbits, as there is in cats.

Van Sluyters and Stewart (1974a, 1974b) provide an intriguing alternative hypothesis to account for the rabbit. They report a favoring of the horizontal and vertical directions for the category of direction-selective cells in binocular cortex, many of which probably fall into the orientation classes of other workers. No such favoring is present for the deprived eye following deprivation. If this tendency is in fact an alignment of fields with the body axes, or with eye movements produced by extraocular muscles, then the hypothesis would fall into the general category of processes subserving functions for which genetic information is inadequate. Experiments aimed at this question in monocular areas of rabbit cortex are in progress.

Until more definite experiments are available we are inclined to reserve judgment on the question of the functional role of orientation experience-sensitivity and therefore on whether it qualifies as an experience-*dependent* process. As we have noted before, orientation specificity certainly develops in the rabbit without visual experience, and may do so in the cat as well. Clearly, in the cat reared under restrictive conditions, selectivities for orientations differing somewhat from those experienced do develop. This leaves us with the uncomfortable feeling that this process relates to some aspect of cortical specificity about which we have no inkling.

VI. The Mechanisms of Experience-Sensitivity

Thus far, we have been concerned with the question of whether available evidence supports the proposition that visual experience participates in the development of the specificity seen in the receptive field organization of neurons in mammalian visual cortex. In this section we want to focus on possible mechanisms of experience-sensitivity, not at the molecular level (cf. Stent, 1973), but rather in terms of the likely variations in neuronal connection patterns that may underlie these processes. We will confine ourselves almost entirely to single-unit physiological studies, on the grounds that to include evoked potential or anatomical studies would require essentially two additional full reviews. There is, however, an extremely important potential limitation in the single-unit physiological approach: its inability to distinguish changes in synaptic effectiveness from changes in anatomical connections. In the final section, we shall briefly mention some anatomical studies in evaluating the seriousness of this limitation.

A. The Locus of Experience-Sensitive Processes

There is a clear feeling in the literature, by omission if not otherwise, that experience-sensitive processes are cortical phenomena, that patterns of connections to neurons in the visual pathways afferent to cortex are indifferent to visual experience. The feeling is based primarily on the fact that the properties of receptive field organization which have been shown to be sensitive to visual experience—orientation specificity in the rabbit, binocularity in the monkey, and both in the cat—are properties not present in the receptive field organization of the relay neurons in the lateral geniculate nucleus.

The only experimental evidence bearing on this question comes from studies on geniculate receptive field organization in lid-sutured cat. There have been no studies of geniculate neurons under any of the other abnormal visual experience regimes described previously. In their original series of studies, Wiesel and Hubel (1963a) reported that, in contrast to cortex, the deprived eye in monocularly lid-sutured animals activated geniculate neurons in a more or less normal fashion. A minority of neurons, however, exhibited larger than normal receptive fields, sluggish responses, and poor peripheral suppression. In addition, fewer units were isolated and overall activity seemed to be reduced. Chow and Stewart (1972) reported no abnormality in geniculate neurons of binocularly deprived cats.

Hamasaki, Rackensperger, and Vesper (1972) and Hamasaki and Winters (1973) confirmed the qualitative normality of geniculate neurons driven by the deprived eye in monocularly deprived animals but noted changes in certain quantitative response characteristics which led them to suggest that there were some changes in synaptic effectiveness either in the geniculate or more peripherally. Sherman and Sanderson (1972) confirmed both the qualitative normality of geniculate neurons in monocularly deprived cats and the apparent reduction in the numbers of neurons isolated. In addition, they showed that the loss of cortical cell activation by the deprived eye could not be accounted for by inhibitory binocular interaction in the geniculate.

The question of geniculate normality in deprived animals has been reinvestigated following the characterization of two classes of receptive field in retina and geniculate [see Sherman & Sanderson (1972) for references; we adopt the terminology used there]. Sherman, Hoffmann, and Stone (1972) reported a significant reduction of the percentage of Y-cells in binocular, but not monocular, segments of geniculate laminae innervated by the deprived eye in monocularly deprived animals. In binocular deprived animals all parts of the laminae exhibited a reduction in percentage of Y-cells.

This observation is quite exciting, both in that it may point to a particular subpopulation of neurons which account for experience sensitivity and in that there are significant anatomical correlates. We shall return to this in the last section. For the moment, we simply note that a loss of a particular cell type from the geniculate, if that is indeed the case, does not necessarily rule out the cortex as the locus of experience-sensitive connections. The original suggestion of Hubel and Wiesel to account for monocular deprivation effects was a competition for synaptic sites by afferents from geniculate laminae representing the two eyes. The resulting failure of neurons in the deprived laminae to form connections could conceivably lead to a retrograde degeneration and a subsequent loss of such cells from the geniculate.

Rapisardi, Chow, and Mathers (1975) have studied the receptive field development of geniculate neurons in the rabbit. While many are apparently normally organized at the time of eye-opening, there are large percentages of nonresponsive and poorly organized cells, the indefinite type, which disappear over subsequent days. Whether this, like the cortical development in rabbit, is experience-sensitive, remains to be determined. A similar study in cat is desirable, especially with regard to the question of whether Y-cells are present at eye-opening or develop subsequently.

Our general feeling is that much of the experience sensitivity shown by cortical neurons has to do with connections in cortex. By this we mean both connections of geniculate afferents and connections intrinsic to the cortex. Nonetheless, the evidence presently available does not even begin to rule out more peripheral loci, and these possibilities need to be evaluated on a case by case basis (cf. Daw & Wyatt, 1974).

B. Excitatory versus Inhibitory Processes

We have already noted that the monocular deprivation experiments provide indirect evidence that excitatory connections from geniculate to cortical cells can be influenced by visual experience. It is unlikely, though not impossible, that this effect could result from suppression of excitatory inputs by increased intracortical inhibition. For this to be the case would require some cortical cells (the inhibitory ones) to be activated by the deprived eye. Some such are seen in monocularly deprived animals, but they are in general rare and poorly responsive.

It seems more likely that geniculostriate excitatory connections themselves are influenced by visual experience. Blakemore and Van Sluyters (1974) report that the effects of monocular deprivation can be fully reversed by reverse suture within the critical period. This implies that there is an ability to reform connections during this period. Perhaps it is a period of continuous formation of connections corresponding to a continuous ingrowth of geniculate afferents. This would account as well for an increase in responsive cells. If such a growth process were experience-sensitive, binocular deprived animals would fail to make such connections and would exhibit the observed high levels of nonresponsive cells.

This particular speculation aside, the disposition of geniculostriate afferents does seem to be experience sensitive. There is likewise indirect evidence that inhibitory connections may be input sensitive. We have already described the evidence of Barlow and Pettigrew (1971) and Pettigrew (1974) that the development of binocular fusion specificity involves appearance of an active suppression of the response due to the dominant eye by a misplace stimulus on the nondominant eye. The transition from neonatal orientation promiscuity to adult specificity may also involve development of inhibition.

C. Time Course of Experience-Sensitive Processes

We have previously noted that very short periods of either monocular deprivation or selective orientation rearing properly timed in otherwise visually inexperienced animals can produce effects comparable to those in animals reared through the entire first few months with abnormal visual experience. This raises the possibility of watching experience dependence in process.

Pettigrew, Olson, and Barlow (1973a) prepared previously visually inexperienced kittens for recording at 18–35 days of age. Once cortical neurons were isolated and their response characteristics determined, controlled visual experience was given in attempt to modify these characteristics. Repeated stimulation of the initially nondominant eye caused it to become the dominant eye for four of 60 binocular cells and produced some increased effectiveness in 43 others. A "not fully convincing" effect was also reported with orientation training. The most successful effects lasted less than 1 hour.

Pettigrew and Garey (1974) used longer training periods and looked at several time periods after training. They also restricted visual experience to one hemisphere by giving visual stimulation in only one hemifield. This mimics the natural situation in the rabbit, providing a control and an experimental cortex in the same animal.

Two previously inexperienced kittens were anesthetized, paralyzed, and given 20 hours of visual stimulation consisting of an oscillating vertical square-wave grating in one hemifield. On the first day subsequent to the stimulation 60 cells were recorded; of these 26 were unresponsive, 7 had weak preferences for vertical stimuli, and 17 were termed "complementary," in that they respond to any stimulus except vertical lines. On the second day, 28 of 52 cells exhibited preferred responsiveness to vertical lines. Five cells were complementary. Units from the nonconditioned hemisphere retained visually naive properties. Results similar to those on the second day were obtained from animals allowed to recover from paralysis and kept in the dark for up to 20 days. However, one animal at 7 weeks of recovery exhibited poor orientation selectivity and two animals at 1 week of recovery showed only small numbers of neurons preferring vertical stimuli.

These experiments are intriguing and undoubtedly worth pursuing. For the moment, we are reluctant to draw strong conclusions from them. An important reservation is that the visual experience is given while the animals are anesthetized and paralyzed. Normal experience-sensitive development may well involve an interaction of visual experience and motor control (see, for example, the work of Hein and Held and collaborators reviewed by Gottlieb in an earlier chapter in this volume).

It is interesting, however, that the response to abnormal visual experience takes some time to appear and that, at least with restricted orientation experience, there seems to be a phase in which responsiveness to the experience orientation is suppressed, rather than favored. This latter observation increases our sense that the orientation experience-sensitive process is not a straightforward enhancement of connections corresponding to a line as the result of linear contours in the environment. It seems rather to involve a more complicated ordering of intracortical circuitry.

D. Experience-Sensitive Processes: Anatomical Reality?

In this review, we have referred to experiments as indicating that "connections" are or are not present under particular circumstances. In so doing, we are using the vernacular of the physiologist, inferring the existence of connections from the response properties of cells. Inferences of this kind are always ambiguous, and we have tried to point out some of these ambiguities in our discussion of mechanisms. In the present context, however, there is a more far-reaching ambiguity.

Recent evidence (Marotte & Mark, 1970; Merrill & Wall, 1972) raises the possibility that there may be synapses which are anatomically normal but physiologically ineffective. This makes it at least conceivable that the changes brought about by visual experience in the physiologist's wiring diagram take place with no change at all in the anatomical pattern of connections. Indeed, a recently proposed model to account for some of the cat data is of this kind (Stent, 1973).

The significance of this reservation is to a large extent undercut by the assumption (perhaps a restricted and chauvinistic view of the physiologist) that what matters is the response properties of the cell. Whether an experience-sensitive process involves actual anatomical changes or simply changes in the effectiveness of existing synapses does not affect its significance for understanding nervous system function. From a developmental point of view, however, the two situations are sufficiently different to warrant mention. The latter would permit experience dependence to operate within a rigid, genetically determined pattern of anatomical connections. The former implies a genetic program in which, at a minimum, experience is used to realize a subset of a set of actual or potential anatomical connections.

It is not our intention here to provide a complete review of the anatomical evidence relating either to development or to deprivation. To do so would double the length of this discussion, and such reviews have been recently written (Chow, 1973; Guillery, 1974). We simply want to mention a few anatomical studies to support the proposition that at least some of the experience sensitivity involves actual changes in anatomical connections.

The earliest described and perhaps best investigated anatomical correlate of a physiologically characterized deprivation effect is the relative reduction of cell size in geniculate laminae receiving afferents from the deprived eye as opposed to laminae receiving from the experienced eye in monocularly deprived cats (Wiesel & Hubel, 1963a). This difference in neuronal growth correlates well with physiological effects of deprivation seen at the cortical level. Effects on growth rate are much less dramatic in binocularly deprived animals (Chow & Stewart, 1972), nor is it present when comparing the monocular segments of the two sides in monocularly deprived animals (Guillery & Stelzner, 1970). In short, it reflects the same competitive relation between inputs from the two eyes that characterizes cortical cells. A particularly elegant demonstration of this effect was made by Guillery (1972), who showed that a small lesion of the retina of the experienced eye abolished much of the reduction of cell size in that portion of the deprived geniculate lamina adjacent to the region in the normal lamina deafferented by the lesion.

The casual relationships of this effect remain to be unraveled. It is not yet clear whether deprived geniculate neurons fail to form functional connections because they are developing more slowly or instead are retarded in their growth because of a competitive disadvantage in making connections. The correlation, however, between cell size and functional connections lends support to the proposition that the connections in experience-sensitive processes have some anatomical reality.

Recently, Guillery and Kaas (1974a, 1974b) have extended these studies to the squirrel. The results of monocular suture in the lateral geniculate are entirely analogous to those in the cat, including the sparing of the monocular segment. Of particular interest, however, are some observations on cortical structure. The cortical cell density contralateral to the sutured eye was higher than in the ipsilateral cortex, conceivably implying a less rich pattern of connections. Particularly important is that cortical areas receiving solely monocular input were no different in this regard than those receiving binocular input. This points to an effect of deprivation different from that related to competition between the two eyes and hence argues, as we have done previously based on receptive field studies, for two experience-sensitive processes. A similar argument applies to the reduction in percentage of Y-cells in binocularly deprived cat geniculate (Sherman et al., 1972).

It is an inference of these studies that the described anatomical changes relate to synapse formation. Lund and Lund have used ultrastructural techniques to look at the development of the rat superior colliculus and the effects of visual deprivation on the development. Though it is not cortex, the study so well illustrates our theme of experience-sensitivity operating within an on-going developmental process that we will include it here as our final example.

R. D. and J. S. Lund (1972) divide development in the rat superior colliculus into three stages based on synaptic morphologies. The first stage ends at eye-opening and is characterized by an initial proliferation of synapses from both optic afferents and intrinsic neurons. The second stage spans the next 10 days and involves further synapse formation from optic axons, including the appearance of multiple contacts and serial synapses. In the third stage, about 10 days, there is a second proliferation of synapse formation by intrinsic axons. J. S. and R. D. Lund (1972) report that the events of stages 1 and 2 occur despite lid suture. The events of stage 3, however, can be delayed by lid suture and, in fact, may be blocked entirely if lid suture is prolonged.

It has not been our intention here to correlate anatomical and physiological data on experience-sensitive processes. Indeed, with the exception of the deprived cat, correlated anatomical and physiological data on the same animal under the same conditions of age and visual experience is rare (cf. Gary & Pettigrew, 1974) and much to be desired. We simply wished to illustrate that anatomical, as well as physiological, properties are sensitive to visual experience. This not only makes more real the likelihood that actual anatomical changes in synapses are the basis of experience-sensitivity processes, it also makes less real the possibility that the receptive field effects produced by abnormal visual experience can be attributed to "soft-ware" processes such as reticular control of transmission through the geniculate or the like. The latter may apply to the recent observation of Fiorentini and Maffei (1974) that the binocularity of simple cells in *adult* cats can be disrupted by immobilization of one eye. In general, we feel that each example of altered physiological function must be tested against all three possibilities, i.e., altered anatomical connections, stable connections but permanently altered synaptic efficacy, and stable connections and synaptic efficacy but transmission that is modifiable by a second neural system.

VII. Summary and Conclusions

The reader will, by this time, be aware that our principal concern in this review has been to provide an overview, rather than to focus on the details of particular experiments, though we hope we have not unduly slighted these. Nor has our primary effort been to understand visual function; indeed we have ignored a large body of correlative behavioral evidence (see chapter by Tees). Instead we have attempted simply to answer the question of whether available evidence supports the proposition that the individual experience of an organism participates in the elaboration of the highly complex patterns of interconnections among neurons. We believe this emphasis to be justified in terms of the importance of the answer both to conceptions of nervous system function and mechanisms of development. It is particularly apt in the present volume, for "specificity" is often loosely opposed to "plasticity," the latter usually encompassing experience-dependent processes. The issue here is not so much how plastic the mammalian visual system is, but whence it derives its normal specificity.

Our emphasis, in turn, justifies at least partially our slighting of both behavior and anatomy. The propostion that individual experience participates in the elaboration of behavior needs no defense and, with respect to detailed connectivity among neurons, behavior is often a poor indicator. The latter statement, it seems, also applies to anatomy. Despite its necessarily inferential character, illustrations of which we have already given, single-unit response properties provide the most sensitive available assay for detailed connectivity. To appreciate this, one need only try to imagine anatomical experiments to evaluate the precision with which afferents representing the two eyes bring together on single cortical cells the same point in visual space.

The experiments we have reviewed, therefore, seem to us the best available ones for resolving the issue at hand. Similar experiments, in systems other than the visual, are notably lacking and badly needed. We have confidence, though that the general principles demonstrated in the mammalian visual system will apply elsewhere and hope that this review may stimulate such studies, if they have not already begun.

Let us then consider the conclusions. Several things are incontestable. The first is that the normal development of receptive field organization is not complete at the time visual experience first becomes available in either cat or rabbit. The second is that normal receptive field development will not occur if the eyes are prevented from opening at the normal time. By this we mean that developmental events which normally follow eye-opening will not occur at the *normal time*, a fact which has again been demonstrated for both cat and rabbit. We defer, for the moment, the question of whether these events will occur at all. Finally, abnormal early visual experience leads to receptive field abnormalities in cats, monkeys, and, at least in binocular areas, in rabbits.

No one of these items is itself sufficient to answer the question of whether connections are formed in part on the basis of individual experience. That some developmental events normally follow eye-opening may be a meaningless coincidence. The perturbation in time course may be a generalized retardation of development. The abnormalities in receptive field organization could, as originally argued, result from a destruction of a normally wired system. The first two observations, however, make very unlikely this interpretation of the third. Taken together, it seems to us that these three observations not only permit, but in fact compel, the conclusion that genetic and ontogenetic information interact in the development of cortical receptive field organization. To put it another way, the genetic program for receptive field development is such as to leave windows through which the process is influenced by individual experience.

The question then becomes: What exactly is it that visual experience is doing for receptive field development and how? At this point the answers become less clear. The evidence from cats reared with abnormal visual experience suggests that there are two experience-sensitive processes. One of these is revealed by experiments using deliberate imbalance, asynchrony, or nonsimultaneity in visual experience of the two eyes. The principal effect is an abnormality in the binocularity of cortical neurons, ranging from a near complete inability of one eye to activate cortical neurons in monocularly deprived cats to an apparent adjustment of the binocular inputs to compensate for slightly misplaced retinal images.

Demonstration of the second experience-sensitive process does not depend on imbalances of visual experience in the two eyes. Instead it is most clearly revealed by experiments in which the visual experience of the two eyes interacts normally, but in which only certain orientations are present in the environment. The principal effect of such experience is an abnormality in the range of orientation specificities exhibited by samples of cortical neurons.

These two effects correspond closely to the information on visually naive animals, both neonatal and appropriately deprived. In the predominant monocular areas of rabbit cortex, orientation specificity does not normally develop until after eye-opening, and the time of this development can be delayed by delaying eye-opening. In the predominant binocular areas of cat cortex, both orientational and fusional specificity normally develop after eye-opening and, again, the time of this development can be delayed by delaying eye-opening. It thus appears to us that the development of both binocular and orientational specificity involves experience-sensitive processes.

This, however, does not provide an adequate answer to what visual experience is normally doing for the animal, much less how. Given that experience-sensitive processes are operating, abnormal visual experience is likely to yield abnormal results. These are not necessarily a good indicator of what the processes normally accomplish. Of the effects demonstrated, only one seems to us to provide an adequate indication of the significance of an experience-sensitive process in normal development and hence to qualify as experience dependent: that obtained in prism-reared cats. This has been thoroughly discussed, and we will only note here two proposed generalizations: (1) experience-dependent processes function to assure the appropriateness of connections when this cannot be assured by genetic information; and (2) they do so by selecting a subset of a set of genetically permitted connections. The permitted set may either be fully realized before experience begins or represent a continuous growth of connections during the operation of the process.

The prism-reared cats illustrate the functional significance of the binocular experience-sensitive process. We have noted several hypotheses fitting the two generalizations for the orientation experience-sensitive process but are not yet satisfied that any of them are correct. Two problems trouble us. Is the process the same in cat and rabbit and, if so, why is the response to selective orientation rearing so much more dramatic in cats? What is the significance of the observation that orientation selectivity develops without visual experience in rabbits? The latter, we have argued, may be the case in cat as well. It is certainly the case in cat that, in some circumstances, selectivities develop to orientations other than those experienced.

There is an intriguing third principle about experience-dependent processes raised by this second problem. We offer it with great hesitation and only because, if true, it will greatly complicate the investigation of such processes. A general feeling, explicitly stated by Shlaer(1971), is that experience-dependent processes act by selecting groups of synapses which tend to be synchronously active. It seems indisputable that it is patterns of activity in the nervous system, rather than the act of seeing per se, that are involved in these processes. "Deprivation," then, may not be a wholly accurate concept when applied to lid-sutured or even dark-reared animals, for these retain some activity in the visual pathways. If experience-sensitive processes represent formation of connection patterns which reflect in some way neuronal activity, there is no reason to believe they do not continue to operate in the "deprived" animal. In short, "deprivation" is itself a form of abnormal visual experience.

These problems, reservations, and cautions aside, the general question seems to us essentially answered: visual experience participates in the development of some of the functional and probably anatomical circuitry underlying receptive field organization in the mammalian visual system. It is almost certainly responsible for the precision with which inputs from the two eyes are fused onto binocular neurons in the cat striate cortex. In this case, an identifiable element of ontogenetic information—which pairs of retinal points are actually simultaneously stimulated—seems to be used to construct functionally appropriate connections. As for orientation specificity, its development is certainly promoted in rabbit and cat by visual experience. We are reluctant to go further and assert that orientation specificity involves an experience-dependent process. On the other hand, we suspect that when we better understand the significance of orientation specificity, that may well turn out to be the case.

All this is by no means a refutation of the work of Sperry and others. Indeed, Sperry (1965) explicitly left open the possibility of "functional shaping of nerve circuits." As we have attempted to make clear, experience-dependent processes operate within a context strictly defined by a genetic program of which they are, in the visual cortex at least, a relatively small part. We have suggested that even this role is played not to relieve the genome of the burden of elaborating neuronal connections, but only when the appropriateness of connections cannot be assured other than by individual experience. The real importance of experience-dependent connections probably lies more centrally, in parts of the nervous system whose very functions are outgrowths of individual experience and in which specificity may be so tied to ontogenetic information as to blur any distinction between it and plasticity.

Acknowledgments

This review was written in connection with research activities supported by the National Institutes of Health (Grants NS 18512 and EY 00691 to K.L.C.). The senior author was an NIH postdoctoral fellow at Stanford during much of its preparation. We gratefully acknowledge the secretarial assistance of P. Vario, E. Brandin, and C. Bailey.

References

Baker, F. H., Grigg, P., & Von Noorden, G. K. Effects of visual deprivation and strabismus on the response of neurons in the visual cortex of the monkey, including studies on the striate and prestriate cortex in the normal animal. *Brain Research*, 1974, **66**, 185–208.

Barlow, H. B., & Pettigrew, J. D. Lack of specificity of neurones in the visual cortex of young kittens. *Journal of Physiology (London)*, 1971, **218**, 98–100.

Blakemore, C. Developmental factors in the formation of feature-extracting neurons. In F. O. Schmitt & F. G. Worden (Eds.), *The neurosciences: Third study program*. Cambridge, Mass.: MIT Press, 1974. Pp. 105–113.

Blakemore, C., & Cooper, G. F. Development of the brain depends on the visual environment. *Nature (London)*, 1970, **228**, 477–478.

Blakemore, C., & Mitchell, D. E. Environmental modification of the visual cortex and the neural basis of learning and memory. *Nature (London)*, 1973, **241**, 467–468.

Blakemore, C., & Van Sluyters, R. C. Reversal of the physiological effects of monocular deprivation in kittens: Further evidence for a sensitive period. *Journal of Physiology (London)*, 1974, **237**, 195–216.

Chow, K. L. Neuronal changes in the visual system following deprivation. In R. Jung (Ed.), *Handbook of sensory physiology* (Vol. 7, part 3A). Berlin and New York: Springer-Verlag, 1973. Pp. 599–630.

Chow, K. L., & Spear, P. D. Morphological and functional effects of visual deprivation on the rabbit visual system. *Experimental Neurology*, 1974, **42**, 429–447.

Chow, K. L., & Stewart, D. L. Reversal of structural and functional effects of long-term visual deprivation in cats. *Experimental Neurology*, 1972, **34**, 409–433.

Chow, K. L., Masland, R. H., & Stewart, D. L. Receptive field characteristics of striate cortical neurons in the rabbit. *Brain Research*, 1971, **33**, 337–352.

Cynader, M., Berman, N., & Hein, A. Cats reared in stroboscopic illumination: Effects on receptive fields in visual cortex. *Proceedings of the National Academy of Sciences of the United States of America*, 1973, **70**, 1353–1354.

Daw, N. W., & Wyatt, H. J. Raising rabbits in a moving visual environment: An attempt to modify directional selectivity in the retina. *Journal of Physiology (London)*, 1974, **240**, 309–30.

Fiorentini, A., & Maffei, L. Change in binocular properties of the simple cells of the cortex in adult cats following immobilization of one eye. *Vision Research*, 1974, **14**, 217–218.

Ganz, L., Fitch, M., & Satterberg, J. A. The selective effect of visual deprivation on receptive field shape determined neurophysiologically. *Experimental Neurology*, 1968, **22**, 614–637.

Garey, L. J., & Pettigrew, J. D. Ultrastructural changes in kitten visual cortex after environmental modification. *Brain Research*, 1974, **66**, 165–172.

Grobstein, P., Chow, K. L., Spear, P. D., & Mathers, L. H. Development of rabbit visual cortex: Late appearance of a class of receptive fields. *Science*, 1973, **180**, 1185–1187.

Grobstein, P., Chow, K. L., & Fox, P. C. Development of receptive fields in rabbit visual cortex: Changes in time course due to delayed eye-opening. *Proceedings of the National Academy of Sciences of the United States of America*, 1975, **72**, 1543–1545.

Guillery, R. W. Binocular competition in the control of geniculate cell growth. *Journal of Comparative Neurology*, 1972, **144**, 117–130.

Guillery, R. W. On structural changes that can be produced experimentally in the mammalian visual pathways. In R. Bellairs & E. G. Gray (Eds.), *Essays on the nervous system*. London: Oxford University Press (Clarendon), 1974. Pp. 299–326.

Guillery, R. W., & Kaas, J. H. The effects of monocular lid suture upon the development of the lateral geniculate nucleus in squirrels (*Sciureus carolinensis*). *Journal of Comparative Neurology*, 1974, **154**, 433–442. (a)

Guillery, R. W., & Kaas, J. H. The effects of monocular lid suture upon the development of visual cortex in squirrels (*Sciureus carolinensis*). *Journal of Comparative Neurology*, 1974, **154**, 443–452. (b)

Guillery, R. W., & Stelzner, D. J. The differential effects of unilateral lid closure upon the monocular and binocular segments of the dorsal lateral geniculate nucleus in the cat. *Journal of Comparative Neurology*, 1970, **139**, 413–422.

Gyllensten, L., Malmfors, T., & Norrlin, M. L. Effects of visual deprivation on optic centers of growing and adult mice. *Journal of Comparative Neurology*, 1965, **124**, 149–160.

Hamasaki, D. I., Rackensperger, W., & Vesper, J. Spatial organization of normal and visually deprived units in the lateral geniculate nucleus of the cat. *Vision Research*, 1972, **12**, 843–854.

Hamasaki, D. I., & Winters, R. W. Intensity-response functions of visually deprived LGN neurons in cats. *Vision Research*, 1973, **13**, 925–936.

Hirsch, H. V. B., & Spinelli, D. N. Visual experience modifies distribution of horizontally and vertically oriented receptive fields in cats. *Science*, 1970, **168**, 869–871.

Hirsch, H. V. B., & Spinelli, D. N. Modification of the distribution of receptive field orientation in cats by selective visual exposure during development. *Experimental Brain Research*, 1971, **13**, 509–527.

Hubel, D. H., & Wiesel, T. N. Receptive fields of cells in striate cortex of very young, visually inexperienced kittens. *Journal of Neurophysiology*, 1963, **26**, 994–1002.

Hubel, D. H., & Wiesel, T. N. Binocular interaction in striate cortex of kittens reared with artificial squint. *Journal of Neurophysiology*, 1965, **28**, 1041–1059.

Hubel, D. H., & Wiesel, T. N. The period of susceptibility to the physiological effects of unilateral eye closure in kittens. *Journal of Physiology (London)*, 1970, **206**, 419–436.

Hughes, A. Topographical relationships between the anatomy and physiology of the rabbit visual system. *Documenta Ophthalmologica*, 1971, **30**, 33–159.

Lund, J. S., & Lund, R. D. The effects of varying periods of visual deprivation on synaptogenesis in the superior colliculus of the rat. *Brain Research*, 1972, **42**, 21–32.

Lund, R. D., & Lund, J. S. Development of synaptic patterns in the superior colliculus of the rat. *Brain Research*, 1972, **42**, 1–20.

Marotte, L. R., & Mark, R. F. The mechanism of selective reinnervation of fish eye muscle. II. Evidence from electron-microscopy of nerve ending. *Brain Research*, 1970, **19**, 53–62.

Mathers, L. H., Chow, K. L., Spear, P. D., & Grobstein, P. Ontogenesis of receptive fields in the rabbit striate cortex. *Experimental Brain Research*, 1974, **19**, 20–35.

Merrill, E. G., & Wall, P. D. Factors forming the edge of a receptive field: The presence of relatively ineffective afferent terminals. *Journal of Physiology (London)*, 1972, **226**, 825–846.

Mize, R. R., & Murphy, E. H. Selective visual experience fails to modify receptive field properties of rabbit striate cortex neurons. *Science*, 1973, **180**, 320–323.

Olson, C. R., & Pettigrew, J. D. Single units in visual cortex of kittens reared in stroboscopic illumination. *Brain Research*, 1974, **70**, 189–204.

Pettigrew, J. D. The effect of visual experience on the development of stimulus specificity by kitten cortical neurons. *Journal of Physiology (London)*, 1974, **237**, 49–74.

Pettigrew, J. D., & Freeman, R. D. Visual experience without lines: Effect on developing cortical neurons. *Science*, 1973, **182**, 599–601.

Pettigrew, J. D., & Garey, L. J. Selective modification of single neuron properties in the visual cortex of kittens. *Brain Research*, 1974, **66**, 160–164.

Pettigrew, J. D., Olson, C. R., & Barlow, H. B. Kitten visual cortex: Short-term stimulus-induced changes in connectivity. *Science*, 1973, **180**, 1202–1203. (a)

Pettigrew, J. D., Olson, C. R., & Hirsch, H. V. B. Cortical effect of selective visual experience: Degeneration or reorganization? *Brain Research*, 1973, **51**, 345–351. (b)

Rapisardi, S. C., Chow, K. L., & Mathers, L. H. Ontogenesis of receptive field characteristics in the dorsal lateral geniculate of the rabbit. *Experimental Brain Research*, 1975, **22**, 295–305.

Riesen, A. H. Sensory deprivation. In E. Stellar & J. M. Sprague (Eds.), *Progress in physiological psychology* (Vol. 1). New York: Academic Press, 1966. Pp. 116–147.

Sherman, S. M., & Sanderson, K. J. Binocular interaction of cells of the dorsal lateral geniculate nucleus of visually deprived cats. *Brain Research*, 1972, **37**, 126–131.

Sherman, S. M., Hoffmann, K. P., & Stone, J. Loss of specific cell type from dorsal lateral geniculate nucleus in visually deprived cats. *Journal of Neurophysiology*, 1972, **35**, 532–541.

Shlaer, R. Shift in binocular disparity causes compensatory changes in the cortical structure of kittens. *Science*, 1971, **173**, 638–641.

Sperry, R. W. Embryogenesis of behavioral nerve nets. In R. L. Deltaan & H. Ursprung (Eds.), *Organogenesis*. New York: Holt, 1965. Pp. 161–186.

Spinelli, D. N., & Hirsch, H. V. B. Genesis of receptive field types in single units of cat visual cortex. Federation Proceedings, *Federation of American Societies for Experimental Biology*, 1971, **30**, 615.

Spinelli, D. N., Hirsch, H. V. B., Phelps, R. W., & Metzler, J. Visual experience as a determinant of the response characteristics of cortical receptive fields in cats. *Experimental Brain Research*, 1972, **15**, 289–304.

Stent, G. A physiological mechanism for Hebb's postulate of learning. *Proceedings of the National Academy of Sciences of the United States of America*, 1973, **70**, 997–1001.

Van Sluyters, R. C., & Blakemore, C. Experimental creation of unusual neuronal properties in visual cortex of kitten. *Nature (London)*, 1973, **246**, 506–508.

Van Sluyters, R. C., & Stewart, D. L. Binocular neurons of the rabbit's visual cortex: Receptive field characteristics. *Experimental Brain Research*, 1974, **19**, 166–195. (a)

Van Sluyters, R. C., & Stewart, D. L. Binocular neurons of the rabbit's visual cortex: Effects of monocular sensory deprivation. *Experimental Brain Research*, 1974, **19**, 196–204. (b)

Wiesel, T. N., & Hubel, D. H. Effects of visual deprivation on morphology and physiology of cells in the cat's lateral geniculate body. *Journal of Neurophysiology*, 1963, **26**, 978–993. (a)

Wiesel, T. N., & Hubel, D. H. Single-cell responses in the striate cortex of kittens deprived of vision in one eye. *Journal of Neurophysiology*, 1963, **26**, 1003–1017. (b)

Wiesel, T. N., & Hubel, D. H. Comparison of the effects of unilateral and bilateral eye closure on cortical unit responses in kittens. *Journal of Neurophysiology*, 1965, **28**, 1029–1040. (a)

Wiesel, T. N., & Hubel, D. H. Extent of recovery from the effects of visual deprivation in kittens. *Journal of Neurophysiology*, 1965, **28**, 1060–1072. (b)

Wiesel, T. N., & Hubel, D. H. Ordered arrangement of orientation columns in monkeys lacking visual experience. *Journal of Comparative Neurology*, 1974, **158**, 307–318.

DEVELOPMENT OF NEURONAL RESPONSES IN THE VISUAL SYSTEM OF CATS

J. D. DANIELS AND J. D. PETTIGREW

Division of Biology
California Institute of Technology
Pasadena, California

I. Introduction

The last two decades have seen considerable progress in our understanding of the mammalian visual system at the single-neuron level. This progress is undoubtedly attributable to man's own visual prowess, but it also stems in large part from the use of behaviorally relevant or "natural" stimuli, an approach presaged by Barlow (1953), generally proselytized by Lettvin, Maturana, McCulloch, and Pitts (1959) and brought to its quintessence by Hubel and Wiesel (1959, 1962, 1963a, 1965a, 1967, 1969). This approach eschews lightning-flash stimuli and the synchronous volleys produced by the electrical stimuli of classical neurophysiology. Instead the experimenter concentrates on the effect of complicated, but carefully controlled, patterns of natural stimuli with familiar parameters like position, movement, color, contrast, and shape.

In the primary visual cortex of a normal adult cat, a given neuron may not fire unless a pattern is present in visual space for which a number of parameters have been carefully set by the experimenter. These parameters include the following:

1. Position of the target on the screen where the neuron's activity is influenced—the *receptive field*.

2. Orientation—unlike the lateral geniculate cells which relay information to the cortex, cortical neurons respond to moving edges only over a narrow range of angles. The optimal angle varies randomly around the clock from cell to cell.

3. Binocularity—nearly every cell can be driven from stimulation of either eye. There is some variation in the relative strength of the inputs from each eye (*ocular dominance*), most cells in a normal animal having balanced binocularity. In addition, under conditions of simultaneous binocular stimulation, each cell is highly selective for the relative retinal positioning or *disparity* between the two retinal images of the target.

4. Movement—both speed and direction of stimulus motion may be important for a vigorous single neuron response.

5. Size—both length and width of the target may be important for the response.

6. Contrast at the moving edge—some neurons respond only to advancing dark edges, others only to light edges, and so on.

And so a particular neuron may respond only to a particular combination of these parameters, corresponding to a target of appropriate position, orientation, and direction of movement in space. This extraordinary specificity of a cell's response is exactly matched for each eye, a property that would enable the cortex to perform one of the first steps in the subtle task of stereopsis, viz., the identification of the two features, one on each retina, which are similar enough to belong to the same external object (Barlow, Blakemore, & Pettigrew, 1967). Because each cell is disparity selective and because the optimal disparity varies from cell to cell, the cortex could also perform the second task required for stereopsis, viz., the calculation of the relative displacement in space of the identified contour.

In summary, the system appears capable of making a binocular *match* on the basis of orientation, velocity, direction, and size and then calculating distance based on *nonmatching* retinal displacements (or disparity).

This extraordinary subtlety and selectivity in adult cortical neuron performance is rivaled by a remarkable degree of plasticity in kitten cortical neuron function, the subject of much study now because of this experience dependence. All the stimulus parameters that are important in the normal adult neuron's ability to match similar parts of the two retinal images (orientation, binocularity, movement, size, and shape) have now been shown to be necessary for a kitten neuron's development.

In the first section of our chapter we review what has been learned in the past decade about the response properties of kitten visual neurons and the susceptibility of those neurons, during a *critical period* (3 weeks to 3 months of age), to environmental factors that can alter the course of their development. The most widely used paradigm for studying this problem has been monocular deprivation; clear-cut effects have been seen in the lateral geniculate (LGN), primary visual cortex, and superior colliculus.

Experiments to demonstrate some effect of experience on the visual system of rabbits are one of the causes of controversy in this field. In the second section we review the organization of the rabbit visual system and the experiments which have shown that rabbit neurons are less susceptible to environmental effects than cat neurons. We offer some ideas as to why this might be so, as do Grobstein and Chow (this volume).

In the third section we discuss briefly some evidence for plasticity in the developing visual systems of frogs, monkeys, and man, comparing the data there to the more extensive data on cats.

Blakemore (1973, 1974) has recently written two short reviews on aspects of the above topics.

II. Responses of Kitten Neurons

A. Visual Cortex

To review the work on kitten visual cortex neurons it is best to proceed chronologically, with perhaps a little hindsight to keep track of the main issues. The main issues are (1) whether the response specificities of single cells in the kitten visual system are different from those of adult cats, and

(2) to what extent can the response specificities of kitten neurons be modified as the consequence of special early visual experiences. The hindsight is that kitten neurons are immature in many respects when compared to adult neurons, and some of their subsequent response specificity comes about as the consequence of visual experience. If that visual experience is appropriately restricted, the adult responses of the cells will likewise be restricted.

Hubel and Wiesel (1959, 1962, 1963a, 1965a, 1967, 1968, 1969, 1971) did the pioneering studies of the responses to patterned stimulation of visual cortex neurons. They found a remarkable change in response properties from the LGN to the cortex. While LGN cell receptive fields are concentric center/surround types which can be plotted with stationary flashing spots from one eye only, cortical fields are asymmetric when plotted with flashing spots, fields can be mapped from both eyes, and most remarkable, the *optimal* stimulus for a cortical neuron is an oriented bar moving in a particular direction. Thus, the geniculostriate connections alone cannot account for the receptive field properties of cortical cells—intrinsic cortical connections must play an important role. Taking account of other cortical response properties (such as size of receptive field, ON–OFF responses, length specificity), Hubel and Wiesel were able to divide cortical neurons into classes: simple, complex, and hypercomplex. There are now many fascinating studies of visual cortex neurons, from several cortical areas of cat, and from rabbits and monkeys too, but discussion of these (see review by Brooks & Jung, 1973, for more details) would sidetrack us from the developmental questions with which Hubel and Wiesel's kitten work deals.

With regard to the first issue (difference between adult and kitten responses), Hubel and Wiesel (1963b) examined the responses of 17 cells from area 17 in two young, visually naive kittens. They found that, although the cells had less spontaneous activity and their evoked responses tended to fatigue more easily, the properties of binocularity and preference for oriented bar stimuli seemed similar to that of an adult cat. They concluded that "... much of the richness of visual physiology in the cortex of the adult cat—the receptive field organization, binocular interaction and functional architecture—is present in very young kittens without visual experience."

A decade later Pettigrew (1974) restudied the visual responses of cortical neurons in young kittens (see also Barlow & Pettigrew, 1971; Pettigrew, 1972). In contrast to Hubel and Wiesel, he found that visually naive kitten neurons do not possess all the specificities of adult cells and that visual experience *is* necessary for the complete development of adult-like responses. For the property of binocularity, Pettigrew agreed with Hubel and Wiesel that visually inexperienced cells can be driven by stimuli from both eyes, but he used an additional technique to show that depth judgment mechanisms, which are functions of signals from both eyes, require a few weeks of visual experience to develop. The technique (Pettigrew, Nikara, & Bishop, 1968) involves horizontal shifting of the receptive fields of the two eyes with respect to each other by prisms in front of the eyes; in an adult, the fields generally need to be precisely aligned to generate the greatest binocular response, and misalignment of the two fields by less than 1° can cause marked inhibition of the binocular response (this is called disparity tuning). In inexperienced kittens no cells with narrow disparity tuning curves are seen. A summary of Pettigrew's data for disparity and two other parameters, orientation and direction preference, is shown in Fig. 1.

Pettigrew used a somewhat different criterion for orientation selectivity than Hubel and Wiesel (1963b). Since testing for orientation selectivity normally involves *moving* an oriented bar through the receptive field, it is possible to confuse orientation selectivity with direction selectivity. Pettigrew tried to differentiate between the two by requiring that an orientation-selective cell at least provide a larger response to an oriented bar than to a small spot (both moved the same direction and speed through the receptive field). Although this is a test easily "passed" by most adult neurons, by this criterion there were no orientation-selective cells in very

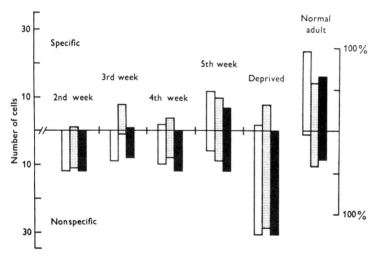

FIG. 1. Development of various response properties of kitten visual cortex neurons during the second to fifth weeks of age, compared to binocularly deprived cats and normal adults. Orientation-specific cells had to show a clear preference for a moving bar over a moving spot. Direction selective cells were seen at all ages. Disparity preference was quite sensitive to experience; no cells in the deprived animals developed disparity specificity. Data from 84 cells are represented in the left portion of the figure; the right portion represents data from a previous study. □, Orientation; □, direction; ■, binocular disparity. Reprinted with permission from Pettigrew (1974).

young kittens (a point disputed by Wiesel & Hubel, 1974). Orientation
selectivity develops over the first few weeks of visual life, as shown in Fig. 1.
On the other hand, direction selectivity is present even in the youngest
kittens studied.

B. Binocular Deprivation

Another way to test whether visual experience is necessary for the proper
development of kitten neurons is to deprive a kitten of visual experience
for some time, then record the responses of the cells, comparing them to
cells from normally reared cats. This sort of experiment allows one to
record from an older, more fit animal, whose optics are clearer and on whom
preparatory surgery, anesthesia, and artificial respiration are not as
traumatic as they would be for a kitten. It must be remembered, however,
that an older binocularly deprived cat is not the same as a visually naive
kitten; in the terms of the developmental mechanisms discussed in Gottlieb's
chapter in Section 1 of this volume, deprivation may hinder *maintenance*
of function, or it may prevent *facilitation* or *induction*. In either case, the
older deprived animal cannot be thought of as just a big version of the
visually naive kitten.

Wiesel and Hubel (1965a) were the first to study single units in binocularly
deprived cats, suturing the lids of both eyes of four kittens around the time
of eye-opening, then recording from cortical neurons about 3 months later.
They found that the cells in these animals were generally sluggish, like
those of a young kitten, and that about 25% of the cells fired spontaneously
but were visually unresponsive. Nevertheless 40% of the cells seemed to
respond normally by adult standards.

On the other hand, Pettigrew, in his later study (1974), found that
virtually none of the cortical neurons of 15 kittens deprived of experience
by lid suture had genuine adultlike properties. Pettigrew's criteria for
adultlike properties were (1) orientation selectivity, (2) binocular disparity
preference, and (3) direction selectivity. His data are summarized in Fig. 1.
Blakemore and Mitchell (1973) also studied a binocularly deprived kitten,
and their findings agree with Pettigrew's. Blakemore (see Lewin, 1974) now
claims to have restudied the problem and to have found a few (15%) truly
adultlike cells in immature cortex. Blakemore and Van Sluyters (1975) report more fully on this.

Besides different criteria for calling a cell's response adultlike, what else
can account for the differences between Wiesel and Hubel's work and
Pettigrew's? Wiesel and Hubel (1965a) recorded from 3-month-old kittens,
whereas all of Pettigrew's binocularly deprived animals were 6 weeks old or
less; perhaps deprivation slows down the *rate* of development (as well as
the eventual level of maturity to which the cells develop). Also possible,

but less likely, is a sampling bias due to different microelectrodes or to different cell sizes in 6-week- and 3-month-old cats.

Pettigrew (1974) notes that Wiesel and Hubel generally use a barbiturate anesthesia for recording, whereas he uses nitrous oxide. Pettigrew (1974) speculates that Wiesel and Hubel's cells may appear more selective because they would be somewhat depressed by the barbiturate.[1] Along these lines, Nicoll (1972) proposed that barbiturates may act by prolonging γ-amino-butyric acid mediated inhibition, and Pettigrew and Daniels (1973) have shown that an antagonist of GABA can eliminate some specificities in cortical neuron responses. Hubel and Wiesel (1962) insisted that anesthesia does not change receptive field organization or selectivity, only responsiveness.

At any rate, it seems that binocularly deprived cats have cortical neuron responses similar to those of kittens whose first visual experience is in the experimental chamber. In both cases most cells can be influenced by stimuli from both eyes and have receptive fields quite different from those of LGN cells, but the responses still seem immature by adult measures. Whether there are *no* cells with adultlike properties is still disputed. Although it may be worthwhile to analyze the developmental mechanisms that underlie the effects of binocular deprivation on cortical neurons, it is perhaps best first to review additional data, both from other visual structures, such as the LGN and superior colliculus, and from other paradigms, such as monocular deprivation, and defer analysis for later.

C. Lateral Geniculate Nucleus (LGN)

Can the responses of area-17 cells in the developing kitten be explained by the responses of the cells that drive them, that is, by the relay cells of the LGN? Probably not, since the responses of cortical neurons are so different from LGN responses that connections *between* the cortical neurons themselves must account for most of the cortical properties. At any rate there are no published studies of the visual responses of single LGN cells in very young visually inexperienced kittens, although work in progress (Norman & Daniels, unpublished observations) indicates that LGN responses in kittens as old as 20 days are not truly adultlike; i.e., some development, probably not dependent on experience, goes on for the first few weeks of life.

There have been LGN studies of binocularly deprived cats; the first by Wiesel and Hubel (1963a) found that the LGN cells they recorded from seemed adultlike, with characteristic concentrically organized receptive

[1] An iceberg effect. A cell normally responsive over a wide range of, say, orientations, may, if artificially depressed, appear to have a range of response over only those orientations to which it responds most vigorously—the tip of the iceberg, so to speak.

fields, surrounds having the opposite response (ON or OFF) of centers, surround illumination inhibiting center response, and center illumination enhancing surround response. Later Sherman and Sanderson (1972) verified this, with the added observation that a subliminal inhibition from the non-dominant eye was somewhat attenuated in deprived cats. Arguing that, even though all the cells recorded from in deprived cats may seem normal, a deficit could still exist if an entire class of cell had dropped out, Sherman, Hoffman, and Stone (1972) restudied the LGN of binocularly deprived cats and showed that there was a reduction in the number of Y-cells (transient) when compared with the percentage in a normal cat. In a normal adult cat about 50% of the LGN relay cells can be classified as Y-type and 50% as X-type (sustained) (Hoffman, Stone, & Sherman, 1972), while in binocularly deprived cats only 25% were Y-type. It is possible that this may have been a sampling bias due to the fact that microelectrodes tend to isolate larger cells, since Wiesel and Hubel (1963a) noted cell shrinkage in the LGN of binocularly deprived cats. Perhaps the Y-cells shrank more than did the X-cells.

In sum then, LGN cells seem little affected (physiologically anyway) by binocular deprivation, which at the same time keeps many, if not all, of the cells in the primary visual cortex from developing properly. Thus a proportion of the LGN-to-area 17 synapses would seem to require some sort of visual experience to become effective. Whether this is a process of atrophy or failure of growth (maintenance versus induction) will be discussed in Section II. In normal kittens, during the first part of the critical period there is a steady increase in the number of synapses in both visual cortex and LGN (Cragg, 1974) (see Fig. 2). Perhaps some of these synapses become repressed (in the sense of Mark, 1974), or eliminated by normal development or special visual experience. Physiological evidence points to this; direct anatomical evidence is lacking.

It might be added that there seems to be no question that the ganglion cells of the retina remain completely normal, physiologically, even after 12–18 months of visual deprivation by lid suture (Sherman & Stone, 1973). However, some structural changes have been seen in cat (Weiskrantz, 1958) and rat (Fifkova, 1972a, 1972b) retina after deprivation, including an increase in the ratio of conventional to ribbon synapses in the inner plexiform layer.

D. Superior Colliculus

To understand further how the responses in the visual cortex develop, one can study structures that receive input from the visual cortex. Besides projecting to other cortical areas, the primary visual cortex (areas 17 and 18)

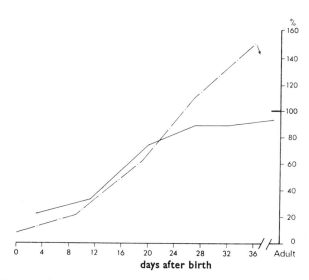

FIG. 2. Density of synapses in developing visual cortex (·—·) and lateral geniculate nucleus (—) of the cat. Adult values are normalized to 100%. From Day 20 to Day 36 represents the first part of the critical period for development of ocular dominance. Note that the density of synapses in the visual cortex rises above future adult values during the critical period. Reprinted with permission from Cragg (1974).

projects to the superior colliculus, which also receives a direct projection from the retina. The properties of binocularity and direction selectivity seen in collicular cells are thought to be mediated by the cortex in a normal adult cat (see Wickelgren, 1972).

Stein, Labos, and Kruger (1973) and Norton (1974) have charted the development of these properties in young kittens. Visually responsive cells could be found in 7-day-old kittens. These cells were easily fatigued, driven only by the contralateral eye, and responded best to stationary flashing stimuli. From the second to the fifth week, an increasing proportion of the cells became binocular and directionally selective, while *losing* their preference for flashing stimuli. The development of directional selectivity in superior colliculus cells correlates well with the development of the same property in cortical cells (see Fig. 1).

Norton (1974) also studied the development of visually guided behavior in the animals he used for recording. Although the eyes would open on Day 10, no visual behavior was seen until Day 15, when orienting responses appeared. Around Day 21 visual placing responses, such as obstacle avoidance, were noted. Thus, light-evoked responses of cells in the visual pathway appear well before visually guided movements.

As with the kitten cortical units, one would like to compare the responses of collicular cells of very young animals with no visual experience to older binocularly deprived animals. Sterling and Wickelgren (1970) found that in binocularly deprived cats almost all the collicular units become monocular (contralateral) and lose direction selectivity, and many of them respond sluggishly (or not at all) to visual stimuli. In decorticate animals Wickelgren and Sterling (1969) made similar observations, including the fact that after removal of the cortex, receptive fields could be plotted with stationary flashing spots. This is a property similar to that described by Stein *et al.* (1973) for immature collicular units. It suggests that the cells are driven predominantly by retinal ganglion cells with similar properties. Thus, collicular units in visually naive kittens, collicular units in binocularly deprived cats, and collicular units in decorticate cats all have similar properties, properties which suggest that the retinal input to the colliculus is present at birth and not dependent upon visual experience for its maintenance or development, whereas the cortical input develops later and depends on experience to make itself felt in the colliculus.

As far as the cat visual system is concerned, then, the retina and the LGN seem to develop properly with or without visual experience (aside from selective loss of Y-cells from the LGN), while the visual cortex and the superior colliculus require visual experience for their neurons to develop the full complement of adult properties. In the absence of visual experience, the neurons in the visual cortex and superior colliculus still can develop visual responses, but the responses are sluggish and nonselective, much like the properties of neurons in very young kittens which have never had visual experience. It is perhaps worth noting that cats deprived sufficiently long of visual experience, though the retina and LGN may be functioning properly, are behaviorally blind (Riesen, 1966).

At this point the reader may want to consult Table I, where the various kinds of visually experienced cat are listed, along with the features of brain structure which have been studied in each kind. In Section III, we shall discuss monocular deprivation, the existence of a critical period for the imprinting of visual experience onto the primary visual cortex, and the possibility of recovery from deficits suffered during the critical period.

III. Monocular Deprivation

A. Cortex

Monocular deprivation can be considered as a sort of special early experience for neurons in the visual cortex. The innately binocular neurons there will receive normal input from one retina and the signal for darkness

TABLE 1
DEVELOPMENT AND DEPRIVATION STUDIES

	Adult cat	Kitten	Visually inexperienced	
			Binocularly deprived	Monocularly deprived
Retina	W, X, Y ganglion cells; majority have concentrically organized receptive fields; surround has opposite response of center	—	Totally normal	Totally normal
LGN[a]	X, Y (and W) input; all cells monocular except for subtle binocular surround inhibition; cells arranged in laminae	—	Essentially normal: some cells sluggish, some binocular inhibition gone, some Y-cells missing	Severe loss of Y-cells in deprived layers; shrinkage of cells in "binocular" regions of deprived layers.
Visual cortex	Most cells binocularly driven; respond best to oriented moving bars Simple Complex Hypercomplex	Binocular excitation innate but disparity preference broad; no preference for moving lines over moving spots; cells easily fatigued	Similar to inexperienced kitten	No cells driven by deprived eye; orientation selectivity normal
Superior colliculus	Cells are movement sensitive, directionally selective; prefer movement toward periphery; binocularly driven; both retinal (W, Y) and cortical input	Binocularity and direction selectivity mature during weeks 2 & 5; at first neurons respond to flashes and fatigue easily	Tends to remove cortical effects; binocularity and direction selectivity attentuated; similar to cortical ablation	No cells driven by deprived eye, but when cortex is ablated, deprived-eye contra-lateral cells are found.
Behavior	Predatory animals relying on stereoscopic visual clues for prey tracking; limited color vision	Eyes open about Day 10; orienting responses appear around Day 15; after Day 25 placing behavior develops	Essentially blind	In deprived eye, only luminosities can be detected; some improvement possible with forced use of deprived eye

[a] Lateral geniculate nucleus.

from the other. Under these conditions, Wiesel and Hubel (1963b) found that the neurons which develop can be driven only by the normal eye. The receptive fields plotted on the normal retina have typical orientation and direction selectivity. Actually the deprived eye is able to drive (though not too reliably), a few cells in the contralateral cortex (Ganz, Fitch, & Satterberg, 1968; Wiesel & Hubel, 1965a).

To be effective the deprivation must occur in a critical period extending from the third week to the third month of the kitten's life. Long monocular deprivation of a normal adult has no effect. Hubel and Wiesel (1970) determined the duration of the critical period by lid-suturing kittens for various times and then recording later from enough cells in each cat to form an ocular dominance histogram, examples of which are shown in Fig. 3 for a normal cat and a monocularly deprived cat (and a strabismic cat).

Hubel and Wiesel (1970) and Olson and Freeman (1975) showed that a very short time of deprivation, 3 days for instance, can shift completely the ocular dominance histogram of a kitten.

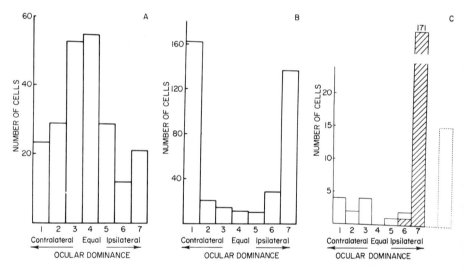

Fig. 3. Ocular dominance histograms from samples of visual cortex cells in (A) normal, (B) strabismic, and (C) monocularly deprived cats. Animals in Groups B and C had altered visual environments during the critical period. Ocular dominance is a measure of the influence of the two eyes on a single cell. Most normal cells can be influenced by both eyes. Animals in Group B had an eye muscle cut so the two eyes looked in abnormally different directions. Animals in Group C (▨, normal; ☐, no orientation; dotted line, no response) had one eye occluded by lid suture. Not shown are the effects of binocular deprivation, after which many cells can still be influenced by both eyes, but the responses of the cells are generally sluggish and immature (see Fig. 1). Reprinted with permission from Hubel and Wiesel (1965a) (A and B), and Wiesel and Hubel (1965b) (C).

Blakemore and Van Sluyters (1974) outlined the critical period in another way by suturing one eye from the time of eye-opening until a variable time later during the critical period. At that time they *reversed* the suture to the other eye and recorded from cortical cells still later to see when reverse-suturing was effective in reversing the effects of the original monocular occlusion. A summary of their data is shown in Fig. 4, where a good agreement is seen with the finding of Wiesel and Hubel that the most sensitive period for ocular dominance determination is around 4 weeks of age. Since work on visually inexperienced kittens had shown that cortical neurons are initially wired to inputs from both eyes, it is clear that monocular deprivation disrupts a maintenance function of normal visual experience. By this reasoning binocular deprivation should lead to loss of responses from both eyes, but it does not, implying that monocular deprivation is actually *more* than disrupted maintenance. It is a demonstration of im-

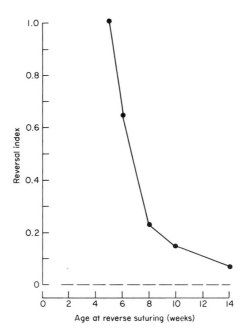

FIG. 4. Time course of the critical period as measured by the percentage of cells that change ocular dominance after *reverse suture* at the times shown on the abscissa. For reverse suture, a kitten is monocularly deprived until the time of reversal, then the first deprived eye is uncovered and the previously free eye is sutured shut. The animal is allowed to develop through the rest of the critical period before single units are sampled. Reversal index is the ratio of cells dominated by the originally sutured eye to the total number of cells studied. Reprinted with permission from Blakemore and Van Sluyters (1974).

balanced *competition* during development, with a winner-take-all outcome. Looked at this way, monocular deprivation can also be seen as a way of *facilitating* the input from the good eye.

B. Lateral Geniculate Nucleus

Wiesel and Hubel (1963a) noted that LGN cells driven by a monocularly deprived eye had normal receptive fields. However, they found a change in the morphology of the LGN: cells in laminae which received input from the deprived eye were smaller than normal by about 25% (cross-sectional area). Guillery (1972) later showed that imbalanced *binocular competition* was responsible for the retarded cell growth in the deprived layers. Specifically, he found that cells in layers receiving projections from the deprived eye grew to normal adult size if they were in a monocular segment of the LGN (a segment which received only deprived eye input) or if they were in a binocular segment whose corresponding input from the normal eye had been destroyed by lesion. Cortical cells could be driven from regions in the deprived eye corresponding to the lesioned regions in the normal eye, further supporting the notion that imbalanced binocular competition was responsible for the suppression of responses from the deprived eye (Sherman, Guillery, Kaas, & Sanderson, 1974).

In another study of the response properties of LGN cells in monocular animals, Sherman, Hoffman and Stone (1972) agreed with Wiesel and Hubel (1963a) that the responses recorded from the cells in deprived layers seemed normal, but they noted a marked absence of Y-cell responses, an absence even more severe (9% versus 55% Y-cell responses in a normal animal) than that seen in binocularly deprived animals.

C. Superior Colliculus

In the superior colliculus, monocular deprivation leads to a situation in which all the cells can be driven only by the normal eye, much like the cortex under the same conditions (Sterling & Wickelgren, 1970). Since the colliculus receives a direct projection from the contralateral retina and since the retina of the deprived eye is perfectly capable of driving cells in the LGN, it seemed odd that the deprived retina was ineffective in the contralateral colliculus. This paradox was explained when Sterling and Wickelgren ablated the cortex in monocularly deprived animals and found a dramatic shift in ocular dominance in the colliculus which received a projection from the deprived eye: all the cells could be driven by the deprived eye and none by the normal eye, much like the situation in a *normally reared animal* with the cortex ablated. So in a monocularly deprived animal not only does the normal eye capture all the cells in the cortex, but the cortical cells then somehow inhibit (perhaps presynaptically) the direct deprived eye input to the colliculus.

D. Behavior

In a behavioral study related to the single unit superior colliculus work on cats, Sherman (1974) showed that cats with unilateral cortical ablations, which cause blindness in half the visual field, can have some return of visually guided behavior in the blinded field if the *contralateral* superior colliculus is also ablated, thus indicating that inhibitory signals from the cortex may first pass through one colliculus on the way to the other.

Dews and Wiesel (1970) conducted behavioral studies on some of the monocularly deprived cats used by Hubel and Wiesel (1970). They found that cats monocularly occluded through the most sensitive part of the critical period are virtually blind in the deprived eye, except for some luminosity detection. Partial recovery of vision is possible when the normal eye is covered and the animal is forced to deal with the visual world through the formerly deprived eye. Comparing their behavioral observations with cortical recordings from animals forced to try to recover vision, they concluded that behavioral recovery does not depend on the originally deprived eye's being able to influence more cortical neurons, since this process may involve the assistance of noncortical visual pathways. [Note that Blakemore and Van Sluyters (1974) reverse-sutured their animals while the animals were still in their critical periods. Wiesel and Hubel waited until *after* the critical period to look at cortical effects of forced recovery.]

Wiesel and Hubel's discovery of the striking effects of monocular deprivation during a critical period on the response properties of cat visual cortex neurons (effects that one could not predict from the results of binocular deprivation) inspired a "second generation" of studies on the perceptual plasticities of visual cortex neurons. The next section will deal with these studies. They show some of the extent to which the environment can shape the development of the nervous system as well as some of the limitations of environmental influence on that development. Table II lists some of these second-generation studies.

IV. Later Plasticity Studies on Kitten Cortical Neurons

A. Binocularity

Hubel and Wiesel (1965b) showed that when both eyes are allowed to see during the critical period but are not allowed to see at the same time (alternating occlusion) or are made to see in abnormally different directions

TABLE II
CRITICAL PERIOD PLASTICITY STUDIES OF CORTICAL NEURONS IN CAT

Property	Changes in area-17 neurons
A. Binocularity	
Squint and alternating occlusion	Cells become monocular: half ipsi, half contra
Prisms	Binocularity preserved, but a regular shift in disparity preference to accommodate prism offset
B. Orientation	
Vertical and horizontal lines	Cells develop preference for orientation to which they were exposed; no preference for lines orthogonal to conditioning lines
Cylindrical lenses (astigmatism)	Bias for orientation of sharp focus
Random dots	Preference for lines lost; many cells become "dot detectors"
C. Movement	
Strobe illumination (no movement)	Movement sensitivity not lost; cells somewhat less specific for orientation; flash responses enhanced
Unidirectional environment	Cells show some directional bias corresponding to exposure

(artificial squint, see Fig. 3), the neurons in the visual cortex lose their binocularity and form two ocular dominance groups, with one group driven exclusively by the right eye and the other by the left. In a more refined experiment concerned with the directions the two eyes see during the critical period, Shlaer (1971) had kittens wear prism goggles, which induced a 2.3° shift in vertical disparity. The 18 cells in two cats he studied later had a shifted disparity histogram in the direction to compensate for the prism-induced misalignment. Shlaer's procedure apparently did not produce populations of monocularly driven cells, as the extreme deviations of strabismus did for Hubel and Wiesel's (1965b) cats.

The monocularly deprived eye need not be occluded for the whole critical period in order for there to be a disruption of normal ocular dominance. Hubel and Wiesel (1970) noted that as few as 3 days of monocular occlusion at the height of the critical period could greatly shift the ocular dominance histogram of a kitten. In a related experiment, Pettigrew, Olson, and Barlow (1973) showed that during the course of an experiment it is possible to induce a temporary shift (i.e., for approximately an hour) in the ocular dominance of a single cell in a kitten. Pettigrew and Garey (1974) demonstrated that more permanent effects resulting from repeated stimulus presentations are possible if several hours of *consolidation time* are allowed before retesting. Along with these more pronounced physiological effects, Garey and Pettigrew (1974) noticed increases in synaptic vesicle densities of stimulated as opposed to unstimulated hemispheres in the same kittens.

B. Orientation

Cortical neurons differ from LGN neurons in two key ways: (1) most cortical cells are binocularly driven; and (2) they are sensitive to the *orientation* of patterns in their receptive fields. The binocular feature can be disrupted by appropriate critical period experience, and, it turns out, so can the orientation feature. Hirsch and Spinelli (1970, 1971) raised kittens which wore goggles with either vertical or horizontal stripes on them and found that the cortical cells from which they recorded all responded either to vertical or to horizontal stimuli, depending on which type of goggles a particular kitten wore. No responses to diagonal patterns were noted. Blakemore and Cooper (1970) obtained similar results by limiting the visual experience of kittens to periods of time in which they were placed in striped cylinders. Blakemore and Mitchell (1973) found that as little as 1 hour of viewing oriented stripes at the most sensitive time of the critical period (4 weeks old), provided that the rest of the time is spent in the dark, can tune most cortical neurons to the orientation seen during the experience (see Fig. 4). Orientation preference is not as easy to alter as ocular dominance. Stryker and Sherk (1975) have been unable to repeat Blakemore and Cooper's original experiment.

Even if there is an in-built bias in cortical cells for oriented bars, critical period experience can override the preference, as was shown in the random-dot experiments of Pettigrew and Freeman (1973) and Van Sluyters and Blakemore (1973). Pettigrew and Freeman, after raising kittens in a planetarium-like environment, found that a majority of the visually responsive cells (27/47) *preferred* a moving small dot to a moving oriented bar. After eliminating the possibilities that these might be LGN or hypercomplex responses, they concluded that early visual experience with straight lines is necessary for the permanent formation of truly orientation selective cells, and that experience without lines can produce a population of cortical cells more responsively tuned to dots than to lines. Unlike binocular deprivation, stripe raising and monocular deprivation do not lead to groups of unresponsive cells among responsive ones. Thus, although some aspects of stripe raising can be thought of as disrupted maintenance (loss of response to many orientations), it is probably best to think of the stripe raising effects as facilitatory, enhancing certain parts of an originally broad orientation curve for each cell. It is important to realize that the high degree of selectivity for small dots exhibited by the "dot-detector" neurons of Pettigrew and

Freeman (1973) cannot be accounted for by a mere failure of development to proceed past the naive kitten stage of poor selectivity for stimulus configuration (a possibility raised in Grobstein and Chow's chapter). As shown clearly in their Fig. 1, the dot-detector gives a very vigorous response to a target much smaller than the receptive field size and virtually no response to a larger target. In contrast, a comparable (in terms of field size and plotability) neuron from a visually inexperienced kitten gives grudging responses to both stimuli, with a preference for the large target, if any. These workers commented on the unusual nature of the "dot-detector" receptive fields and on the vigor of their responses. In addition, electron microscopic study of these animals (Garey & Pettigrew, 1974) revealed none of the signs (such as low vesicle density) indicative of immaturity or lack of visual experience.

C. Motion

In an effort to give kittens visual experience with patterns but not with motion, Cynader, Berman, and Hein (1973) raised two kittens in stroboscopic illumination (10-μsec flash every 2 seconds). The strobe-reared pair was found to have some directionally selective cells (38%), but this percentage was much less than the 83% found in a group of normal animals. Some of the cells in the strobe-raised group responded *only* to strobe flashes, but there were none like this in the control group. In an independent study, Olson and Pettigrew (1974) observed similar effects, though they saw somewhat more directionally selective units than Cynader *et al.* (56% versus 38%). They also noted that no cells responded exclusively to strobe flashing. Because there is a substantial, though less than normal, number of directionally selective cells in strobe-raised cats, it seems that direction sensitivity cannot be easily manipulated by critical period experience. Two studies have shown that the distribution of preferred directions of cortical neurons can be shifted to reflect a unidirectional, moving environment (Cynader, Berman, & Hein, 1975; Tretter, Cynader, & Singer, 1975).

Grobstein and Chow (this volume) have suggested that a truly adaptational role for kitten neuron plasticity might require the demonstration of Gottlieb's principle of induction for some neurons. This would require the demonstration of some special neuronal property, produced by a particular experience, and not observed in normal nor in visually inexperienced cortex. There may in fact be a few examples of this.

1. Spinelli, Hirsch, Phelps, and Metzler (1972) have described remarkable, grating-shaped, receptive fields whose dimensions closely match the conditioning stimulus viewed by the animal. While "multimodal" receptive

fields are occasionally reported in the literature, no one has seen one (let alone several) examples of vertical, grating-shaped receptive fields with 6° spacing, either in normal cats or visually inexperienced kittens. Pettigrew and Garey (1974) have a similar finding.

2. Pettigrew and Freeman (1973) describe dot-detectors that have a number of properties not shared by any neurons so far described in the cortex of normal cats or in visually inexperienced kittens.

3. There are a number of reports (Pettigrew, unpublished; Van Sluyters & Blakemore, 1973) of binocular neurons that have *different* properties in the two eyes (e.g., different preferred orientations or directions). Finally, the early work of Hubel and Wiesel (1963b) suggested, and subsequent work by Blakemore and Van Sluyters (1974) and Movshon and Blakemore (1974) abundantly confirms, that the ocular dominance changes following eye closure are not merely due to a failure of maintenance, with binocular and occluded-eye-driven cells dropping out. Rather there is a reorganization, with new groups of cells gradually coming to prefer the open eye. After a reverse suture experiment, Movshon and Blakemore described neurons driven by the newly opened eye in small islands which gradually expand (100–200 μm/day) to cover the whole cortex. Similarly, wholesale visible expansion of ocular dominance columns is seen in monkey visual cortex after neonatal eye removal (LeVay, Hubel, & Wiesel, 1975).

D. Summary

Wiesel and Hubel's observations concerning the effects of monocular deprivation on ocular dominance in cortical neurons were the fountainhead for a still-continuing series of experiments by laboratories around the world, experiments which are showing that experience during a critical period of development can markedly influence later adult properties of cortical neurons, either by the reorganization of innate tendencies or by the imprinting of new experiences on previously uncommitted cells.

Until now, researchers have been busily finding one parameter after another that can leave its lasting impression on the cortex. In the future, attention will probably be turned to the mechanisms by which the critical period starts and stops. Does experience, cell growth, hormones, or innate genetic programming govern the time course of the critical period? Can a factor be found that will extend the critical period or return older neurons to a state of plasticity? Specific theories (e.g., Stent, 1973) have been advanced to explain how monocular deprivation may work at the cell membrane level, but the theories still assume an unknown force that ends the critical period.

TABLE III

GANGLION CELL CLASSIFICATION

Classification		Visual streak (%)	Peripheral retina (%)
Rabbit[a]			
Concentric:	Off-center	25.2 } 41.6	36.1 } 60.0
	On-center	16.4	23.9
Direction-selective:	On-Off-type	10.5 } 17.5	21.1 } 25.0
	On-type	7.0	4.9
Orientation-selective:	Horizontal	6.6 } 11.1	0.7 } 1.1
	Vertical	4.5	0.4
Large-field		4.5	6.2
Local-edge detector		19.5	2.4
Uniformity detector		2.6	1.2
Unclassified		3.2	3.1
Total no. in sample:		154 (100%)	577 (100%)

		Total retina	
		No.	(%)
Cat[b]			
Concentrically organized		887	(92)[c]
A. Brisk		774	(80)
1. Transient		243	(25)
(a) On-center		115	
(b) Off-center		128	
2. Sustained		531	(55)
(a) On-center		271	
(b) Off-center		260	

B. Sluggish	113	(12)
1. Sustained	44	
(a) On-center	22	
(b) Off-center	22	
2. Transient	27	
(a) On-center	13	
(b) Off-center	14	
Not concentrically organized	73	(8)
1. Local edge detector	45	(5)
2. Direction selective	11	(1)
3. Color coded	6	(< 1)
4. Uniformity detector	5	(< 1)
5. Edge inhibitory off-center	3	(< 1)
6. Unclassified	3	(< 1)
	Total: 960 (100%)	

[a] From Levick (1967) and Oyster (1968).
[b] From Cleland & Levick (1974b).
[c] Percentage of 960.

V. Rabbits

The work with neuronal development in the cat visual system is fascinating, but we must be cautious about generalizing the results until data from other animals confirm or qualify them. The visual system of rabbits, from the retina to the cortex, has been carefully studied by several groups, and some of the same developmental and deprivation experiments performed on cats have been done on rabbits. Grobstein and Chow (this volume) review some of the features of neurons in the rabbit cortex. In this section we want to compare the rabbit data with the cat data and try to account for some of the differences, differences which imply that the rabbit visual system is less susceptible to environmental influences, even though rabbit visual neuron responses are equally as complex as those of the cat.

A. Ganglion Cells

Rabbit ganglion cells include all the types seen in cat, as well as others (see reviews by Levick, 1972; Rodieck, 1973). Some features extraction reserved for the cortex in cats is done in the retina in rabbits. Table III presents a summary of receptive field types for rabbit and cat ganglion cells (data from Cleland & Levick, 1974b; Levick, 1967; Oyster, 1968). One of the striking differences is that the simple concentrically organized ON- or OFF-center types account for over 90% of the cat cells and only about 50% of the rabbit cells. One can note that between 1968 and 1974 subclasses of the ON- and OFF-center types were distinguished, namely the sustained/transient types and the brisk/sluggish types (Cleland & Levick, 1974a), but this in no way detracts from the fact that, for the cat, ganglion cells show few of the more complex features seen in many rabbit cells.

Of the more complex features extractors in the rabbit retina, the largest group is the directionally selective cells. These cells have been carefully studied by Barlow and co-workers (Barlow & Hill, 1963; Barlow, Hill & Levick, 1964; Barlow & Levick, 1965; Oyster, 1968; Oyster & Barlow, 1967; Oyster, Takahashi, & Collewijn, 1972). Depending on their responses to flashes of light, these directionally selective cells fall into one of two groups: those that give both ON and OFF responses throughout their receptive fields, and those that give only ON responses.

The pure ON types give better responses to slower moving stimuli and are more prevalent in the central visual streak. An important detail concerning the directionally selective cells of the rabbit retina is that their preferred directions are not distributed around the clock but are confined to four directions (see Fig. 6) These are the four directions of pull of the extraocular muscles of the rabbit, and it has been speculated (Oyster &

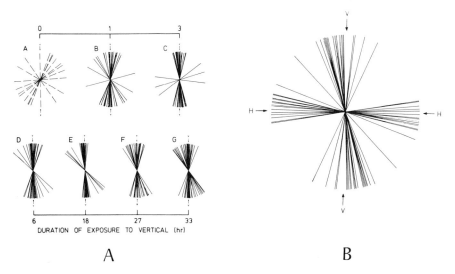

FIG. 5. (A) Polar graph of orientation preferences of cells from kittens exposed only to vertical stripes for various numbers of hours. The control animal in (A) was totally deprived of visual experience. Note that as little as 1 hour of experience to the vertical stripes can create a population of cells preferring vertical; some narrowing of preference is seen after more hours of exposure. Each polar plot represents data from a different animal. (B) Orientation preferences of 37 cells from a kitten exposed to both vertical and horizontal stripes. Fifty hours of experience to each stripe during the critical period, around the Day 28th of age. Reprinted with permission from Blakemore (1973).

Barlow, 1967) that the ON–OFF directionally selective cells are involved in controlling rabbit eye movements.

Note that the distribution of preferred directions in rabbit retinal cells is similar to the distribution of preferred orientations in cortical neurons of cats that have been raised in an environment of only vertical and horizontal stripes. In another comparison with the cat, note from Fig. 1 that in area 17 of the cortex, 60% of an adult cat's cells are directionally selective while only 1% of its ganglion cells are directionally sensitive.

Daw and Wyatt (1974), using the directionally selective cells in rabbit retina, wanted to see if the presence of "complex" responses was sufficient to make a cell sensitive to environmental modification. They knew that cat cortical cell responses could change after special early experience, but retinal ganglion cells could not, one difference being that the cortical cells have more complicated response properties. In the rabbit, complicated responses appear in the retina (direction and orientation selective cells, etc.). In a carefully controlled study, Daw and Wyatt allowed rabbit pups to see only the lateral movement of vertical stripes in a rotating cylinder

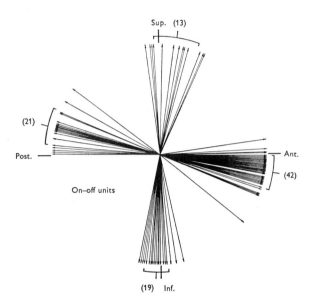

FIG. 6. Rabbit data. Preferred directions of movement for a sample of ON–OFF directionally selective ganglion cells in rabbit retina. Ant.-Post. is used to describe lateral motion because a rabbit's eyes are on the *side* of its head. The pure ON directionally selective units in rabbit retina have a somewhat different, three-lobed distribution (not shown). The ON–OFF rabbit cells are direction selective, but not necessarily orientation selective, as are the cat cells shown in Fig. 5. Reprinted with permission from Oyster (1968).

for the first 60 days of their lives. The stripes rotated around the rabbits fast enough to ensure that optokinetic nystagmus did not allow the image to move "backward" on the retina, but slow enough to ensure that most ON–OFF directionally selective cells would still be responding (about 50°/sec). Recording the responses of 135 directionally selective neurons in rabbits from five different litters, they found absolutely no change in the ratio of (a) directionally selective cells responding to the *conditioning* direction to (b) cells responsive to movement in the *opposite* direction (these would be two of the four classes of ON–OFF directionally selective cells). They concluded that either the rabbit visual system is less plastic than that of the cat or the retina is less plastic than the cortex. They further noted that the two conclusions are related, since some of the complicated response properties found in cat cortical cells are found in rabbit retinal ganglion cells.

In the course of their experiments Daw and Wyatt also presented their rabbits with stripes of the same orientation in much the same way as Blakemore and Cooper (1970) presented stationary stripes to kittens. Since there are also orientation-sensitive ganglion cells in rabbit retina (although here again they are innately tuned only to horizontal and vertical), Daw and Wyatt looked for some of these and found several horizontally tuned cells, indicating that vertical experience does not imprint all orientation-sensitive cells, as it does in the cats. Mize and Murphy (1973) raised rabbits in stationary striped drums. They obtained no evidence that the orientation specificity of cortical cells had been modified, finding normal numbers of both vertically and horizontally sensitive cells. These findings are striking when compared to the cat. The differences are absolute in a sense; in cats, *all* the cortical neurons can be tuned for vertical by a striped environment, while in rabbit *no* cells change preference.

B. Monocular Deprivation

Rabbits have also been monocularly deprived with no obvious effect on the cells in the cortex. Rabbits have little binocular vision, so the results of monocular deprivation in rabbits to some extent confirm the idea that the effects of monocular deprivation in cats are due to binocular competition between the synaptic inputs to a "potentially" binocular cortical cell. Chow and Spear (1974) saw no behavioral deficits or any electrophysiological effects on monocularly driven cortical cells. Van Sluyters and Stewart (1974b) examined the effect of monocular deprivation on *binocular* neurons in the rabbit cortex and also failed to find that input from the deprived eye had been eliminated. One would think that monocular deprivation would have an effect on binocular cells in rabbits if the binocular competition hypothesis were true for all binocularly driven cells and not in just some species. Van Sluyters and Stewart's observations indicate that the results of monocular deprivation in cats may be more than simply the effects of binocular competition, since in the normal cat some (10%) of the cells are exclusively driven by one or the other eye. Why, then, are not these cells still seen after monocular deprivation? In fact, only 1% of cat cortical cells can be influenced by the deprived eye (Wiesel & Hubel, 1965a).

Chow and Spear (1974) also found responses in the rabbit superior colliculus to be normal (i.e., cells could be driven by the deprived eye), and they found a small (10%) but significant decrease in the size of LGN neurons after monocular deprivation. However, this decrease was much smaller than the decrease observed in the binocular section of cat LGN after monocular deprivation ($\approx 30\%$).

C. Development

In the preceding section we noted that by the fifth postnatal week kittens have many cortical neurons with adultlike specificities, although they still do not have the full complement of a grown cat. In rabbits, there are two studies of the development of visual neurons which confirm that rabbit cells develop somewhat more rapidly than cat cells. Spear, Chow, Masland, and Murphy (1972) showed that even before the rabbit pup's eyes open (normally around Day 10) neurons in the superior colliculus have developed most of their adult specificities (direction selectivity, etc.), and that by the end of the third week the superior colliculus is completely developed. This should be compared to Norton (1974), who showed that *cat* superior colliculus cells require more than 6 weeks to develop adultlike ocular dominance and direction selective properties. Grobstein, Chow, Spear, and Mathers (1973) studied the development of response properties in rabbit cortical neurons and found that although some of the more elaborate asymmetric receptive fields, (i.e., directionally selective, complex, and simple) did not appear until after the eyes opened (Day 10), the cortex was essentially adult-like by the third week. Compare this to kittens (Pettigrew, 1974), where at least 5 weeks of development are necessary before cells in the visual cortex acquire their adultlike specificities. The adult rabbit striate cortex is organized somewhat differently from that of the cat. Responses do not seem to be grouped into columns (Van Sluyters & Stewart, 1974a), and although simple, complex, and hypercomplex fields are seen in rabbit, about 30% of the visually responsive cells have less elaborate fields, responding dependably to simple motion or flashed spots, with no intricate trigger features (Chow, Masland, & Stewart, 1971).

The *development* of the rabbit LGN has not been studied, but Levick, Oyster, and Takahashi (1969) noted that adult LGN cells in rabbit have narrower ranges of response than directionally selective ganglion cells. Thus, they sharpen the already selective set of orientations over which directionally sensitive ganglion cells respond. Chow *et al.* (1971), however, found that this fine tuning was lost in the cortex, where directionally selective cells responded over various ranges and directions.

D. Discussion of Apparent Lack of Plasticity in Rabbit Visual System

There are a number of considerations that might help to account for the apparent difference in plasticity shown by the developing rabbit and cast visual systems.

The first of these relates to the question: Why have a critical period during which neural connectivity is visual-experience dependent? This difficult question will be taken up in greater detail at the end of the chapter, where it is argued that genetic prespecification may not be sufficient for a stereoscopic visual system whose tolerances are extremely fine. If this idea proves to be correct, it could be argued that the rabbit has not acquired a high degree of postnatal dependence on visual experience because this was not necessary for a nonstereoscopic system during evolution. In this regard, one recalls Aubrey Manning's (1975) example of the two closely related species of tern, one of which learns to recognize the individual patterns of its own eggs in the nest, while the other lacks this learning ability. The ability of the first can be related to the need to discriminate its own nest among its closely spaced neighbors in the crowded colony. The second species' lack of learning ability can apparently be related to its nesting site on a tiny rocky ledge separated from other nests by a yawning chasm.

One can reason further along such ecological lines that a long critical period of environmental dependence becomes advantageous only in those species, such as the carnivores and primates, which enjoy a similarly long period of parental protection. It would clearly be disastrous for a zebra foal to be born on the veldt without a visual apparatus sufficiently prewired to allow recognition and appropriate response to a threat. A rabbit might likewise be regarded as a protypical prey species with the need for "prewiring" outweighing the value of "soft wiring."

The foregoing arguments may not be necessary if it should prove to be wrong to assume that the rabbit's geniculocortical system is less plastic than the cat's. The crucial experiments may have yet to be performed. We can hardly pretend to understand the function of rabbit visual cortex in the sort of detail available for cat and monkey visual cortex. It is possible that postnatal plasticity could be demonstrated in rabbit visual cortex if we knew more about the relevant parameters to control in the early visual environment. Consider for a moment the transformations performed by cat cortical neurons upon the matrix of inputs they receive from the LGN. Each cortical neuron responds to a complex spatiotemporal sequence of activity in the input matrix, each of whose elements is relatively nonselective except for spatial position. Thus from a series of position-coded inputs a cortical response is generated which is specific for orientation, direction, binocular disparity, and so on. It is difficult to imagine what the results of a similar transformation might be in the rabbit's visual cortex where the input elements from the lateral geniculate have much more complex properties than those of the cat. Orientation and direction selectivity are properties of retinal cells in the rabbit, and if this information is passed on to the cortex[2], neurons there may perform some higher-order analysis which is beyond our

[2] The direction selectivity certainly is (Levick, Oyster, & Takahashi, 1969), and it seems not unlikely that orientation-selective cells will eventually be found in the deep layers of the rabbit LGN, in view of the recent discovery of W-cell input to very small, hard-to-record neurons in the deep layers of the cat LGN (Cleland, Morstyn, Wagner, & Levick, 1975).

present understanding. Such an understanding might be required before one could perform a more crucial test of the hypothesis that cortical properties are experience dependent. To put this viewpoint another way: Is it surprising that rabbit visual cortical neurons fail to show changes in orientation preference when it has been shown that the rabbit's eye contains neurons that are orientation selective and whose preferences are unchanged by the orientations present in the early environment?

Our limited understanding of rabbit visual cortex may help explain another apparent difference in the organization of rabbit and cat visual system. This difference concerns the role of the corticotectal pathway from deep pyramidal cells of the visual cortex back to the superior colliculus. In the cat this pathway is very important for the function of collicular neurons since it conveys both binocularity and direction selectivity. Collicular neurons are severely disrupted after cortical ablation in the cat with a loss of binocular input and loss of direction selectivity (Wickelgren & Sterling, 1969). In contrast, the rabbit colliculus appears to be much less dependent upon cortical input, and cortical ablation appears to have little effect on the properties of collicular neurons (Masland, Chow, & Stewart, 1971).

The most likely explanation for this difference is that the corticotectal pathway *is* indeed much less important for the rabbit than the direct retino-tectal pathway, from which the brain stem can derive a considerable amount of information directly from the highly specialized retinal ganglion cells. However, the failure to demonstrate the role of the corticotectal pathway in the rabbit may be further evidence that we still have much to learn about the function of rabbit visual cortex.

VI. Frogs, Monkeys, and Humans

Critical period neuronal plasticity has been observed at the single unit level in frogs and monkeys and has been inferred psychophysically in astigmatic humans. We want to provide a short review of this work to give the reader a perspective on the comparison we have made between cats and rabbits.

A. Frogs

Keating and Gaze (1970; reviews by Keating, 1974; and this volume) found a modifiable ipsilateral projection in the tectum of *Xenopus* (an aquatic African frog). All the ganglion cell axons in *Xenopus* cross to the contralateral tectum. One tectum then projects to the other to form the retinotopically organized binocular mapping of visual space common to both eyes. If one eye is rotated 180° before larval stage 62, the ipsilateral projections stay in register, resulting in a *rotated* ipsilateral projection through the normal eye and a *normal* projection through the rotated eye, which is the complete opposite of what one would expect if the ipsilateral projections did not have the property of plasticity. Keating and Gaze also found that the ipsilateral registration does not readjust if the animals are kept in the dark. Thus, they have demonstrated a stimulation-dependent plasticity with a larval-stage critical period.

Showing that choice of species is important (as we have suggested with cats and rabbits), Jacobson and Hirsch (1973) found no such plasticity in the binocular projection of the frog *Rana pipiens*. They did notice that prolonged deprivation of one eye could impair the ipsilateral projection, and said: "These results show that neither patterned visual stimulation nor functional correspondence between the eyes is required for the initial development of ipsilateral visuotectal projections (which are subserved by intertectal connections) during metamorphosis. However, the maintenance of the ipsilateral projections requires symmetrical (but not patterned) stimulation of both eyes during the onset of metamorphosis" (p. 683). The reader should see Skarf and Jacobson (1974) for further evidence of the lack of plasticity in the frog tectum.

B. Monkeys

Hubel and Wiesel (1970) suggested that monkeys may have a critical period for the establishment of ocular dominance. von Noorden and co-workers (Baker, Grigg, & von Noorden, 1974) explored this possibility at the single neuron level in rhesus monkey striate and prestriate cortex, using animals von Noorden had previously tested behaviorally after monocular occlusion and surgically induced crossed eyes. In their normally reared control animals they noted (as did Hubel & Wiesel, 1963b) that many (77%) cells in striate cortex were driven by both eyes, though with little specificity for retinal disparity. In prestriate cortex even more (88%) of the cells were binocularly driven, and many of these required precise alignment of targets on both retinas to achieve good binocular activation (i.e., stereopsis cells were common in prestriate cortex). Monocularly deprived animals had very few (5/150) cells that could be influenced by the deprived eye. Cross-eyed animals had cells which could be influenced by either eye, but very few cells which could be influenced by both eyes, as one would expect from the cross-eyed (artificial squint) cats studied by Hubel and Wiesel (1965b). From his behavioral data von Noorden thought the critical period extended from birth (when the eyes are open and the optics clear) to about 8 weeks.

Wiesel and Hubel (1974) studied ocular dominance and orientation specificity in a very young (2-day-old) macaque monkey and in four binocularly deprived macaques. In the 2-day-old monkey (monkeys' eyes are open at birth) they observed an ocular dominance pattern (23 cells) not unlike that of an adult and recorded from several truly orientation-specific cells. The deprived monkeys showed a lack of binocular cells, suggesting to Wiesel and Hubel that the deprivation had disrupted the innately binocular connections seen in the 2-day-old monkey. Wiesel and Hubel did not test for disparity tuning in the binocular cells, as Pettigrew (1974) did in his kitten development study. Of the binocularly deprived monkeys they said, "... there were several groups of cells amounting to about 10–15% of the total, that could only be driven with difficulty, or whose orientation seemed less critical than unusual." They attributed the abnormal responsiveness of these cells also to the effects of deprivation, since no such cells were seen in either control animals of the same age or the 2-day-old monkey.

C. Humans

Mitchell, Freeman, and co-workers (Freeman, Mitchell, & Millodot, 1972; Freeman & Thibos, 1973; Mitchell, Freeman, Millodot, & Haegerstrom, 1973) reasoned that astigmats[3] who had uncorrected vision during childhood would provide good tests for the presence of a sensitive period for visual development in humans. By correcting optically the astigmatism in their subjects (so test images on the retina were completely in focus) and demonstrating that the subjects still had an acuity deficit on the originally blurred axis, they obtained evidence that, indeed, early experience influenced later performance (for orientation sensitivity, at least) in humans. Of course some parts of the human (and other animals') visual system must remain modifiable and remodifiable for a lifetime. Note Kohler's work (see Kohler, 1962 for review) on the ability of humans to adapt to various sorts of goggles which distort normal vision (invert it, etc.).

VII. Why a Critical Period?

Despite the controversy over just how much selectivity can develop in cat visual cortex in the absence of visual experience, there is unanimous agreement that marked changes in cortical organization can be wrought by

---

[3] Astigmatism: One visual meridian is more out of focus than the others because of a distortion of the eye's lens. For example, horizontal lines may be blurred while verticals are in focus.

alterations of the visual input during the critical period. What could be the selective advantage of a modifiable system when the potential handicap is so great? For example, permanent loss of binocular vision might follow accidental, brief, monocular occlusion at the peak of the sensitive period. Two major forms of hypotheses can be entertained.

The first might be called a "world-model" or "superacuity" hypothesis: The properties of cortical neurons are modifiable in early development so that these properties will eventually be an accurate reflection of the statistics of the visual world. This idea follows naturally from the useful, if oversimplifying, concept that cortical neurons are "feature detectors," tuned to particular stimulus combinations. Since there are very many more stimulus combinations in the visual world than there are cortical neurons, and since the proportions of such stimulus combinations can vary from one environment to another, it might be advantageous to allow the proportions of different feature detectors to be determined by the early environment rather than by genes. In this way the animal would have more feature detectors for the commonly occurring stimuli. Signal detection theory then predicts that his discrimination will be better for those stimuli (as a function of the square root of the increase in number of neurons) and he might be said to show "superacuity." For example, if the kittens raised in vertical stripes can be shown to have more neurons responding selectively to vertical than normal kittens, it should also be possible to show that their performance on some aspects of a task involving vertical contours is superior to normal, despite their proven inferiority on horizontal tasks.

No clear statement about such "superacuity" can yet be made about specially reared animals because of the large variation of the "normal" value from one individual to another, although there are some suggestive pieces of evidence. For example, it is known that most humans have higher resolution for vertical and horizontal gratings than for obliques and that this may be related to the incidence of contours in the environment since the difference at obliques is not shown by Cree Indians raised far from Western architecture (Annis & Frost, 1973). A number of studies (Henry, Dreher, & Bishop, 1974; Pettigrew et al., 1968) have reported that urban cats have increased numbers of cortical neurons for horizontal and vertical, a possible neurophysiological counterpart to the human anisotropy, although there is no support for this from behavioral studies of cats so far (Bisti & Maffei, 1974).

There are a number of problems with the "superacuity" hypothesis, quite apart from the lack of direct evidence to support it. To begin with, the limits of performance for basic visual functions such as resolution are determined by the optical properties of the retinal image. No amount of extra neural processing can improve human visual resolution beyond the limits set by diffraction, and these limits have certainly been discovered during the course of evolution and incorporated into the genome (cf. photoreceptor spacing in the retina of any species, which is exactly what one would expect from the optical quality of the retinal image in that species).

Moreover, for basic aspects of the visual world like contour density and orientation, there is not likely to be such large and unpredictable variation from one environment to another. While one could argue a very strong case for experience dependence of the higher-order visual functions involved in, say, facial recognition, there seems to be no good reason why basic contour-processing circuitry cannot be prewired, as it appears to be in rabbit retina and monkey visual cortex.

A second hypothesis links the role of the critical period to the special demands made by a visual system which subserves stereopsis. In such a system the input-array from one eye has to be placed in close register with the array from the other eye so that cross-correlation can be performed to detect the horizontal differences (or disparities) between the inputs, which are the basis of stereopsis. This detection task has a staggering accuracy, since the threshold disparity for humans is 10 sec-arc, six times more accurate than can be accounted for by the grain of the retinal photo-receptors, which are each separated by about 1 min-arc. This accuracy is accompanied by an extraordinary subtlety of the cross-correlative process which can binocularly extract patterns invisible to either eye alone (for more details and references, see Pettigrew, 1972).

While it cannot be claimed that we have a full understanding of the way in which a binocular visual system achieves stereopsis, it is possible to suggest a number of reasons why such a system should be experience dependent in the early neonatal period.

In the first place the performance has such fine tolerances that it would be degraded by such factors as slight differences between the optical pro-perties of each eye and the relative positions of the eyes in the head. Not only are these factors difficult to predict in advance, they change constantly with age. An experience-dependent system would allow continuous adjust-ment to be made during growth of the head, as well as providing a means of correcting for unpredictable errors that might arise during development. In this regard one might speculate that one reason for the higher degree of organization of monkey visual cortex observed at birth, both anatomically (Rakic, 1974) and physiologically (Wiesel & Hubel, 1974) when compared to the cat (Blakemore & Van Sluyters, 1975; Cragg, 1972; Hubel & Wiesel, 1963b; Pettigrew, 1974); is related to the higher precision with which eye position can be specified in the bony orbits of the monkey, the cat's eye position varying considerably during development (Pettigrew, 1974; Sherman, 1972) and ultimately being determined by soft tissue rather than bone.

Blakemore and Van Sluyters (1975) have placed further stress on the role of the critical period in the establishment of neural connections involved in stereopsis. These workers found that the most highly selective neurons in very young kitten cortex tended to be monocular and suggested that normal development of these cells involved the experience-dependent establishment of a set of connections with the nondominant eye, which was very closely matched to the properties of the prespecified dominant eye. In this way the optimal stimulus requirements with respect to orientation, velocity, size, and shape could be made very close in each eye, an important characteristic for binocular neurons involved in disparity detection, as already pointed out by Barlow, Blakemore, and Pettigrew (1967). In support of their idea, Blakemore and Van Sluyters find binocular neurons which have *different* properties in each eye in conditions of pattern deprivation.

In summary, then, the high degree of plasticity of kitten visual cortex may be related to the special demands of a binocular visual system involved in stereopsis. If this is true, further studies on the critical period and on the neural basis of stereopsis may be mutually illuminating.

Acknowledgments

Preparation of the chapter was supported by a grant from the Spencer Foundation. The authors thank Harry Tschopik for a critical reading of the manuscript, and Elizabeth Hanson for secretarial assistance.

References

Annis, R. C. & Frost, B. Human visual ecology and orientation anisotropies in acuity. *Science*, 1973, **182**, 729–731.

Baker, F. H., Grigg, P., & von Noorden, G. K. Effects of visual deprivation and strabismus on the response of neurons in the visual cortex of the monkey, including studies on the striate and prestriate cortex in the normal animal. *Brain Research*, 1974, **66**, 185–208.

Barlow, H. B. Summation and inhibition in the frog's retina. *Journal of Physiology (London)*, 1953, **119**, 69–88.

Barlow, H. B., & Hill, R. M. Selective sensitivity to direction of movement in ganglion cells of the rabbit retina. *Science*, 1963, **139**, 412–414.

Barlow, H. B., & Levick, W. R. The mechanism of directionally selective units in the rabbit's retina. *Journal of Physiology (London)*, 1965, **178**, 377–407.

Barlow, H. B., & Pettigrew, J. D. Lack of specificity of neurons in the visual cortex of young kittens. *Journal of Physiology (London)*, 1971, **218**, 8P–100P.

Barlow, H. B., Hill, R. M., & Levick, W. R. Retinal ganglion cells responding selectively to direction and speed of image motion in the rabbit. *Journal of Physiology (London)*, 1964, **173**, 377–407.

228   J. D. DANIELS AND J. D. PETTIGREW

Barlow, H. B., Blakemore, C., & Pettigrew, J. D. The neural mechanism of binocular depth discrimination. *Journal of Physiology (London)*, 1967, **193**, 327–342.
Bisti, S., & Maffei, L. Behavioral contrast sensitivity of the act in various visual meridians. *Journal of Physiology (London)*, 1974, **241**, 201–210.
Blakemore, C. Developmental factors in the formation of feature extracting neurons. In F. O. Schmitt & F. G. Worden (Eds.), *The neurosciences: Third study program.* Cambridge, Mass.: MIT Press, 1973. Pp. 105–113.
Blakemore, C. Development of the mammalian visual system. *British Medical Journal,* 1974, **30**, 152–157.
Blakemore, C., & Cooper, G. F. Development of the brain depends on visual environment. *Nature (London)*, 1970, **228**, 477–478.
Blakemore, C., & Mitchell, D. E. Environment modification of the visual cortex and the neural basis of learning and memory. *Nature (London)*, 1973, **241**, 467–468.
Blakemore, C., & Van Sluyters, R. C. Reversal of the physiological effects of monocular deprivation in kittens: Further evidence for a sensitive period. *Journal of Physiology (London)*, 1974, **237**, 195–216.
Blakemore, C., & Van Sluyters, R. C. Innate and environmental factors in the development of the kitten's visual cortex. *Journal of Physiology (London)*, 1975, **248**, 663–716.
Brooks, B., & Jung, R. Neuronal physiology of the visual cortex. In R. Jung (Ed.), *Handbook of sensory physiology* (Vol. 7, part 3B). Berlin and New York: Springer-Verlag, 1973. Pp. 325–440.
Chow, K. L., & Spear, D. D. Morphological and functional effects of visual deprivation on the rabbit visual system. *Experimental Neurology,* 1974, **42**, 429–447.
Chow, K. L., Masland, R. H., & Stewart, D. L. Receptive field characteristics of striate cortical neurons in the rabbit. *Brain Research,* 1971, **33**, 337–352.
Cleland, B. G., & Levick, W. R. Brisk and sluggish concentrically organized ganglion cells in the cat's retina. *Journal of Physiology (London)*, 1974, **240**, 421–456. (a)
Cleland, B. G., & Levick, W. R. Properties of rarely encountered types of ganglion cells in the cat's retina and an overall classification. *Journal of Physiology (London)*, 1974, **240**, 457–492. (b)
Cleland, B. G., Morstyn, R., Wagner, H., & Levick, W. R. *Rarely encountered receptive field types in the LGN of the cat.* Paper presented at the national meeting of the Association for Research in Vision and Ophthalmology, Sarasota, Florida, May 1975.
Cragg, B. G. The development of synapses in cat visual cortex. *Investigative Ophthalmology,* 1972, **11**, 377–385.
Cragg, B. G. Plasticity of synapses. *British Medical Journal,* 1974, **30**, 141–145.
Cynader, M., Berman, N., & Hein, A. Cats reared in stroboscopic illumination: Effects on receptive fields in visual cortex. *Proceedings of the National Academy of Sciences of the United States of America,* 1973, **70**, 1353–1354.
Cynader, M., Berman, N., & Hein, A. Cats raised in a one-directional world: Effects on receptive fields in visual cortex and superior colliculus. *Experimental Brain Research,* 1975, **22**, 267–280.
Daw, N. W., & Wyatt, H. J. Raising rabbits in a moving visual environment: An attempt to modify directional sensitivity in the retina. *Journal of Physiology (London)*, 1974, **240**, 309–330.
Dews, P. B., & Wiesel, T. N. Consequences of monocular deprivation on visual behavior in kittens. *Journal of Physiology (London)*, 1970, **206**, 437–455.
Fifkova, E. Effect of light and visual deprivation on the retina. *Experimental Neurology,* 1972, **35**, 450–457. (a)
Fifkova, E. Effect of visual deprivation and light on synapses of the inner plexiform layer. *Experimental Neurology,* 1972, **35**, 458–469. (b)

Freeman, R. D., & Thibos, L. N. Electrophysiological evidence that abnormal early visual experience can modify the human brain. *Science*, 1973, **180**, 876–878.

Freeman, R. D., Mitchell, D. E., & Millodot, M. A neural effect of partial visual deprivation in humans. *Science*, 1972, **175**, 1384–1386.

Garey, L. J., & Pettigrew, J. D. Ultrastructural changes in kitten visual cortex after environmental modification. *Brain Research*, 1974, **66**, 165–172.

Ganz, L., Fitch, M., & Satterberg, J. A. The selective effect of visual deprivation and receptive field shape determined neurophysiologically. *Experimental Neurology*, 1968, **22**, 614–637.

Grobstein, P., Chow, K. L., Spear, P. D., & Mathers, L. H. Development of rabbit visual cortex: Late appearance of a class of receptive fields. *Science*, 1973, **180**, 1185–1187.

Guillery, R. W. Binocular competition in the control of geniculate cell growth. *Journal of Comparative Neurology*, 1972, **144**, 117–130.

Henry, G. H., Dreher, B., & Bishop, P. O. Orientation specificity of cells in cat striate cortex. *J. Neurophysiol.*, 1974, **37**, 1394–1409.

Hirsch, H. V. B., & Spinelli, D. N. Visual experience modifies distribution of horizontally and vertically oriented receptive fields in cats. *Science*, 1970, **168**, 869–871.

Hirsch, H. V. B., & Spinelli, D. N. Modification of the distribution of receptive field orientation in cats by selective visual exposure during development. *Experimental Brain Research*, 1971, **12**, 509–527.

Hoffmann, K.-P., Stone, J., & Sherman, S. M. Relay of receptive-field properties in dorsal lateral geniculate nucleus of the cat. *Journal of Neurophysiology*, 1972, **35**, 518–531.

Hubel, D. H., & Wiesel, T. N. Receptive fields of single neurones in the cat's striate cortex. *Journal of Physiology (London)*, 1959, **148**, 574–591.

Hubel, D. H., & Wiesel, T. N. Receptive fields, binocular interaction and functional architecture in the cat's visual cortex. *Journal of Physiology (London)*, 1962, **160**, 106–154.

Hubel, D. H., & Wiesel, T. N. Shape and arrangement of columns in the cat's striate cortex. *Journal of Physiology (London)*, 1963, **165**, 559–568. (a)

Hubel, D. H., & Wiesel, T. N. Receptive fields of cells in striate cortex of very young visually inexperienced kittens. *Journal of Neurophysiology*, 1963, **26**, 994–1002. (b)

Hubel, D. H., & Wiesel, T. N. Receptive fields and functional architecture in two nonstriate visual areas (18 and 19) of the cat. *Journal of Neurophysiology*, 1965, **28**, 229–289. (a)

Hubel, D. H., & Wiesel, T. N. Binocular interaction in striate cortex of kittens reared with artificial squint. *Journal of Neurophysiology*, 1965, **28**, 1041–1059. (b)

Hubel, D. H., & Wiesel, T. N. Cortical and callosal connections concerned with the vertical meridian of visual fields in the cat. *Journal of Neurophysiology*, 1967, **30**, 1561–1573.

Hubel, D. H., & Wiesel, T. N. Receptive fields and functional architecture of monkey striate cortex. *Journal of Physiology (London)*, 1968, **195**, 215–243.

Hubel, D. H., & Wiesel, T. N. Visual area of the lateral suprasylvian gyrus (Clare-Bishop-Area) of the cat. *Journal of Physiology (London)*, 1969, **202**, 251–260.

Hubel, D. H., & Wiesel, T. N. The period of susceptibility to the physiological effects of unilateral eye closure in kittens. *Journal of Physiology (London)*, 1970, **206**, 419–436.

Hubel, D. H., & Wiesel, T. N. Aberrant visual projections in the Siamese cat. *Journal of Physiology (London)*, 1971, **218**, 33–62.

Jacobson, M., & Hirsch, H. V. B. Development and maintenance of connectivity in the visual system of the frog. I. The effects of eye rotation and visual deprivation. *Brain Research*, 1973, **49**, 47–65.

Keating, M. J. The role of visual function in the patterning of binocular visual connexions. *British Medical Journal*, 1974, **30**, 145–151.

230   J. D. DANIELS AND J. D. PETTIGREW

Keating, M. J., & Gaze, R. M. Rigidity and plasticity in the amphibian visual system. *Brain, Behavior and Evolution*, 1970, **3**, 102–120.

Kohler, I. Experiments with goggles. *Scientific American*, 1962, **208**, pp. 62–72.

Lettvin, J. Y., Maturana, H. R., McCulloch, W. S., & Pitts, W. H. What the frog's eye tells the frog's brain. *Proceedings of the Institute of Radio Engineers*, 1959, **47**, 1940–1959.

LeVay, S., Hubel, D. H., & Wiesel, T. N. The pattern of ocular dominance columns in Macaque visual cortex revealed by a reduced silver stain. *Journal of Comparative Neurology*, 1975, **159**, 559–576.

Levick, W. R. Receptive fields and trigger features of ganglion cells in the visual streak of the rabbit's retina. *Journal of Physiology (London)*, 1967, **188**, 285–307.

Levick, W. R. Receptive fields of retinal ganglion cells. In M. G. F. Fuortes (Ed.), *The handbook of sensory physiology* (Vol. 7, part 2). Berlin and New York: Springer-Verlag, 1972. Pp. 531–566.

Levick, W. R., Oyster, C. W., & Takahashi, E. Rabbit lateral geniculate nucleus: Sharpener of directional information. *Science*, 1969, **165**, 712–714.

Lewin, R. Developing brains. *New Scientist*, 1974, 686–689.

Manning, A. Varieties of animal learning and adaptation, ethological approaches. In M. R. Rosenzweig & E. R. Bennett (Eds.), *Proceedings of the Asilomar Conference on neural mechanisms of memory*. Cambridge, Mass.: MIT Press, 1975. Pp. 65–74.

Mark, R. F. *Memory and nerve cell connections*. London: Oxford University Press, 1974.

Masland, R. H., Chow, K. L., & Stewart, D. L. Receptive field characteristics of superior colliculus neurons in the rabbit. *Journal of Neurophysiology*, 1971, **34**, 148–156.

Mitchell, D. E., Freeman, R. D., Millodot, M., & Haegerstrom, G. Meridonal amblyopia: Evidence for modification of the human visual system by early visual experience. *Vision Research*, 1973, **13**, 535–558.

Mize, R. R., & Murphy, E. H. Selective visual experience fails to modify receptive field properties of rabbit striate cortex neurons. *Science*, 1973, **180**, 320–323.

Movshon, A. J., & Blakemore, C. Functional reinnervation in kitten visual cortex. *Nature (London)*, 1974, **251**, 504–505.

Nicoll, R. A. The effects of anaesthetics on synaptic excitation and inhibition in the olfactory bulb. *Journal of Physiology (London)*, 1972, **223**, 803–814.

Norton, T. T. Receptive-field properties of superior colliculus cells and development of visual behavior in kittens. *Journal of Neurophysiology*, 1974, **37**, 674–690.

Olson, C. R., & Freeman, R. D. Progressive changes in kitten striate cortex during monocular vision. *Journal of Neurophysiology*, 1975, **38**, 26–33.

Olson, C. R., & Pettigrew, J. D. Single units in visual cortex of kittens reared in stroboscopic illumination. *Brain Research*, 1974, **70**, 189–204.

Oyster, C. W. The analysis of image motion by the rabbit retina. *Journal of Physiology (London)*, 1968, **199**, 613–635.

Oyster, C. W., & Barlow, H. B. Direction-selective units in rabbit retina: Distribution of preferred directions. *Science*, 1967, **155**, 841–842.

Oyster, C. W., Takahashi, E., & Collewijn, H. Direction-selective retinal ganglion cells and control of optokinetic nystagmus in the rabbit. *Vision Research*, 1972, **12**, 183–193.

Pettigrew, J. D. The importance of early visual experience for neurons of the developing geniculostriate system. *Investigative Ophthalmology*, 1972, **11**, 386–394.

Pettigrew, J. D. The effect of visual experience on the development of stimulus specificity by kitten cortical neurons. *Journal of Physiology (London)*, 1974, **237**, 49–74.

Pettigrew, J. D., & Daniels, J. D. GABA antagonism in visual cortex: Different effects on simple, complex, and hypercomplex neurons. *Science*, 1973, **182**, 81–83.

Pettigrew, J. D., & Freeman, R. D. Visual experience without lines: Effect on developing cortical neurons. *Science*, 1973, **182**, 599–601.

Pettigrew, J. D., & Garey, L. J. Selective modification of single neuron properties in the visual cortex of kittens. *Brain Research*, 1974, **66**, 160–164.

Pettigrew, J. D., Nikara, T., & Bishop, P. O. Binocular interaction on single units in cat striate cortex: Simultaneous stimulation by single moving slit with receptive fields in correspondence. *Experimental Brain Research*, 1968, **6**, 391–410.

Pettigrew, J. D., Olson, C. R., & Barlow, H. B. Kitten visual cortex: Short-term, stimulus-induced changes in connectivity. *Science*, 1973, **180**, 1202–1203.

Rakic, P. Neurons in rhesus monkey visual cortex: Systematic relation between time of origin and eventual disposition. *Science*, 1974, **183**, 425–427.

Riesen, A. H. Sensory deprivation. In E. Stellar & J. M. Sprague (Eds.), *Progress in physiological psychology.* New York: Academic Press, 1966. Pp. 117–147.

Rodieck, R. W. *The vertebrate retina: Principles of structure and function.* San Francisco, Cal. Freeman, 1973.

Sherman, S. M. Development of interocular alignment in cats. *Brain Research*, 1972, **37**, 187–198.

Sherman, S. M. Visual fields of cats with cortical and tectal lesions. *Science*, 1974, **185**, 355–357.

Sherman, S. M., & Sanderson, K. J. Binocular interaction on cells of the dorsal lateral geniculate nucleus of visually deprived cats. *Brain Research*, 1972, **37**, 126–131.

Sherman, S. M., & Stone, J. Physiological normality of the retina in visually deprived cats. *Brain Research*, 1973, **60**, 224–230.

Sherman, S. M., Hoffman, K.-P., & Stone, J. Loss of a specific cell type from dorsal lateral geniculate nucleus in visually deprived cats. *Journal of Neurophysiology*, 1972, **35**, 532–541.

Sherman, S. M., Guillery, R. W., Kaas, J. H., & Sanderson, K. J. Behavioral, electrophysiological and morphological studies of binocular competition in the development of the geniculo-cortical pathways of cats. *Journal of Comparative Neurology*, 1974, **158**, 1–18.

Shlaer, R. Shift in binocular disparity causes compensating change in the cortical structure of kittens. *Science*, 1971, **173**, 638–641.

Skarf, B., & Jacobson, M. Development of binocularly driven single units in frogs raised with asymmetrical visual stimulation. *Experimental Neurology*, 1974, **42**, 669–686.

Spear, P. D., Chow, K. L., Masland, R. H., & Murphy, E. H. Ontogenesis of receptive field characteristics of superior colliculus neurons in the rabbit retina. *Brain Research*, 1972, **45**, 67–86.

Spinelli, D. N., Hirsch, H. V. B., Phelps, R. W., & Metzler, J. Visual experience as a determinant of response characteristics of cortical receptive fields in cats. *Experimental Brain Research*, 1972, **15**, 289–304.

Stein, B. E., Labos, E., & Kruger, L. Sequence of changes in properties of neurons of superior colliculus of the kitten during maturation. *Journal of Neurophysiology*, 1973, **36**, 667–679.

Stent, G. S. A physiological mechanism for Hebb's postulate of learning. *Proceedings of the National Academy of Sciences of the United States of America*, 1973, **70**, 997–1001.

Sterling, P., & Wickelgren, B. Function of the projection from the visual cortex to the superior colliculus. *Brain, Behavior & Evolution*, 1970, **3**, 210–218.

Stryker, M. P., & Sherk, H. *Modifying cortical orientation selectivity by restricted visual experience: A reexamination.* Presented at the national meeting of the Association for Research in Vision and Ophthalmology, Sarasota, Florida, May 1975. (Abstract)

Tretter, F., Cynader, M., & Singer, W. Modification of direction selectivity of neurons in the visual cortex of kittens. *Brain Research*, 1975, **84**, 143–149.

Van Sluyters, R. C., & Blakemore, C. Experimental creation of unusual neuronal properties in visual cortex of kitten. *Nature (London)*, 1973, **246**, 506–508.

Van Sluyters, R. C., & Stewart, D. L. Binocular neurons of the rabbit's visual cortex: Receptive field characteristics. *Experimental Brain Research*, 1974, **19**, 166–195. (a)

Van Sluyters, R. C., & Stewart, D. L. Binocular neurons of the rabbit's visual cortex: Effects of monocular sensory deprivation. *Experimental Brain Research*, 1974, **19**, 196–204. (b)

Weiskrantz, L. Sensory deprivation and the cat's optic nervous system. *Nature (London)*, 1958, **181**, 1047–1050.

Wickelgren B. Some effects of visual deprivation on the cat superior colliculus. *Investigative Ophthalmology*, 1972, **11**, 460–467.

Wickelgren B., & Sterling, P. Influence of visual cortex on receptive fields in the superior colliculus of the cat. *Journal of Neurophysiology*, 1969, **32**, 16–23.

Wiesel, T. N., & Hubel, D. H. Effects of visual deprivation on morphology and physiology of cells in the cat's lateral geniculate body. *Journal of Neurophysiology*, 1963, **26**, 978–993. (a)

Wiesel, T. N., & Hubel, D. H. Single cell responses in striate cortex of kittens deprived of vision in one eye. *Journal of Neurophysiology*, 1963, **26**, 1003–1017. (b)

Wiesel, T. N., & Hubel, D. H. Comparison of the effects of unilateral and bilateral eye closure on cortical unit responses in kittens. *Journal of Neurophysiology*, 1965, **28**, 1029–1040. (a)

Wiesel, T. N., & Hubel, D. H. Extent of recovery from the effects of visual deprivation in kittens. *Journal of Neurophysiology*, 1965, **28**, 1060–1072. (b)

Wiesel, T. N., & Hubel, D. H. Ordered arrangement of orientation columns in monkeys lacking visual experience. *Journal of Comparative Neurology*, 1974, **158**, 307–318.

Section 4

BEHAVIORAL SPECIFICITY

INTRODUCTION

As we move from neural specificity to a consideration of the development of species-specific behavior, we continue to be faced with the problem of the proper interpretation of the role which experience plays in the process (when it does play a role).

In the first chapter in this section, the writer is concerned with the question of whether normally occurring embryonic auditory experience is involved in the species-specific auditory perception of young, hatchling birds, while in the second chapter Richard Tees reviews the pros and cons of experience vis-à-vis the development of auditory and visual perception in a variety of mammals. It is in Tees' chapter in particular that crucial methodological issues and experimental design problems once again surface in such a troublesome way as to make unequivocal interpretation difficult, despite the large volume of research on perceptual development in mammals. While the deprivation procedure is certainly the method of choice with which to begin an analysis of perceptual development, in the event that deficiencies result from the procedure, longitudinal analysis and controlled experiential substitutions must be undertaken if the actual contribution of normally occurring stimulation is to be delineated. According to Tees' review, these later steps are all too often neglected in the mammalian literature on behavioral specificity, as they sometimes are in the literature on neural specificity.

EARLY DEVELOPMENT OF SPECIES-SPECIFIC AUDITORY PERCEPTION IN BIRDS

GILBERT GOTTLIEB

Psychology Laboratory
Division of Research
North Carolina Department of Mental Health
Raleigh, North Carolina

I. Introduction

The problem of the development of species-specific behavior shares many of the conceptual difficulties involved in neural specificity. This kind of adaptive behavior occurs with such regularity and high predictability that many of the early workers in the area could not see any necessary role for experience in its development; hence, it was—and still is—often regarded as instinctive or innate behavior (meaning that it develops in the absence of experience). Thus, the earliest conceptual model for the development of innate behavior can be depicted in this way:

Genes ——→Innate Behavior

Now, everyone realizes that genes cannot construct behavior, so, to think somewhat more realistically about the problem in developmental terms, one must envision the genetic material somehow influencing cells to enter into certain arrangements with each other during the course of early maturation. This process ultimately leads to the formation of particular organs and organ systems, and to particular connections within and between these systems, and, thence, to innate behavior. As far as innate behavior goes, then, in this view the genes provide an essential controlling or determinative impetus to the development of the nervous system, including peripheral sense organs and muscles. In a word, genes are thought to somehow be at the base of neural maturation, which, in turn, leads to the manifestation of innate behavior:

Genes ——→Neural Maturation ——→Innate Behavior

This oversimplified way of schematizing the problem at least shows in a gross way the rather different levels of analysis which are involved. It will be recognized that the actual study of the activities of genes during development is in the domain of the molecular biologist, neural maturation is in the domain of the developmental neurobiologist, and innate behavior is in the province of the animal behaviorist or biopsychologist (or psychobiologist). We all overlap somewhat in each other's areas. For example, here I will be writing a bit about the development of the nervous system and innate behavior, while in the chapters in this volume by Keating and by Meyer and Sperry, which are concerned with how the nervous system gets itself put together at very early stages of maturation, one finds occasional references to DNA, on the one hand, and to innate behavior, on the other. But, to return to the theme, in the view expounded above the basic notion is that somehow or other (chemoaffinity and so on) the nervous system gets itself organized "prefunctionally" (i.e., nonexperientially) as a precursor to the development of innate behavior (Meyer & Sperry, this volume, for example).

This particular view has rather wide currency, particularly in the biological literature, where, instead of the term innate, one is more apt to read that certain features of behavior are under genetic control (or stem from genetic determination) when the writer feels that experience plays no significant role in the development of the behavioral feature in question. Since neural maturation processes are considerably more proximal to the development of behavior than are genes, I think it may be preferable from an analytic standpoint to emphasize the supposedly endogenous character of the neural maturation process vis-à-vis these behavioral features, rather than to speak of the much more remote processes of genetic determination. An additional reason for not distinguishing innate behavior by its genetic determination is the widely recognized fact that an animal's ability to respond to experience is no less genetically determined than its ability to develop behavior independent of experience.

II. Theories of Innate Behavioral Development

A. Neural Theory

Developmental neurobiologists sometimes speak of the nervous system as being "hard-wired" and "soft-wired." The former neural arrangements are thought to undergird innate behavior, while the latter are believed to be responsible for learning. These casual but widely held notions were first formalized into a theory by Altman (1967) and subsequently applied to development by Jacobson (1974). These authors theorize that there are two different types of neurons in the nervous system. As defined by Altman, these two types (macroneurons and microneurons) can be distinguished on the basis of their structure, function, ontogeny, phylogeny, and plasticity. Macroneurons have long axons which conduct impulses from the peripheral sensory surfaces into the central nervous system and, on the motor side, from the central nervous system out to muscle. Such neurons also serve to connect different areas of the brain to each other. Microneurons, on the other hand, have rather short axons and are found inside the central nervous system, where they interconnect *within*—but not between—areas of the brain. Macroneurons are said to mature earlier in ontogeny than microneurons; by virtue of their later development and their profuse and highly local interconnection, microneurons are believed to be more dependent on, and responsive to, exogenous factors such as hormones and sensory experience, and they have often been hypothesized to underlie learning, memory, and intelligent behavior. From an ontogenetic standpoint, the present notion is that the developmental course of macroneurons is under strict maturational determination, whereas the developmental course of microneurons is subject to individual experience during ontogeny. As Jacobson puts it, there are "two modes of neuronal ontogeny." Thus, experience is believed to play no role whatsoever in the maturation of macroneurons, whereas experience is important in the development of the microneurons. The former undergird the innate, phylogenetically adapted components of behavior; the latter, learning and the more modifiable, individually adapted components of behavior. As Jacobson himself expresses it:

The essential thesis is that neurons develop in two complementary modes which together permit all possible neuronal functions to be represented: functions that are innately predetermined as well as those that develop as a result of individual experience. In the first mode of development, neurons can express their functions only in a predetermined way as highly predictable patterns of behavior which are characteristic of each species. In the second mode of development, neurons form populations with such diverse potentials that all possible contingencies of function can be realized, including forms of behavior that are unpredictable or aleatory [1974, p. 152].

B. Behavioral Theory

The assumptions of the neural theory of innate behavior square precisely with the assumptions of certain *behavioral* theories of innate behavioral development. For example, Lorenz (1965), one of the foremost exponents of the innate component in behavior, holds that the terms innate and learned refer to two entirely different, dichotomous *sources* of behavioral adaptation: the former refers to information acquired by the species through evolution via mutation and natural selection, and the latter refers to information acquired by the individual in interaction with its environment during ontogenetic development. Lorenz suggests that there can be behavior patterns which owe their adapted quality exclusively to information acquired during the evolution of the species, and that learning itself is also based on phylogenetically acquired information. Lorenz's main point is that these two modes of adaptation are physiologically distinct, in the sense of the notions of "hard-wired" and "soft-wired" described above. He writes:

... there is no evidence and no logical reason for assuming that all phylogenetically adapted machinery of behavior must unconditionally be susceptible to adaptive modification. Quite the contrary, there are strong arguments in favor of the assumption that certain mechanisms of behavior, for the simple reason that they do contain the phylogenetic programming of learning processes, must themselves be refractory to any modificatory change.

... [While] phylogenetic adaptation must unconditionally be contained in every learning process, ... the hypothesis that learning must enter into all phylogenetically adapted behavior is entirely unfounded [Lorenz, 1965, p. 104].

Besides the two channels represented (*a*) by the adaptive processes of evolution, and (*b*) by individual acquisition of information, no third possibility exists for information being "fed into" the organic system ...

Nor must the functional analogies which exist between the two types of acquiring information mislead anyone into thinking them to be physiologically the same. Indeed, we know that they are not [Lorenz, 1965, pp. 18–19. © 1965 by The University of Chicago. All rights reserved. Published 1965. Printed in the United States of America].

C. Critique

A good bit of fur has flown over the nature–nurture dichotomy, and there is no need to recapitulate the entire history of the controversy here, especially since the first chapter in this volume (Lippe) covers a good bit of that ground. Since my own orientation to the problem of behavioral development is in the intellectual tradition initiated by Z.-Y. Kuo in the 1920s (summarized in Kuo, 1967) and very much extended in the writings of Lehrman (1953, 1970) and especially Schneirla (1956, 1966), I do feel constrained to review their viewpoint and explain how and why I am departing from it at the moment.

Kuo was the first psychologist to realize that postulating ultimate "sources" of adaptation, be they genetic *or* represented by the blanket term learning, was to short-circuit developmental analysis. In his view, and the view of Schneirla and Lehrman, that was to take a nonanalytic position vis-à-vis an interesting and significant *analytic* problem; namely, the developmental processes whereby the behavior in question was realized during ontogeny. It is my opinion that the reason Schneirla defined the term experience as broadly as he did (described in my earlier chapter in this volume) was to make certain that extended developmental analysis was forced upon anyone who wanted to assert that a given behavior was innate.

At the present time in our science, I think there is little danger of the developmental basis of innate behavior going uninvestigated at any level (anatomical, physiological, behavioral), so in my earlier chapter I chose to redefine the term experience rather narrowly to include only events involving neurosensory or neuromotor function. This does not mean that I feel organism—environment interactions (or interactions within the developing organism) are unimportant for neural or behavioral development if they happen to fall outside my definition of experience; it is just that I think it might be useful to be more precise in our use of the term experience at the present time, and to become correspondingly more precise in our delineation of the other factors that influence development. I want to ask exactly the same question that my colleagues were obsessed with (Is innate behavior truly free of the effects of *all* earlier experience?), but I want to ask the question in a more narrow and strictly defined way.

Perhaps this is a good place to mention the point of all this careful linguistic and conceptual maneuvering. I think the mechanism by which phylogenetically adapted behavior gets "fixed" into the developmental scheme of the species may not be as encapsulated as Lorenz seems to think. It must be recalled that we do not actually know how this happens, so one hypothesis could be as plausible as another, provided it does not violate any known facts. Certainly, in some sense genes must be at the basis of behavior which is considered innate, otherwise there would be no basis for the consistent and regular appearance of the behavior from generation to generation—there would be no way "to inherit the potential" of developing the behavior. (The same can be said for frankly learned behavior.) So far I have merely stated my agreement with Lorenz's viewpoint—there is nothing here to disagree on. Where I think there is room for another opinion concerns Lorenz's (and Jacobson's) hypothesis on the totality of factors controlling the ontogenetic expression of innate behavior.

Innate behavior is a phenotype. The behavioral phenotype is an outcome of development. Natural selection operates on the phenotype. As long as the phenotype has a genetic basis, it does not make any difference how the phenotype developed. Natural selection is not restricted to only certain kinds of developmental programs. There could be many programs; there might only be one; no one can know in advance of inquiry. The point is the program for innate behavioral development could involve experience— there is nothing to say that it cannot involve experience. Innate behavior could even be modifiable (in Lorenz's sense).

Thus, with respect to the evolution of species-specific behavior, natural selection could have involved a selection for the entire developmental manifold, including not only the organic but the normally occurring experiential features of ontogeny. In terms of the simple diagram presented earlier, the present hypothetical sequence of events would look like this:

Genes ———→ Neural Maturation ←—— Experience ———→ Innate Behavior

The experience in question could be facilitative or inductive, and thus operate prior to completion of the maturation process, or it could be of a maintenance character and operate merely to preserve the end product of maturation.

III. Development of Species Identification in Ducklings

Ducklings hatched in incubators in the laboratory are able to respond preferentially to the maternal (nest exodus or assembly) call of their species in simultaneous auditory choice tests (i.e., tests in which their own species maternal call is pitted against the maternal call of another species). The fact that the ducklings evince this capability in the absence of previous exposure to stimulation normally provided by the mother presents a particularly interesting phenomenon for developmental analysis. The phenomenon is especially interesting because it bears all the classical hallmarks of "instinctive" or innate behavior: it is adaptive, species-typical or species-specific, appears at the appropriate time, and, most important, appears in the absence of prior experience with the object to which the behavior is addressed. Since the early part of this century (e.g., Kuo, 1921), the question has continually been raised whether instinctive behavior is truly free of the effects of *all* earlier experience, the implication being that prior experiences other than direct contact with the object might be essential to the development of the instinctive behavior in question. For example, Kuo's (1932) empirical work seemed to suggest that, in birds at least, the adaptive motor behavior seen after hatching was possibly a consequence of a variety of behavioral events which occurred *in embryo*. This suggestion was never demonstrated experimentally, however. I raise the matter not only for historical perspective, but because the question of the influence of normally occurring embryonic experience on the development of innate behavior has not in fact been resolved and it was this question, and the conceptual issues related to it, which inspired the present experiments.

A. Present Status of Problem

The only auditory experience of a vocal nature to which an incubator-hatched duckling has been exposed before entering the maternal-call test situation is its own vocalizations and those of its conspecific siblings. The Peking duckling (*Anas platyrhynchos*), a domestic form of mallard (*Anas platyrhynchos*), begins vocalizing as an embryo several days before hatching when it begins to move into the air-space at the large end of the egg. In an effort to determine whether exposure to these embryonic and perinatal vocalizations influences the duckling's response to the species maternal call, communally incubated and brooded Peking ducklings were given enhanced exposure to these vocalizations via a tape recorder before being tested with the maternal call (Gottlieb, 1966). The ducklings so exposed did show an enhanced response to the maternal call compared to those not so exposed. The matter was left there for a period of several years, during which time an embryonic devocalization procedure was perfected (Gottlieb & Vandenbergh, 1968). Briefly described, the procedure involves painting the embryo's syringeal ("voicebox") membranes with a surgical glue so that the membranes cannot vibrate and thus the embryo (and the duckling) is prevented from vocalizing. With the devocalization procedure in hand the reverse experiment (total auditory deprivation) was conducted to determine if the absence of exposure to the embryonic and neonatal vocalizations[1] was detrimental to the development of the duckling's discriminative preference for the species maternal call in simultaneous auditory choice tests after hatching (Gottlieb, 1971a). The devocalized-isolated ducklings gave a "yes and no" answer: their preference for the species maternal call was as highly perfected as that of intact vocal-communal ducklings in many different tests, but it was definitely deficient in one of these tests. For some reason, presumably an overlap in certain critical acoustic features, the devocalized-

---

[1] The embryonic and neonatal vocalizations are very similar from an audiospectrographic point of view. There are three basic vocalizations, commonly called alarm-distress, contact-contentment, and brooding-like calls. The first two can be reliably differentiated by context and by striking differences in loudness, duration of notes, frequency range, peak frequencies, and frequency modulation. The brooding-like call resembles the contact-contentment call more closely than it does the alarm-distress call. A detailed analysis of each call is presented in Gottlieb and Vandenbergh (1968).

isolated ducklings confused the species maternal call (mallard) with the chicken maternal call in simultaneous choice tests, whereas sham-operated ducklings did not do so, and most important, devocalized-isolated ducklings themselves did not do so if the embryonic devocalization procedure was delayed so that they had about 24 hours of exposure to their own vocalizations before being muted (Gottlieb, 1971a, pp. 141–142).

Thus, the ducklings' ability to respond selectively to the maternal call of their species becomes very highly developed even in the complete absence of prior exposure to normally occurring auditory stimulation of a vocal nature, but it does not become (or does not remain) fully developed under such circumstances. From the enhancement and deprivation studies mentioned above, we do not yet know, of course, whether the ducklings' vocalizations provide any distinctive or special contribution to the development of its auditory perceptual system, or whether the forward impetus of the system could be maintained by exposure to almost any sound. If the precise nature of the auditory perceptual deficit in the devocalized-isolated ducklings could be determined, then it might be possible to delineate the contribution of the duckling's own vocalizations to the duckling's normal, completely differentiated perception of the maternal call. The first experiments thus concern the nature of the auditory perceptual deficit which auditory deprivation causes in Peking ducklings vis-à-vis the species maternal call (mallard).

B. Hypothesized Perceptual Deficit in Devocalized Peking Ducklings

In examining the possibly important perceptual differences between the mallard maternal call and the chicken maternal call, it seemed relevant that while the calls share a peak energy band around 800 Hz, the chicken maternal call has virtually no energy above that point, whereas the mallard call contains frequency bands at around 1100 Hz, 1600 Hz, and 2300 Hz (see Figs. 1 and 2).[2] The fact that the chicken call shares the lower-frequency component with the mallard call but lacks the higher-frequency components suggests the possibility that the devocalized-isolated ducklings may be relatively insensitive to the presence of these higher-frequency components in the mallard call and thus tend to "confuse" the two calls in a simultaneous choice test. The possibility that the confusion is based on the devocalized-isolates' relative insensitivity to higher frequencies is strengthened by the fact that the devocalization procedure deprives the embryo and hatchling of

[2] Although the Brüel and Kjaer frequency analysis (Fig. 2) portrays peak frequency much more precisely and accurately than the Kay Sonagraph (Fig. 1), the Brüel and Kjaer analyses do tend to obscure the fact that the mallard call is composed of discrete (discontinuous) bands of energy at each peak hertz. The discontinuities are depicted very clearly by the Sonagraph. Since the Sonagraph is highly inexact with respect to frequency (and gives no information on dB), these analytic procedures complement each other.

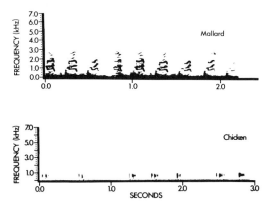

FIG. 1.   Sonagraphic analysis of mallard and chicken maternal calls. (Figure 2 shows the specific peak frequencies in each call.)

hearing their own vocalizations, and it happens that all of the embryo's and hatchling's vocalizations fall in the high-frequency part of the vocal spectrum (1500–5000 Hz: Gottlieb & Vandenbergh, 1968). Thus, it is possible that preventing the ducklings from hearing their own vocalizations may cause the devocal ducklings' threshold for perceiving high-frequency stimulation to be more elevated than it would under normal conditions. The ducklings' exposure to their own vocalizations—given that it is involved at all—could make a *constructive* contribution by increasing sensitivity to the higher frequencies, or, alternatively, the vocal stimulation could be required merely to *maintain* an end point achieved by the sheerly intrinsic maturation of the auditory system.

Since the chicken call has other elements in it which make it different from the mallard call, the best (purest) test of a high frequency perceptual deficit in the devocal ducklings would be one in which they are simultaneously presented with two mallard calls: a normal mallard maternal call and the

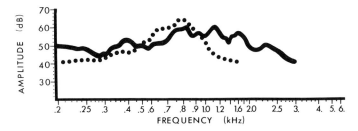

FIG. 2.   Peak frequency (Hz) bands in mallard (—) and chicken (● ● ●) maternal calls.

same mallard call with its higher frequencies removed by selective filtering. If it is correct that the devocal ducklings are relatively insensitive to the higher frequencies of the mallard call, they should be more apt than vocal ducklings to choose the filtered call in such a test. The present experiments examine that prediction by testing devocal and vocal ducklings in simultaneous auditory choice tests with (1) the normal mallard maternal call versus the same call with frequencies over 825 Hz attenuated and (2) an even finer test involving the normal mallard call versus the same call with only the frequency band over 1800 Hz attenuated.

If it is correct that the perceptual deficit in the devocalized ducklings is confined more to the higher Hz than to the lower Hz bands, then one would predict that, while the devocalized ducklings would perform worse than vocal ducklings on choice tests with high-frequency attenuated mallard calls, they would be as apt as vocal ducklings to detect a mallard call which had its *lower* frequencies attenuated. Thus, to examine this prediction, the performance of vocal and devocal ducklings is examined in a simultaneous choice test in which (3) the normal mallard call is pitted against the same call with frequencies less than 825 Hz attenuated. If the hypothesis is correct, there should be no differences between vocal and devocal ducklings in that test because the auditory deprivation resulting from embryonic devocalization has not impaired their perceptual sensitivity to the lower frequencies of the mallard call. Thus, in this third test, the devocalized ducklings should be as apt as vocal ducklings in selecting the normal mallard call, whereas in the first two tests (i.e., the ones in which the *high* frequencies have been diminished), the devocal ducklings should be less apt than the vocal ducklings in selecting the normal mallard call.

By way of briefly summarizing the experimental procedure, which is described in complete detail elsewhere (Gottlieb, 1975a, 1975b, 1975c), at the stage indicated in Fig. 3, just before they begin vocalizing, the ducklings are devocalized during the first 6 hours of Day 24 of embryonic development and placed in individual soundproof incubator compartments, where they remain till they are tested at 24 hours after hatching. These ducklings have never been exposed to advanced embryos of a vocal age, so they have not heard any vocalizations prior to being tested. The vocal-communal ducklings, on the other hand, have been exposed to their own vocalizations and to those of siblings, both before and after hatching. To assure a minimum amount of auditory stimulation of a vocal nature, these ducklings are maintained in groups of no less than 20 before and after hatching. (After hatching, the ducklings are placed in individual brooder cartons, so they can hear but not see one another.)

At 24 hours after hatching, the ducklings are placed in a simultaneous auditory choice test situation in the apparatus depicted in Fig. 4.

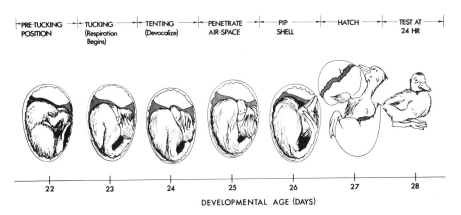

FIG. 3.   Late embryonic and early postnatal stages in Peking duckling. Devocalization takes place in tenting stage.

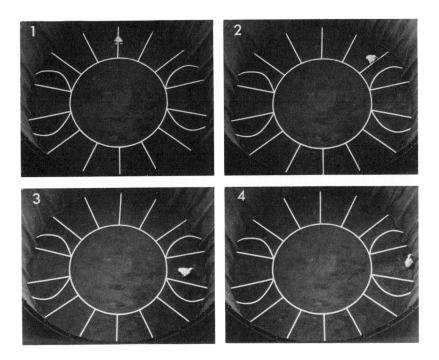

FIG. 4.   Simultaneous auditory choice test. (1) Duckling is placed equidistant between two speakers (not visible), in front of which are painted elliptical (approach) areas. (2) Duckling makes its way toward approach area on its left. (3) Duckling is in approach area and (4) snuggles next to curtain and orients to nonvisible speaker broadcasting maternal call of its species.

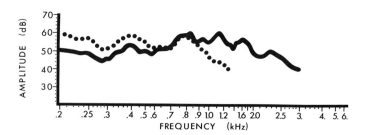

FIG. 5. Peak frequency (Hz) bands in normal mallard (—) and attenuated > 825 Hz mallard
(● ● ●) maternal call.

1. TEST OF HIGH-FREQUENCY PERCEPTUAL DEFICIT IN THE DEVOCALIZED-ISOLATED PEKING DUCKLINGS

In this experiment, one group of devocal-isolated ducklings and one group of vocal-communal ducklings were given a simultaneous auditory choice test with the normal mallard maternal call versus a high-frequency attenuated (> 825 Hz) mallard maternal call (Fig. 5), while other groups of devocal-isolated and vocal-communal ducklings were given a simultaneous auditory choice test with the normal mallard maternal call versus a low-frequency attenuated (< 825 Hz) mallard maternal call (Fig. 6). If the hypothesized selective high-frequency deficit in the mute ducklings is correct, the devocal ducklings should be less able than the vocal ducklings to detect the absence of the higher frequencies in the > 825 Hz attenuated call and therefore choose it more often than the vocal ducklings. In addition, if the auditory perceptual deficit of the mute ducklings is indeed selective and relegated to the higher frequencies of the maternal call, they should be as able as vocal ducklings to choose the normal maternal call over the low-frequency (< 825 Hz) attenuated one in a simultaneous auditory choice test.

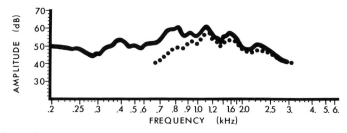

FIG. 6. Peak frequency (Hz) bands of normal mallard (—) and attenuated < 825 mallard
(● ● ●) maternal call.

TABLE I

DEVOCAL-ISOLATED AND VOCAL-COMMUNAL DUCKLINGS' PREFERENCES IN SIMULTANEOUS
AUDITORY CHOICE TEST WITH NORMAL VERSUS HIGH-FREQUENCY (> 825 Hz)
ATTENUATED MALLARD MATERNAL CALLS[a]

Groups	n	Responded	Preference		Both
			Normal mallard call	> 825 Hz attenuated mallard call	
Vocal-communal ducklings	77	51	46	4	1
Devocal-isolated ducklings	83	47	34	13	0

[a]According to the chi-square test, more of the ducklings in the devocal-isolated group chose the attenuated maternal call than in the vocal-communal group ($p = .01$). Table II shows latency and duration of response to these calls in both groups.

a. Normal versus High-Frequency (> 825 Hz) Attenuated Mallard Maternal Calls. As can be seen in Table I, in comparison to the vocal-communal ducklings, a greater proportion of the devocal-isolated ducklings chose the high-frequency (> 825 Hz) filtered mallard maternal call in the simultaneous auditory choice test with the normal mallard maternal call. Also, as shown in Table II, the devocal ducklings showed a longer latency and a shorter

TABLE II

LATENCY AND DURATION OF RESPONSE OF DEVOCAL-ISOLATED AND VOCAL-COMMUNAL
DUCKLINGS IN SIMULTANEOUS AUDITORY CHOICE TEST WITH NORMAL VERSUS HIGH-
FREQUENCY (> 825 Hz) ATTENUATED MALLARD MATERNAL CALLS[a]

Groups	n	Latency (sec)				Duration (sec)			
		Normal call		Attenuated call		Normal call		Attenuated call	
		Mean	SD	Mean	SD	Mean	SD	Mean	SD
Vocal-communal ducklings	51	100.6	88.0	281.0	58.7	162.9	94.5	9.1	37.4
Devocal-isolated ducklings	47	149.6	110.6	239.2	102.9	113.3	103.6	35.4	68.2

[a]According to the Mann–Whitney test, the devocal-isolated ducklings had a longer latency ($p = .01$) and a shorter duration ($p = .006$) of response to the normal maternal call than the vocal-communal ducklings, and they had a shorter latency ($p = .01$) and a longer duration ($p = .01$) of response to the high-frequency call than the vocal-communal ducklings. (Although nonparametric statistics are used throughout, means and standard deviations are presented for their informational value.)

TABLE III
DEVOCAL-ISOLATED AND VOCAL-COMMUNAL DUCKLINGS' PREFERENCES IN SIMULTANEOUS
AUDITORY CHOICE TEST WITH NORMAL VERSUS LOW-FREQUENCY (<825 Hz)
ATTENUATED MALLARD MATERNAL CALLS[a]

Groups	n	Responded	Preference Normal mallard call	Preference <825 Hz attenuated mallard call	Both
Vocal-communal ducklings	72	47	38	7	2
Devocal-isolated ducklings	62	30	24	5	1

[a] According to the chi-square test, there are no differences between the groups in the proportion favoring each call.

duration of response to the normal mallard call than the vocal ducklings, and, conversely, they showed a shorter latency and a longer duration of response to the high-frequency attenuated mallard maternal call than the vocal ducklings.

b. *Normal versus Low-Frequency (<825 Hz) Attenuated Mallard Calls.* As shown in Table III, there were no differences between the devocal and vocal ducklings in the proportion favoring the normal and low-frequency (< 825 Hz) filtered mallard maternal calls. Also, in Table IV, there were no differences between the devocal and vocal ducklings in latency and duration of response to either call.

TABLE IV
LATENCY AND DURATION OF RESPONSE OF DEVOCAL-ISOLATED AND VOCAL-COMMUNAL
DUCKLINGS IN SIMULTANEOUS AUDITORY CHOICE TEST WITH NORMAL VERSUS
LOW-FREQUENCY (<825 Hz) ATTENUATED MALLARD MATERNAL CALLS[a]

Groups	n	Latency (sec) Normal call Mean	Latency (sec) Normal call SD	Latency (sec) Attenuated call Mean	Latency (sec) Attenuated call SD	Duration (sec) Normal call Mean	Duration (sec) Normal call SD	Duration (sec) Attenuated call Mean	Duration (sec) Attenuated call SD
Vocal-communal ducklings	47	116.7	103.2	249.6	94.4	138.0	98.2	20.7	50.6
Devocal-isolated ducklings	30	116.5	89.7	262.7	82.8	124.5	99.4	12.3	30.1

[a] There are no differences between the groups in latency and duration of response to either call.

2. Further Test of High-Frequency Perceptual Deficit in the Devocalized Ducklings

The first experiment bore out the prediction of a selective perceptual deficit in the devocal ducklings, one confined to the higher rather than the lower frequencies of the species maternal call. The present experiment extends that finding by examining the devocal-isolated ducklings' ability to choose the normal mallard maternal call in a simultaneous choice test in which it is paired with the same call with only its very highest frequency component (> 1800 Hz) diminished (see Fig. 7). The highest frequency component of the mallard maternal call (around 2300 Hz) is not very marked relative to the 800, 1100, and 1600 Hz bands, so this test calls for particularly fine high-frequency discrimination. Thus, it could prove somewhat difficult even for vocal-communal ducklings. Should that be the case, devocal-isolated ducklings might not even be able to discriminate between the calls in this particular test.

a. Normal versus Very-High-Frequency (> 1800 Hz) Attenuated Mallard Calls. As indicated in Table V, according to the binomial test, the devocal-isolated ducklings did not discriminate between the calls, whereas the vocal-communal ducklings did (favoring the normal mallard call by a ratio of three to one). According to the chi-square test, however, there is no difference *between* the devocal and vocal ducklings in the proportion choosing each call. Fewer devocal than vocal birds responded in this test.

With respect to latency and duration of response to the calls (Table VI), there are no differences between the groups in latency of response to either call, but the vocal-communal ducklings had a longer duration of response to the normal mallard call than the devocal ducklings. Also, whereas the devocal ducklings did not show any differences in latency or duration of response to the two calls, the vocal-communal ducklings showed a shorter latency and a longer duration of response to the normal maternal call in comparison to the attenuated one.

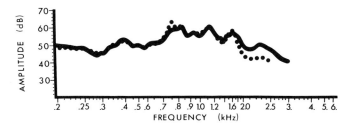

Fig. 7. Peak frequency (Hz) bands of normal mallard (—) and attenuated > 1800 Hz mallard (● ● ●) maternal call.

TABLE V

DEVOCAL-ISOLATED AND VOCAL-COMMUNAL DUCKLINGS' PREFERENCES IN SIMULTANEOUS
AUDITORY CHOICE TEST WITH NORMAL (0–2300 Hz) VERSUS VERY HIGH-FREQUENCY
(>1800 Hz) ATTENUATED MALLARD MATERNAL CALL[a]

| | | | Preference | | |
Groups	n	Responded	Normal mallard call	>1800 Hz attenuated mallard call	Both
Vocal-communal ducklings	98	69	52	17	0
Devocal-isolated ducklings	85	42	26	16	0

[a] There is no difference between the groups in the proportion choosing each of the calls, but, according to the binomial test, the devocal-isolated ducklings did not discriminate between the two calls in this test ($p = .16$), whereas the vocal-communal ducklings did ($p = .00006$). (Both p-values are two-tailed.) Fewer devocal than vocal ducklings responded in this test ($p = .004$).

TABLE VI

LATENCY AND DURATION OF RESPONSE OF DEVOCAL-ISOLATED AND VOCAL-COMMUNAL
DUCKLINGS IN SIMULTANEOUS AUDITORY CHOICE TEST WITH NORMAL (0–2300 Hz)
VERSUS VERY HIGH-FREQUENCY (>1800 Hz) ATTENUATED MALLARD MATERNAL
CALLS[a]

| | | Latency (sec) | | | | Duration (sec) | | | |
| | | Normal call | | Attenuated call | | Normal call | | Attenuated call | |
Groups	n	Mean	SD	Mean	SD	Mean	SD	Mean	SD
Vocal-communal ducklings	69	151.6	109.0	247.2	97.9	118.9	104.3	37.5	78.8
Devocal-isolated ducklings	42	180.9	115.5	226.7	100.4	74.5	90.6	51.4	83.1

[a] There are no statistically reliable differences between the groups in latency of response to either call, but the vocal-communal ducklings did show a longer duration of response ($p = .01$) to the normal Mallard call than the devocal ducklings. According to the Wilcoxon test, the devocal-isolated ducklings did not show any differences in latency or duration of response to the two calls, whereas the vocal-communal ducklings showed a shorter latency ($p < .0003$) and a longer duration ($p < .0002$) of response to the normal maternal call in comparison to the attenuated one.

3. Summary and Conclusions

In simultaneous choice tests with normal and selectively attenuated maternal calls, devocal-isolated ducklings were much more likely than vocal-communal ducklings to select the mallard maternal call in which the higher frequencies were severely attenuated, thus indicating their relative insensitivity to the higher frequency components of the maternal call. On the other hand, the devocal ducklings were as apt as vocal ducklings in selecting the normal mallard maternal call when it was pitted against a low-frequency attenuated mallard call. Thus, the perceptual deficiency resulting from embryonic (and postnatal) auditory deprivation is selective in the sense of being relegated to the higher frequency components of the maternal call. Therefore, as hypothesized earlier, the original failure of the devocalized ducklings to discriminate the mallard maternal call from the chicken maternal call (Gottlieb, 1971a) may very well have stemmed from their relative inability to detect the frequencies above 800 Hz in the mallard call (both calls sharing a component around 800 Hz and the chicken call having virtually no energy above that frequency range). It just so happens that the other calls with which the devocal ducklings were tested (Gottlieb, 1971a) did not present this particular problem. Namely, the wood duck maternal call had its energy centered around 1300 Hz with no frequencies lower than 1100 Hz, the pintail maternal call had a very-low-frequency peak at 440 Hz, and the duckling call had a very-high-frequency peak at 3400 Hz. Naturally, the present set of experiments does not eliminate the possibility of still other perceptual deficits in devocalized ducklings.

The rather important possibility that the specific deficit in frequency (Hz) perception in the devocalized ducklings may be a consequence of a specific lack of auditory stimulation (rather than a general one) is raised by two considerations. (1) As shown in Fig. 8, according to Konishi's (1973) neurophysiological analysis of auditory development in the Peking duck embryo, the neurons in the cochlear nuclei are first responsive to low frequencies (< 1000 Hz) and then become progressively responsive to higher frequencies with age. The progressive change in frequency range is accompanied by a gradual decrease in neuronal threshold, so it is not until 24–48 hours after hatching that the vocal-communal duckling becomes maximally sensitive to frequencies in the region of 1500–2500 Hz (cf. Saunders, Gates, & Coles, 1974). Thus, according to Konishi's findings, the neuronal basis of maximal high frequency sensitivity is maturing in the duck embryo during that stage of development coincident with the onset of embryonic vocalization and mutual auditory stimulation between communally incubated conspecifics. (2) Devocalization of the embryo prohibits it from hearing its own vocalizations, all of which happen to be in the high-frequency range at 1500

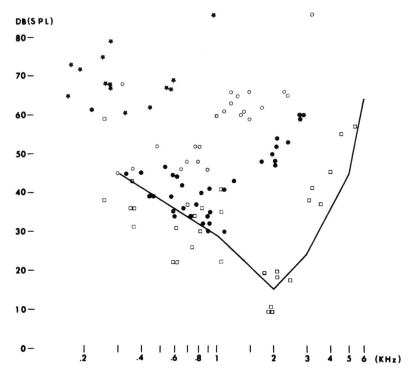

FIG. 8. Developmental changes in thresholds of auditory neurons at their characteristic frequencies in the Peking duck embryo. (Single-unit recordings from the cochlear nuclei, *N. magnocellularis* and *N. angularis*.) ★, Day 20 (6–7 days before hatching); ○, Day 23; ●, immediately after hatching; □, 2 days after hatching; ——, behavioral audiogram of an adult male mallard from Trainer (1946). From Konishi (1973).

Hz and above. With these two facts in mind, it is noteworthy that, in the present experiments, the devocalized-isolated ducklings completely failed to discriminate the > 1800 Hz attenuated maternal call from the normal maternal call.

Considering the neurophysiological and behavioral evidence, the relative insensitivity of the devocal ducklings to higher frequencies presents an excellent experimental opportunity to come to grips with certain key theoretical problems in the development of perception as well as developmental neurobiology. These questions concern the role of experience in the development of behavior, which is regarded (correctly or incorrectly) as instinctive or innate. Does embryonic experience play a *constructive* role (adding functional improvements that would not otherwise be manifest) or does it play merely a permissive or maintenance role with respect to the development of innate behavior? Is exposure to the embryonic vocalizations per se required for normal auditory perceptual development, or is the auditory experiential requirement relatively nonspecific?

C. Experiential Prevention of Perceptual Deficit in Devocalized Peking Ducklings

A most important question is whether the selective high-frequency perceptual deficit of the devocalized-isolated Peking ducklings results from a specific lack of prior auditory experience with their own vocalizations, or whether exposure to almost any sound would be sufficient to support or maintain what could be an entirely intrinsic neural auditory maturation process (as the process of innate perceptual development is usually envisaged). The next experiments were designed to answer these questions.

EMBRYONIC AND NEONATAL VOCALIZATIONS

The Peking embryo and hatchling make three distinctive vocalizations: contact-contentment, alarm-distress, and brooding-like calls. The first two differ radically with respect to spectral (Hz) content, frequency modulation, etc., whereas the brooding-like call is similar though not identical to the contact-contentment call. The contact-contentment call is especially interesting in the present context because its peak energy content falls into the region of greatest insensitivity in the devocalized duckling (1500–2500 Hz; see Fig. 9). The alarm-distress call, on the other hand, is composed mostly of very high frequencies extending up to 5000 Hz and peaking around 4000 Hz (Fig. 10). Thus, as far as natural calls are concerned, it would be of interest to determine whether embryonic exposure to either of these two very different vocalizations would prove equally effective in rectifying the high-frequency perceptual deficit of devocalized and otherwise aurally

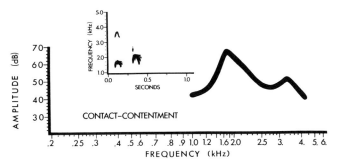

FIG. 9.   Peak frequency band and Sonagraphic analysis (inset) of contact-contentment vocalization.

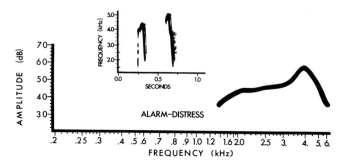

FIG. 10. Peak frequency band and Sonagraphic analysis (inset) of alarm-distress vocalization.

isolated ducklings. Given the fact that the devocalized-isolated ducklings show their perceptual deficit in the higher-frequency (> 825 Hz) range of the maternal call, to test the notion that exposure to almost any sound would be sufficient to maintain the forward impetus of the maturing auditory system, it was decided to fabricate a low-frequency "white noise" sound between approximately 300 and 1800 Hz, otherwise pulsed exactly like the contact-contentment call (note duration and interpulse interval), to see it embryonic exposure to this sound would be as effective as the contact-contentment call in remedying (or preventing) the high-frequency perceptual deficit of the devocalized duckling. The low-frequency white noise is depicted in Fig. 11.

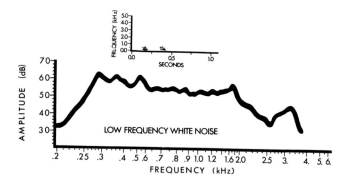

FIG. 11. Peak frequency band and Sonagraphic analysis (inset) of low frequency white noise. Note that the Sonagram does not show any energy above 1000 Hz. This is probably due to the fact that the frequency analysis was made acoustically as the sound was broadcast inside a soundproof incubator compartment, whereas the Sonagram was made by electrical means, i.e., via a direct electrical connection between the tape recorder and the Sonagraph machine. Since this is the conventional way to make a Sonagram, the major discrepancy between the two modes of analysis in this particular case is very significant: Acoustic and electrical analyses are sometimes not at all comparable. It is for that reason that each call in the present experiments was analyzed by the acoustic method.

D. Hypotheses

Aside from its motivational connotations, the energy of the contact-contentment vocalization falls completely in the region of greatest perceptual insensitivity in the devocalized duckling (1500–2500 Hz). Therefore, assuming the necessity of a fairly specific match between the deficit to be remedied and the remedial experience, it would be expected that embryonic exposure to the sound of the contact-contentment call would be more effective in remedying or preventing the postnatal perceptual deficiency than exposure to the low-frequency white noise (300–1800 Hz). This hypothesis is examined in a simultaneous auditory choice test situation with the normal mallard maternal call versus the high-frequency (> 825 Hz) attenuated mallard maternal call, with the specific prediction that the contact-contentment call will enhance the devocalized ducklings' response to the normal mallard call more than the low-frequency white noise.

The rationale for this prediction can better be appreciated if one examines Fig. 5, showing the normal versus > 825 Hz attenuated mallard maternal call, and compares that information to Fig. 12, where the Hz energy distribution of the contact-contentment call and the low-frequency white noise is contrasted with the normal maternal call. (It is important to note that all these frequency analyses are *acoustic* analyses taken from the point where the embryo would be stimulated in its soundproof incubator compartment in the case of the contact-contentment call and the low-frequency white noise, and from the spot where the devocalized duckling is placed in the test apparatus in the case of the maternal call.) In Fig. 12, it can be seen that the distribution of energy in the contact-contentment call corresponds to the area of the maternal call in which the devocalized ducklings are least sensitive, whereas the low-frequency white noise is confined primarily to frequencies below 1800 Hz, where the devocal ducklings exhibit no deficiency vis-à-vis the maternal call.

To make an even sharper test of the efficacy of the contact-contentment call, the second experiment places it in competition with the alarm-distress

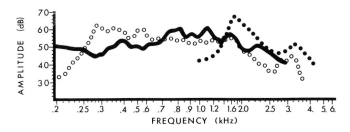

Fig. 12. Peak frequency bands of normal mallard maternal call (■), contact-contentment call (● ● ●), and low-frequency white noise (○ ○ ○).

258

GILBERT GOTTLIEB

call and examines the behavior of devocal-isolated ducklings in a simultaneous choice test involving the normal mallard maternal call versus a very-
high-frequency (> 1800 Hz) attenuated mallard maternal call. In this test,
whereas the vocal-communal ducklings show a statistically reliable preference for the normal maternal call over the attenuated one (binomial
test), the unstimulated devocal-isolated ducklings completely fail to detect
a difference between the calls and therefore fail to show a preference for
the normal maternal call. However, the vocal-communal ducklings do make
enough errors in this test so that there was no difference *between* them and
the devocal-isolated ducklings in their preference for the normal maternal
call (chi-square test). Accordingly, to take that eventuality into account,
the present prediction would be that embryonic exposure to the contact-
contentment call would be sufficiently effective to allow the devocal
duckling to discriminate between the maternal calls, whereas the alarm-
distress call would be no more effective than no prior stimulation (i.e., the
devocal ducklings so stimulated would fail to prefer the normal maternal
call over the very-high-frequency attenuated one). In other words, although
the differential effectiveness of the prior auditory exposure can be predicted
and distinguished, the previous lack of a statistically reliable difference
between the devocal-isolated and vocal-communal ducklings in this test
precludes the expectation of a between-group difference in preference in
the present circumstance. Once again, examination of the two maternal
calls (Fig. 7) and the energy distribution of the two embryonic vocalizations
(Fig. 13) shows the concrete basis for the predicted differences in the efficacy
of the two embryonic vocalizations. In short, the distribution of energy in
the contact-contentment call is more favorably matched to the devocal
ducklings' high-frequency perceptual deficit than is that of the alarm-distress
call.

More generally speaking, the present predictions are based on the assumption than a selective perceptual deficit requires a closely matched or

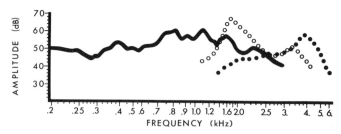

FIG. 13. Peak frequency bands of normal mallard maternal call (➜), contact-contentment call (o o o), and alarm-distress call (● ● ●).

relatively specific experience for rectification, even when the behavior in question is considered innate and thus primarily endogenous in its development. For conceptual clarity, it should be said that the present assumption does not entail the belief that the prior auditory experience *induces* the preference for the maternal call, but only that it sharpens the discriminative basis of the preference. Whether this is in fact an active (facilitative) effect of experience or merely a more passive (maintenance) process is a separate question.

The ducklings in the present experiments were treated and maintained in the same fashion as those in the vocal-communal and devocal-isolated groups in the previous experiments. The embryonic auditory stimulation with one or another of the calls commenced on Day 24, 18 hours for 5 minutes an hour through Day 26, 18 hours. The ducklings were tested at around 24 hours after hatching. (The experiments are described in detail in Gottlieb, 1975b.)

1. Efficacy of Contact-Contentment Call and Low-Frequency White Noise in Preventing Perceptual Deficit of Devocal-Isolated Ducklings

To examine the prediction that the contact-contentment call would be more efficacious than the low-frequency white noise in preventing the high-frequency perceptual deficit in devocal-isolated ducklings, in this experiment 76 such ducklings were exposed to the contact-contentment call and 94 were exposed to the low-frequency white noise before being tested with the normal mallard maternal call versus the high frequency (> 825 Hz) attenuated maternal call at 24 hours after hatching.

As shown in Table VII, according to the binomial test, each group of ducklings, including the nonexposed control group, favored the normal maternal call over the attenuated one. According to the chi-square test, however, the ducklings which were exposed to the contact-contentment call chose the normal maternal call more often than the nonexposed ducklings ($\chi^2 = 3.54, p = .03$), whereas the preference of the ducklings exposed to the low-frequency white noise did not differ from the nonexposed ducklings ($\chi^2 = 1.80, p = .18$). There were no differences in preference between the two stimulated groups.

In terms of latency and duration of response (Table VIII), the ducklings which responded in each group showed a shorter latency and a longer duration of response to the normal maternal call compared to the attenuated call. According to the Mann–Whitney U-test, there were no differences between the groups in latency and duration of response to either call.

TABLE VII

PREFERENCE OF DEVOCAL-ISOLATED DUCKLINGS IN SIMULTANEOUS AUDITORY CHOICE TEST WITH NORMAL VERSUS HIGH-FREQUENCY (> 825 Hz) ATTENUATED MALLARD MATERNAL CALLS AFTER EMBRYONIC EXPOSURE TO CONTACT-CONTENTMENT VOCALIZATION OR LOW-FREQUENCY WHITE NOISE

| Embryonic auditory experience | n | Responded | Preference | | Both |
			Normal mallard call	> 825 Hz attenuated mallard call	
No vocal exposure	83	47	34^a	13	0
Exposed to contact-contentment vocalization	76	49	43^c	5	1
Exposed to low-frequency white noise	94	54	46^b	8	0

$^a p = .004$, binomial test.
$^b p < .00006$, binomial test.
$^c p < .00003$, binomial test.

TABLE VIII

LATENCY AND DURATION OF RESPONSE OF DEVOCAL-ISOLATED DUCKLINGS IN SIMULTANEOUS AUDITORY CHOICE TEST WITH NORMAL VERSUS HIGH-FREQUENCY (> 825 Hz) ATTENUATED MALLARD MATERNAL CALLS AFTER EMBRYONIC EXPOSURE TO CONTACT-CONTENTMENT VOCALIZATION OR LOW-FREQUENCY WHITE NOISE[a]

| Embryonic auditory experience | n | Latency (sec) | | | | Duration (sec) | | | |
| | | Normal call | | Attenuated call | | Normal call | | Attenuated call | |
		Mean	SD	Mean	SD	Mean	SD	Mean	SD
No vocal exposure	47	149.6^b	110.6	239.2	102.9	113.3^b	103.6	35.4	68.2
Exposed to contact-contentment vocalization	49	128.0^b	82.6	270.4	72.4	122.9^b	81.1	17.9	52.5
Exposed to low-frequency white noise	54	130.3^b	95.5	274.8	63.2	122.8^b	84.8	13.4	36.6

^{a} Although the Wilcoxon matched-pairs signed-ranks test and the Mann–Whitney U-test do not use means and standard deviations, these figures are presented here and in Table IV for their informational value. (N includes only ducklings which responded.)

$^b p \leq .01$, Wilcoxon test (shorter latency or longer duration than score for opposing call).

2. Efficacy of Contact-Contentment Call and Alarm-Distress Call in Preventing Perceptual Deficit of Devocal-Isolated Ducklings

The simultaneous choice test with > 1800 Hz attenuated mallard maternal call is a much more difficult test than the previous one (> 825 Hz attenuated maternal call), so it could provide an even better basis for evaluating the efficacy of the contact-contentment call than did the previous test. As mentioned earlier, it is important to recall that in this test vocal-communal ducklings do favor the normal maternal call over the attenuated one, but not to the extent that they are (statistically) significantly better than devocal-isolated ducklings, which fail to distinguish between the two calls. The point is that the absence of a between-group difference in preference in the vocal-communal–devocal-isolate comparison precludes the expectation of a between-group difference here, the present prior auditory experience being considerably less in extent and variation than that provided by the vocal-communal condition.

As shown in Table IX, the nonexposed control group and the group exposed to the alarm-distress vocalization failed to show a preference between the normal and very-high-frequency attenuated maternal calls, whereas more of the ducklings in the group exposed to the contact-contentment vocalization chose the normal maternal call over the attenuated one. As anticipated, there were no differences between the groups on this measure.

TABLE IX

PREFERENCE OF DEVOCAL-ISOLATED DUCKLINGS IN SIMULTANEOUS AUDITORY CHOICE
TEST WITH NORMAL VERSUS VERY-HIGH-FREQUENCY (> 1800 Hz) ATTENUATED
MALLARD MATERNAL CALLS AFTER EMBRYONIC EXPOSURE TO CONTACT-CONTENTMENT
VOCALIZATION OR ALARM-DISTRESS VOCALIZATION

Embryonic auditory experience	n	Responded	Preference		
			Normal mallard call	> 1800 Hz attenuated mallard call	Both
No vocal exposure	85	42	26	16	0
Exposed to contact-contentment vocalization	85	46	32^a	13	1
Exposed to alarm-distress vocalization	83	37	23	12	2

$^a p = .004$, binomial test.

With respect to latency and duration of response (Table X), the non-exposed group showed neither a shorter latency nor a longer response to the normal maternal call, the group exposed to the alarm-distress vocalization showed a shorter latency but not a longer duration of response to the normal maternal call, and the group exposed to the contact-contentment call showed both a shorter latency and a longer duration of response to the normal maternal call compared to the attenuated one. There were no differences between the groups on these measures.

3. SUMMARY AND CONCLUSIONS

Although failing to provide striking or large differences between the groups, the outcome of both experiments indicates the consistent superiority of the contact-contentment call in preventing the high-frequency perceptual deficit in the devocal-isolated ducklings. In the first experiment, the ducklings exposed to the contact-contentment call showed an increased preference (Table VII) for the normal maternal call in comparison with the nonexposed devocal-isolated ducklings. In the second experiment, although there were no differences between the groups due to the aforementioned ceiling effect (i.e., the preferences of vocal-communal ducklings do not differ from nonexposed devocal-isolates in that particular test), the only group which showed a preference for the normal maternal call over the very-

TABLE X

LATENCY AND DURATION OF RESPONSE OF DEVOCAL-ISOLATED DUCKLINGS IN SIMULTANEOUS AUDITORY CHOICE TEST WITH NORMAL VERSUS VERY-HIGH-FREQUENCY (> 1800 Hz) ATTENUATED MALLARD MATERNAL CALLS AFTER EMBRYONIC EXPOSURE TO CONTACT-CONTENTMENT VOCALIZATION OR ALARM-DISTRESS VOCALIZATION

| Embryonic auditory experience | n | Latency (sec) | | | | Duration (sec) | | | |
| | | Normal call | | Attenuated call | | Normal call | | Attenuated call | |
		Mean	SD	Mean	SD	Mean	SD	Mean	SD
No vocal exposure	42	180.9	115.5	226.7	100.4	74.5	90.6	51.4	83.1
Exposed to contact-contentment vocalization	46	159.8[b]	111.6	241.3	94.8	91.2[b]	86.1	29.0	60.2
Exposed to alarm-distress vocalization	37	156.7[a]	115.5	226.7	96.0	69.0	80.9	49.1	80.2

[a] $p = .02$, Wilcoxon test (shorter latency than score for opposing call).
[b] $p = .002$, Wilcoxon test (shorter latency and longer duration than score for opposing call).

high-frequency attenuated one was the group exposed to the contact-contentment call (Table IX). Prior exposure to the alarm-distress was *somewhat* effective in this test in that those ducklings did show a shorter latency of response to the normal maternal call in comparison to the attenuated call. Prior exposure to the contact-contentment call promoted both a shorter latency and a longer duration of response to the normal maternal call.

The experimental results gain some strength when one considers the highly (and deliberately) "mechanical," invariant, and noncontingent nature of the prior stimulation conditions. The devocalized embryos were exposed to only two notes (and the same two notes) of a given call for 5 minutes an hour for 48 hours. The ducklings played no role in the production of the sound imposed upon them, in the sense that it was not contingent on their behavior and the sound itself was not produced by them. The effects achieved, modest as they may be, would seem to be among the "purest" cases of sheerly perceptual learning. Although it cannot be ruled out that the possible motivational and/or emotional "connotations" of the contact-contentment call may have enhanced its effectiveness, the call was selected in the present context merely on the basis of its frequency characteristics, which happen to match the region of the devocal ducklings' greatest high-frequency insensitivity. If one wanted to try to rule out the possible connotations of the call, narrow-band white noise in the same spectral region (1500–2500 Hz) could be employed. Whether or not the psychological aspects of the contact-contentment call, other than its spectral content, enhanced the effectiveness of the call, the conclusion would still hold that not any sound (e.g., low-frequency white noise) is capable of preventing the high-frequency perceptual deficit in the devocalized duckling, and, in this regard, certain normally occurring embryonic sounds (e.g., contact-contentment call) are more effective than others (e.g., alarm-distress call). An important characteristic of the "therapeutic" value of the sound pattern is its match with that region of the frequency spectrum in which the perceptual deficiency occurs.

As pointed out by Bateson (1975), some theorists (e.g., Lorenz, 1965) who concern themselves with innate behavior assume that the development of such behavior is not critically linked to any specific prior experience, but rather that it will exhibit itself provided only that rather general (nonspecific) life-sustaining conditions prevail during ontogeny. The assumption that innate behavior derives from the process of neural maturation without the benefit or necessity of experience is not confined to classical ethological thought—it would seem to be a fairly widely held view in the psychological field as well. The present results call for a revision in that view, and offer some support for the contention that, during the evolution of species-specific perception, natural selection would seem to have involved a selection for the entire developmental manifold, including not only the neuroembryological component, but also the normally occurring sensory stimulative features of ontogeny (Gottlieb, 1971a). This contention is in accord with recent advances in developmental neurobiology, which call for an appreciation of the experiential component in realizing or maintaining species-typical neural end products (e.g., Berry, 1974). As mentioned earlier, for conceptual clarity it is important to note that the embryonic auditory experience is not required to bring about (induce) the preference for the maternal call in this species; rather, such experience merely contributes to the sharpness of the discriminative basis of the preference at 24 hours after hatching.

A very important question, one that has ramifications for developmental neurobiology as well as the development of species-specific perception, concerns the nature of the effect of the embryonic auditory stimulation in the present experiments. Does it sharpen later discrimination by, say, adding to the effects of intrinsic neural maturation per se, or does it merely preserve or maintain a level of perceptual development which is entirely a consequence of strictly endogenous neural events? The answer to this question can come from a behavioral analysis of the gradual or full-blown character of perceptual development in the embryo, and that information is not yet in hand (the research is in progress). Another question of considerable moment is whether the embryonic (and postnatal) auditory deprivation caused by devocalization merely induces a lag in neural maturation and species-specific perceptual development, such that perceptual deficiencies evident at early ages disappear at older ages, or whether such deficiencies are persistent and are not subsequently rectified sheerly by internal neural maturation processes. That matter will be explored in the next experiments in this series.

E. Maturational Rectification of Perceptual Deficit in Devocalized Peking Ducklings

The experiments specifying the devocal ducklings' perceptual deficit and the experience required to prevent the deficit have been restricted to 24-hour-old ducklings: All the ducklings were tested at 24 hours after hatching. The neural maturation processes underlying the development of innate behavior are usually considered to be self-sufficient (i.e., self-differentiating). Thus, an important question is whether the perceptual deficit present at 24 hours represents merely a temporal lag in a primarily endogenous process of neural maturation, such that the deficiency would eventually rectify itself at some later age even in the absence of auditory experience. In this view, the normally occurring embryonic auditory stimulation would merely play a temporal regulative role in the appearance of the behavior in question; if the embryonic auditory experience plays a stronger role (e.g., sharpening perception beyond the degree achieved by intrinsic maturational factors alone), the aforementioned perceptual insensitivity would not completely rectify itself in the absence of auditory experience. Given that it takes exposure to a highly specific pattern of auditory stimulation to rectify the high-frequency perceptual deficit at 24 hours of age, it would seem doubtful that the deficit could rectify itself without experience. Thus, it would be predicted that, in the absence of auditory experience, the high-frequency sensitivity of the devocal-isolated ducklings would always be inferior to the vocal-communal ducklings regardless of the age at testing.

The next experiments examine the question of whether the high-frequency perceptual deficit in the devocal ducklings can rectify itself without auditory experience. This question can be answered by testing devocal ducklings at progressively later ages after hatching; that is, by allowing more time for neural maturation to take place in the ducklings' auditory system before giving them the first simultaneous choice tests with the normal mallard maternal call versus the high-frequency attenuated mallard maternal calls used in the previous experiments. Based on electrophysiological studies, the auditory system of the Peking duck is known to be undergoing the final stages of neural maturation (specifically involving increasing sensitivity to high frequencies) during the late embryonic and early neonatal periods (Konishi, 1973; summarized here in Fig. 8 in Section III). Consequently, in these experiments, the devocal Peking ducklings' performance in the choice tests with the normal maternal call versus the > 825 Hz and > 1800 Hz attenuated maternal calls was examined at 24 hours, 48 hours, and 65 hours after hatching. Given the rather specific auditory input that is required to rectify their high-frequency insensitivity at 24 hours, it was expected that, in the absence of auditory experience, the devocal ducklings would fail to show sufficient improvement to bring them up to the level of perceptual competence of the vocal-communal ducklings at any age.

1. PERFORMANCE OF VOCAL-COMMUNAL AND DEVOCAL-ISOLATED
   DUCKLINGS IN TEST WITH NORMAL MALLARD MATERNAL CALL
   VERSUS HIGH-FREQUENCY (> 825 Hz) ATTENUATED MALLARD
   MATERNAL CALL AT THREE DIFFERENT AGES

To determine if the devocal ducklings' perceptual deficiency eventually rectifies itself after hatching, a total of 168 vocal-communal and 201 devocal-isolated ducklings were tested either at 24 hours, 48 hours, or 65 hours after hatching with the normal versus high-frequency (> 825 Hz) attenuated maternal calls (Fig. 5). Each duckling was tested once at only one age because test–retest performance has been found to be erratic with these particular calls, whereas the results of the first test at any age are consistent (reliable).

As shown in Table XI, according to the binomial test, both the vocal-communal and devocal-isolated ducklings preferred the normal maternal call at all ages. Proportionately more of the vocal than devocal ducklings selected the normal call at 24 hours ($p = .01$) and at 65 hours ($p = .009$), but not at 48 hours, at which age the devocal ducklings' preference for the normal maternal call was equivalent to that of the vocal ducklings. The devocal ducklings' selection of the normal call improved from 24 hours to 48 hours ($p = .04$), but their performance tended to deteriorate between 48 hours and 65 hours ($p = .06$). Incidentally, the over-all incidence of response in the vocal ducklings took a remarkable rise from 66% to 94% between 24 hours and 48 hours ($p < .001$), and more of the vocal than the devocal ducklings responded at that age ($p = .001$) and at 65 hours ($p = .04$) in this test.

With respect to latency and duration of response (Table XII), both groups of ducklings showed a shorter latency and a longer duration of response to the normal maternal call compared to the > 825 Hz attenuated call at all ages. Most important, in the comparison between the vocal and devocal ducklings on latency of response to the normal call, the former outper-

TABLE XI

PREFERENCE OF VOCAL-COMMUNAL DUCKLINGS AND DEVOCAL-ISOLATED DUCKLINGS IN
SIMULTANEOUS AUDITORY CHOICE TEST WITH NORMAL VERSUS HIGH-FREQUENCY
(> 825 HZ) ATTENUATED MALLARD MATERNAL CELLS

| | | | Preference | | |
| | | | Normal mallard call | > 825 Hz attenuated mallard call | |
Groups	n	Responded			Both
Vocal-communal ducklings					
24 Hours	77	51	46^b	4	1
48 Hours	50	47	42^b	4	1
65 Hours	41	34	32^b	1	1
Devocal-isolated ducklings					
24 Hours	83	47	34^a	13	0
48 Hours	58	39	36^b	3	0
65 Hours	60	39	28^a	10	1

[a] $p < .006$, binomial test.
[b] $p < .00006$, binomial test.

TABLE XII
LATENCY AND DURATION OF RESPONSE OF VOCAL-COMMUNAL DUCKLINGS AND
DEVOCAL-ISOLATED DUCKLINGS IN SIMULTANEOUS AUDITORY CHOICE TEST WITH
NORMAL VERSUS HIGH-FREQUENCY (>825 Hz) ATTENUATED MALLARD MATERNAL
CALLS[a]

| | | Latency (sec) | | | | Duration (sec) | | | |
| | | Normal call | | Attenuated call | | Normal call | | Attenuated call | |
Groups	n	Mean	SD	Mean	SD	Mean	SD	Mean	SD
Vocal-communal ducklings									
24 Hours	51	100.6[d]	88.0	281.0	58.7	162.9[d]	94.5	9.1	37.4
48 Hours	47	39.6[d]	49.1	271.1	77.4	185.3[d]	95.7	12.6	46.6
65 Hours	34	66.1[d]	61.4	278.6	63.8	173.6[d]	88.7	10.3	45.7
Devocal-isolated ducklings									
24 Hours	47	149.6[b]	110.6	239.2	102.9	113.3[c]	103.6	35.4	68.2
48 Hours	39	83.3[d]	93.5	287.0	46.1	126.9[d]	105.6	4.4	20.1
65 Hours	39	106.1[c]	107.4	236.2	107.5	98.8[c]	97.8	27.6	62.5

[a] The p-values for Wilcoxon test refer to shorter latency or longer duration than score for opposing call.
[b] $p = .01$, Wilcoxon test.
[c] $p \leq .003$, Wilcoxon test.
[d] $p < .00006$, Wilcoxon test.

formed the latter at 24 hours ($p = .02$) and 48 hours ($p = .01$), but there was no difference between the groups on this measure at 65 hours. The devocal ducklings showed an improvement in latency of response to the normal maternal call between 24 hours and 48 hours ($p = .002$) which slipped only slightly thereafter, so that at 65 hours the latency figure to the normal maternal call was still shorter than at 24 hours ($p = .058$) and no different from the 48-hour figure. The vocal ducklings also showed a similar improvement in latency to the normal call between 24 hours and 48 hours ($p < .00006$), but they slipped enough between 48 hours and 65 hours for that difference to be significant ($p = .004$), which virtually put them back to their 24-hour value ($p > .05 < .10$).

With respect to duration of response to the normal call, neither the devocal or the vocal ducklings showed any change over age, and the vocal ducklings excelled the devocal ducklings at all ages ($p = .007$, .004, and .0002 at 24, 48, and 65 hours, respectively).

In summary, the devocal ducklings' perception of the normal maternal call improved sufficiently between 24 hours and 48 hours so that the number of devocal ducklings exhibiting a preference for the normal call was equivalent to the vocal ducklings at that age. However, the preference of the devocal ducklings for the normal call declined between 48 hours and 65 hours so that there was once again a difference between them and the vocal ducklings at 65 hours (as at 24 hours). The devocal ducklings' latency of response to the normal call was inferior to that of the vocal ducklings at 24 and 48 hours but not at 65 hours. The devocal ducklings' duration of response to the normal maternal call was inferior to that of the vocal ducklings at all ages. Of the three response measures (preference, latency, duration), the ability of the birds to select (prefer) the normal maternal call over the attenuated one is clearly of most importance. In this regard the devocal ducklings are inferior to the vocal ducklings at 24 hours and at 65 hours but not at 48 hours. (These findings are summarized in Fig. 14.) In sum, the devocal ducklings "caught up" to the vocal ducklings at least one age on all measures except duration of response to the normal maternal call.

2. PERFORMANCE OF VOCAL-COMMUNAL AND DEVOCAL-ISOLATED
   DUCKLINGS IN TEST WITH NORMAL MALLARD MATERNAL CALL VERSUS
   VERY HIGH-FREQUENCY (> 1800 Hz) ATTENUATED MALLARD
   MATERNAL CALL AT THREE DIFFERENT AGES

The devocal ducklings are able to discriminate the normal maternal call from the > 825 Hz attenuated one, so, in that sense the previous test is easier than the present one, in which they are faced with the normal maternal call versus a very-high-frequency (> 1800 Hz) attenuated call; i.e., 24-hour-old devocal ducklings do not distinguish between these calls. Thus, the

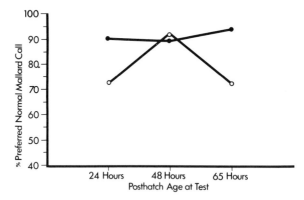

FIG. 14. Proportion of responding vocal-communal (●———●, N = 132) and devocal-isolated (○———○, N = 125) ducklings which selected the normal maternal call in the normal mallard maternal call versus > 825 Hz attenuated mallard maternal call test at 24 hours, 48 hours, and 65 hours after hatching.

present experiment makes an even greater demand for improvement in high-frequency perceptual differentiation than the previous test, and so should provide even more conclusive evidence as to whether the high-frequency perceptual deficit is ultimately rectified by maturation.

As shown in Table XIII, according to the binomial test, the vocal ducklings preferred the normal maternal call at all ages. Although the devocal ducklings failed to show such a preference at 24 hours or 65 hours, they did show it at 48 hours. [There are no differences in preference between the vocal and devocal ducklings at any age in this test. The question of interest is whether the devocal ducklings' perception improves sufficiently to allow them to discriminate between the calls at any age, and the answer (above) is *yes*.] Incidentally, both groups showed a statistically reliable increase in the number of responding birds between 24 hours and 48 hours ($p < .001$ for the vocal ducklings and $p = .009$ for the devocal ducklings). Whereas the devocal ducklings resumed their original low incidence of response between 48 hours and 65 hours ($p = .02$), the vocal ducklings' incidence of response remained relatively high at all ages. In fact, the vocal ducklings had a greater incidence of response than the devocal ducklings at all ages ($p = .008$, $<.001$, and $<.001$ at each age).

With respect to latency and duration of response (Table XIV), the vocal ducklings showed a shorter latency and a longer duration of response to the

TABLE XIII

PREFERENCE OF VOCAL-COMMUNAL DUCKLINGS AND DEVOCAL-ISOLATED DUCKLINGS IN SIMULTANEOUS AUDITORY CHOICE TEST WITH NORMAL VERSUS VERY-HIGH-FREQUENCY (> 1800 HZ) ATTENUATED MALLARD MATERNAL CALLS

			Preference		
Groups	n	Responded	Normal mallard call	> 1800 Hz attenuated mallard call	Both
Vocal-communal ducklings					
24 Hours	98	69	52^c	17	0
48 Hours	51	49	38^c	7	4
65 Hours	57	48	31^a	14	3
Devocal-isolated ducklings					
24 Hours	85	42	26	16	0
48 Hours	93	65	45^b	17	3
65 Hours	74	38	19	14	5

$^a p = .017$, binomial test.
$^b p < .0006$, binomial test.
$^c p < .00006$, binomial test.

TABLE XIV

LATENCY AND DURATION OF RESPONSE OF VOCAL-COMMUNAL DUCKLINGS AND
DEVOCAL-ISOLATED DUCKLINGS IN SIMULTANEOUS AUDITORY CHOICE TEST WITH
NORMAL VERSUS VERY-HIGH-FREQUENCY (> 1800 HZ) ATTENUATED MALLARD
MATERNAL CALLS[a]

		Latency (sec)				Duration (sec)			
		Normal call		Attenuated call		Normal call		Attenuated call	
Groups	n	Mean	SD	Mean	SD	Mean	SD	Mean	SD
Vocal-communal ducklings									
24 Hours	69	151.6[c]	109.0	247.2	97.9	118.9[c]	104.3	37.5	78.8
48 Hours	49	60.1[d]	79.5	218.2	118.7	146.9[d]	96.2	30.7	63.7
65 Hours	48	129.2	115.5	165.1	129.8	90.8	94.4	73.4	111.6
Devocal-isolated ducklings									
24 Hours	42	180.9	115.5	226.7	100.4	74.5	90.6	51.4	83.1
48 Hours	65	123.4[b]	115.5	215.5	118.7	97.2[c]	100.7	30.1	60.4
65 Hours	38	145.8	126.6	189.9	119.7	89.4	101.1	46.3	81.5

[a] The p-values for Wilcoxon test refer to shorter latency or longer duration than the score for opposing call.
[b] $p < .001$, Wilcoxon test.
[c] $p < .0004$, Wilcoxon test.
[d] $p < .00006$, Wilcoxon test.

normal maternal call at 24 and 48 hours but not at 65 hours, whereas the devocal ducklings showed such differences only at 48 hours. The vocal ducklings showed a shorter latency to the normal call than the devocal ducklings at 48 hours ($p < .0002$), but not at 24 hours or 65 hours. Both groups showed an improvement in latency to the normal call between 24 and 48 hours ($p < .00006$ for the vocal ducklings and $p = .02$ for the devocal ducklings). The vocal ducklings did not sustain their remarkably short latency between 48 hours and 65 hours ($p < .001$).

With respect to duration of response to the normal maternal call, the vocal ducklings were superior to the devocal ducklings at 24 hours ($p = .01$) and 48 hours ($p = .002$), but not at 65 hours. The vocal ducklings showed a deterioration on this measure between 48 hours and 65 hours ($p = .003$).

As summarized in Fig. 15, the devocal ducklings became able to distinguish the normal maternal call at 48 hours, although they did not sustain this improvement at 65 hours. Whereas the vocal ducklings were able to distinguish the normal from the attenuated call at all ages (Fig. 15), they showed signs of deterioration in their latency and duration of response at 65 hours. Thus, the devocal ducklings' response to the normal maternal call

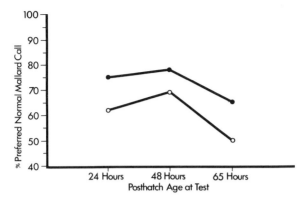

FIG. 15. Proportion of responding vocal-communal (●———●, N = 166) and devocal-isolated (○———○, N = 145) ducklings which chose the normal maternal call in the normal mallard maternal call versus > 1800 Hz attenuated mallard maternal call test at 24 hours, 48 hours, and 65 hours after hatching.

became comparable to the vocal ducklings' at one or more ages on all measures except incidence, whereon the vocal ducklings exceeded the devocal ducklings at all ages.

3. SUMMARY

The results of both experiments clearly show a significant, maturationally mediated rectification of the devocal ducklings' high-frequency perceptual deficit between 24 and 48 hours after hatching. In the first experiment, their performance in terms of preference became as differentiated as that of the vocal ducklings at 48 hours, whereas in the second experiment they became able to distinguish the normal call from the attenuated one at 48 hours. In both instances, however, the devocal ducklings' performance showed a significant deterioration in their selection of the normal maternal call between 48 hours and 65 hours, indicating that they are unable to sustain the improvement in the absence of auditory stimulation. In both experiments the devocal ducklings "caught up" to the vocal ducklings on most measures but not all: in the first experiment their duration of response to the normal maternal call did not equal the vocal ducklings' at any age, while in the second experiment their incidence of response failed to equal the vocal ducklings' at any age.

As demonstrated earlier in this series of experiments, embryonic exposure of the devocal ducklings to the (sibling) contact-contentment call prevented the high-frequency perceptual deficit from manifesting itself at 24 hours (Section III, D). It is a matter of considerable interest to determine whether that same experience might prevent the deterioration in perception observed between 48 hours and 65 hours in the present experiments. The next experiment was designed to address that problem.

4. EFFICACY OF EMBRYONIC EXPOSURE TO CONTACT-CONTENTMENT CALL IN PREVENTING PERCEPTUAL DETERIORATION OF DEVOCAL DUCKLINGS AT 65 HOURS AFTER HATCHING

In the previous study of the auditory experience required to prevent the high-frequency perceptual deficit in devocal ducklings, embryonic exposure to the contact-contentment call proved more efficacious than other sounds (Section, III, D). Thus, that vocalization was chosen for use in the present experiment. In the previous study the exposure took place for 5 minutes each hour for 48 hours between Day 24, 18 hours (beginning about 12 hours after embryonic devocalization) and Day 26, 18 hours (continuing to about 10 hours after hatching), with the birds being tested at 24 hours after hatching. It was decided to employ the same schedule in the present experiment, despite the fact that the birds would be tested at 65 hours after hatching rather than at 24 hours. If the same exposure proved as efficacious at the older age as it did at the younger age, the significance of the early auditory experience would be considerably broadened. Since there was a statistically reliable difference between the devocal and vocal ducklings' preferences at 65 hours in the normal maternal call versus > 825 Hz attenuated maternal call test, that test was used here, with a two-pronged prediction: namely, that the prior auditory experience would sustain the devocal ducklings' pre-ference for the normal mallard call such that (1) they would perform significantly better than the nonexposed devocal ducklings and (2) thereby nullify the difference between the devocal and vocal ducklings at 65 hours.

As shown in Table XV, the aurally stimulated devocal ducklings were as proficient as the vocal ducklings in choosing the normal maternal call, thereby erasing the previous difference between the devocal and vocal ducklings in this test at 65 hours. Also, there was no difference between the present devocal ducklings and the vocal ones on incidence of response, thereby eliminating that difference at 65 hours. Further, as predicted, the aurally stimulated devocal ducklings' preference for the normal maternal call tended to be greater than the nonstimulated ducklings, but that differ-ence just failed to be statistically reliable ($p = .06$).

With regard to latency and duration of response (Table XVI), there was no difference between the present devocal ducklings and the vocal ducklings on latency of response to the normal maternal call, but there was no differ-ence on this measure in the previous experiment either, so this result does not add anything material to the question. The previous difference in dura-

TABLE XV

Preference of Vocal-Communal Ducklings and Devocal-Isolated Ducklings in Simultaneous Auditory Choice Test with Normal versus High-Frequency (>825 Hz) Attenuated Mallard Maternal Calls at 65 Hours after Hatching

			Preference		
Groups	n	Responded	Normal mallard call	>825 Hz attenuated mallard call	Both
Vocal-communal ducklings	41	34	32^b	1	1
Devocal-isolated ducklings: no prior auditory experience	60	39	28^a	10	1
Devocal-isolated ducklings: exposed to contact-contentment call	76	53	47^b	6	0

$^a p = .006$, binomial test.
$^b p < .00006$, binomial test.

TABLE XVI

Latency and Duration of Response of Vocal-Communal Ducklings and Devocal-Isolated Ducklings in Simultaneous Auditory Choice Test with Normal versus High-Frequency (>825 Hz) Attenuated Mallard Maternal Calls at 65 Hours after Hatching[a]

		Latency (sec)				Duration (sec)			
		Normal call		Attenuated call		Normal call		Attenuated call	
Groups	n	Mean	SD	Mean	SD	Mean	SD	Mean	SD
Vocal-communal ducklings	34	66.1^c	61.4	278.6	63.8	173.6^c	88.7	10.3	45.7
Devocal-isolated ducklings: no prior auditory experience	39	106.1^b	107.4	236.2	107.5	98.8^b	97.8	27.6	62.5
Devocal-isolated ducklings: exposed to contact-contentment call	53	102.8^c	93.2	268.5	78.3	108.5^c	92.3	12.9	45.3

[a] The p values for Wilcoxon test refer to shorter latency or longer duration than the score for opposing call.
$^b p \leq .003$, Wilcoxon test.
$^c p < .00006$, Wilcoxon test.

274   GILBERT GOTTLIEB

tion of response to the normal call persisted ($p = .001$), however, so the
auditory experience did not wipe that out. While the present devocal
ducklings did not excel the previous devocal ducklings in either latency or
duration of response to the normal maternal call, they were significantly
less responsive to the attenuated maternal call than were those ducklings.
Specifically, the aurally stimulated ducklings had a longer latency and
shorter duration of response to the > 825 Hz attenuated maternal call as
compared to the aurally inexperienced devocal ducklings in the first experiment in this subsection ($p \leq .02$ for both comparisons).

In summary, there were three differences between the devocal and vocal
ducklings in the test with the normal versus > 825 Hz attenuated maternal
call at 65 hours in the first experiment in this subsection, and giving devocal
ducklings in the present experiment prior exposure to the contact-contentment call erased two of those differences (preference for the normal
maternal call and incidence of response). Although the aurally stimulated
devocal ducklings' preference for the normal maternal call improved
sufficiently to erase the previous difference with the vocal ducklings, it did
not improve quite enough to be reliably better than the nonstimulated
devocal ducklings ($p = .06$). The prior auditory stimulation did make the
devocal ducklings less responsive (latency and duration) to the attenuated
maternal call, however. In conclusion, the same auditory experience which
prevents the high-frequency perceptual deficit in devocal ducklings from
manifesting itself at 24 hours is also partially effective in preventing the
deterioration in high-frequency sensitivity that usually occurs in these
ducklings between 48 hours and 65 hours.

5. SUMMARY AND CONCLUSIONS

The hypothesis that, in the absence of auditory experience, the devocal
ducklings would fail to show sufficient improvement in high-frequency
perceptual sensitivity to bring them up to the level of competence of the
vocal ducklings at any age has been resoundingly disconfirmed. The proportion of devocal ducklings showing a preference for the normal maternal
call over the > 825 Hz attenuated one became equivalent to the vocal
ducklings at 48 hours after hatching, as did their ability to discriminate
the normal call from > 1800 Hz attenuated maternal call. In view of the fact
that the devocal ducklings were maintained in auditory isolation, this
improvement in high-frequency sensitivity must be ascribed virtually wholly
to the operation of neural maturational events which can bring the high-
frequency elements of the auditory system up to essentially normal functioning in the absence of experience by 48 hours after hatching. The qualification
of "virtually wholly" is necessary because the devocal ducklings have not

been reared in the complete absence of all auditory stimulation. For example, some slight mechanical noises inevitably arise when the doors of the soundproof incubator compartments are opened and closed. When the compartments are opened to check the progress of the hatch and the state of the duckling, and when the ducklings are removed from their compartment for transport to the test apparatus, they are briefly exposed to the 120-Hz drone of an air conditioner motor, a sound to which the embryos have also been exposed before being devocalized. When the devocal ducklings move about in their compartments, the contact of their body with the interior surfaces (floor and walls) sometimes produces noise, however fleeting and low intensity it may be.

Although the devocal ducklings manifest deficiencies on one measure or another at all ages, and they are not comparable to vocal ducklings on all measures even at 48 hours, the finding of most general significance is the extent of the maturational rectification of their high-frequency perceptual deficit at 48 hours, as demonstrated by the proportion of ducklings choosing the normal maternal call at that age.

Although prior embryonic auditory experience obviously plays little role in the maturation of the ducklings' high-frequency perceptual sensitivity at 48 hours, its influence is important at 24 hours and at 65 hours. As summarized in Fig. 16, prior embryonic exposure to the contact-contentment call serves to make the devocal ducklings' ability to select the normal maternal call equivalent to that of the vocal ducklings at 24 hours and at 65 hours. If these results are surveyed *in toto*, the interpretation of the role

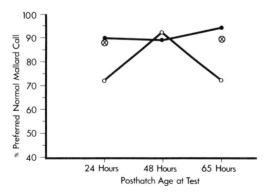

FIG. 16.   Proportion of responding devocal ducklings which showed a preference for the normal maternal call in the normal mallard maternal call versus > 825 Hz attenuated mallard maternal call test after exposure to the sibling contact-contentment call ($\otimes$, $N = 102$) (designated stimulated devocal groups above). ●——●, normal communal ($N = 132$); ○——○, devocal-isolated ($N = 125$).

of experience in the development of this particular innate behavior is rather interesting; namely, at 24 hours the ducklings' normally highly differentiated behavior could be said to be partially a consequence of perceptual learning because the requisite prior auditory experience was of a rather specific character (i.e., it had to have in it acoustic features that overlapped with the higher frequencies of the maternal call). There is an interesting difference here with the usual procedure for bringing about perceptual learning in that the prior experience was not with the particular stimulus pattern or object to be later discriminated. This has particularly interesting implications for the developmental analysis of other innate behaviors, especially ones involving "naive" perceptual preferences, because it shows that sensory experience other than that with the pattern to be later discriminated or preferred can be consequential. Schneirla's (1965) theory of perceptual development is founded on the premise that such relationships routinely occur between embryonic experience and early postnatal behavior, but evidence has been lacking heretofore.

As noted in Section III, D, 3 and in my earlier article in this volume, the term "perceptual learning" is used here in the sense of a previous specific sensory experience *facilitating* perceptual development by increasing the animal's ability to differentiate among stimulus patterns; the term is not being used in the sense of an inductive or *determinative* influence whereby the perceptual preference itself is established or acquired. Devocal Peking ducklings have a preference for the maternal call of their species. Auditory experience with the contact-contentment call sharpens the discriminative basis of that preference; auditory experience does not induce the preference in this particular species, although it may do so in the wood duck, *Aix sponsa* (Gottlieb, 1974). Unfortunately, the terminological distinctions being made here are sometimes blurred in treatments of perceptual learning and imprinting [e.g., see Gibson (1969) and Sluckin (1965)]. The term imprinting refers to an *inductive* influence of experience in determining perceptual preferences, whereas perceptual learning refers to a *facilitative* influence of experience in fostering an increased differentiation of perceptual (discriminative) abilities. For analytic and conceptual clarity, it seems useful to distinguish between these different influences of experience.

So at 24 hours the ducklings' usual level of perceptual selectivity is partially a function of perceptual learning as well as sheerly endogenous maturational events. At 48 hours the ducklings' high level of perceptual selectivity can be ascribed almost solely to endogenous maturational events. At 65 hours prior auditory experience is necessary to maintain the highly selective performance exhibited at 48 hours. There is an interesting difference here with the usual experiential procedures for maintaining behavior in that the experience comes *earlier* in development than the behavior which is maintained by the experience (i.e., the experience antedates the maturational basis of the behavior). That kind of relationship between experience and the development of perception does not fit very readily into conventional conceptions of neurobehavioral development, which usually call for experience to maintain neural or behavioral abilities *after* they have developed. The finding that a given level of perceptual functioning is partially a consequence of perceptual learning at one stage (24 hours) of development, while the same high level of functioning is a consequence of "entirely innate" factors at another stage (48 hours) is not quite as difficult to comprehend. I think this can be accounted for by assuming that the absence of relevant early experience causes a lag in species-specific perceptual development and, thus, that experience plays an important temporal regulative (facilitative) role which seems particularly significant in the development of other basic sensory and perceptual functions as well (e.g., Gottlieb, 1971b). The fact that the experiential requirement is so specific in the present instance is unanticipated, and the specificity of the experience and its consequences fits the paradigm, if not the precise operations, of perceptual learning.

According to the present results, high-frequency perceptual differentiation in the embryo probably develops gradually such that the embryo would be relatively insensitive to the higher frequencies in the maternal call. That prediction is supported by the available electrophysiological evidence on the development of peripheral auditory function in the Peking duck embryo (Konishi, 1973) (Fig. 8). (A study in progress addresses that question from a behavioral point of view.)

A final *caveat*. The three studies in this series (Section III, B, III, C, and III, E) stemmed from the hypothesis that the original finding (Gottlieb, 1971a) of a perceptual deficiency in the devocal ducklings, the one in which they failed to discriminate between the mallard maternal call and the chicken maternal call, was attributable to a lessened sensitivity in the higher frequencies. That hypothesis has been supported, but there remain other perceptual deficiencies in the 48-hour-old devocal Peking duckling. That is, the tests with the chicken versus the mallard call were conducted at 48 hours, so the present maturational rectification of high-frequency perceptual sensitivity by 48 hours suggests that still other perceptual deficiencies were responsible for the devocal ducklings' failure to discriminate the mallard call in the mallard versus chicken call test in the original experiments (Gottlieb, 1971a). Thus, the perceptual competence of the devocal ducklings is not entirely rectified in the absence of auditory experience. If the perceptual basis of the vocal ducklings' discrimination of the mallard and chicken calls was known, that would permit the specification of the possibly remaining perceptual deficiencies in the devocal duckling at 48 hours. Repetition rate and frequency modulation are likely candidates.

IV. Bearing of the Present Findings on the Assumptions of Innate Behavioral Development Theory

The present results support one of the key assumptions of the theory of innate behavioral development, while calling for a revision of other assumptions. The fact that the devocalized-isolated Peking ducklings' high-frequency sensitivity improved sufficiently in the absence of specific auditory experience to be equivalent to that of the vocal-communal ducklings at 48 hours supports the self-differentiating character of that feature of innate behavior development. Self-differentiation in this context refers to the primarily endogenous character of the neural maturational events underlying high-frequency perceptual development in this species, in the sense of their lack of dependence on exogenous sources of experience to realize their full function. (This neural maturational process could very well be dependent on spontaneous neural activity in the auditory system—that possibility was not investigated here.) The present conclusion also does not rule out the possibility that the maternally naive ducklings' attraction to certain features of the maternal call (e.g., repetition rate) may be some consequence of earlier experience (e.g., rhythms) in other sensory modalities, interoceptive or exteroceptive. In the absence of evidence to the contrary, the possibility of these kinds of cross-modality effects should be held open for developmental analysis.

The most distinctive and significant feature of innate behavior is its ontogenetically preadapted quality, such that the developing organism becomes capable of an appropriate and adaptive response to a particular object in advance of contact (experience) with the object. This distinctive defining feature would not change even if the behavior in question were shown to be partially dependent upon certain earlier experiences. The investigative question, it will be recalled, is whether there are such experiential precursors in the development of innate behavior, and this is perhaps where the most serious changes need to be made in the assumptions underlying innate behavioral development. Extant theory, whether behavioral (Lorenz, 1965) or neural (Jacobson, 1974), does not allow for experience to play a facilitating role, for example, as it actually does in the case of the temporal regulation of the Peking ducklings' ability to respond to the high-frequency components of the maternal call at 24 hours after hatching. Also, the finding that a maintenance experience can antedate the behavior to be maintained is an entirely novel result which does not fit into the existing conception of innate behavioral development.

Another assumption that may call for some liberalization is the notion that innate behavior is unmodifiable. This assumption coordinates with the "hard-wiring" of the developmental neurobiologist and Lorenz's notion of phylogenetic adaptation. Although the present results do not bear on that question, we may find that innate behavior is to a certain extent experience-sensitive as well as experience-dependent, to use the terminology of Grobstein and Chow (this volume). As pointed out in the introductory sections of this article, much of the controversy surrounding the innate component in behavior seems to stem from particular theories of how natural selection "fixes" the developmental basis of a behavioral trait in a species' repertoire. The fact that experience may be involved in the development of innate behavior does not undermine its genetic basis nor make it any less a consequence of phylogenetic adaptation. The various developmental programs by which adaptive behavioral phenotypes actualize themselves are largely unknown to us.

Acknowledgment

The author's research described in this article is supported by the North Carolina Department of Mental Health and Research Grant HD-00878 from the National Institute of Child Health and Human Development.

References

Altman, J. Postnatal growth and differentiation of the mammalian brain, with implications for a morphological theory of memory. In G. Quarton, T. Melnechuk, & F. O. Schmitt (Eds.), *The neurosciences: A study program*. New York: Rockefeller University Press, 1967. Pp. 723–743.

Bateson, P. P. G. Specificity and the origins of behavior. In J. S. Rosenblatt, R. A. Hinde, E. Shaw, & C. Beer (Eds.), *Advances in the study of behavior* (Vol. 6). New York: Academic Press, 1976. Pp. 1–20.

Berry, M. Development of the cerebral neocortex of the rat. In G. Gottlieb (Ed.), *Aspects of neurogenesis*. New York: Academic Press, 1974. Pp. 7–67.

Gibson, E. J. *Principles of perceptual learning and development*. New York: Appleton, 1969.

Gottlieb, G. Species identification by avian neonates: Contributory effect of perinatal auditory stimulation. *Animal Behaviour*, 1966, **14**, 282–290.

Gottlieb, G. *Development of species identification in birds*. Chicago, Ill.: University of Chicago Press, 1971. (a)

Gottlieb, G. Ontogenesis of sensory function in birds and mammals. In E. Tobach, L. R. Aronson, & E. Shaw (Eds.), *The biopsychology of development*. New York: Academic Press, 1971. Pp. 67–128. (b)

Gottlieb, G. On the acoustic basis of species identification in Wood ducklings (*Aix sponsa*). *Journal of Comparative and Physiological Psychology*, 1974, **87**, 1038–1048.

Gottlieb, G. Development of species identification in ducklings. I. Nature of perceptual deficit caused by embryonic auditory deprivation. *Journal of Comparative and Physiological Psychology*, 1975, **89**, 387–399. (a)

Gottlieb, G. Development of species identification in ducklings. II. Experiential prevention of perceptual deficit caused by embryonic auditory deprivation. *Journal of Comparative and Physiological Psychology*, 1975, **89**, 675–684. (b)

280   GILBERT GOTTLIEB

Gottlieb, G. Development of species identification in ducklings. III. Maturational rectification of perceptual deficit caused by auditory deprivation. *Journal of Comparative and Physiological Psychology*, 1975, **89**, 899–912. (c)

Gottlieb, G., & Vandenbergh, J. G. Ontogeny of vocalization in duck and chick embryos. *Journal of Experimental Zoology*, 1968, **168**, 307–325.

Jacobson, M. A plentitude of neurons. In G. Gottlieb (Ed.), *Aspects of neurogenesis*. New York: Academic Press, 1974. Pp. 151–166.

Konishi, M. Development of auditory neuronal responses in avian embryos. *Proceedings of the National Academy of Science of the United States of America*, 1973, **70**, 1795–1798.

Kuo, Z.-Y. Giving up instincts in psychology. *Journal of Philosophy*, 1921, **18**, 645–664.

Kuo, Z.-Y. Ontogeny of embryonic behavior in Aves. I. The chronology and general nature of the behavior of the chick embryo. *Journal of Experimental Zoology*, 1932, **61**, 395–430.

Kuo, Z.-Y. *The dynamics of behavior development*. New York: Random House, 1967.

Lehrman, D. S. A critique of Konrad Lorenz's theory of instinctive behavior. *Quarterly Review of Biology*, 1953, **28**, 337–363.

Lehrman, D. S. Semantic and conceptual issues in the nature-nurture problem. In L. R. Aronson, E. Tobach, D. S. Lehrman, & J. S. Rosenblatt (Eds.), *Development and evolution of behavior*. San Francisco, Cal.: Freeman, 1970. Pp. 17–52.

Lorenz, K. *Evolution and modification of behavior*. Chicago, Ill.: University of Chicago Press, 1965.

Saunders, J. C., Gates, G. R., & Coles, R. B. Brain-stem evoked responses as an index of hearing thresholds in one-day-old chicks and ducklings. *Journal of Comparative and Physiological Psychology*, 1974, **86**, 426–431.

Schneirla, T. C. Interrelationships of the "innate" and the "acquired" in instinctive behavior. In P.-P. Grassé (Ed.), *L'Instinct dans le comportement des animaux et de l'homme*. Paris: Masson, 1956. Pp. 387–452.

Schneirla, T. C. Aspects of stimulation and organization in approach/withdrawal processes underlying vertebrate behavioral development. In D. S. Lehrman, R. A. Hinde, & E. Shaw (Eds.), *Advances in the study of behavior* (Vol. 1). New York: Academic Press, 1965. Pp. 1–74.

Schneirla, T. C. Behavioral development and comparative psychology. *Quarterly Review of Biology*, 1966, **41**, 283–302.

Sluckin, W. *Imprinting and early learning*. Chicago: Aldine, 1965.

Trainer, J. E. *The auditory acuity of certain birds*. Unpublished doctoral dissertation, Cornell University, 1946.

PERCEPTUAL DEVELOPMENT IN MAMMALS

RICHARD C. TEES

Department of Psychology
The University of British Columbia,
Vancouver, British Columbia

I. Introduction

A. Nativism versus Empiricism

Although the classical controversy between nativism and empiricism has profoundly influenced psychological theory, in contemporary research it is largely a matter of emphasis. Earlier in this century, however, Gestalt psychologists argued that the perceptual capacities of the organism were exclusively determined by inherited neural mechanisms (Koffka, 1935), while behaviorists maintained "by definition" that these capacities were almost all acquired (Hull, 1943). Since neither side had a respectable collection of relevant behavioral evidence, the controversy persisted.

Substitution of careful experimentation for dependence on dogma was the first step in the destruction of this polarization, and research in perceptual development has become increasingly empirically oriented. As research efforts unfolded, questions about the role environment and heredity played in the case of a particular perceptual capacity began to be framed a little differently. The idea of these variables as alternative to each other instead of collaborative faded. Theoretically, one might distinguish between these different kinds of influences, but in practice they were inseparable. There was no behavior that was independent of an animal's heredity or its supporting environment. A further change in perspective may also be taking place (Hebb, 1972). Having recognized that both heredity and environment affect a capacity, some investigators believed it necessary to specify how important each variable is (e.g., 80% heredity, 20% environment). Clearly, the relationship is not additive but multiplicative. Asking how much heredity contributes to an ability is like asking how much the width of the field contributes to its area or how much its length contributes. Neither contributes anything by itself.

One should really think about the collaboration of five or six factors that influence behavioral development (Hebb, 1972) (Table I). Factor I is obviously the hereditary variable in behavior. Although this paper is concerned with Factors IV and V, Factors II through V represent the environmental variables.

B. Perceptual Learning

A by-product of the early debate between nativistic and empiristic explanations of perceptual phenomena was the neglect of perceptual learning (Beach, 1955; Hebb, 1949). One of the chief reasons why theorists slighted sensory–sensory (S–S) integration was the inconsistency with which they employed the term "stimulus." A stimulus could be the event at one receptor or, for example, the array of energy inherent in a facial expression that

TABLE I

CLASSES OF FACTORS IN BEHAVIORAL DEVELOPMENT[a]

No.	Class	Source, mode of action, etc.
I	Genetic	Physiological properties of the fertilized ovum
II	Chemical, prenatal	Nutritive or toxic influence in the uterine environment
III	Chemical, postnatal	Nutritive or toxic influence: food, water, oxygen, drugs, etc.
IV	Sensory, constant	Pre- and postnatal experience normally inevitable for all members of the species
V	Sensory, variable	Experience that varies from one member of the species to another
VI	Traumatic	Physical events tending to destroy cells: an "abnormal" class of events to which an animal might conceivably never be exposed, unlike Factors I–V

[a] From Hebb (1972).

excites the whole sense organ. This flexibility represented a tacit acceptance of certain Gestalt principles about the functional unity of the stimulus for the organism. Thus, in the confrontation with Gestalt theory, learning was solely represented by sensorimotor theory in which the association between an incredibly flexible stimulus with an equally inclusive response was all that was learned.

With the publication of Hebb's *Organization of Behavior* (1949) and the dissolution of the constraints of the prevailing theoretical controversy, the importance of early sensory preconditioning, or S–S integration involving learning according to a contiguity principle, was recognized as an antecedent of mammalian visual development (Riesen, 1958, 1961a).

Because sensory integration between and within sense modalities can occur without overt responses that can be measured directly, a somewhat indirect method was necessary to attack its role in perception—manipulation from an early age of sensory input. In this way an increase or decrease in the number of possible S–S pairings is achieved, and the effect of such restriction or enrichment on the organism's discriminative and integrative capacities is later assessed by comparing its behavior with that of subjects reared under normal environmental conditions. Fundamentally, the differences or lack of differences found in behavioral tasks have been used to establish the relative contribution normally made by experiential factors in the development of the species-typical discriminative behavior in question (Riesen, 1961a). Although most such comparisons have involved a two-group experimental design, the advantages of a four-group design in which additional groups are pretested in order to gain information as to "initial" capacities have been pointed out and incorporated in several investigations (Solomon & Lessac, 1968). The mammalian species most often employed in variations of this paradigm have been the rat, rabbit, cat, monkey, and chimpanzee.

C. Procedures and Methods of Controlled Rearing

The visual modality is unique in the degree to which afferent processes may be controlled experimentally. For this reason, and because of the stress that Hebb (1949) placed on early visual experience, the visual system has been utilized most often in studies of exclusion and manipulation of early sensory stimulation.

These manipulations have involved several procedures, each with its own goals, advantages, and disadvantages. The most frequently used method of restriction has been dark-rearing; i.e., raising the organism from birth or shortly thereafter to adulthood in total darkness (Riesen, 1947). Its goal is the elimination of light-produced activity in the visual system until, and usually through, testing, with the animal's visual experience restricted to only that activity occurring in the test situation itself. Its advantages lie in its relative convenience and its potential comparability in many other respects (e.g., handling) to "normal" rearing conditions. A potential disadvantage is basic deterioration or atrophy of the visual system that would interfere with normal functioning, such as retinal disc pallor (Chow, Riesen, & Newell, 1957). To prevent this from happening, light-rearing conditions, consisting of either white translucent contact lenses (Ganz & Riesen, 1962) or translucent globes (Fig. 1a) in which the animal's head is secured (Riesen, 1965b), have been used. In addition to eliminating patterned light stimulation, the light intensity itself is also reduced by 1–2 log units. Such a diffuse light "supplement" usually has been given for a limited period of time daily, with the organism remaining in the dark the rest of the time. These conditions result in less severe changes than complete dark-rearing in the more obvious measures of the neural substrate (Riesen, 1965b) but are time consuming, entail potential damage due to the occluders, and involve the introduction of differences in other experiential variables into the situation. Diffuse light-rearing conditions also have been produced by suturing the eyelids together (which reduces light intensity to the eyes by 4–5 log units) as a more expeditious strategy (Wiesel & Hubel, 1965). In conjunction with both diffuse light- or dark-rearing, animals have also been given restricted exposure during initial testing as adults, in which eye movements related to the stimulus array and retinal location (Fig. 1b) have been controlled (Ganz & Riesen, 1962; Ganz & Wilson, 1967).

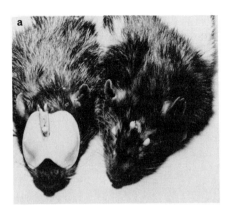
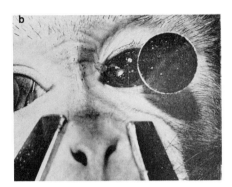

FIG. 1.   (a) Rats wearing two diffuse light-producing occluders. From Miller & Cooper (1974).

(b) Rhesus macaque with a clear contact lens in the left eye. The dark disc is a front surface mirror mounted at the end of a light-weight stalk and is part of the system to "stabilize" stimulus material onto a particular retinal locus. From Ganz & Wilson (1967).

The technique of limited and/or biased exposure to patterned light stimulation has also been employed in other ways. "Dark-reared" animals, presented with a normal visual environment for a short (e.g., 1 hour) daily period during which they might move freely, have been compared with other animals, exposed to the same visual environment but prevented from moving during the exposure period by head-holders or similar devices (Held & Hein, 1963; Riesen & Aarons, 1959).

More recently, the stimulus array presented during a limited daily exposure to patterned light (Blakemore & Cooper, 1970; Hirsch & Spinelli, 1971) has been restricted to a particular shape or pattern (Fig. 2) or even a particular direction of stimulus movement (Daw & Wyatt, 1974). The importance of such manipulations is readily evident if an investigator can show substantial changes in perceptual functioning and/or the neural substrate which relate in a predicted or specific way to the controlled exposure history of the organism.

A potentially interesting modification of the controlled rearing paradigm resulted from an attempt to test theories emphasizing the importance of ocular scanning on the development of normal vision. Animals were reared in a room that was illuminated for 1/15 second once every 7 seconds, totaling 10 minutes of patterned light daily (Orbach & Miller, 1969).

Other restrictive manipulations of visual input have included early versus late exposure to patterned light involving alternation for periods of several

FIG. 2. (a) A kitten wearing one of the masks used to provide selective visual stimulation. The stimulus patterns are mounted on the inside surface of the black rectangular sheet of plastic at the end of the two white cylinders. From Hirsch & Spinelli (1971).

(b) Selective visual stimulation is presented by a visual display consisting of an upright plastic tube about 2 m high with an internal diameter of 46 cm. The kitten, wearing a black muff to mask its body from its eyes, stands on a glass plate supported in the middle of the cylinder. The stripes on the wall are illuminated from above by a spotlight. From Blakemore & Cooper (1970).

months to dark and light (Riesen, 1965b), alternating monocular occlusion to patterned light stimulation (Riesen & Mellinger, 1956), prism displacement or rearrangement of the visual input (Bishop, 1959), and surgically induced artificial squint (Hubel & Wiesel, 1965).

Enrichment represents a second experimental strategy to test propositions related to perceptual development. If early restrictive manipulation is hypothesized to impede perceptual development, then enrichment involving exposure to augmented stimulus input complexity and/or variability can also be examined as to the possibility of accelerated development (facilitation). Enrichment has been less frequently used than restriction; however, cut-out "complex" stimulus patterns or three-dimensional shapes have been preexposed on cage walls or floors, both early and late in the life history of the organism (Forgus, 1956; Gibson & Walk, 1956), both with and without the opportunity for tactual and self-regulated motor experiences with the stimuli (Forgus, 1955). Exposure to regularly changed stimulus objects and shapes has also been incorporated into experimental designs (Rosenzweig, 1971). Unfortunately, many of the experiments employing enrichment have tended to confound manipulations of visual experience with manipulation of opportunities for social interactions and general motor experience (Rosenzweig, 1966, 1971).

Interpretations of the effects of any of these manipulations are sometimes inconsistent or even contradictory. Differences in the relative maturity of particular species at birth, in life-span, in methods and duration of controlled rearing, as well as disparity in measures of behavioral consequences, all contribute to this apparently confusing picture. Moreover, in trying to measure effects of a deprived or enriched environment on behavioral development, the problem of an appropriate base line or "normal" sensory environment can become of concern. If the control group is actually "impoverished," then the normal (N) condition may produce all or most of the important effects of deprivation, leaving no appreciable effect for the condition labeled deprived (D). Conceivably, the condition that is enriched (E), or supposedly above base line, may also be impoverished on an absolute scale of sensory environments (Rosenzweig, 1971). If the terms D, N, and E have some validity but the rearing conditions representing them do not, then potentially sharp, qualitative differences in perceptual development due to rearing might be missed (though presumably graded effects would not be).

D. General Theoretical Positions

Besides the classic Hebbian and Gestaltist positions, there are several other important theoretical traditions that have influenced studies of mammalian perceptual development in general, in particular, studies involving controlled rearing. Developmental biologists (e.g., Kuo, 1967) have taken positions regarding the behavioral as well as the neural plasticity of the developing organism and the extent to which phenotype might differ from genotype in regard to species-typical responses and sensory-perceptual processes. These positions have either reflected the nativist viewpoint that behavior is predetermined by invariant organic factors of growth and neural maturation or the view that behavior is a probabilistic result of the collaboration of genetic, maturational, and experiential factos that are present during the course of ontogeny (Gottlieb, 1971; Kuo, 1967; Schneirla, 1965). In common with others interested in sensory development, the developmental biologists have had as one of their goals the search for units—building blocks out of which behavior is established (Gottlieb, 1971). However, their search has not concentrated on the ontogeny of anything but rudimentary species-typical behaviors (see Section I, E). On the other hand, a second interest in the sequence of intermodal sensory development has added some interesting theoretical and potentially rewarding research ideas that have yet to be followed up (Gottlieb, 1971; Schneirla, 1965). The history of the deprivation experiment and concern for the modifiability of behavior have also included the ethologists. For the most part, the study of the phenomenon of imprinting has emphasized the elucidation of mechanisms related to the development of social attachments rather than the ontogeny of the sensory-perceptual behavior—although the potential use of the paradigm by ethologists to provide answers related to perceptual capacities has been pointed out (Kovach, Fabricius, & Falt, 1966).

Several models of behavioral development with strong biological or neuropsychological orientations (other than Hebb's) have postulated sequential developmental stages in which particular kinds of sensory stimulation would be critical or optimal at different ages in their effects on the course of behavioral development (e.g., Scott, 1962; Thompson & Grusec, 1970). Finally, a number of essentially psychological models of development and early experience bear on the kind of research and interpretations of data made in this area. These positions differ from each other along several dimensions including the relative emphasis of selective or responsive aspects (Gibson, 1969) or "cognitive" aspects (Kagan, 1967). To some extent the same themes are expressed by individuals from all major theoretical perspectives and disciplines (e.g., concerns with stages or sequences, basic units of behavior, relative emphasis in either nativistic or experiential contributions).

E. Problems of Definition

In attempting to examine available evidence as to potential support or rejection of any of these theoretical ideas, it is clear that many investigations are conducted without clear reference to a particular theoretical position. The theories themselves are often ambiguous as to what specific predictions they make regarding the outcome of any particular piece of research (Bond, 1972). More important is that they are not mutually exclusive, but often in fact complement each other. Part of the explanation of this lies in the difficulty of defining perception. For example, perception has a phenomenal aspect involving the awareness of events presently occurring in the organism's immediate surroundings. It also has a responsive aspect; it entails discriminative or selective responses to the stimuli or events in the immediate environment. By avoiding the problem of definition or by restricting one's examination to one aspect of perceptual development, particular investigators and their theories can relate to the ontogeny of quite different behavioral patterns that have general phenomenal similarity but differ in terms of underlying mechanisms. In doing so they avoid a possible distinction between a number of processes including sensation and perception. In the case of the perceptual development of an organism, such distinctions can be theoretically valuable.

Where behavior is under immediate sensory control, no problem of perception need arise, theoretically. The "response" of sweating in a warm room does not depend on perception; perception of warmth may accompany it, but one often realizes that the room is warm only after finding himself sweating. The question of perception appears only when a stimulus gives rise to central or mediating processes (Hebb, 1972). Hence, we need terms to distinguish between two theoretically known processes, different in kind: one tied to activity of receptors, of afferent pathways and primary projection areas; the other, central, and though initiated by their first, not completely determined by it. Sensation and perception meet this need. Awareness of the potential complexity of the species-typical discriminative behavior being studied could lead to greater care and sophistication in behavioral testing and interpretation of data.

A similar analysis can also be made regarding the term "attention." A number of investigators of developmental processes have defined their interest in terms of the ontogeny of visual attention rather than visual perception, and one can make a case for two theoretically useful kinds of attentional processes—shading into one another as do sensory and perceptual processes. Several studies (e.g., Ames & Silfan, 1965) have indicated that young, unlike older, organisms seem to be "captured by stimuli." This shift from obligatory attention to stimuli to greater control over the stimuli attended to is also accompanied by a developmental change in the nature of the stimuli characteristics attended to—from relatively simple characteristics, such as edges, to more spatially complex stimulus properties. Propositions regarding the different neural substrates underlying these two theoretically distinct attentional processes could be made similar to that of Hebb's (1972) analysis regarding sensation and perception.

Such distinctions become important when we consider the interpretation of experiments dealing with the development of a species-typical behavior. For example, Fantz (1967) has shown that the newborn infant's eye are directed selectively at parts of the visual environment, but this may be a reflexive response, an important factor in the development of perception and attention in the adult sense, but not itself evidence of "perception" in the newborn. At this age, the behavior may be controlled directly by sensory processes functioning "reflexively." Similarly, Riesen (1960) has argued that the optokinetic nystagmus response involves mechanisms which may not be identical with those underlying pattern perception—the central retina and cortex are not necessary for optokinetic nystagmus to "patterned" stimuli, such as vertical lines. Statements about the ontogeny of pattern perception or visual attention may be unwarranted when they are based on faulty assumptions about what is being measured by such techniques.

II. Specific Visual Capacities and Sensory Experience

In light of these initial considerations and cautions regarding methodology, definition, and theory, the following section examines investigations relating to the role played by experience in the development of specific visual functions in mammals, notably those mediating acuity, visual guidance, intensity, depth, and form discrimination. The emphasis will be on experiential contributions since the studies reviewed involve manipulations of environmental, not of genetic, variables. Moreover, the consequences of unimodal manipulations of visual or auditory stimulation will be the limited focus of concern. A number of other reviews (Rosenzweig, 1971; Thompson & Grusec, 1970) have attempted to assess the available information on the effects of "controlled" rearing involving social or general multimodal restriction, stimulation, and enrichment on the ontogeny of emotionality, learning and problem-solving abilities, and underlying neural mechanisms.

A. Visual Acuity

The question of the role of maturational and experiential factors in the development of visual acuity has been examined in the case of the visually deprived rabbit (Van Hof & Kobayashi, 1972), cat (Ganz & Fitch, 1968), monkey (Riesen, Ramsey, & Wilson, 1964; Wilson & Riesen, 1966), and chimpanzee (Riesen, 1958) using either the elicitation of optokinetic nystagmus or a learned response to striations of varying widths. Irreversible loss is reported in the case of chimpanzees deprived of patterned light for 18 months or longer. On the other hand, although diffuse light- or dark-rearing of the cat or monkey for shorter periods does produce a slight deficit when visual acuity is first tested, there is a rapid development to normal levels with exposure for brief periods to patterned light (Riesen, 1958, 1961b). The time course of this development is no more, and sometimes less, than that observed for their controls kept under normal light conditions from birth (Fig. 3). Although little has been reported on the effects of an enriched visual environment on the development of acuity, Vestal and King (1971) do report an acceleration of developmental rate in deermice by stimulus augmentation involving supplementary exposure to moving striations, but this exposure made no difference in final levels of capability. Enrichment in this case seemed to act as a hothouse forcing an "early bloom," which nevertheless did not differ from a normal flower (Vandenberg, 1968); that is, a facilatative effect of experience as defined by Gottlieb in the second chapter of this volume.

One study that seems not to fit in with the pattern of evidence is that of Van Hof and Kobayashi (1972), who report a slight but persistent deficit in

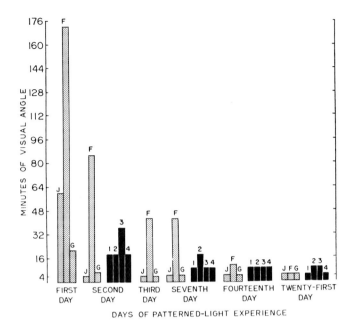

FIG. 3.   Improving visual resolving capacities of infant monkeys after 20 days of patterned light deprivation (stippled bars) compared with those of normally reared monkeys (black bars). The normally reared monkeys were studied by Ordy, Massopust, and Wolin (1962). Data for the monkeys reared in diffuse light are from Riesen, Ramsey, and Wilson (1964). From Riesen, Ramsey, & Wilson (1964).

visual acuity for dark-reared (DR) rabbits 5 months after removal from an initial 7-month period in the dark. This seems paradoxical in light of neurophysiological as well as behavioral evidence that the visual system of the rabbit may be different from that of the cat and other mammals in its ability to resist changes caused by sensory deprivation or biased rearing (Mize & Murphy, 1973), at least in terms of development of its basic sensory capacities (but see Grobstein & Chow, this volume).

The consequences of monocular, patterned light-deprivation for the cat (Ganz & Fitch, 1968) and monkey (Von Noorden, Dowling, & Ferguson, 1970) are more severe and persistent in measures of acuity through the deprived eye. However, if use of the deprived eye is forced by reversal of the monocular deprivation, then recovery is effected within a period compatible with or longer than the initial period of deprivation (Ganz & Fitch, 1968). This is consistent with the general proposition that asymmetrical exposure to significant visual input results in a competitive disadvantage for the deprived eye in terms of the developing neural substate. This leaves the eye in a poorer position in terms of visual capacity than if the light deprivation had been more complete but symmetrical(e.g., Chow & Stewart, 1972; Ganz & Fitch, 1968). It is also consistent with a second general proposition that appropriate sensory experience can lead to recovery of function, and hence supports the idea of an optimum rather than critical period regarding the development of this particular capacity and the timing of patterned light stimulation (see Section VI, F).

A number of investigations have utilized biased rearing as a technique to test notions concerning the potential modifiability of neurons in visual cortex (see Grobstein and Chow, this volume). Most of these studies have employed cats which were selectively exposed to a field of either vertical or horizontal striations for daily periods of several hours during the first few months or weeks of life (e.g., Blakemore & Cooper, 1970). The dramatic finding that even a limited exposure of several hours at an early age to a selected line orientation would result in an absence of cortical neurons having a preferred orientation perpendicular to that of the experienced contours led to experiments in which the perceptual consequences of such modification were measured (Hirsch, 1972; Muir & Mitchell, 1973). Cats reared during the first few weeks of life in environments in which only contours in a single orientation were presented showed diminished ability to resolve striations of the orthogonal orientation in later testing (Muir & Mitchell, 1973). Several points should be made about these results. No study has attempted to test recovery of function after a deliberate reversal of contour orientation presentation. Although the perceptual deficits are persistent in the sense that they remained after a year of exposure to normally lighted colony environments, they initially are considerably smaller than one would expect from the neurophysiological evidence. The consequences of early selective rearing is not blindness for lines perpendicular to the contours presented in the initial environment, but only a slight deficit in acuity comparable to that of an optically corrected human astigmatism.

Finally, the literature on the limited comparable data in humans suggests that scattering of light and obscuring of the retinal image by congenital cataracts does not prevent the development of foveal fixation and normal acuity after removal of cataracts later in life. Moreover, the extent and time course of the reduced visual acuity associated with strabismus and the recovery resulting from prolonged occlusion of the dominant eye is comparable to that obtained in monocularly deprived cats and monkeys (Flom, 1970). Evidence of modification of human visual systems by early experience due to meridional amblyopia caused by astigmatism is also available. Optically corrected astigmatic subjects whose early visual environment was one in which contours in a particular orientation were imaged considerably less sharply than others were found to show the slight but significant acuity deficits similar to those found in cases of selectively reared cats (Mitchell, Freeman, Millodot, & Haegerstrom, 1973).

B. Binocularity

Patterned light deprivation also interferes with or interrupts the development of relatively simple binocular skills, but the relative contribution of genetic and maturational variables appears greater than that of sensory experience. For 60-day-old, diffuse light-reared monkeys to show convergence to an approaching object, 18 hours of patterned light are necessary—a rate of development faster than in normally reared monkeys (Wilson & Riesen, 1966). Eight-month-old, diffuse light-reared chimpanzees and cats require several weeks of patterned light to show such convergence—somewhat longer in the case of some of the deprived chimpanzees than their normally reared controls (Riesen, 1958, 1965b). There have not been any attempts to examine the possibility that enriched visual experience might appearance of basic visual skills such as convergence. Eye coordination in the cat does not even seem to depend on an early history of binocularly driven cortical cells, since specially reared cats (e.g., alternating monocular deprivation) showed only very mild strabismus and reliable eye convergence upon presentation of novel objects following their deprivation period (Riesen, 1966).

C. Visually Guided Behavior

One of the recent trends in the study of the visual system has been the partial dissociation of those neural mechanisms underlying visual information processing, "perception," or discrimination and those underlying visually elicited location, orientation, or locomotion (Held, 1968).

Normal adult vision employs both localization and perception simultaneously or in close interaction. The capacity to orient to parts of the environment may have its own developmental history, which intuitively must precede (with some overlap) the development of perception. It is the presence of this "orienting" behavior to stimulus change that leads directly to the acquisition of the species-typical representative processes that function in a perceiving adult organism (Section V).

Investigation of the consequences of experiential manipulations of the ontogeny of these visual-motor capacities have primarily employed tasks such as visual placing or reaching. As an organism is carried toward a visible surface, its limbs extend to avoid hitting the surface. This visual placing response has been used for a long time as an indicator of the integrity of mechanisms underlying visual-motor behavior. If, in addition to the presence or absence of a response, one is interested in and measures accuracy, the term visual reaching is used.

In the case of the cat and primate, dark- or diffuse light-rearing during the first few weeks delays visual placing at the time of emergence in the light. Five hours of patterned light experience is required for the visually deprived cats, and 18 hours for the deprived monkeys (Riesen, 1958, 1965b). Once again, the interaction between maturational and experiential processes is evident. For example, a visual placing response is not exhibited by the normally reared kitten which has had longer patterned light experience until days 28–30 of age. Interaction between maturational and experiential sources of development is also evident in the case of eye and head orientation to light stimuli in the chimpanzee. Reports on chimpanzees after several months of patterned light deprivation indicate that although visual fixation and refixation to a moving target of light appear relatively quickly after exposure to patterned light, mature (accurate) visual pursuit movements and reaching require much longer exposure to patterned light, as well as coordinated visual–motor interactions (Riesen, 1961a). Interestingly, a short daily period of exposure to patterned light will maintain the integrity of this unit of visually guided behavior as well as others (e.g., avoidance of obstacles). Chow (1955) "dark-reared" two monkeys for 8 months with a 5–10-minute daily period of exposure to patterned light. Measures of visually guided behavior were normal.

In terms of accurate eye–hand coordination, Wilson and Riesen (1966) reported that 60-day-old diffuse-light-reared monkeys developed abilities equivalent to their normal (LR) counterparts within 21 days of patterned light experience—a period of time roughly comparable to that the normal animal would take to show accurate reaching. With longer periods of deprivation, it is evident that recovery of such functions is either much slower or absent (Riesen, 1966). For example, Sherman (1973) reported, after 6 months of diffuse light-rearing (involving eye suturing), persistent monocular visual field deficits in which cats failed to show visually guided behavior in the ipsilateral hemifield.

The most extensive series of investigations involving the role played by experience in the development of visually guided behavior have come from the laboratories of Held, Hein, and their co-workers. Initially, they showed that the requirements for adequate visual placing included "free" locomotion in patterned light. Rearranging the normal relationship between self-produced movements and patterned light experience prevented the appearance of the behavior (Held & Hein, 1963). More recent research indicates that visually coordinated movements can be segregated into somewhat independent components—each perhaps with its own developmental history. These components include visually elicited extension, locomotion, and visually guided reaching. Dark-reared kittens do not display visually triggered extension of the forelimbs at first exposure to patterned light (Riesen, 1961a). However, exposure to diffuse light or monocular exposure to patterned light without opportunity to locomote freely is sufficient to support the development of the response (Hein & Diamond, 1971b; Hein,

Gower, & Diamond, 1970). Other visually guided behaviors, such as accurate reaching, were absent when the cats used the visually deprived eye. Selected experience with visual feedback from the forelimbs revealed that accurate guidance of each limb by each eye represented an independently acquired component of reaching. This specificity was also found in the case of the development of visually guided reaching in the infant monkey (Held & Bauer, 1967). Hence, the development of visual reaching was specified (or limited) by these precise and biased experiences of visual–motor feedback. For example, neonatal exposure of freely moving kittens at low levels of illumination demonstrates that the visually guided behavior can be acquired independently by scotopic and photopic systems (Hein & Diamond, 1971a).

Finally, dependence of the development of one component of visually coordinated guided reaching on another has been demonstrated. Kittens acquired guided reaching when provided with visual feedback from limbs in an otherwise dark surrounding after—but not before—they had acquired visually guided locomotion (Hein & Diamond, 1972). Kittens dark-reared at birth for 1–3 months and then exposed to a luminously painted limb for 10 days, failed to exhibit appropriate visual reaching responses. Only after 30 hours of visual stimulation, systematically associated with free locomotion and hence after the development of guided locomotion, did a second short test experience with a luminous limb result in appropriate visual guided reaching. Clearly this particularly elegant experiment revealed a sequential developmental scheme in terms of acquisition of guided locomotion and guided reaching and is clearly consistent with the theoretical analysis of Gottlieb (1971).

D. Intensity Discrimination

Cats reared entirely in the dark and those receiving 1 hour of diffuse light experience daily learn a visual intensity discrimination task as rapidly as normally reared animals. If trained monocularly, they show immediate interocular transfer to an eye that has never received light stimulation (Aarons, Halasz, & Riesen, 1963; Riesen, 1965a; Riesen & Aarons, 1959). Similar findings have been obtained for the diffuse light-reared monkey (Wilson & Riesen, 1966).

Differential responsiveness to light and dark appears in the rat before its eyes are open (Crozier & Pincus, 1937). It is also observed in rats reared in darkness either until their eyes are open or until maturity, when they are tested for visual orientation (Hebb, 1937; Turner, 1935). These findings have suggested that responses to visual intensity differences in mammals do not require prior visual experience. All the above tests of visual intensity discrimination were relatively easy for the normal animal, involved large differences in intensity, and took few trials to learn. However, visually deprived rats can learn a difficult intensity discrimination as rapidly as LR controls (Tees, 1968a). Such a difficult discrimination utilized a small difference in light intensity—one close to threshold—and took more trials to learn than a complex visual pattern discrimination. A differential response to such stimuli may be made on the basis of either luminous flux (total amount of light) or luminance (amount of light per unit area). In all of the above experiments, either or both cues might have been used to discriminate between the targets. Further experimentation has indicated that although visually deprived animals can learn a discrimination based on both luminous flux and luminance as rapidly as their LR controls, LR rats use luminance differences in learning the two-cue discrimination significantly more than the DR rats. Moreover, inferior performance by DR rats on a second intensity discrimination in which only luminance differences were relevant revealed the specific role of visual experience in terms of processing luminance information (Tees, 1971). Fragmentary evidence of such a difference in cue utilization also exists for the diffuse light-reared cat (Riesen & Aarons, 1959).

Bland and Cooper (1970) tested rats on an 8:1 intensity discrimination after they were laboratory reared until 90 days of age and they given 3 months of experience either in a visually improverished or a regular laboratory environment. They found no significant difference due to later rearing conditions in terms of which cue the animals utilized to acquire the discrimination. Both groups used luminance cues. This study suggests that the difference found in the Tees (1971) study was due to the qualitative difference of early experience and not solely related to the 90 days of visual experience per se.

There is not a great deal of definitive evidence concerning the visual capacities of mammals following biased and enriched rearing. In a study by Hirsch (1972), the visual experience of cats was limited for 3 months to either horizontal or vertical striations, and only a relatively easy flux discrimination was employed. There was no significant differences between their performance and that of normally reared cats. Similarly, Rosenzweig (1971) failed to find any significant difference in performance between any of his groups of visually impoverished and enriched rats in an "easy" light–dark discrimination. Given the insensitive nature of the tests employed in both studies, the failure to differentiate animals on the basis of exposure history is not surprising. However, this evidence (such as it is) is consonant with the findings and interpretations reported in the case of comparisons of LR and DR mammals; namely, discrimination of intensity is not affected by controlled rearing unless it is based on luminance cues.

E. Depth Perception

Investigation of the role played by experiential and maturational factors in the ontogeny of depth perception has had a long history (Lashley & Russell, 1934; Spalding, 1873). A great deal of this research has concerned the role experience plays in the performance of various mammalian species on the visual cliff apparatus (reviewed by Walk & Gibson, 1961). In the case of the rabbit and cat it is apparent that they do not show evidence on the cliff of depth perception at eye opening but develop it over the next several weeks (Karmel, 1968; Karmel & Walk, 1965; Stewart & Riesen, 1972). Moreover, photic stimulation has been shown to be essential for the occurrence of depth discrimination since DR young and adolescent rabbits do not discriminate depth until after several weeks of light experience following initial testing (Raskin & Walk, 1963). In the case of the monkey there is less than satisfactory evidence of its ability to discriminate depth at eye-opening, but there is clear evidence of the "unfolding" of this ability after only 20 days of diffuse light- or dark-rearing from birth (Walk & Gibson, 1961; Wilson & Riesen, 1966). Deficits in visual cliff performance are clearly related to age at the time of the deprivation period. Adult cats and monkeys dark-reared for 3 months show no deleterious effects on the cliff (Jones & Pasnak, 1970; Slomin & Pasnak, 1972).

Early experiments found that 90-day-old DR rats avoided the optically deep side as accurately as their LR counterparts (e.g., Walk, Gibson, & Tighe, 1957). Walk and Gibson (1961) repeated their studies for 30-day-old and 90-day-old DR rats while controlling for texture density cues. On the basis of their results they concluded that the visually inexperienced rat could discriminate depth even when motion parallax was the only remaining major cue and offered the widely held interpretation that (unlike the other mammals cited above) depth perception in the rat was "innate" and required neither experience nor maturation beyond eye opening for its development.

Most of the investigations of depth perception in mammals have not involved a systematic examination of performance on the cliff as a function of age. Moreover, in most studies a "deep" side is employed with the pattern 20 or 53 inches below the glass surface, depths that do not provide a sensitive measure of ability at any age. In order to examine the ontogenetic development of depth discrimination, a modification of the visual cliff (Fig. 4) in which the depth of the deep side can be varied would be most useful (Booher & Walk, 1968). Walk and Bond (1968) used such a modified cliff to demonstrate that 90-day-old DR rats prefer the shallow side at 10 inches, but not at 4 inches of differential visual depth. Such a result reveals an impairment of fine discrimination but not gross motion or depth discrimination due to

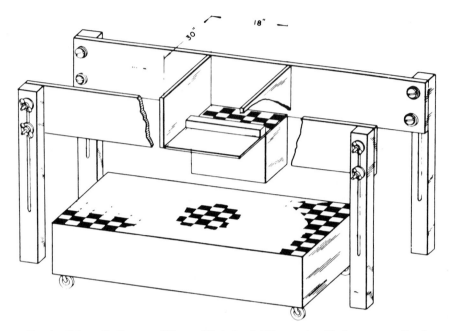

FIG. 4. Schematic diagram of the modified visual cliff apparatus. The box representing the deep side can be raised (or the shallow side lowered) to adjust the deep pattern to a particular depth below the glass. From Booher & Walk (1968).

the restricted experience, but it does not reveal whether this is a result of retarded development, nondevelopment, or deterioration of processes underlying the capacity (Fig. 5). A recent experiment involving the modified visual cliff and systematic testing at a variety of ages beginning at 20 days does give such evidence (Tees, 1974).

The ontogeny of depth perception in the rat as outlined in this study involves the collaboration of a number of factors (see Fig. 6). The influence of an "innate" component is reflected in the ability of both the LR and DR 20-day-old rats to discriminate depth on the cliff at 8 inches of differential depth. The contribution of maturational and nonvisual experiential factors is demonstrated in the improvement in depth perception by older DR rats. The influence of visual experience perhaps can be said to take two forms: the first (facilitative) involving a sharpening or augmenting of the ability of the visually experienced rat to make fine discriminations of motion and depth as evidenced in the decreasing differential thresholds obtained by the maturing LR rat; the second (maintenance) reflected in the role visual experience plays in tonic stimulation of underlying neural structures (Hebb, 1963)—the lack of which is evident in the deterioration in performance

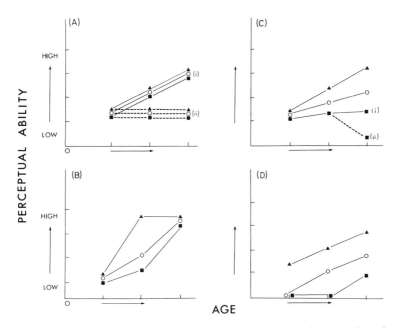

FIG. 5. The effect of stimulation history on a perceptual capacity: some hypothetical outcomes. Environments: ▲——▲, Enriched; ○——○, normal; ■——■, deprived. (A) Controlled rearing results in little alteration on either (i) a capacity showing age-related changes (ii) a relatively stable capacity. (B) A transient effect involving impeded or accelerated development but no appreciable differences in adult levels of ability. (C) Augmented or reduced levels of ability either through (i) lack of development or (ii) deterioration. (D) Delayed or advanced appearance of capacity (as well as adult levels).

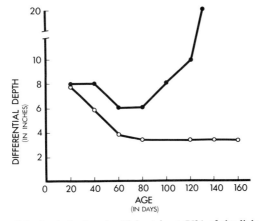

FIG. 6. Differential visual depths at which at least 75% of the light-reared (○——○) and dark-reared (●——●) animals descended to the optically shallow side. From Tees (1974).

after prolonged dark-rearing. The latter result has also been found using a standard visual cliff by other investigators (Nealey & Riley, 1963; Walk, Trychin, & Karmel, 1965). Since visual experience did play a part in the development of depth perception in the rat, it suggests that the difference between the hooded rat and other mammals in the interaction of experiential and other factors is quantitative rather than qualitative.

It would be interesting to see whether or not augmented or enriched visual experience would result in better depth discriminative abilities. Held and Hein (1963) showed that depth perception in the cat not only depended on patterned visual experience, but that this exposure must be concurrent with and systematically dependent upon self-produced movement. It is not clear with respect to performance on the visual cliff whether or not a distorted relationship between self-produced movements and visual stimulation has a specially disruptive effect (i.e., a case of induction). The restricted (e.g., passive) cat is learning during its daily exposure to light that its own movements are unrelated to perceived motion, lines, etc., in the environment. It is conceivable that performance differences may be directly related to this aberrant association rather than to a lack of ability to distinguish depth cues.

F. Form Perception

Cats reared entirely in the dark and those receiving 1 hour of diffuse light experience daily require three times as many trials as normally reared animals to learn an N versus X discrimination (Riesen, 1965b). Retarded performance on a triangle versus circle discrimination has been obtained for the visually deprived rat (Michels, Bevan, & Strasel, 1958), monkey (Wilson & Riesen, 1966), and chimpanzee (Riesen, Chow, Semmes, & Nissen, 1951). These results have been used to illustrate the important contribution of experience to the ontogeny of form perception in mammals (Hebb, 1949; Riesen, 1961a). One of the criticisms (McCleary, 1960; Melzack, 1962) leveled at the interpretation of this deficit is that it is related to the difficulty of the task itself rather than to any particular kind of discrimination (i.e., form). These critics have argued that the DR animal is intellectually and/or emotionally inferior to its LR counterpart, and the more difficult the discrimination (of whatever kind), the more deleterious the effect of this deprivation on performance. In support of such a suggestion is the fact that visually naive mammals learn to discriminate between vertical and horizontal striations as rapidly as visually experienced animals. This has been demonstrated for the visually deprived rat (Woodruff, 1955), rabbit (Van Hof & Kobayashi, 1972), cat (Riesen, 1965a), monkey (Wilson &

Riesen, 1966), and chimpanzee (Riesen, 1961a). In such a task, the difficulty of form discrimination is greatly reduced since the differences between stimuli are large and are replicated throughout the figures.

Evidence has been provided that the duplication of the vertical stripes is not critical in the resulting similarity in performance between LR and DR animals (Tees, 1968b). Visually inexperienced rats learn to discriminate between a single horizontal rectangle and a vertical rectangle as rapidly as their LR controls. Moreover, visual experience plays no more of a role when the stimuli employed are two oblique rectangles, or a vertical and an oblique, or when such tasks are more difficult for the normal rat than an N versus X discrimination (see Table II). It is apparent that an important distinction must be made between the mechanisms responsible for form discriminations that can be made on the basis of orientational cues and those requiring some further degree of spatial and temporal integration on the part of the organism (Tees, 1968b).

The above experiments illustrate a frequently employed technique of studies on the effects of early experience. Evidence is collected about the mechanisms underlying the way normal and, for example, restricted animals classify shapes and process visual information by looking at the relative ease of difficulty with which these animals are able to distinguish two shapes.

An additional procedure, which has been employed less frequently, is the use of transfer or stimulus equivalence tests in which the deprived and normally reared animals, having been exposed to one or two shapes during preliminary training, are then tested to see which other shapes or discriminative characteristics are perceived as similar to or different from the original stimuli. This procedure thus examines the more subtle question of differences between visually experienced and inexperienced animals in what is

TABLE II

TRIALS TO CRITERION FOR NORMALLY REARED AND VISUALLY DEPRIVED RATS ON THE VISUAL DISCRIMINATION PROBLEMS[a]

Problems	Rearing condition	Mean	SD
Horizontal versus vertical	Light	144.17	42.71
	Dark	168.33	38.04
Vertical versus oblique	Light	314.17	81.28
	Dark	318.13	85.81
Oblique versus oblique	Light	250.83	77.27
	Dark	293.33	121.78
Pattern (N versus X)	Light	261.67	121.98
	Dark	420.00	244.64

[a]$N = 12$ for each group.

learned from specific exposures to particular shapes and forms, and what degree of cue control results in each case. For example, in a recent study (Tees, 1972) DR rats learned to discriminate a single rectangle from an equally "bright" target with no rectangle as rapidly as LR controls. Moreover, the ability of DR animals to discriminate between rectangles in different angular orientation after training with a single orientation was found to be different from that of LR rats. Both groups showed peaked generalization gradients, hence weakening the proposition (Ganz, 1968; Lashley & Wade, 1946) that a necessary condition for cue control along a stimulus dimension is differential reinforcement, and hence experience, along that dimension. Exposure to the two rectangle orientations did not result in a significant rearing difference in ability to transfer to rectangles differing in orientation from the original training stimulus. It is significant that visually naïve rats learn these discriminations and transfer to other stimuli along the dimension of angular orientation as efficiently as visually experienced animals. They seem to possess not only the "predisposition" to isolate and unify a figure from its ground (Hebb, 1937) and some capacity to respond differentially to vertical, oblique, and horizontal stimuli, but also the ability to generalize from that experience to lines in different angular orientations.

On the other hand, with more complex identifications involving forms differing only in their elements' relationship to one another (e.g., N versus X), DR animals learn more slowly (Tees, 1968b) and learn less (as evidenced in stimulus equivalence tests) about these concatenations of lines in different orientations than do LR animals (Tees, 1972). Rotation of these complex shapes by 22.5° resulted in significant differences due to experience in successfulness of transfer. It is likely that spatial integration necessary in the case of form (N versus X) perception involves a higher order neural substrate which does require visual experience for its development and/or maintenance.

Other evidence has accumulated in relation to experience and generalization after edge and contour training in mammals. Ganz and Wilson (1967) found that after training on a horizontal versus vertical line discrimination, the visually naïve monkey generalized as well as the LR monkey to horizontal and vertical stimuli involving fragmentation of the figure, reversal of figure-ground brightness relations, and shifts of the stimuli to the contralateral retina. These investigators suggested the operation of an "innate" line-recognition mechanism based on findings concerning the receptive fields of simple cortical cells in the visual system whose properties paralleled their generalization data. However, the scaling of rectangles along the dimension of angular orientation by experienced and stimulus-naïve rats reveals the operation of a mechanism more complex than the simple line-detection system involving receptive fields selectively sensitive to a single orientation suggested to explain the transposition behavior in the stimulus-naïve monkey.

Forms represent multidimensional stimulus arrays that can be distinguished on the basis of other dimensions. Some evidence exists that visual experience might play a part in the discrimination when an attempt is made to restrict the task to a size discrimination, at least in the case of the chimpanzee (Riesen, 1965a) and rat (Michels, Bevan, & Strasel, 1958). However, most experiments have not employed transfer testing as a means of determining more precisely what cue was being utilized. Usually in size-discrimination tasks, either luminous flux or luminance is available as a cue, and in one study it was clear that both DR and LR rats did use flux (or luminance) rather than size in such a task after acquiring the original problem (in an equivalent number of trials) (Tees, 1971). Heller (1968) has indicated that DR rats can learn a size discrimination in terms of retinal image size, though, unlike LR rats, they fail to show size constancy. Heller reports that size constancy developed quickly in 10 days of exposure to a normal laboratory environment.

There is a great deal of experimental evidence that early, but not later, exposure to shapes such as triangles and circles can facilitate later discrimination between the forms (Forgus, 1956; Gibson & Walk, 1956). Although the evidence is not as clear-cut as one would like, it appears that the effect of this enrichment might be rather specific, i.e., effective only in the case of later discrimination training involving the preexposed forms or shapes very similar to them (Bennett, Anton, & Levitt, 1971; Gibson, Walk, Pick, & Tighe, 1958). However, McCall and Lester (1969) found that exposure to angled line stimuli facilitated learning of both a square versus triangle and a circle versus ellipse discrimination task by rats. Brown and King (1970) also report that increasing the variety and number of preexposed complex forms resulted in greater facilitation of performance on later specific complex-form discrimination tasks. Neither finding is consistent with the "specific" facilitation idea stated above (Rosenzweig, 1971). However, preexposed and test shapes have, for the most part, been rather limited, and *all visual stimuli are not necessarily equally enriching.*

It appears that preexposure to such forms as horizontal and vertical striations is not effective in terms of later discrimination performance, while the exposure to more complex patterns is (McCall & Lester, 1969; Oswalt, 1972). For example, Oswalt found that rats reared from birth to 50 days of age with circles and triangles (complex patterns) exposed on the cage walls learned to discriminate between the two forms significantly faster than control animals. Rearing with horizontal and vertical striations had no such effect on later discrimination of these striation patterns. Such findings are clearly consistent with the previous interpretation of visual deprivation studies and the differential role played by sensory experience in particular kinds of form-discrimination mechanisms. As indicated earlier (Section II, A), even biased rearing with such lines reveals little difference in later ability to process information about these and related contours, in spite of the apparent dramatic and long-term effects of such biased rearing on cortical neurophysiology. There are only slight differences due to such biased rearing in the cat (Hirsch, 1972) and the rat (Calahan, 1973) on acuity measures; and performance is even less affected on discrimination tasks involving orientation of lines, including mirror images, complex forms such as square versus X, and interocular transfer.

In reviewing the work of Held and Hein earlier, the importance of "active" movement-produced stimulation in the development of visually guided behavior was clearly outlined. However, interpretation of these previously reported results must be somewhat restricted. For example, enrichment studies with rodents, in which tactual-kinesthetic feedback with visual stimulation was provided, indicate no additional gain in discriminability beyond that obtained from exposure to the stimuli themselves (Anton & Bennett, 1972). In the ontogeny of complex visual information processing, the development of a basic visually guided response is necessary and normally precedes it; however, an exposure history involving a variety of complex stimuli is of considerable importance.

III. Auditory Perception

Although vision has been the chosen modality for almost all sensory deprivation experiments, a comparable experimental design may be used involving manipulation of auditory stimulation, and several studies have examined the effects of early auditory restriction on later adult behavior (Batkin & Ansberry, 1964; Gauron & Becker, 1959; MacDougall & Rabinovitch, 1971; Wolf, 1943). Several points must be made about these studies. The methods of Wolf and of Gauron and Becker to achieve temporary auditory deprivation involved the use of ear plugs, which entails the possibility of damage to the ears; evidence does exist that ear plugs can produce such damage (Sterritt & Robertson, 1964). If some degree of hearing loss occurred because of damage to the ear structures, this fact would limit possible interpretations of their findings.

Although the results of both studies cited above, as well as the report by Batkin and Ansberry, could support the principle that early sensory deprivation is followed by an inability to use information presented later in the affected modality, more effective and more meaningful methods of testing auditory discrimination have been devised by Neff (1961) and his co-workers in their studies of the effects of ablation of the cat's auditory cortex. These discrimination tests involve conditioned avoidance response (CAR) training to changes in either the intensity, frequency, or duration of a pulsing tone, or in the pattern of a sequence of tones.

Such tests have demonstrated that cumulative auditory experience with temporal patterns is necessary for the development of the temporal integrative capacities of the rat and does facilitate the organism's performance in learning specific auditory pattern as well as duration discriminations, but such experience does not play any appreciable role in discrimination of changes in either intensity or frequency of pulsing tones (Tees, 1967a, 1967b). The only other evidence regarding auditory discrimination, and more particularly the effects of auditory deprivation, is the clinical data on deafness. Unfortunately, much of the focus of inquiry has been on the adjustment of the deaf, not on their learning or perceptual capacities; but a considerable amount of research has been carried out on the effect of deafness on nonspecific cognitive ability. To some extent this evidence is important because it implies that the deficit obtained on form discrimination with visual deprivation reflects a more general cognitive loss rather than one specific to visual function (Axelrod, 1959).

IV. Intermodal Consequences of Early Sensory Deprivation

An early hypothesis about the consequences of visual deprivation was that, although no deficit existed with regard to visual perception, the DR animal learned to rely on nonvisual cues, and these earlier learned responses interfered with acquisition of new responses or decreased the probability of using visual cues. To some extent the evidence supports this hypothesis. For example, DR rats use spatial cues more than visual cues in a Krech Hypothesis Apparatus, while the reverse is true for LR subjects (Gamboni, 1964).

However, it is evident that DR animals learn easy and difficult brightness discriminations as well as do LR animals (Section II, D). Presumably, they are as able as control animals to direct their attention to that aspect of their visual world. Earlier learned responses do not appear to interfere with acquisition. They are also able to attend to striations and single stripes as well as control subjects, and yet these are the elements of the X and N discrimination which they then learn at a significantly slower rate than control animals. Additionally, DR cats that receive only 1 hour of patterned light daily learn pattern discriminations as rapidly as controls; 23 hours a day of relying on nonvisual cues does not adversely affect performance (Riesen, 1965a).

However, a number of observations, including the fact that sensory systems do not become functional at the same time in development (Gottlieb, 1971), have renewed interest in the more general question of how sensory systems and their stimulation histories relate to one another. Although the systems may develop relatively independently so that interference with one would not result in significant consequences on the operation of others, adult organization in one modality may depend in some way on the functioning of another developing modality (Schneirla, 1965). For example, several investigators have argued that the DR animal is intellectually inferior to its LR counterpart (e.g, Melzack, 1962). Similarly, early blindness in humans has occasionally been shown to produce impairments in a variety of nonvisual perceptual and learning tasks (Axelrod, 1959), and these findings have been used as evidence of a reduced general intellectual functioning in early-blind subjects.

The proposition that visually deprived organisms show greater "sensitivity" in other senses than visually experienced subjects has also been suggested (Drever, 1955). Some fragmentary evidence exists which supports this "sensory compensation" hypothesis (Spigelman & Bryden, 1967). Rats blinded early in life tend to perform better than late-blinded and sighted animals on a nonspatial auditory learning task. Spigelman and Bryden interpreted the inferior performance in terms of a failure to attend to the relevant auditory cues.

However, surprisingly, there is not a great deal of systematic evidence available on potential developmental interdependence. What is clear is that none of the above general statements as to intermodal consequences of unimodal deprivation is fully supported by available evidence. For example, Tees and Cartwright (1972) clearly demonstrated that the DR rat could acquire a CAR to auditory tonal stimuli as rapidly as the LR rat. In this particular study involving processing of auditory information, the DR rat was no more or no less capable than his LR counterpart. Similarly, Mac-Dougall and Rabinovitch (1971) reported that performance of rats deafened at birth and of congenitally deaf mice do not differ from normals on either a visual intensity or a horizontal versus vertical striation discrimination task.

Specific differences do appear to result from early (but not from late) blindness. In addition to finding that rats peripherally blinded by enucleation shortly after birth performed better as adults on a nonspatial auditory learning task, Spigelman found that these animals performed more poorly than did the late blinded on an auditory localization (spatial learning) task (Spigelman, 1969; Spigelman & Bryden, 1967). The initial appearance of tactually directed grasping by thumb–finger opposition was delayed for monkeys reared under diffuse light conditions (Wilson, 1964). One is faced with the possibility that sensory deprivation within a late developing (visual) system can result in either acceleration, deceleration, or no change in the development of behaviors mediated by earlier developing (tactual and auditory) systems.

Turkewitz, Gilbert, and Birch (1974) have undertaken the study of the consequences of manipulating the experiential history of the first sensory system to develop, which bears directly on Schneirla's (1965) hypothesis of interdependence. Tactile experience was reduced by clipping the vibrissae (i.e., whiskers) of kittens in the first postnatal day and measuring the effect of this manipulation on the development of visual cliff behavior. Unfortunately, although the performance of the tactually deprived animals on the visual cliff was superior to that of nonclipped animals at 28 days of age, the appropriate control group (clipped at time of testing) was not run. Thus, the effects of the reduced tactual input could easily be regarded as primarily due to the difference at time of testing rather than as support for the developmental interpretation in which early lack of tactile stimulation led to precocial use of visual cues due to decreased competition between sensory systems (Turkewitz et al., 1974). Clearly, additional, carefully planned research on the intermodal consequences of controlled rearing needs to be done, particularly in regard to the stimulation histories of early developing sensory systems.

V. Stimulus-Seeking Behavior

A number of investigators have provided support for the proposition that stimulus change itself mediates preference and approach behavior (Bindra, 1959; Walker, 1970). A correlate of most theoretical assumptions about this role of sensory stimulation is that deprivation should result in an increase in stimulus-seeking behavior. Fox (1962) reported that the rate of bar-pressing for light did increase with the duration of previous light deprivation, with an asymptote at 4 hours.

Some evidence is available as to the role stimulation history might play in terms of these motivational properties of the deprived sensory input. Deprived mammals show initial motivation equal to or greater than that of controls to obtain the theretofore missing source of sensory stimulation. In cases of self-regulated exposure to unpatterned light, 3 months of dark-rearing from birth did not significantly change the bar-pressing of rats to turn the light source on or off (Lockard, 1963). Bar-pressing for light stimulation in long-term (3 years) deprived monkeys (given 1 hour of diffuse light daily) was considerably greater than normal or adult light-deprived monkeys (Lindsley, Wendt, Lindsley, Fox, Howell, & Adey, 1964).

A second basic theoretical consideration involves spatial complexity, within stimulus change (Walker, 1970). Stimuli slightly more complex than the organism's own "psychological" complexity will be preferred, and stimuli too complex or too simple will be neutral. The maturation and development of these preferential responses to visual stimuli have been examined, and levels of preferred complexity have been shown to increase with age in the human (Thomas, 1965) as well as the monkey (Fantz, 1967). In an examination of the consequences of differential rearing on stimulus-seeking behavior, Sackett (1967) raised rats in metal fruit cans from Days 15 to 60 in either darkness, alternating dark-light, or light. In the latter two conditions the walls were either painted black, white, or in a black–white checkerboard. When placed in a choice situation, the DR rats preferred the homogeneous black to the checks, and the LR rats, regardless of rearing conditions, preferred the checks. After 30 days of normal colony experience, all three groups preferred the check pattern. Although this study indicated that gross manipulation of early experience affected initial complexity preference, the study had a number of methodological problems. In a more recent study, in which brightness and complexity of stimuli were not confounded and preference ordering of individual subjects was utilized, DR rats at 60 days of age were found to be at a lower level of "psychological" complexity with respect to visual stimuli than were LR rats. Although both LR and DR animals shifted in preference over 6 days of testing in the direction of increasing complexity, the LR rats showed a faster and/or greater degree of shift to higher complexity (Creighton, 1969). In the case of monkeys reared in diffuse light for several months, less stimulation seeking was also evident than in the case of control monkeys when very complex visual patterns were used as stimuli, even after several months of normal visual experience (Levison & Levison, 1971; Levison, Levison, & Norton, 1968). In these experiments no attempts were made to scale stimuli or to obtain individual preference orders. In general, however, adult visual complexity preference in the rat and monkey were found to be a function of the complexity of early rearing condition—at least as far as the relatively crude evidence is concerned.

Two additional points should be made. First, 10 minutes of limited exposure (or enrichment) to the laboratory resulted in elevated stimulus-seeking in the Levison experiments, a finding similar to that of Wendt, Lindsley, Adey, and Fox (1962), who found that monkeys reared in darkness for 16 months (except for 1 hour of daily exposure to patterned light) showed higher than normal rates of self-maintained stimulation when allowed to press to obtain light. Riesen (1965b) also showed that such a limited exposure resulted in excellent complex pattern discrimination in the DR cat. Even a daily brief period of perhaps 10–60 minutes of unrestricted pattern vision can establish and maintain the neural substrate underlying the perceptual and motivational processes related to complex form discrimination.

Second, the use of a longitudinal (rather than a two-group cross-sectional) design involving several groups of animals would provide better information. In such a study, Fantz (1965) measured preference in monkeys for patterned or unpatterned visual targets using the amount of visual fixation as his indicator of motivational properties of stimuli. He found that more than 2 months of dark-rearing resulted in a "deterioration" in the development of preference for increasing stimulus complexity (see Fig. 7). Moreover, the longer-deprived infants did not cease to have preferences but may have developed abnormally with a shift toward a preference for color and larger size (induction). There are certain methodological problems with this study regarding what differential visual fixation signified in the situation (see Section I, E) and how the targets differed from each other in terms of stimulus dimensions. However, the results are consistent with those reported by Tees (1974) on the ontogeny of depth perception in the rat in regard to collaborative contributions of several sources of development.

A final qualifying point about the role early experience plays in the development of the motivational properties of visual stimuli has been made by Sackett (1966). The dependence on specific sensory experience in the ontogeny of stimulus-seeking may hinge on the nature of the visual stimuli them-

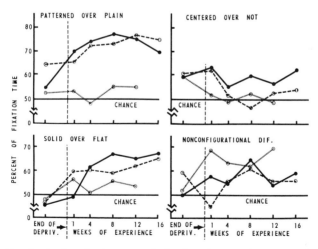

Fig. 7. Postdeprivation development of visual preferences in each of four categories of stimulus variables by groups of infant rhesus monkeys with different lengths (●——●, 0–3 weeks; O---O, 5–6 weeks; O···O, 8–16 weeks) of dark-rearing (the most significant category is patterned over plain). From Fantz (1965).

selves. Sackett reared monkeys in social isolation and found that they began to show differential behaviors, including bar-pressing, toward specific types of visual stimulation (picture of infant and "threatening" monkeys) at 2.5–4 months of age in spite of their lack of experience with such complex visual stimuli. The motivational mechanisms underlying the evocation of these differential behaviors (approach and avoidance) seem to represent the maturation of a species-specific structure (and behavior) similar to releasing mechanisms, such as those identified by ethologists for avian species.

VI. Additional Considerations and Reflections

A. The Importance of Early versus Late Experience

A number of investigators have outlined how one can operationally define the importance (or lack of it) of the consequences of early enrichment or deprivation (Thompson & Grusec, 1970; Thompson & Schaefer, 1961). Importance is determined by the size, generality, and potential reversibility of these alterations in the course of behavioral development, and over all the information outlined previously (Section II) is consistent with the idea of early experience being relatively more important than later. Clearly, early experiences are especially important by these standards because they represent initial experiences that can preempt neural mechanisms and hence continue to have an effect through ontogeny.

There are several cautions that should be applied to such a picture. One of these has to do with the short-term effects of sensory deprivation. An entire literature on the effects of relatively short-term manipulation of sensory experience in mammals, focusing on the role of variability in sensory stimulation later in the life of an organism, has been produced (reviewed by Zubek, 1969). Clear-cut (sometimes transient) effects on stimulus-seeking behavior, discrimination performance, etc., have been found in these research efforts, but there has been little attempt to integrate or compare these findings with those reported in the case of early manipulation of stimulus variability.

Second, the paradox between the "fact" that early experience has important consequences for adult behavior and the "fact" that many early acquired behaviors appear to be quickly forgotten (Campbell & Jaynes, 1969) needs to be considered. Obviously central issues in our research area are the specification of mechanisms by which a residue of early experience may be stored and a resolution of the apparent contradiction in the consequences of such experience.

Solutions to this apparent problem would seem to lie (1) in more detailed propositions of sequences or stages in which particular kinds of experience are more or less effective (Thompson & Grusec, 1970) and hence leave more or less of a residue depending on their actual time of exposure; (2) in more sensitive behavioral tests used to measure the consequences of the early experience; and (3) in the reinstatement of the theory of Campbell and Jaynes (1969). To ensure retention of a given experience, Campbell and Jaynes proposed that reinstatement or the periodic partial repetition of an experience is necessary to maintain the experience through time. Although this modification of the paradigm has not been utilized in the traditional controlled rearing experiment, both nonspecific as well as specific experiences plus reinstatement can enhance later discrimination learning (Wachs, 1972).

B. Species and Strain Differences

One should expect the susceptibility of an organism to change as a result of environmental manipulation to vary with genetic constitution of species. Some organisms should be expected to be strongly buffered and others, weakly buffered against the lack of sensory stimulation (Thompson & Grusec, 1970). In terms of multimodal sensory restriction and isolation as well as enrichment, Melzack's (1968) work reveals real within-species differences between the consequences of such rearing for Scottish terriers versus beagles. Rhesus monkeys and dogs may also be more susceptible to arousal disorders due to light deprivation than are cats and rats (Riesen, 1961b, 1966). Genetic differences with respect to "buffering" also appear to be the case in terms of rat strains. Strains, genetically selected for maze ability (or lack of it), are differentially responsive to early environmental manipulation (Cooper & Zubek, 1958). The "dull" rat strain gains much more than the "bright" strain in maze ability as a result of exposure to an enriched early environment. In a restricted environment "brights" lose much more than "dulls."

Some other examples of species differences have been mentioned previously in outlining the available evidence as to the development of specific visual capacities. However, in general, the proposition that mammals higher in the class seem to suffer more severely in terms of development than lower ones seems to be widely accepted (Riesen, 1961a). In large part the evidence for this assumption is anatomical rather than behavioral, e.g., the relative degree of cell loss or shrinkage in the peripheral visual system suffered after early visual deafferentation by rat, rabbit, cat, and monkey (Riesen, 1966). Moreover, the dependence on sensory experience within a species differs according to the precise capacity being examined, and one would expect the same to hold true in terms of between-species and strain comparisons.

Only in the case of depth perception are the effects of comparable periods of controlled rearing in various mammalian species measured; it is clear that performance on the visual cliff does require visual experience in the cat and monkey, but the evidence is not so clear for the rat and rabbit (Walk & Gibson, 1961). Even in this case, visual experience does play a role in the rat's development of fine optical motion or depth discrimination (Tees, 1974). The point is not that species and strain differences do not exist, but rather that (1) similarities within the class have been underestimated, and (2) differences are often based on relatively insensitive behavioral tests in which the lack of comparability (e.g., length of deprivation or enrichment) across studies is in evidence. The most noticeable trend is a common mammalian response to environmental restriction which transcends differences among species and perhaps even minor variations in rearing conditions. The implication is that developing mammals have similar requirements for processing sensory information if one is focusing on adult abilities, such as those related to complex pattern discrimination.

C. Perceptual Abilities

Evidence outlined previously is consistent with the idea that some basic information processing capacities are not dependent on visual experience for their development. Due to failure to test at an early age or inability of the young organism to respond suitably to stimulus differences, there is not always direct evidence as to whether the capacities of visually inexperienced and experienced animals both remain constant from birth to adulthood or whether both show similar improvement over that period (Fig. 5). It is clear that early visual experience plays a limited (perhaps maintenance) role in the adult's ability to discriminate between slight differences in certain kinds of information, for example, contour orientation. These "basic" capabilities might be roughly subserved under the rubric of feature detectors (Sutherland, 1968).

On the other hand, the capacity to discriminate between patterns such as N versus X, in which integration of visual information such as contours over space and time is required, is clearly dependent upon visual experience. Whether one views the neural representatives of such stimuli as reflecting stored descriptions (Sutherland, 1968) or semiautonomous central processes (Hebb, 1963), their establishment requires early visual experience which facilitates later discriminations based on them.

To the extent to which evidence is available, the findings in regard to the processing of auditory information are consistent with those reported in the visual modality. However, one would wish for data from more sophisticated behavioral testing.

The phylogenetic and ontogenetic evidence of a strong trend toward increasing capacity to respond to or extract higher-order structural and relational properties of stimuli (visual, auditory, and intermodal) is much better than that available in regard to a developmental trend toward overall increasing specificity, i.e., differentiation along all stimulus dimensions (Gibson, 1969). For example, the response of an organism to similarity between stimuli in which the complexity of the invariant from stimulus array to array is great would more clearly place it along species, age, and stimulation history continuums than its response to fineness of line stimuli. Tasks such as matching-to-sample, and discrimination of oddity, or intermediate size in tristimulus arrays would likely be sensitive to even slight differences in stimulation history (see also Sections VI, D and VI, E).

D. Attentional Processes Revisited

A number of investigators have suggested that, by one mechanism or another, the primary effect of controlled rearing is related to the development of attentional processes (Fantz, 1967; Ganz, 1968; Gibson, 1969; Melzack, 1968). Discussion of this position and related evidence has appeared previously (Sections I, E, II, E, II, F); however, there are a number of additional points that should be made.

Melzack (1962, 1968) proposed an explanation of sensory deprivation based on a model in which failure to establish an interpretative organization (mediating processes) is crucial to supervene incongruent sensory input. Excessive behavioral arousal results from the abrupt change from deprived to normal conditions and leads to difficulty in attending selectively and failure to inhibit irrelevant response patterns. If the deprived mammal is more susceptible to "arousal disorders," and there is some evidence that it is (Melzack, 1962; Riesen, 1961b), the explanation is not so simple. Deprivation should interfere with performance on difficult intensity and striation problems as well as complex form discrimination. Performance is not so affected. Even worse for this position is the fact that "enriched" beagles (raised on a farm) exhibited excessive excitability which did not subside for months (Melzack, 1968).

Earlier (Section II, D) the interpretation was offered that the discriminations based on luminance represent tasks which, like complex form discriminations (N versus X), require some degree of spatial integration on the part of the animal, and the development and/or maintenance of the capacity to integrate visual information across space depends, to some extent, on early visual experience (Tees, 1971). The findings of that particular experiment were also consistent with two-stage models of discrimination learning in which sensory input is processed by a limited number of analyzers arranged in a hierarchy, with the hierarchy itself depending, to some extent, on experience (Dodwell, 1970; Sutherland, 1968).

For example, examination of the type of errors made by LR and DR rats illustrates the significant difference in terms of cue utilization in acquisition of a task in which luminance was rewarded and flux was available but irrelevant (Fig. 8). On those trials in which the rewarded luminance (e.g., bright) and "related" luminous flux (e.g., "high") were opposed, DR animals made more errors. On those trials in which the rewarded luminance value varied with the corresponding flux value, the DR animals made significantly fewer errors. The visually inexperienced animals were responding primarily to flux rather than luminance differences early in the course of training, while the LR seemed to "attend" to luminance earlier. Such a difference in the relative dominance of the two cues facilitated faster acquisition by LR animals, and speed of learning about a cue depends on the cue's relative dominance in a population of available cues. Such speculations are consistent with earlier analysis. A difference in the ability to process certain kinds of visual information would logically result in differences in the relative attention paid to particular stimulus dimensions (and vice versa).

In later work we have examined attentional processes other than those reflecting the hierarchy of sensory analyzers. We have taken the position

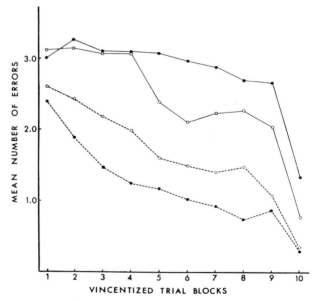

FIG. 8.   Effect of rearing conditions on two types of errors over vincentized trial blocks. ●, Dark-reared; ○, light-reared; ——, flux errors; ---, other errors. From Tees (1971).

that some of these processes can be regarded as relatively autonomous central or mediating processes (Hebb, 1963; Melzack, 1968) related to visual information that would be effective or ineffective across all sensory analyzers provided that the behavioral tests were such as to give them "expression." Hence, one could expect differences due to rearing even across a hierarchy of analyzers or dimensions (e.g., contour orientation) which had previously been shown to be little affected by dark-rearing. Comparison of optional intra- and extradimensional and overtraining reversal shift behavior of DR and LR rats, involving stimulus dimensions along which no differences in acquisition were obtained which were ascribable to rearing, did nonetheless reveal significant differences in shift performance, thus reflecting the dependence of attentional (or mediating) processes on visual experience (Creighton & Tees, 1973; Schwartz, Schwartz, & Tees, 1971). Such a conclusion would be complementary with previous statements as to other central processes, such as "stored descriptions" of complex visual patterns, and illustrate the importance of an awareness of the complexity of the processes underlying discriminative behavior.

E. Sensory Preconditioning and Development

As indicated earlier (Section I, B), impetus to the use of the controlled rearing paradigm came from the introduction of the idea that early sensory preconditioning (SPC) was characteristic of mammalian visual development. The phenomenon of SPC itself has been of theoretical interest since Brogden's (1939) initial demonstration of its effect. Traditionally, it has been explained in terms of a S-S learning approach (Birch & Bitterman, 1951), but SPC is also, in part, an attentional phenomenon (Adamec & Melzack, 1970). Recently, LR and DR hooded rats were given one of three SPC experiences (Tees & Cartwright, 1972). In each, animals were presented with two stimuli, either paired or unpaired, followed by conditioning to one and extinction of the other. Two auditory stimuli were utilized in the first experiment. Since the association formed between the two auditory stimuli paired in close temporal contiguity was no less effective for the visually deprived rat, and since it acquired the CAR to an auditory signal as rapidly as the LR rat, the DR animal was not less capable than its LR counterpart in terms of processing nonvisual (auditory) information.

In the second experiment, involving intermodal stimuli (light and tone), the S-S association was effective for both LR and DR animals; hence the development of the neural processes underlying such associations is not entirely dependent on experiential factors. However, unlike the first experiment there was an effect due to rearing condition. The difference between LR and DR animals was not reflected in performance on the initial CAR to either the tone or the light but rather on the subsequent SPC test. The SPC experience was more effective in the case of the LR rats. Such a finding suggests that it is the association between visual and auditory stimuli that does not initially result in the same degree of "sensory associative efficiency" (Riesen, 1961b) in the case of the DR rat. It is possible that the modification in central neural activity, when two or more intermodal signals are paired, is either less stable or has less access to response processes in the inexperienced rat. Thompson and Kramer (1965) have reported on the essential role of polysensory association cortical areas in crossmodal SPC. Similar polysensory areas have also been found in the normally reared rat (Meikle, 1968). Recently, Mayers, Robertson, Rubel, and Thompson (1971) have reported that the percentage of polysensory cells in the association cortex of normally reared kittens increases gradually through day 50 of life. Evidence of such postnatal development would provide a means whereby the development of neural responses underlying intermodal information processing could be modified by sensory experience or lack of it.

    In a third experiment, rectangle stimuli were employed. The effect of the SPC was evidenced in the LR animals; however, performance of DR animals was not significantly different from that of LR or DR controls. The visually experienced animals benefited more from the association between the two rectangle stimuli in spite of the fact that no significant differences between LR and DR animals have been found on discriminations involving single or paired rectangles differing in angular orientation. Significantly slower acquisition by visually deprived rats of discriminations involving concatenations of rectangle stimuli (e.g., N versus X) in different orientations has been reported (Tees, 1968b). In such discrimination learning involving two collections of line stimuli, one of the kinds of learning that takes place is the S–S association between vertical, horizontal, and oblique rectangles. The findings in the above study indicate that such associations proceed at a slower rate in the visually deprived than in the normally reared rat. Ganz, Fitch, and Satterberg (1968) have found that directionally selective cells in the visually deprived cats are less responsive and more easily fatigued than those of LR cats. Evidence of the late appearance of particular classes of receptive fields in normally reared rat and rabbit visual cortex and superior colliculus is also available (see Grobstein & Chow, this volume). Such findings are consistent with the idea that, for the DR animal, the pairing of the vertical and horizontal rectangle stimuli resulted in a less stable association between the neural representatives of the two stimuli, and hence less of a modification results than would occur normally from spatial contiguity of the two stimuli.

    In summary, the cumulative effect of early sensory preconditioning, involving extensive combinations of environmental stimulus sequences, appears to be a fundamental factor in the development of certain kinds of perceptual capacities, especially those in which temporal or spatial relationships between cross-modal and intramodal stimulus information are important.

F. Problems of Multiple Determination, Interaction, and Interpretation

As Riesen (1971) has so lucidly pointed out, one of the basic problems in regard to developmental neuropsychological research is the fact that behavior is clearly overdetermined. There appears to be evidence that many antecedent conditions are necessary but not sufficient in regard to behavior. Physiological and anatomical substrates are interchangeable to some extent, and moreover may shift during development so that structures (or changes in these structures) that were critical at one stage are not at another. Many measures of neural functions show gradual and consistent changes with particular behavior (e.g., measures of perceptual capacity). These correlations may be incidental. Independence can sometimes be revealed through selective experimental manipulations such as the ones we have been discussing here. Failure to appreciate these observations about multiple determination and interaction have led to some naïve and overoptimistic statements about cause and effect in regard to a particular perceptual capacity, its neural substrate, and the role visual experience might play in its development. For example, clearly the deleterious effects of later removal of neural structures such as cortex and superior colliculus (Aarons, Haslaz, & Riesen, 1963; Wickelgren & Sterling, 1969) on visually deprived animals should preclude the possibility of interpreting the consequence of visual deprivation in terms of an absence of functioning of these structures yet such ideas have been advanced (Sherman, 1973).

Some have suggested that visual deprivation produces pathological side effects that interfere with the visual processes that would otherwise be fully operative (Gibson, 1969). Studies such as Riesen's early work (1947) with prolonged dark-rearing in the chimpanzee revealed a pronounced pallor of the optic disc, and histological examination showed degeneration of retinal ganglion cells (Chow, Riesen, & Newell, 1957). While this particular criticism is relevant to several earlier experiments, it cannot be applied with the same force to later research involving shorter periods of deprivation or diffuse light-rearing conditions. The key question is the relative importance of such consequences in terms of behavioral development. "Physiological" side effects, such as RNA depletion at the retinal level, can be separated from the behavioral. As previously mentioned, cats that receive 1 hour of unrestricted visual stimulation and remain in the dark for 23 hours a day for over a year perform a form discrimination as well as LR animals; however, their RNA levels are low in comparison to those of their normally reared counterparts (Rasch, Swift, Riesen, & Chow, 1961). In the case of the effects of enrichment, as both enriched and deprived rats grow older, some of the neurochemical differences, thought earlier to have an important relationship to the observed behavioral differences, disappear, while the behavioral differences persist (Rosenzweig, Bennett, & Diamond, 1967).

Moreover, the absence of some competing condition(s) may also be a crucial requirement for normal development, and this simple idea has also been overlooked on occasion. The naive notion that monocular deprivation might produce through one eye of an organism the effect normally produced by binocular deprivation, and through the other, the effect of normal experience was such a case (Wiesel & Hubel, 1963). Such ideas about competing conditions and ontogeny are certainly coming into focus in terms of investigations of dramatic alterations of neural development produced by biased rearing (Pettigrew & Freeman, 1973). Yet these dramatic differences in cortical unit responses apparently yield only slight differences in perceptual behavior (Hirsch, 1972). Either the importance of these neural processes or the representativeness of the recorded units will have to be reassessed.

A final point about the interpretation of controlled rearing studies has to do with the proposition that deficits due to deprivation result because a critical period has been passed. A true critical period hypothesis would demand irreversibility of the effects of early deprivation, and several examples of developmental arrest being overcome by later enriched environments have been reported (Chow & Stewart, 1972; Riesen, 1961b, 1966). The more "neutral" optimum period hypothesis often seems more appropriate (Riesen, 1961c). Empiricists argue that the stimulation is more important than the age period, and serial order of sequence is more crucial than absolute age during maturation. Obviously, the species and the behavior being observed are also important. But in mammals a case can be made for optimum periods for a number of categories of behavior in which timing is important, but less important than the proper sequence of stimulation.

VII. Conclusions

Investigations of behavioral effects of sensory deprivation rest on the fundamental premise that behavior (as well as neural structure) is modified by function. The initial appearance of some forms of behavior awaits prior sequences of sensory activation, which thereafter are not necessary for the recurrence of the behavior.

Riesen (1965a) generated several general hypotheses pertaining to perceptual development. He stated that the available evidence supported the conclusions that a parallel exists between neural development and perceptual development in which (a) percepts are a function of an organism's stimulation history; (b) changes in neural structure during development reflect the organism's stimulation history; and (c) prolonged minimal levels of stimulation induce permanent perceptual arrest and irreversible cell loss.

In this paper an attempt has been made to outline some additional statements as to the ontogeny of mammalian perceptual development. If one is interested in further determining the behavioral consequence of manipulations of experiential variables, including patterned light stimulation, it should be clear that the following are most necessary: (1) a precise idea of what psychological processes underlie a particular species-typical behavior; (2) a degree of sophistication about behavioral testing techniques; (3) a multigroup or longitudinal design in which some control and experimental animals are pretested as well as posttested; and (4) a design in which recovery of function is examined.

These elementary considerations will enable one to make a better experimental description of the role played by sensory stimulation and help determine whether, for example, deprivation results in (1) slower or nondevelopment, (2) deterioration, (3) no difference, or (4) aberrant or different development with regard to a particular kind of capacity related to perceptual ontogeny (Fig. 5). In this way one would be in a better position to relate neural and behavioral age-related changes.

Acknowledgments

This review was written in connection with research activities supported by the National Research Council of Canada (Research Grant APA 0179). The assistance of S. Langlois, G. Midgley, K. Mucha, and K. F. Tees in preparing the manuscript is gratefully acknowledged.

References

Aarons, L., Halasz, H. K., & Riesen, A. H. Interocular transfer of visual intensity discrimination after ablation of striate cortex in dark-reared kittens. *Journal of Comparative and Physiological Psychology*, 1963, **56**, 196–199.

Adamec, R., & Melzack, R. The role of motivation and orientation in sensory preconditioning. *Canadian Journal of Psychology*, 1970, **24**, 230–239.

Ames, E. W., & Silfan, C. K. *Methodological issues in the study of age differences in infant's attention to stimuli varying in movement and complexity.* Paper presented to the Society for Research in Child Development, Minneapolis, March 1965.

Anton, B. S., & Bennett, T. L. Role of tactual-kinesthetic feedback in transfer of perceptual learning in the golden hamster. *Psychomonic Science*, 1972, **28**, 157–158.

Axelrod, S. Effects of early blindness: Performance of blind and sighted children on tactile and auditory tasks. *American Foundation for the Blind Research Series*, 1959, (Whole No. 7), Vol. IX, 83 pp.

Batkin, S., & Ansberry M. Effect of auditory deprivation. *Journal of the Acoustical Society of America*, 1964, **36**, 598.

Beach, F. A. The descent of instinct. *Psychological Review*, 1955, **62**, 401–410.

Bennett, E. L., Anton, B. S., & Levitt, L. Stimulus recovery and transfer of perceptual learning. *Psychonomic Science*, 1971, **25**, 159–160.

Bindra, D. *Motivation: A systematic reinterpretation.* New York: Ronald Press, 1959.

Birch, H. G., & Bitterman, M. F. Sensory integration and cognitive theory. *Psychological Review*, 1951, **58**, 355–361.

Bishop, H. E. *Innateness and learning on the visual perception of direction.* Unpublished doctoral dissertation, University of Chicago, 1959.

Blakemore, C., & Cooper, G. F. Development of the brain depends on the visual environment. *Nature (London)*, 1970, **228**, 477–478.

Bland, B. H., & Cooper, R. M. Experience in vision of the posterior neo-decorticate rat. *Physiology and Behavior*, 1970, **5**, 211–214.

Bond, E. K. Perception of form by the human infant. *Psychological Bulletin*, 1972, **72**, 225–245.

Booher, H. R., & Walk, R. D. Apparatus for the differential visual depth threshold and its determination in the hooded rat. *Psychonomic Science*, 1968, **12**, 187–188.

Brogden, W. J. Sensory preconditioning. *Journal of Experimental Psychology*, 1939, **25**, 323–332.

Brown, C. P., & King, M. G. Developmental environment: Variables important for later learning and changes in cholinergic activity. *Developmental Psychobiology*, 1970, **4**, 275–286.

Calahan, M. *The effects of dark-rearing and selective exposure on pattern discrimination in rats* Unpublished B.A. thesis, Queen's University, Kingston, Ontario, Canada, 1973.

Campbell, B. A., & Jaynes, J. Effect of duration of reinstatement on retention of a visual discrimination learned in infancy. *Developmental Psychology*, 1969, **1**, 71–74.

Chow, K. L. Failure to demonstrate changes in the visual system of monkeys kept in darkness or in colored light. *Journal of Comparative Neurology*, 1955, **102**, 597–606.

Chow, K. L., Riesen, A. H., & Newell, F. W. Degeneration of retinal ganglion cells in infant chimpanzees reared in darkness. *Journal of Comparative Neurology*, 1957, **107**, 27–42.

Chow, K. L., & Stewart, D. L. Reversal of structural and functional effects of long-term visual deprivation in cats. *Experimental Neurology*, 1972, **34**, 409–433.

Cooper, R. M., & Zubek, J. P. Effects of enriched and restricted environments on the learning ability of bright and dull rats. *Canadian Journal of Psychology*, 1958, **12**, 159–164.

Creighton, D. E. *Complexity perferences and preference shifts in rats as a function of early visual experience.* Unpublished Master's thesis, University of British Columbia, 1969.

Creighton, T., & Tees, R. C. *The effects of early visual deprivation on selective attention in the rat.* Paper presented at the meeting of the Canadian Psychological Association, Victoria, June 1973.

Crozier, W., & Pincus, G. Photic stimulation of young rats. *Journal of Genetic Psychology*, 1937, **17**, 105–111.

Daw, N. W., & Wyatt, H. J. Raising rabbits in a moving visual environment: An attempt to modify directional sensitivity in the retina. *Journal of Physiology (London)*, 1974, **240**, 309–330.

Dodwell, P. C. *Visual pattern recognition.* New York: Holt, 1970.

Drever, J. Early learning and the perception of space. *American Journal of Psychology*, 1955, **68**, 605–614.

Fantz, R. L. Ontogeny of perception. In A. M. Schrier, H. F. Harlow, & F. Stollnitz (Eds.), *Behavior of non-human primates: Modern research trends* (Vol. 2). New York: Academic Press, 1965. Pp. 365–403.

Fantz, R. L. Visual perception and experience in early infancy: A look at the hidden side of behavior development. In H. W. Stevenson, E. H. Hess, & H. L. Rheingold (Eds.), *Early behavior: Comparative and developmental approaches.* New York: Wiley, 1967. Pp. 181–224.

Flom, M. C. Early experiences in the development of visual coordination. In F. A. Young & D. B. Lindsley (Eds.), *Early experience and visual information processing in perceptual and reading disorders.* Washington, D.C.: National Academy of Science, 1970.

Forgus, R. H. Early visual and motor experience as determiners of complex maze-learning ability under rich and reduced stimulation. *Journal of Comparative and Physiological Psychology,* 1955, **48,** 215–220.

Forgus, R. H. Advantage of early over later perceptual experience in improving form discrimination. *Canadian Journal of Psychology,* 1956, **10,** 147–155.

Fox, S. S. Self-maintained sensory input and sensory deprivation in monkeys: A behavioral and neuropharmacological study. *Journal of Comparative and Physiological Psychology,* 1962, **55,** 438–444.

Gamboni, W. R. Visual deprivation and hypothesis behavior in rats. *Perceptual and Motor Skills,* 1964, **19,** 501–502.

Ganz, L. An analysis of generalization behavior in the stimulus deprived organism. In G. Newton & S. Levine (Eds.), *Early experience and behavior.* Springfield, Ill.: Thomas, 1968. Pp. 365–411.

Ganz, L., & Fitch, M. The effect of visual deprivation on perceptual behavior. *Experimental Neurology,* 1968, **22,** 638–660.

Ganz, L., Fitch, M., & Satterberg, J. A. The selective effect of visual deprivation on receptive field shape determined neurophysiologically. *Experimental Neurology,* 1968, **22,** 614–637.

Ganz, L., & Riesen, A. H. Stimulus generalization to hue in dark-reared macaque. *Journal of Comparative and Physiological Psychology,* 1962, **55,** 92–99.

Ganz, L., & Wilson, P. D. Innate generalization of a form discrimination without contouring eye movements. *Journal of Comparative and Physiological Psychology,* 1967, **63,** 258–269.

Gauron, E. F., & Becker, W. C. The effects of early sensory deprivation on adult rat behavior under comparative stress. *Journal of Comparative and Physiological Psychology,* 1959, **52,** 322–328.

Gibson, E. J. *Principles of perceptual learning and development.* New York: Appleton, 1969.

Gibson, E. J., & Walk, R. D. The effect of prolonged exposure to visually presented patterns on learning to discriminate them. *Journal of Comparative and Physiological Psychology,* 1956, **49,** 239–242.

Gibson, E. J., Walk, R. D., Pick, H. L., & Tighe, T. J. The effect of prolonged exposure to visual patterns on learning to discriminate similar and different patterns. *Journal of Comparative and Physiological Psychology,* 1958, **51,** 584–587.

Gottlieb, G. Ontogenesis of sensory function in birds and mammals. In E. Tobach, L. R. Aronson, & E. Shaw (Eds.), *The biopsychology of development.* New York: Academic Press, 1971. Pp. 67–128.

Hebb, D. O. The innate organization of visual activity. I. Perception of figures by rats reared in total darkness. *Journal of Genetic Psychology,* 1937, **51,** 101–126.

Hebb, D. O. *The organization of behavior.* New York: Wiley, 1949.

Hebb, D. O. The semiautonomous process: Its nature and nurture. *American Psychologist,* 1963, **18,** 16–27.

Hebb, D. O. *Textbook of psychology* (3rd ed.). Philadelphia, Penn.: Saunders, 1972.

Hein, A., & Diamond, R. M. Independence of the cat's scotopic and photopic systems in acquiring control of visually guided behavior. *Journal of Comparative and Physiological Psychology*, 1971, **76**, 31–38. (a)

Hein, A., & Diamond, R. M. Contrasting development of visually triggered and guided movements in kittens with respect to interocular and interlimb equivalence. *Journal of Comparative and Physiological Psychology*, 1971, **76**, 219–224. (b)

Hein, A., & Diamond, R. M. Locomotory space as a prerequisite for acquiring visually guided reaching in kittens. *Journal of Comparative and Physiological Psychology*, 1972, **81**, 394–398.

Hein, A., Gower, E., & Diamond, R. M. Exposure requirements for developing the triggered component of the visual-placing response. *Journal of Comparative and Physiological Psychology*, 1970, **73**, 188–192.

Held, R. Dissociation of visual functions by deprivation and rearrangement. *Psychologische Forschung*, 1968, **31**, 338–348.

Held, R., & Bauer, J. A., Jr. Visually guided reaching in infant monkeys after restricted rearing. *Science*, 1967, **155**, 718–720.

Held, R., & Hein, A. Movement-produced stimulation in the development of visually guided behavior. *Journal of Comparative and Physiological Psychology*, 1963, **56**, 872–876.

Heller, D. P. Absence of size contancy in visually deprived rats. *Journal of Comparative and Physiological Psychology*, 1968, **65**, 336–339.

Hirsch, H. V. B. Visual perception in cats after environmental surgery. *Experimental Brain Research*, 1972, **15**, 405–423.

Hirsch, H. V. B., & Spinelli, D. N. Modification of the distribution of receptive field orientation in cats by selective visual exposure during development. *Experimental Brain Research*, 1971, **12**, 509–527.

Hubel, D. H., & Wiesel, T. N. Binocular interaction in striate cortex of kittens reared with artificial squint. *Journal of Neurophysiology*, 1965, **28**, 1041–1059.

Hull, C. L. *Principles of behavior.* New York: Appleton, 1943.

Jones, G., & Pasnak, R. Light deprivation and visual-cliff performance in the adult cat. *Psychonomic Science*, 1970, **21**, 278–279.

Kagan, J. The growth of the "face" schema: Theoretical significance and methodological issues. In J. Hellmuth (Ed.), *Exceptional infant* (Vol. I. *The normal infant*). Seattle: Special Child Publications, 1967. Pp. 335–414.

Karmel, B. Z. *Texture density and normal development of visual cliff depth avoidance.* Paper presented at the meetings of the Western Psychological Association, San Diego, March 1968.

Karmel, B. Z., & Walk, R. D. *The development of depth perception in the cat.* Paper presented at the meeting of the Eastern Psychological Association, Atlantic City, April 1965.

Koffka, K. *Principles of gestalt psychology.* New York: Harcourt, 1935.

Kovach, J. K., Fabricius, E., & Falt, L. Relationships between imprinting and perceptual learning. *Journal of Comparative and Physiological Psychology*, 1966, **61**, 449–454.

Kuo, Z. Y. *The dynamics of behavioral development.* New York: Random House, 1967.

Lashley, K. S., & Russell, J. T. The mechanism of vision: XI. A preliminary test of innate organization. *Journal of Genetic Psychology*, 1934, **45**, 136–144.

Lashley, K. S., & Wade, M. The Pavlovian theory of generalization. *Psychological Review*, 1946, **53**, 72–87.

Levison, C. A., & Levison, P. K. Effects of early visual conditions on stimulation-seeking behavior in young rhesus monkeys, II. *Psychonomic Science*, 1971, **22**, 145–147.

Levison, C. A., Levison, P. K., & Norton, H. P. Effects of early visual conditions on stimulation-seeking behavior in infant rhesus monkeys. *Psychonomic Science*, 1968, **11**, 101–102.

Lindsley, D. B., Wendt, R. H., Lindsley, D. F., Fox, S. S., Howell, J., & Adey, W. R. Diurnal activity, behavior and EEG responses in visually deprived monkeys. *Annals of the New York Academy of Sciences*, 1964, **117**, 564–587.

Lockard, R. B. Some effects of light upon the behavior of rodents. *Psychological Bulletin*, 1963, **60**, 509–529.

MacDougall, J. C., & Rabinovitch, M. S. Early auditory deprivation and sensory compensation. *Developmental Psychology*, 1971, **5**, 368.

Mayers, K. S., Robertson, R. T., Rubel, E. W., & Thompson, R. T. Development of polysensory responses in association cells of kitten. *Science*, 1971, **171**, 1037–1038.

McCall, R. B., & Lester, M. L. Differential enrichment potential of visual experience with angles versus curves. *Journal of Comparative and Physiological Psychology*, 1969, **69**, 644–648.

McCleary, R. A. Type of response as a factor in interocular transfer in the fish. *Journal of Comparative and Physiological Psychology*, 1960, **53**, 311–321.

Meikle, M. B. *Unit activity in rat association cortex in response to auditory, visual and tactile stimulation*. Paper presented at the meeting of the Western Psychological Association, San Diego, April 1968.

Melzack, R. Effects of early perceptual restriction on simple visual discrimination. *Science*, 1962, **137**, 978–979.

Melzack, R. Early experience: A neuropsychological approach to heredity-environment interactions. In A. Newton & S. Levine (Eds.), *Early experience and behavior*. Springfield, Ill.: Thomas, 1968. Pp. 65–82.

Michels, K. M., Bevan, W., & Strasel, H. C. Discrimination learning and inter-dimensional transfer under conditions of systematically controlled visual experience. *Journal of Comparative and Physiological Psychology*, 1958, **51**, 788–781.

Miller, L. G., & Cooper, R. M. Translucent occluders and the role of visual cortex in pattern vision. *Brain Research*, 1974, **79**, 45–59.

Mitchell, D. E., Freeman, R. D., Millodot, M., & Haegerstrom, G. Meridional amblyopia: Evidence for modification of the human visual system by early visual experience. *Vision Research*, 1973, **13**, 535–558.

Mize, R. R., & Murphy, E. H., Selective visual experience fails to modify receptive field properties of rabbit striate cortex neurons. *Science*, 1973, **180**, 320–323.

Muir, D. W., & Mitchell, D. E. Visual resolution and experience: Acuity deficits in cats following early selective visual deprivation. *Science*, 1973, **180**, 420–422.

Nealey, S. M., & Riley, D. A. Loss and recovery of discrimination of visual depth in dark-reared rats. *American Journal of Psychology*, 1963, **76**, 329–332.

Neff, W. D. Role of the auditory cortex on sound discrimination. In W. A. Rosenblith (Ed.), *Sensory communications*. New York: Wiley, 1961. Pp. 259–278.

Orbach, J., & Miller, M. H. Visual performance of infra-human primates reared in an intermittently illuminated room. *Vision Research*, 1969, **9**, 713–716.

Ordy, J. M., Massopust, L. C., & Wolin, L. R. Postnatal development of the retina, ERG and acuity in the Rhesus monkey. *Experimental Neurology*, 1962, **5**, 364–382.

Oswalt, R. M. Relationship between level of visual pattern difficulty during rearing and subsequent discrimination in rats. *Journal of Comparative and Physiological Psychology*, 1972, **81**, 122–125.

Pettigrew, J. D., & Freeman, R. D. Visual experience without lines: Effect on developing cortical neurons. *Science*, 1973, **182**, 599–601.

Rasch, E., Swift, H., Riesen, A. H., & Chow, K. L. Altered structure and composition of retinal cells in darkreared mammals. *Experimental Cell Research*, 1961, **25**, 348–363.

Raskin, L. M., & Walk, R. D. *Depth perception in the light-reared and in the dark-reared rabbit.* Paper presented at the meeting of the Eastern Psychological Association, New York, April 1963.

Riesen, A. H. The development of visual perception in man and chimpanzee. *Science*, 1947, 106, 107–108.

Riesen, A. H. Plasticity of behavior: Psychological aspects. In H. F. Harlow & C. N. Woolsey (Eds.), *Biological and biochemical bases of behavior.* Madison: University of Wisconsin Press, 1958. Pp. 425–450.

Riesen, A. H. Brain and behavior: Session I. 4. Effects of stimulus deprivation on the development and atrophy of the visual sensory system. *American Journal of Orthopsychiatry*, 1960, 30, 23–35.

Riesen, A. H. Stimulation as a requirement for growth and function in behavioral development. In D. W. Fiske & S. R. Maddi (Eds.), *Function of varied experience.* Homewood, Ill.: Dorsey Press, 1961. Pp. 57–80. (a)

Riesen, A. H. Studying perceptual development using the technique of sensory deprivation. *Journal of Nervous and Mental Disorders*, 1961, 132, 21–25 (b).

Riesen, A. H. *Is the critical period hypothesis useful?* Paper presented at the meeting of the American Psychological Association, New York, September 1961. (c)

Riesen, A. H. Effect of visual deprivation on perceptual function and neural substrate. In J. Ajuriaguerra (Ed.), *Désafférentation expérimentale et clinique.* Geneva: Georg et Cie, 1965. Pp. 47–66. (a)

Riesen, A. H. Effects of early deprivation of photic stimulation. In S. F. Osler & R. R. Cooke (Eds.), *The biosocial basis of mental retardation.* Baltimore: Johns Hopkins Press, 1965. Pp. 61–85. (b)

Riesen, A. H. Sensory deprivation. In E. Steller & J. M. Sprague (Eds.), *Progress in physiological psychology* (Vol. I). New York: Academic Press, 1966. Pp. 116–147.

Riesen, A. H. Problems in correlating behavioral and physiological development. In M. B. Sterman, D. J. McGinty, & A. M. Adinolfi (Eds.), *Brain development and behavior.* New York: Academic Press, 1971. Pp. 59–70.

Riesen, A. H., & Aarons, L. Visual movement and intensity discrimination in cats after early deprivation of pattern vision. *Journal of Comparative and Physiological Psychology*, 1959, 52, 142–149.

Riesen, A. H., & Mellinger, J. C. Interocular transfer of habits in cats after alternating monocular visual experience. *Journal of Comparative and Physiological Psychology*, 1956, 49, 516–520.

Riesen, A. H., Chow, K. L., Semmes, J., & Nissen, H. W. Chimpanzee vision after four conditions of light deprivation. *American Psychologist*, 1951, 6, 282.

Riesen, A. H., Ramsey, R. L., & Wilson, P. D. The development of visual acuity in rhesus monkeys deprived of patterned light during early infancy. *Psychonomic Science*, 1964, 1, 33–34.

Rosenzweig, M. R. Environmental complexity, cerebral change, and behavior. *American Psychologist*, 1966, 21, 321–332.

Rosenzweig, M. R. Effects of environment on development of brain and of behavior. In E. Tobach, L. R. Aronson, & E. Shaw (Eds.), *Biopsychology of development.* New York: Academic Press, 1971. Pp. 303–342.

Rosenzweig, M. R., Bennett, E. L., & Diamond, M. C. *Transitory components of cerebral changes induced by experience.* Paper presented at the meeting of the American Psychological Association, Washington, September 1967.

Sackett, G. P. Monkeys reared in isolation with pictures as visual input: Evidence for an innate releasing mechanism. *Science*, 1966, 154, 1470–1473.

Sackett, G. P. Response to stimulus novelty and complexity as a function of rats' early rearing experiences. *Journal of Comparative and Physiological Psychology*, 1967, **63**, 369–375.

Schneirla, T. C. Aspects of stimulation and organization in approach withdrawal processes underlying vertical behavior development. In D. S. Lehrman, R. A. Hinde, & E. Shaw (Eds.), *Advances in the study of behavior* (Vol. I). New York: Academic Press, 1965. Pp. 1–74.

Schwartz, R. M., Schwartz, M., & Tees, R. C. Optional intradimensional and extradimensional shifts in the rat. *Journal of Comparative and Physiological Psychology*, 1971, **77**, 470–475.

Scott, J. P. Critical periods in behavior development. *Science*, 1962, **138**, 949–958.

Sherman, S. M. Visual field defects in monocularly and binocularly deprived cats. *Brain Research*, 1973, **49**, 25–45.

Slomin, V., & Pasnak, R. The effects of visual deprivation on the depth perception of adult and infant rats and adult squirrel monkeys (Saimiri scurea). *Vision Research, 1972,* **12**, 623–626.

Solomon, R. L., & Lessac, M. S. A control group design for experimental studies of development processes. *Psychological Bulletin*, 1968, **70**, 145–150.

Spalding, P. A. Instinct—With original observation on young animals. *Macmillan's Magazine*, 1873, **27**, 282–293. (Reprinted in the *British Journal of Animal Behaviour*, 1954, **2**, 2–11.)

Spigelman, M. N. Effects of age at onset and length of blindness on auditory spatial learning in the rat. *Canadian Journal of Psychology*, 1969, **23**, 292–298.

Spigelman, M. N., & Bryden, M. P. Effects of early and late blindness on auditory spatial learning in the rat. *Neuropsychologia*, 1967, **5**, 267–274.

Sterritt, G. M., & Robertson, D. G. Pathology resulting from chronic paraffin ear plugs. Methodological problem in auditory sensory deprivation research. *Perceptual and Motor Skills*, 1964, **19**, 662.

Stewart, D. L., & Riesen, A. H. Adult versus infant brain damage: Behavioral and electrophysiological effects of striatectomy in adult and neonatal rabbits. In G. Newton & A. H. Riesen (Eds.), *Advances in psychobiology* (Vol. I). New York: Wiley, 1972. Pp. 171–211.

Sutherland, N. S. Outlines of a theory of visual pattern recognition in animals and man. *Proceedings of the Royal Society*, 1968, **71**, 296–317.

Tees, R. C. Effects of early auditory restriction in the rat on adult pattern discrimination. *Journal of Comparative and Physiological Psychology*, 1967, **63**, 389–393. (a)

Tees, R. C. The effects of early auditory restriction in the rat on adult duration discrimination. *Journal of Auditory Research*, 1967, **7**, 195–207. (b)

Tees, R. C. Effect of early visual restriction on later intensity discrimination in rats. *Journal of Comparative and Physiological Psychology*, 1968, **66**, 224–227. (a)

Tees, R. C. Effect of early restriction on later form discrimination in the rat. *Canadian Journal of Psychology*, 1968, **22**, 294–298. (b)

Tees, R. C. Luminance and luminous flux discrimination in rats after early visual deprivation. *Journal of Comparative and Physiological Psychology*, 1971, **74**, 292–297.

Tees, R. C. Effects of visual restriction in rats on generalization along the dimension of angular orientation. *Journal of Comparative and Physiological Psychology*, 1972, **3**, 494–502.

Tees, R. C. Effect of visual deprivation on development of depth perception in the rat. *Journal of Comparative and Physiological Psychology*, 1974, **86**, 300–308.

Tees, R. C., & Cartwright, J. Sensory preconditioning in rats following early visual deprivation. *Journal of Comparative and Physiological Psychology*, 1972, **81**, 12–20.

Thomas, H. Visual-fixation responses of infants to stimuli of varying complexity. *Child Development*, 1965, **36**, 629–638.

Thompson, R. F., & Kramer, R. F. Role of association cortex in sensory preconditioning. *Journal of Comparative and Physiological Psychology*, 1965, **60**, 186–191.

Thompson, W. R., & Grusec, J. E. Studies of early experience. In P. H. Mussen (Ed.), *Carmichael's manual of child psychology* (Vol. I). New York: Wiley, 1970. Pp. 565–654.

Thompson, W. R., & Schaefer, T., Jr. Early environmental stimulation. In D. W. Fiske & S. R. Maddi (Eds.), *Functions of varied experience*. Homewood, Ill.: Dorsey Press, 1961. Pp. 81–105.

Turkewitz, G., Gilbert, M., & Birch, H. G. Early restriction of tactile stimulation and visual functioning in the kitten. *Developmental Psychobiology*, 1974, **7**, 243–248.

Turner, W. D. Development of perception. I. Visual disorders: The first eidoscopic orientation of the albino rat. *Journal of Genetic Psychology*, 1935, **47**, 121–140.

Vandenberg, S. G. The nature and nurture of intelligence. In D. C. Glass (Ed.), *Genetics*. New York: Rockefeller University Press, 1968. Pp. 3–58.

Van Hof, M. W., & Kobayashi, K. Pattern discrimination in rabbits deprived of light for seven months after birth. *Experimental Neurology*, 1972, **35**, 551–557.

Vestal, B. M., & King, J. A. Effect of repeated testing on development of visual acuity in prairie deermice. *Psychonomic Science*, 1971, **25**, 297–298.

Von Noorden, G. K., Dowling, J. E., & Ferguson, D. C. Experimental amblyopia in monkeys. *Archives of Opthamology*, 1970, **84**, 206–214.

Wachs, T. D. Reinstatement of early experiences and later learning: An animal analogue for human development. *Developmental Psychobiology*, 1972, **6**, 437–444.

Walk, R. D., & Bond, E. K. Deficit of depth perception of 90-day-old dark-reared rats. *Psychonomic Science*, 1968, **10**, 383–384.

Walk, R. D., & Gibson, E. J. A comparative and analytic study of visual depth perception. *Psychology Monographs*, 1961, **75**, 1–44.

Walk, R. D., Gibson, E. J., & Tighe, T. J. Behavior of light- and dark-reared rats on a visual cliff. *Science*, 1957, **126**, 80–81.

Walk, R. D., Trychin, S., Jr., & Karmel, B. Z. Depth perception in dark-reared rat as a function of time in the dark. *Psychonomic Science*, 1965, **3**, 9–10.

Walker, E. L. Complexity and preference in animals and men. *Annals of the New York Academy of Sciences*, 1970, **169**, 619–654.

Wendt, R. H., Lindsley, D. F., Adey, W. R., & Fox, S. S. Self-maintained stimulation in monkeys after long-term visual deprivation. *Science*, 1962, **139**, 336–338.

Wickelgren, B., & Sterling, P. Effect on the superior colliculus of cortical removal in visually deprived cats. *Nature (London)*, 1969, **224**, 1032–1033.

Wiesel, T. N., & Hubel, D. H. Single cell responses in striate cortex of kittens deprived of vision in one eye. *Journal of Neurophysiology*, 1963, **26**, 1003–1017.

Wiesel, T. N., & Hubel, D. H. Comparison of the effects of unilateral and bilateral eye closure on cortical unit responses in kittens. *Journal of Neurophysiology*, 1965, **28**, 1029–1040.

Wilson, P. D. *Visual development in Rhesus monkeys neonatally deprived of patterned light*. Unpublished doctoral dissertation, University of Chicago, 1964.

Wilson, P. D., & Riesen, A. H. Visual development in Rhesus monkeys neonatally deprived of patterned light. *Journal of Comparative and Physiological Psychology*, 1966, **66**, 87–95.

Wolf, A. The dynamics of the selective inhibition of specific functions in neurosis. *Psychosomatic Medicine*, 1943, **5**, 27–38.

Woodruff, A. B. The effect of severe restriction of visual experience of learning and perception in the white rat. *Ohio State University Dissertation Abstracts*, 1955, **66**, 397–403.

Zubek, J. D. (Ed.) *Sensory deprivation: Fifteen years of research*. New York: Appleton, 1969.

Section 5

EPILOGUE

From the accounts in the present volume, the problem of the development of neural specificity requires the postulation of not only a molecular or biochemical component (chemoaffinity) but also an experiential one. In the very early stages of neurogenesis one envisages some sort of chemical communication between nerve cells which influences them to aggregate in certain patterns and also to form connections with one another in specific ways. At a later stage of neural maturation, spontaneous and evoked function (experience) begins to play a role, not only in selectively maintaining already formed connections and characteristic cellular activities, but perhaps also in facilitating or even inducing their further maturation. No one knows precisely when during neurogenesis the prefunctional, chemical stage begins to become susceptible to the influence of experience, but there is no disagreement in these pages that at some point experience usually plays a role in the "final fashioning" of the developing nervous system in all species studied to date. The most critical and significant disagreements arise in connection with the precise roles that experience plays in this process, especially its role in normal (i.e., species-typical) development.

There are at least three roles that experience can play in the development of neural specificity. It can *maintain* already achieved (or to-be-achieved) end-states (i.e., keep the system going, functional, intact); it can *facilitate* development in a quantitative sense (e.g., influencing development on such dimensions as early-late; smaller-bigger; few-many; fine-gross; low-high threshold; and so on); or it could conceivably *induce* development in a qualitative sense (e.g., making a cell function in *this* way rather than *that* way, possibly causing *this* connection to be made rather than *that* one). To further complicate matters, it is at present far from clear whether or how the physiological effects of experience are mirrored in changes at the level of neuroanatomy.

There is no disagreement on the modifiability of neural connections and neural cellular functions by experience. This has been demonstrated time and again by deprivation studies, on the one hand, and by stimulus substitution or biased rearing studies, on the other. Although not all cells at all levels of the nervous system are modifiable, neural plasticity is a fact. Thus, plasticity is not necessarily the antithesis of specificity. For example, developmentally plastic cells could inevitably realize species-specific outcomes if they were invariably exposed to the standard (species-typical) range of experiential conditions during ontogenesis.

But the fact of plasticity is much surer than an understanding of its status during development. It is in this connection that Grobstein and Chow (this volume) have introduced the felicitous division of *experience-sensitive* and *experience-dependent* processes. The former refer to plasticity, the latter to the question of whether particular neural connections and/or functions require certain kinds of experience to develop (mature) normally. Within this framework, one could see how experience *could* play a role in normal development (-sensitivity) but not be necessary (-dependence). According to this view, the phenotype (a given neural specificity) would merely appear earlier in development with experience and later in development without experience. Or abnormally restrictive early experience during formative periods might modify development away from the species-typical or species-specific norm.

The conceptual problems relating to the development of species-specific or species-typical behavior are much the same as those having to do with the development of neural specificity. Instead of applying notions such as morphogenetic fields and chemoaffinity to the early "prefunctional" stages of species-specific behavioral development, we use the conceptually related notion of the *innate* component in behavior. Such behavioral activities are of course adaptive and species-specific (or, at the very least, species-typical), they appear at the appropriate stage of development, but their hallmark is that they appear without the animal's having engaged in them before. These activities include motor performances as well as sensory-perceptual feats, even though in the present volume the latter have been emphasized. The question has always been whether *other*, not obviously relevant activities (experiences) that the animal has engaged in earlier in development influence the development of innate behavior in any way (maintenance, facilitation, or induction). I refer here to the possibility of "nonobvious" experiential precursors to innate behavior. Perhaps we have so few examples of these because our thinking has been too constrained. An excellent example is the highly specific visual and locomotor precursors to visually guided reaching in the kitten (reviewed in the second chapter in this volume). If one had hypothesized such an intricate and nonobvious experiential background to visually guided reaching, it would have seemed indeed a far-fetched theory in advance of the facts.

As reviewed elsewhere in this volume, there are instances of maintenance, facilitation, and possibly induction in the species-specific behavior of birds (e.g., the auditory perceptual development of young ducklings; song in certain species of songbird) as well as in the visual perceptual development of a variety of mammalian species (reviewed extensively by Tees in this volume). Perhaps the ontogenetic analysis of innate behavior is more apt to be undertaken when that behavior is not defined as independent of prior experience but rather, more precisely, as behavior which the animal has not engaged in beforehand. Any aspect of the behavior is thus a candidate for inquiry with respect to its relationship to the earlier experiences of the animal. This is not to minimize the obvious importance of intrinsic interactions within the maturing nervous system vis-à-vis the development of innate behavior, but merely to call attention to the fact that an investigation of the development of innate behavior is not solely a matter of either molecular biology or neurobiology—it is, as C. Judson Herrick would have had it, a matter of psychobiology.

AUTHOR INDEX

Numbers in italics refer to the pages on which the complete references are listed.

SUBJECT INDEX

CONTENTS OF PREVIOUS VOLUMES

351